Consumer Awareness & Consumer Protection: An Empirical Evidence

Parkash Chandel & Shammi Minhas

ISBN: 10:1723301108
ISBN-13: 978-1723301100

DEDICATION

To God, Friends and Family

CONTENTS

PREFACE

Consumer protection has become the topic of debate at all levels. The reason behind this has been the lack of awareness of consumers and the malpractices of business world. In order to maximize profits, many businessmen exploit consumers by supplying poor qual-ity goods at higher prices. They adopt unfair trade practices such as adulteration, boarding, black-marketing, etc. As a result consumers do not get value for their money. Big business houses use their power for private gain and to the detriment of consumers. Consumers are exposed to physical, environmental and other hazards. They need to be protected from spurious, duplicate and adulterated products, pollution of air, water and noise, and misleading advertising. Consumer protection, however, is only possible if two steps are taken. First is to frame rules, legislations and set up machinery like courts to assure that laws are implemented in their true spirits. Second is to make the stakeholders aware of such laws so that they might defend themselves when required. Keeping these two steps in mind, this study has been undertaken. It covers the evaluation of consumer protection machinery and assesses the level of awareness of consumers in Himachal Pradesh. A brief outline of the thesis is as below.

Chapter – I deals with the introduction to consumer protection. It discusses meaning of consumer, consumer protection and consumerisms. It also discusses the consumer's rights, needs and consumer's responsibilities. *Chapter – II* reviews the literature concerning the problem in hand. It also presents a picture of research design formulated for the present research work. It discusses the selection of the problem, importance, scope, objectives, hypotheses and research methodology of the present study. Finally, limitations and the future scope of study have been shown. *Chapter – III* discusses consumerism and consumer protection movements at the international and national level. *Chapter – IV* is an attempt to examine various legislations for consumer protection at the international level as well at the national level in India. *Chapter – V* reviews the frameworks for consumer dispute resolution and redress in India. *Chapter – VI* examines the organizational setup for the consumer protection along with its evaluation in Himachal Pradesh. *Chapter – VII* deals with the analyses of opinion and perception about consumer awareness and consumer alertness with regard to consumer protection. *Chapter – VIII* highlights the summary and major findings of the study. It also explains suggestions to improve the implementation of consumer protection laws and awareness among people.

It is the most pleasant duty to acknowledge my sincere gratitude, thanks to those who helped, encouraged, and guided us in the formation and presentation of this this.

First, we are highly grateful to God who always bestowed upon us His love and '*Ashirwad*' to attain what we deserved. May His name be exalted, honoured and glorified!

We are extremely thankful to our family members and friends without whom encouragement and inspiration the task of writing the book would never be completed.

We are indebted to many scholars and authors whose scholarly writings and viewpoints have been made use of at various stages in this study. We should be failing in our duty if we do not place on record our gratitude to the respondents for their cooperation and help in extracting the primary data.

Last but not least, we are highly grateful to Dr. Vinod Kumar for his help in formatting this book

Parkash Chandel & Shammi Minhas

ACRONYM AND ABBREVIATION

ACASH	Association for Consumers Action on Safety and Health
AERB	Atomic Energy Regulation Board
AGMARK	Agricultural Marketing
APL	Above Poverty Line
BIS	Bureau of Indian Standards
BIS	Bureau of Indian Standards
BPL	Below Poverty Line
CAG	Consumer Action Group
CAI	Consumers Association of India
CCC	Consumer Coordination Council
CERC	Consumer Education and Research Centre
CERC	Consumer Education and Research Centre
CGSI	Consumer Guidance Society of India
CI	Consumers International
CPCB	Central Pollution Control Board
CU	Consumer Union
CUTS	Consumer Unity and Trust Society
Ed./eds.	Edition/editions (when preceding the title)
Ed./eds.	Editor/editors (when preceding author(s) name)
FAO	Food and Agriculture Organization
FCI	Food Corporation of India
FMCG	Fast Moving Consumer Goods
FPO	Fruit Products Order
FPS	Fair Price Shops
GM	Genetically Modified
HUDCO	Housing and Urban Development Corporation
IAC	Indian Association of Consumer
Ibid	Ibidem (in the same place)
ILO	International Labour Organization
IOCU	International Organization of Consumer Unions
ISI	Indian Standards Institute
KCSS	Karnataka Consumer Services Society
Kg	Kilogram
Loc.cit.	Loco citato (in the place sited)
LPG	Liquefied Petroleum Gas
MRTP	Monopolies and Restrictive Trade Practices
NHHP	National Housing and Habitat Policy
Op.cit	Opera citato (in work cited)
PAC	Public Accounts Committee

PATRA	Passengers and Traffic Relief Association
PDS	Public Distribution System
Rs.	Rupee
SPCB	State Pollution Control Board
TV	Television
U.K.	United Kingdom
UN	United Nation
UNCTAD	National Conference on Trade and Development
UNESCO	United Nations Educational, Scientific and Cultural Organization
UNICEF	United Nations Children's Fund
US/USA	United State / United State of America
USSR	United States Soviet Russia
UT	Union Territory
VCC	Visaka Consumer Concil
WGU	Women Graduate Union
WHO	World Health Organization
Jt.	Joint
Add/.	Additional
F & A	Finance and Account
H.Q.	Head Quarter
Govt.	Government
AAY	Antodaya Ann Yojana
MT	Million Tones
Deptt.	Department
Ltd.	Limited
Co.	Company

LIST OF FIGURES

LIST OF GRAPHS

LIST OF TABLE

CHAPTER – 1
INTRODUCTION

The moment a person comes into this world, he starts consuming. He needs milk, clothes, oil, soap, water and many more things and these needs keep taking one form or the other all along his life. Thus, we all are consumers. When we approach the market as a consumer, we expect value for money, i.e., right quality, right quantity, right prices, information about the mode of use, etc. But there may be instances where a consumer is harassed or cheated. He may be supplied with goods which do not perform as per their description or have one or more defects. Likewise, in case of services, there may be deficiency.

In the early times, consumer was considered as King of the market but in the contemporary society, consumers are no longer safe against the mal practices such as, substandard goods and unsatisfactory services. The consumer has every right to reject any product or services rendered by any manufacturer in the market and can mould them to produce goods of their choice. Indian Consumer are ignorant, illiterate and do not know the role of consumption vis-a-vis economic system as well as quality of life. When they are ignorant of their rights, they cannot know their responsibility as consumers. Consumers in the market find themselves deceived by wrong weights and measures, adulterated and substandard products causing great damages to health (Selvasdas, 1998). Neelkanta and Anand (1992) found that people prefer to absorb and endure the wrong done to them rather than fight against injustice. This is because consumers do not know the ways and means of facing them confidently (Acharya, 2007).

At present the consumer movement in India is in its infancy. Vast majority of the people are not even aware of consumerism as a movement closely connected with the protection of their interest. Many constitutional provisions have been made by government to protect the consumers. Until and unless these provisions are availed of by the consumers, the protection of consumer become inevitable. There is a great need to make them aware of their rights and responsibilities. The current investigation has been undertaken to seek answers to key aspects such as level of consumer awareness regarding legislation and organizations with the specific objective to assess the awareness of male and female respondents towards consumer legislation organization and consumer protection laws (Siddiq 2009).

The growing interdependence of the world economy and international character of many business practices have contributed to the development of universal emphasis on consumer rights protection and promotion. Consumers, clients and customers' world over, are demanding value for money in the form of quality goods and better services (Kaynak, 1982).

Modern technological developments have no doubt made a great impact on the quality, availability and safety of goods and services. But the fact of life is that the consumers are still victims of unscrupulous and exploitative practices. Exploitation of consumers assumes numerous forms such as adulteration of food, spurious drugs, dubious hire purchase plans, high prices, poor quality, services, deceptive advertisements, hazardous products, black marketing and many more. In addition, with revolution in information technology newer kinds of challenges are thrown on the consumer like cyber crimes, plastic money etc., which affect the consumer in even bigger way. 'Consumer is sovereign' and 'Customer is the King' are nothing more than myths in the present scenario particularly in the developing societies. However, it has been realized and rightly so that the Consumer protection is a socio- economic programme to be persuade by the government as well as the business as the satisfaction of the consumers is in the interest of both. In this context, the government, however, has a primary responsibility to protect the consumers' interests and rights through appropriate policy measures, legal structure and administrative framework (Padma, 1990).

The maxim relieved the seller of the obligation to make disclosure about the quality of the product. In addition, the personal relation between the buyer and the seller was one of the major factors in their relations. But with the growth of trade and its globalization the rule no more holds true. It is now impossible for the buyer to examine the goods beforehand and most of the transactions are concluded by correspondence (Fernando, 2009).

In the age of revolutionized information technology and with the emergence of c-commerce related innovations the consumers are further deprived to a great extent. As a result buyer is being misled, duped and deceived day in and day out. Mahatma Gandhi, the father of nation, attached great importance to what he described as the "poor consumer", who according to him should be the principal beneficiary of the consumer movement. He said:

"A Consumer is the most important visitor on our premises. He is not dependent on

us we are on him. He is not an interruption to our work; he is the purpose of it. We are not doing a favour to a consumer by giving him an opportunity. He is doing us a favour by giving an opportunity to serve him. (Chandra 2004) "

In present situation, consumer protection, though as old as consumer exploitation, has assumed greater importance and relevance. Consumerism is a recent and universal phenomenon. It is a social movement. Consumerism is all about protection of the interests of the consumers.

1.1. Concept of Consumer and Consumer Protection

The Latin term 'Consumo' means, "eat up completely" which understandable to the current use of the term consumer. There is no dispute that every person is a consumer. We need food to eat, clothes to wear and house to live in and therefore, these basic things are to be purchased by every human being unless he is the producer of the same. 'Consumer' means any person who (i) buys and goods for a consideration which has been paid or promised or partly paid and partly promised, or under any system of deferred payment and includes any user of such goods other than the person who buys such goods for consideration paid or promised or partly paid or partly promised, or under any system of offered payment when such use is made with the approval of such person, but does not include a person who obtains such goods for resale or for any commercial purpose; or (ii) hires or avails of any services for a consideration which has been paid or promised or partly paid and partly promised, or under any system of deferred payment and includes any beneficiary of such services other than the person who hires or avails of the services for consideration paid or promised, or partly paid and partly promised, or under any system of deferred payment, when such services are availed of with the approval of the first mentioned person (Krishan, 2002).

Consumer protection means protecting the interests and rights of consumer in the business place. The consumer protection includes the physical protection, protection against cheating, environmental protection and protection against monopoly. It includes protection against marketing of goods and services which are hazardous to life and property, protection against unfair trade practices by providing information about quality, quantity, potency, purity, standard and price of goods and services, protection to the consumers by providing access to a variety of goods and services at competitive prices, protection to the consumers by bringing their interests and grievances at the appropriate Forums (Selvada, 1998).

Consumer protection means and aims at protecting consumers from various unfair trade practices. In India, business organizations have certain advantages in form of well-organized firms, better informed and a better dominating position. Because of this, the companies are understandably in a position to easily exploit consumers. Many Indian consumers are still semi-literate and unaware of consumer protection and consumer rights. These consumers are highly vulnerable to business malpractices. Recent global scenario has contributed to increased awareness of consumer rights among consumers. Consumers are gradually becoming more and more conscious towards deficiencies in products and services. Consumers, world over, are demanding value for money in the form of quality goods and better services (Joseph, 2004).

In simple words consumer protection is a form of social action which is created to attain the well-being of consumers. Since an individual consumer is considered more vulnerable in the modern world, to exploitation and harassment by the manufacturers and distributors or sellers, it is necessary that the various groups of society such as government, judiciary, voluntary associations of consumers play their role to protect the consumer interest (economic, social and environmental).

1.2. Need for Consumer Protection

The necessity of adopting measures to protect the interest of consumers arises mainly due to their helpless position and the unfair business practices. No doubt consumers have the basic right to be protected from the loss or injury caused on account of defective goods and deficiency of services. However, consumers are unable to make use of their rights due to lack of awareness and ignorance. For example, as consumers we have the right to choose the goods of right quality from a variety of similar goods available in the market. But often we fail to make the right choice because of misleading advertisements by which we are carried away and buy sub-standard goods. Under certain circumstances, we are helpless in the sense of our inability to verify the quality of products. The clever shopkeeper can deceive us by his persuasive words. If the date of expiry on a strip of medicinal tablets is not legible, we may be in a hurry and depend on what the seller tells us. If the medicine does not have the desired effect, we may go to the doctor again and request him to prescribe some other medicine, we forget that the medicine we bought might not have had the effect as we were supplied the medicine after its date of expiry. Often, we are guided by some of our beliefs without any basis. For instance, many of us believe that 'higher price indicates better quality' and so do not mind paying higher price for a product if the salesmen recommend it to be of good quality. Again, it is a common belief that imported goods are inevitably of a superior quality. So, if there is a printed label or a mark that shows a product is made in a foreign country, we may buy it at a higher price without verifying its place of manufacture (Herrmann, 1980).

Processed food sold in packets, like potato chips, are not good for health. But young boys and girls buy these because they are tasty. Certain brands of soft drink are popular with young people as the brand ambassadors shown on the TV are popular film artists or cricketers and what they say carries lot of weight with their fans. Excessive use of soft drinks is also not good for health. If seems we have forgotten fresh lime water with sugar or salt as a good drink. Producers of goods often put standard certification marks like ISI on the package which are genuinely certified. Similarly, if packaged good are sold short of weight we pay for, it is very difficult to verify always the weights before buying. Sometimes the weighing machines are defective. Above all, consumers are not fully aware of remedies open to them if goods are defective or there is deficiency of service. So, one can very well realize why steps must be taken to protect consumers from business practices which are unfair and may cause loss and injury to health and other dangerous effects (Ramesh, 1989).

The fundamental cause of consumer movement in any country has been the consumer dissonance. Dissonance means after – purchase doubts, disillusionment, disappointment and dissatisfaction. Dr. Peter Drucker rightly put 'consumerism' as 'the shame of modern marketing'. There will be no scope for consumerism in the case all marketers practice marketing concept in its real sense and entirety because, true marketing is 'consumer oriented' (Drucker, 1987). Prof. Philip Kotler, treated consumerism as the final expression of the marketing concept. According to him it is the philosophy which forces the product managers and services purely from the eyes and brains of consumers. The real need for consumer protection arises because of the following:

1. Consumer needs physical protection against products and services that are spurious, unsafe and endanger health and property.
2. Consumer needs protection against deceptive and unfair trade practices followed by unscrupulous business community.
3. Consumer needs protection against the abuse of monopoly and restrictive trade practices.
4. Consumer needs protection against sellers. In most of the cases the receipt as a documentary proof makes it clear that goods once sold will not be taken back.
5. Consumer needs protection against pollution of all kinds.

1.3. Problems Faced by Consumers

Consumers may be deceived in various ways by unscrupulous businessmen including traders, dealers, producers and manufacturers as well as service providers. Some of the following unfair practices must have come to one's notice sometime or the other:

1) **Adulteration** that is, adding something inferior to the product being sold. This is a practice consumers come across in the case of cereals, spices, tea leaves, edible oil, petrol, etc. For example, mustard oil may be adulterated with rape seed oil or argemone oil, blace pepper is

known to be adulterated with dry papaya seeds, petrol is mixed with kerosene oil, vanaspati may be mixed with ghee/butter. Sometimes, the inferior material used with the product may be injurious to health (Thorelli, 1988).

2) **Sale of spurious products**, that is, selling something of no value instead of the real product. This is often found in the case of medicines and drugs or health care products. Cases have been reported where ampoules for injections contained only water or glucose water in bottles contained only distilled water (Thorelli, 1988).

3) **Use of false weights and measures** is another malpractice which some traders adopt while selling the goods. Goods which are sold by weight (kg.) like vegetables, cereals, sugar, etc., those sold by measures (meter) like textile fabrics, suit pieces, are sometimes found to be less than the actual weight or length. False weights (Kg, 500 grams, 250 grams, etc.) or measuring tapes or sticks having false markings are used for the purpose and buyers are cheated. Sometimes packaged goods and sealed containers (tins) contain less quantities, than what is stated on the label or packet (Saraf, 1990). This cannot be easily verified. Sweets are often weighed along with the card board box which may weigh upto 50-100 grams. One pays for it at the same rate as the sweets.

4) **Sale of duplicates**, that is, goods that indicates a mark which shown it is of superior quality than what it actually is. For example, goods which are locally made, are sold at a higher price as imported items expected to be of superior quality. Certain products like washing soap, detergent powders, tube lights, jams, edible oil, even medicines, carry well-known brand names although these are made by others.

5) **Hoarding and black-marketing** is another problem that consumer often face. When any essential commodity is not made available in the open market and stocks are intentionally held back by dealers it is known as hoarding. Its purpose is to create an artificial scarcity, to push up the prices. Black marketing is the practice of selling hoarded goods, secretly at a higher price. These practices are sometimes adopted when there is short supply of any product. People may have read in the newspapers sometime back about scarcity of onions in the open market in some states and high prices being charged by traders who had stocks (Fernando, 2009).

6) **Tie-in-Sales**: Buyers of durable consumer goods are sometimes required to buy some other goods as a pre-condition to sale or may be required to pay after-sales service charges for one year in advance. Consumers may have heard about tying up of new gas connections with the sale of gas stoves (burners). Also TV sets are sometimes sold

on the condition that the buyers will make advance payment of a year's service charge (Daniel, 1988).

7) **Offering gifts**: Offering gifts having no additional value or coupons to collect a gift on the next purchase of some product are practices aimed at alluring consumers to buy a product. Often gifts are offered after the price of the product on sale has been increased. Dealers also announce contests or lottery among buyers of a product without the intention of awarding any prize (Shah, 1990).

8) **Misleading advertisement** is yet another practice by which consumers are deceived. Such advertisements falsely represent a product or service to be of superior quality, grade or standard, or falsely asserts the need for or usefulness of a product or service. A pharmaceutical company advertised that use of its paracetamol tablet did not have any side effects like aspirin, but it suppressed the experts' report that the use of paracetamol had adverse effect on the liver. A company announced in its advertisement that it was manufacturing 150 cc. scooters in technical collaboration with a foreign company, although no such collaboration had been entered into. In another case, a company used the trademark of a well-known company 'Philips' in its advertisement for TV sets. On enquiry it was found that the company did not have the necessary permission from Philips for the use of its trade mark on TV sets. It was a case of misrepresentation of facts although that company was authorized to use the trademark 'Philips' on its audio products (radio sets) only (Sing, 1990).

9) **Sale of sub-standard goods**: Sale of goods which do not conform to prescribed quality standard particularly for safety. Such products include pressure cookers, stoves, electric gadgets (heaters, toasters, etc.), and cooking gas cylinders (Shah, 1987).

These are some instances of consumer helplessness even if he is a wise buyer. So, to safeguard the interest of consumers it is felt that some measures are necessary to help the common-man. Thus, consumer protection refers to the steps necessary to be taken or measures required to be accepted to protect consumers from business malpractices. It may be regarded as a movement like consumerism. This is necessary primarily because businessman aim at maximizing profits and this is often done at the expense of consumers.

1.4. Parties to Consumer Protection

Consumer Protection has a wide agenda. It not only includes educating consumers about their rights and responsibilities, but also helps in getting their grievances redressed. It not only requires judicial machinery for protecting the interests of consumers but also requires the consumers to get together and form themselves into consumer associations for protection and promotion of their interests (Acharya, 2007). At the same time, consumer protection has a special significance for businesses too. Actually, for effective consumer protection, it is essential that all the parties must be involved, that is, (a) Consumers; (b) Business; (c) Government ; (d) Media; (e) Organizations and societies(f) Legal protection to consumers and (g) Jurisdiction of consumer courts . Let us consider what each of the parties:

1.4.i. Consumers

Self-help is the best help. Therefore, consumers should, as far as possible, take care of their own interest and protect themselves from market malpractices. For this purpose, it is necessary that they should try to know about their rights and exercise them. They should not depend on the good sense of businesspersons. Consumers have a right to education and a right to be heard. They should attend training programmes for consumers arranged by local consumer associations or by their own association and invite consumer, activists to speak to them on consumer rights and remedies available under the law to protect them (Abbokar, 2009). The importance of consumer protection from the consumers' point of view can be understood from the following points:

(i) **Consumer Ignorance:** In the light of widespread ignorance of consumers about their rights and reliefs available to them, it becomes necessary to educate them about the same to achieve consumer awareness (Abbokar, 2009).

(ii) **Unorganized Consumers:** Consumers need to be organized in the form of consumer organizations that would take care of their interests. Though, in India, we do have consumer organizations which are working in this direction, adequate protection is required to be given to consumers till these organizations become powerful enough to protect and promote the interests of consumers (Abbokar, 2009).

(iii) **Widespread Exploitation of Consumers:** Consumers might be exploited by unscrupulous, exploitative and unfair trade practices like defective and unsafe products, adulteration, false and misleading advertising, hoarding, black-marketing etc. Consumers need protection against such malpractices of the sellers (Sarkar, 1989).

1.4.ii. Business

As regards businesspersons, it is expected that producers, distributors, dealers, wholesalers as well as retailers should pay due regard to consumer rights in their own interest. They should ensure supply of quality goods and services at reasonable prices. To prevent unfair practices, associations of traders, chambers of commerce and industry, and manufacturers' associations should entertain consumer complaints against their members and take proper action against those guilty of malpractice (Adamson, 1982).

A business must also lay emphasis on protecting the consumers and adequately satisfying them. This is important because of the following reasons:

(i) **Long-term Interest of Business:** Enlightened businesses realize that it is in their long-term interest to satisfy their customers. Satisfied customers not only lead to repeat sales but also provide good feedback to prospective customers and thus, help in increasing the customer-base of business (Brigittee, 1987). Thus, business firms should aim at long-term profit maximization through customer satisfaction.

(ii) **Business uses Society's Resources:** Business organizations use resources that belong to the society. They, thus, have a responsibility to supply such products and render such services, which are in public interest and would not impair public confidence in them (Gupta and Anurag, 1989).

(iii) **Social Responsibility:** A business has social responsibilities towards various interest groups. Business organizations make money by selling goods and providing services to consumers. Thus, consumers form an important group among the many stakeholders of business and like other stakeholders, their interest has to be well taken care of (Fetterman and Schiller, 1978).

(iv) **Moral Justification:** It is the moral duty of any business to take care of consumer's interest and avoid any form of their exploitation (Gupta & Anurag, 1988). Thus, a business must avoid unscrupulous, exploitative and unfair trade practices like defective and unsafe products, adulteration, false and misleading advertising, hoarding, black marketing etc.

1.4.iii. Government

For Government, consumer protection is a responsibility to be undertaken in the general interest of society. Enforcement of various laws and amending existing laws to protect consumer interests are required to be taken up in the light of viewpoints of consumer associations. Representations of consumer groups should also be associated with the policy-making bodies set up by government at the center and the states. A number of measures have been taken by Government from time to time.

A business engaging in any form of exploitative trade practices would invite government intervention or action. This can impair and tarnish the image of the company. Thus, it is advisable that business organizations voluntarily resort to such practices where the customers' needs and interests will well be taken care of. In view of the above, the government of India has enacted several regulations designed to provide adequate protection to consumers (Sivazaman, 1991).

1.4.iv. Consumer Co-operatives Societies

Consumer Co-operatives are sometimes mentioned as the starting point of the Consumer Movement. In general, consumer co-operatives have been successful in halting some of the abuses of the monopolies and in improving conditions of the lower-income classes. They have undertaken consumer education, elementary product improvement and other projects of interests to members as well as to other low income consumers (Sivazaman, 1991). However, in contrast to activities to which the term 'Consumer Movement' has been applied, co-operatives have sought to perform certain services for themselves, thus replacing private enterprises in these areas. On the other hand, movement activities have been directed towards modification of business practices, either with or without the aid of government.

Decontrol and de-rationing in 1951-52 meant a setback to the co-operative movement. Revival came in 1962. In 1960, an all India seminar on consumer co-operatives was held in Bombay for a critical appraisal of the entire consumer scenario. From the Third Five Year plan onwards, there has been much emphasis on the development of consumer co-operatives by the governments to make them viable. In 1975-76, Rs. 5.5 crores was invested for consumer co-operatives in accordance with the 20 point programme. Consumer co-operatives are very important for improving the distribution of essential goods through Public Distribution System (PDS) and combating inflation. It has been announced that 10 to 20% of the supplies of baby foods, bicycles, blades, cloth and students needs etc. would be through co-operatives. At present, in the distribution of consumer goods the co-operatives under P.D.S. account for about 28% of retail outlets (fair price shops) in rural areas. Nearly 51,000 village societies and their various branches distributed Rs. 2500 crores worth of consumer articles in rural areas in 1989-90 (Riswadkar, 1983). However, the co-operative movement treaded its path among the consumers and as was the case in the West, in India the co-operative movement was not organised as a measure for consumer protection of the modern type. Consumer movement did not make its presence felt in India till the 1960's when organised consumer groups came up.

1.4.v. Consumers Organizations

Consumer movement in India had its beginning in the early part of this century. The first known collective body of consumers in India was set up in 1915 with the 'Passengers and Traffic Relief Association' (PATRA) in Bombay. Women Graduate Union (WGU). Bombay was another organisation started in 1915. One of the earliest consumer co-operatives was the 'Triplicane Urban Co-operative Stores' started in late 40's in Madras. It has about 150 branches all over the city. The Indian Association of Consumer (IAC) was set up in Delhi in 1956. This was an All India Association for consumer interests with the government's support. However, even IAC did not make any headway (Lizzy, 1996).

The first organisation to really make an impact was the Consumer Guidance Society of India (CGSI), Bombay started by nine housewives in 1966 with Mrs. Leela Jog as its founder secretary. Instead of just holding conferences and meetings and asking questions like earlier consumer associations, it started testing and reporting the quality of items of daily use of foodstuffs and handling' consumer complaints. It has 8 branches at various places carrying on publicity, exhibitions and education. It publishes a magazine called 'Keemat', in English, for consumer information. The second consumer organisation which made quite an impact in making the cause of consumers known throughout the country is the Karnataka Consumer Services Society' (KCSS) formed in 1970. The main strength of the KCSS was Mrs. Mandana who spread the word of the movement throughout the country, especially among government circles at a time when the word 'consumer' was not familiar to many. It is based in Bangalore (Karmatala, 1976). Visaka Consumers Council (VCC) started in 1973 in Vishakhapatnam, Andhra Pradesh, 'is another pioneering consumer organisation which has made a significant contribution to the consumer movement. It represented the plight of the poor ration card holders and LPG gas users, who had to stand in long queues because of the irresponsible attitude of the concerned authorities.

The Eighties of the 20thcentury saw the dawn of a new era in consumer movement in India. There was mushrooming of consumer organizations, many floated by politicians to earn additional income and capture a gullible vote bank! However some associations were really committed to the cause of the consumers (Selvadas, 1998).

1.4.vi. Media

The role of media has two-fold significance in modem life. Its multifaceted facilities are used to inform, educate and raise awareness on one hand and on the other; it is used as a commercial tool by the advertisers. Advertisers fund the media, so they use money for influencing the media they depend upon. Advertisers up their quest to improve sales, manipulate both the media and consumer. Since advertising is used for sales promotion, it tells only partial truths, highlighting the positive and suppressing the negative. In a country like India, with its complex social structures, media can be a very important tool for mass education on a variety of issues. Media plays a crucial role in changing and influencing the thoughts of the people. Media has a great power to influence what we think about things happening around. The role of media is not only to seek solution to the many problems of the country, but the task of media is also to inform and educate people so that a critical awareness among the people is encouraged.

Today it is rightly said that a consumer makes a good citizen and ultimately a good Democrat. Promoting awareness through the dissemination of information is the fundamental task that the media can make towards the development of consumerism. Media has played a vital role in welfare of consumer through books, magazines, newspaper, broadcasting, radio, telephone, TV, movies, documentaries etc.

The exploitation of consumers is due to the absence of such a key role in providing right information at the right time for consumers. Ignorance about prices and price behavior of market structure and fluctuations in the economy changes is not understood by ordinary consumers and therefore are victims of exploitation and consumer malpractices. Therefore there is a need for greater role of media to regulate consumer protection mechanism for the betterment of consumers in this changing era. Media in any form, printed or electronic, is a mirror of the times and society we live in connects us with the world and the world to us. Media also plays a useful role in establishing good relations or friendship between the merchants and shoppers. The promotion of fair trade practices, the establishment of codes of conduct for businessmen is the task that the media can only assume.

Nevertheless, the same population segments can become targets of media manipulation. As consumers, people need to be aware of the role that advertising can play in the hands of market forces. Once the consumer has been sensitized to the tricks that advertisers can resort to, he can use his discretion to stay in control.

1.5. Consumer Rights: Indian Perspective

Due to globalization and opening of Indian markets to foreign players, Indian consumers today have an access to innumerable brands. In every industry whether it is fast moving consumer goods (FMCG) or durable goods or service industry there are more than twenty brands at national level catering to the needs of the consumers. This situation of plenty is giving the consumer an opportunity to choose goods and services from a wide spectrum

Further liberalization of our economy in 1991 gave opportunity to Indian consumers to get quality products at competitive prices. Earlier in order to protect our own industries government restricted foreign competition. This led to a situation where consumers were getting very few choices and quality wise also our products were inferior (Chandra, 2004). For purchase of car there used to be a huge booking and there were only two brands available. Nobody bothered about consumer interests and the attitude was towards protecting our own industry.

Thus, the need for consumer satisfaction and consumer protection was recognized. A consumer is considered as an inevitable part of a socio-economic–political system, where the exchange initiated and transaction realized between two parties, namely buyers and sellers has an impact on a third party i.e. society. However, the inherent profit motive in mass production and sales also offers the opportunity to many manufacturers and dealers to exploit consumers. Problems of defective goods, deficiency in service, spurious and duplicate brands, misleading advertisements are rampant and often the gullible consumer falls prey to it.

1.5.i.   A Brief History of Consumer Rights

Before discussing the various consumer rights it is important to discuss history of consumer rights. Thus, a brief history has been illustrated as under:

On April 9, 1985 the General Assembly of the United Nations passed a Resolution adopting a set of guidelines for consumer protection and authorized Secretary General, United Nations to persuade the member countries, especially the developing ones to adopt policies and laws for better protection of the interests of the consumers. Consumers today want value for money, a product or service that would meet reasonable expectations, should be safe in use and full disclosure of the product specification (Peterson, 1987). These expectations are termed as 'Consumer Rights'. 15th March is observed as the World Consumers' Day. The United Nations adopted a set of Guidelines for Consumer Protection to address the interest and needs of consumer, worldwide and to provide a framework for Governments, particularly those of developing and newly independent countries, to use for elaborating and strengthening their consumer protection policies and legislation. The UN Guidelines have outlined eight areas for developing policies for consumer protection, which have been translated into eight consumer rights for this discussion and the enforceability and the present state of affairs of these rights in India is looked into. The eight consumer rights that are analyzed for the present study are, consumers right to basic needs, consumers right to education, consumers right, consumers right to redressed, consumers right to representation and consumers right to healthy environment (Harland, 1988).

This date has a historic importance as it was on this day in 1962, when the Bill for Consumer Rights was moved in the US Congress. During his speech President John F. Kennedy had remarked:"If a consumer is offered inferior products, if prices are exorbitant, if drugs are unsafe or worthless, if the consumer is unable to choose on an informed basis, then his dollar is wasted, his health and safety may be threatened, and national interest suffers (Ramesh, 1989)."

The Consumers International (CI), formerly known as International Organization of Consumer Unions (IOCU), the umbrella body, for 240 organizations in over 100 countries, expanded the charter of consumers rights contained in the US Bill to eight, which in a logical order reads:

1. Basic Needs
2. Safety
3. Information
4. Choice
5. Representation
6. Redress
7. Consumer Education and
8. Healthy Environment.

This charter had a universal significance as they symbolized the aspirations of the poor and disadvantaged. On this basis, the United Nations, in April 1985, adopted its Guidelines for Consumer Protection. Consumers play a vital role in the economic system of a nation because in the absence of effective demand that emanates from them, the economy virtually collapses. Mahatma Gandhi said, "A consumer is the most important visitor on our premises. He is not dependent on us, we are on him. He is not an interruption to our work, he is the purpose of it. We are not doing a favour to a consumer by giving him an opportunity. He is doing us a favour by giving us opportunity to serve him. But, of late, unfortunately cheating by way of overcharging, black marketing, misleading advertisements, etc. has become the common practice of greedy sellers and manufacturers to make unreasonable profits. In this context, it is the duty of the government to confer some rights on consumers to safeguard their interests (Jha, 2003).

In the 20th century, the presence and influence of the market grew dramatically in consumer life. We began to purchase things from the market for a price. Soon, mass production and industrial production came into being, giving the consumer world an entirely new dimension. Has one ever wondered how much urban consumers depend on the market for fulfillment of even their basic needs. This over-dependence on the market and the inherent profit motive in mass production and sales has given manufacturers, and dealers a good reason to exploit consumers. As a consumer, one would know how market products are constantly under-weight, of inferior quality and do not prescribe to quality standards specified by quality-control agencies. Consumers not only do not get value for their money but also often have to suffer losses and inconvenience due to market manipulations (Chandra, 2004).

In a developing country like India the population faces a number of problems, especially in the consumer related issues. As consumer rights are the pivotal of consumer movement, it generally covers all types of rights such as social rights, political rights, human rights and the economic rights of the people in general. The term consumer embraces both poorest and the richest human beings in the society and the greatest sufferers of the atrocities of the providers of goods and services are the poorest who are denied their rights, including rights to basic needs (Singh, 1978). The concentration of the market in the hands of a select few has affected consumer's behavior over time. It is not the consumer who is the king, but it is the large corporation which is the king in the economy. Whatever happens is not because the consumer wants it that way, but simply because large powerful corporations prefer it that way.

The legal basis for consumer protection can be seen in the Fundamental Rights and the Directive Principles of State Policy in our Constitution. The Constitution of India provides for economic justice and consumer protection is its constituent element. Thus, a constitutional duty is imposed on the state to protect consumers from the unscrupulous activities of the well organized and powerful business lobby. The consumer welfare measures have achieved much importance since 1985. When India became one among the 185 odd countries which agreed to adopt the United Nations Guidelines for Consumer protection. But it would be unfair to say that the consumer protection measures were not in existence before 1985.

Some 40 bits of legislations were enacted or strengthened over time to protect the interest of the consumers. Some of them belong to the British era. But neither of them provided a comprehensive coverage of consumers right nor properly implemented and redressed of consumers grievances through the existing civil court system is difficult and time consuming. The first concrete effort to enact comprehensive consumer protection legislation was made in March 1985. A 28-member National Consumer Protection Council consisting of various ministry representatives, after two meetings, decided to convene a National workshop on Consumer Protection on March 11-12-1985 with consumer representatives. Following this, a draft bill was disused at another meeting on January 20-21, 1986 and the unique consumer redressal and representation system came in to existence when the Parliament enacted the Consumer Protection Act on December 17, 1986 (Garg, 1990)).

The Act was notified in May 1987. The pro-consumer steps that took place in 1986 paved the way for a radical change in India's history of consumer protection. The Consumer Protection Act, 1986 is unique in the world, because exclusive courts for consumer disputes were established with superior courts at the state and the apex consumer disputes were established with superior courts at the state and the apex consumer court at the national level, six consumer rights were spelt out in a statute and consumer protection councils were established in all the states with a central one at the national level (Agarwal, 1989).

1.5.ii. Consumer Rights

In order to safeguard consumer interest, 6 consumer rights were initially envisioned by consumer rights activists of the West, namely:

1   Right to Safety
2   Right to Information
3   Right to Choice
4   Right to be Heard
5   The Right to Redress
6   The right to consumer education

These rights were conceptualized in the developed world's consumer context where consumers are wealthy and completely dependent on the market to fulfill their needs. These rights had to be redefined keeping in mind the realities of a developing country like India. Consequently, two very important rights were added viz.:

- The Right to Basic Needs and
- The right to a healthy and sustained environment.

These two rights are very closely linked with the realities of developing countries where environment plays a very important role as a resource and support-structure for the people. In a country like India, a large section of the population looks for food security, assured safe water supply, shelter, education and health services. Most consumers relate very little to imported goods stacked in supermarkets or for choice among latest models of cars, as is the case in the developed world (Borrie, 1984). For India's one billion populations, food security and a safe environment are more pressing needs than any other consumer options and rights. The developing country natural resources also serve as a resource base for the developed world's industrial output. The consumer rights have been discussed as under.

1.5.ii.(a)   Right to Basic Needs

The very survival of the people (consumers) of a country depends on the fulfilling of the basic needs of the people. The dignified living of consumers depends upon how well these basic needs are met. In an under developed country, like India, basic needs are traditionally related to food. Clothing and shelter. Without the fulfillment of these basic needs it would be impossible for any human being to have a dignified life. Access to food, water and shelter are the basis of any consumer's life. Without these fundamental amenities, life cannot exist (Fetterman, and Schiller, 1978). In September 2001, India's stock of foodgrains were around 60 million tonnes, yet one third of the Indian population lives below the poverty line and consumers often go hungry or remain severely malnourished, leading to poor health. The recent starvation deaths in Orissa are a case in point. A very crucial objective of the conceptualisation and existence of consumer rights is to ensure that consumers have an assured food supply, safe and permanent dwellings, basic amenities of life like sanitation and potable water, and power supply (Ministry of Information & Broadcasting, 1990).

Urbanization is seen as a mark of development but for rural migrant

16

population, living conditions in cities is very poor. The population of cities is growing rapidly in India and after 1988, the percentage of urban poor has been more than that of the rural poor. Around 20 to 25 per cent of the urban households live in slums, make-shift colonies or refugee settlements due to non-availability of affordable and decent habitat in urban areas. According to some estimates, in urban areas alone, there is a housing shortage of 17 million units. This has led to a habitat crisis in Indian cities. In rural India, the situation is equally bad, with a large part of the population still living in make-shift dwellings and hutment. With non-permanent housing comes lack of sanitation facilities and other amenities like running water and electricity supply. Due to burgeoning population, most people do not have access to dry toilets in rural and urban areas (Ministry of Food & Civil Supply Department,1990).

1.5.ii.(b)   Right to Food/ Food Security for Consumers

The deaths of poor people in Orissa due to starvation in August 2001 have indicated that food security is still a myth of a section of the Indian consumers. To solve this food scarcity problem, the Government of India mooted the PDS (Public Distribution System) to help reach foodgrain to the masses at subsidized rates through government-run 'Fair Price Shops'. There are about 4.5 lakh Fair Price Shops all over India of which 3.05 are in rural areas and 0.94 in urban areas. On an average there is one PDS shop for every 2000 consumers. Yet, many parts of India still suffer from food shortages. Poor distribution and under-utilization of food grains has led to artificially-created food scarcities in the country. Presently, there are 60 million tonnes of foodgrain in terms of buffer stock in Indian godowns. This foodgrain is rotting due to un-utilization and improper storage facilities. The need of the hour is to channelize this stock towards needy consumers and offer them 'food for work' programmes, which will not only give them employment but also money. Besides making sure that there is enough food accessible to consumers at all times, nutrition is another area which the health of children and the vulnerable sections of population is at stake. This is an area where consumers can take responsibility for ensuring that quality is added to their basic food supply.

The right to food is nothing but food security. It can be achieved only by making the food available. The instrument for ensuring food security for the people of India, particularly for the poorer sections of society, is through the Public Distribution System (PDS). Presently, the PDS follows a three tier pricing structure: for Families above poverty Line (APL), for families Below Poverty Line (BPL). And a special category for representing the poorest of the poorest of the poor, called Antodaya. The PDS in India was started during the Second World War to prevent misallocation of food grains between urban and rural areas and the idea of ensuring food availability to rural areas through statutory urban rationing was mooted. But after independence the situation has changed and so also the objective of the PDS. Since the mid-1960s, here were two major objectives for the PDS. First was reducing food insecurity and the second was achieving self-sufficiency in food production through guaranteed outlets for farmers. The first was achieved through creation of a wide network of Fair Price Shops (FPS), supplying products at subsidized prices. The second objective was accomplished through the creation of the Food Corporation of India (FCI) in 1964, and by setting up of a system to determine agricultural procurement prices in 1970 (Ministry of Food & Civil Supply Department,2004).

The right to food is not directly stated in the constitution of India. But the chapters on Fundamental Rights and Directive Principles of State Policy enacted certain justifiable as well as non-justifiable rights. Article 21 (Fundamental Right) states that no person shall be deprived of his life and personal liberty except according to procedure established by the law. Commenting on Francis Carbolic Vs. The Union Territory of Delhi (1981 I SCC 608, AIR 1981, SC 746) case, the former Chief Justice of India, P.N. Bhagwati remarked that the right to life includes the right to live with human dignity and all that goes along with it, namely, the bare necessities of life such as adequate nutrition, clothing and shelter over the head.

The objective of the Directive Principles is to achieve a welfare State (among others, ensuring basic needs) by supplementing Fundamental Rights. Article 39 (Directive Principles of State Policy) states that the State shall, in particular, direct its policy towards securing that the citizen, men and women equally, have the right to adequate means of livelihood. Article 47 (Directive Principles of State Policy) calls upon the State to raise the level of nutrition and the standard of living and to improve public health (Shobhana, 1983).

For regulating the market, there are a few laws governing food. The Essential Commodities Act, 1955 has the objective of ensuring equitable distribution and making available the essential commodities at fair prices. The production, supply and distribution of any essential commodity can be regulated or prohibited by the Union Government by an order under this Act. A supporting legislation in this respect is the Prevention of Black marketing and Maintenance of Supplies of Essential Commodities Act, 1980. In 1964 the Food Corporation of India Act was passed and its object is to ensure minimum prices to primary producers and protecting consumers from the speculative trade. The Food Corporation of India has the primary function to undertake the purchase, storage, movement, transport, distribution and sale of food grains and other foodstuff.

The objective of the PDS is to enhance the welfare of the poor by steady availability of food grains at affordable prices. However the PDS has failed to address its objective due to the following reasons. The majority of the states have not been able to lift their full allotment of food quotas from the food Corporation of India due to their financial problems. The field level studies show that on an average only about 25 percent of the poor are availing the benefits of the PDS system. This of course, varies across state to state. Besides, the mismanagement of the FCI has also added to its economic cost, which in recent years has been nearly 50percent of the procurement cost. This has led to a huge drain on the government exchequer. The micro aspects of the failure of the PDS relate to factors such as low margins of the FPS owners, thereby leading to the corruption, transportation bottlenecks, shops not being opened at convenient times etc (Ministry of Food & Civil Supply Department, 2007).

1.5.ii.(c)   Right of Clothing

Clothing is an essential requirement for livelihood. So, it is inherently related with the textile industry. The textile industry in India is predominantly cotton-based. It consists of three sectors: mill, power loom, and handloom. The latter two come under the decentralized sector. Over the years, the government has given various incentives for the growth of the decentralized sector, which is important for the fulfillment of the right to clothing.

In India the right to clothing has been considered as one of the basic needs as per the 20 - Point Programme and also per the Supreme Court judgment in Francis Coralie vs. Union Territory of Delhi (1981 1 SCC 608, AIR 1981. SC 746). The right to clothing is covered indirectly within the right to life and personal liberty as per Article 21 of Constitution. In 1978, the Government of India launched a new scheme called "Janata cloth scheme" helps the poor. The scheme aimed at providing employment to the unemployed and the under-employed handloom weavers and making cloth available to the poor at subsidized rates. The Textile Policy. 1985, has stated that the primary objective of the policy is consumer satisfaction and consumer protection. The government of India introduced textile regulation in 1988 and went a bit ahead in de-licensing of the textile sector in August 1991. It also introduced the Small Enterprise Policy in 1991. These policies were not only aimed at ensuring increased availability of clothing, but also aimed to help the poor to have better access to clothing at affordable prices.

The public distribution system through which the right to clothing at the local level is implemented is growl incapable of addressing the issue. The Janatha Cloth Scheme faced the same drawbacks that are prevalent in the public distribution system. The Public Accounts Committee (PAC) of the Union Parliament criticized the scheme in its report of 1996. The PAC report stated that instead of creating more jobs, it caused more unemployment, more avenues for corruption and left the poor deprived of an affordable price of cloth (PAC, 2000).

1.5.ii.(d)   Right to Shelter

Shelter is fundamental for dignified living. With the growing rate of urbanization, lack of housing is increasing is increasingly becoming a social problem apart from the economic stress associated with it. The need for housing has become so great that all lands in the periphery of towns and cities are under the threat of becoming slums for construction works. According to housing census data in 1991, there was a housing shortage of 18.5 mn units (13.7mn in rural and 4.8 mn in urban areas). These figures had shot up to over 21mn units in 1996 (13.66 mn in urban areas and 7.57mn units in urban areas). This shows an increasing trend of shortage of shelter. Thus, the problem of shelter represents challenges, risks and uncertainties.

The right to shelter is not covered is not covered under any particular Fundamental Right in India. But Article 21 (Right to life and personal liberty) under the Chapter on Fundamental Rights deals indirectly with this matter. However, under the old 20-Point Programme (adopted by Government of India in 1975) The right to shelter was recognized. The national Housing Policy, 1988 did not pay enough attention to the serious problem of high Land Costs in urban areas, but as per the 1994 Housing Policy, the Government shifted its role from that of a builder to that of a facilitator. The Central Government has prepared a new housing policy titled National Housing and Habitat Policy (NHHP), By this, emphasis was given in forging partnership between private, public and cooperative sectors for enhancing the capacity of the construction industry to participate in housing as well as in empowering the Panchayati Raj Institutions (PRI) and village cooperatives to mobilize credit for rural housing.

In India, the implementation measures relating to the demand for and supply of housing are handled by the Housing and Urban Development Corporation (HUDCO) Ltd., and its subsidiary, the National Housing Bank (NHB). Whereas the NHB, which was established in 1989, is responsible for financing of housing schemes, the planning and actual implementation is being done by HUDCO.

The National Housing and Habitat Policy (NHHP), 1998, has given many promises with regard to housing in general and more particularly for the poorer sections of society. But it is pity to note that, majority of the poor and disadvantaged sections are not able to afford housing even if it is subsidized. Moreover, the Government has not given the construction activities the status of an industry thereby depriving the sector all benefits available to an industry.

1.5.ii.(e)   Right to Safe and healthy Environment

The environment covers everything that surrounds us. The environmental legislation can therefore theoretically cover a very vast range of human activities that may have a possible impact on life. The resources used in the production and consumption of goods and services should be utilized in a healthy and ecologically sound manner. This is the rationale behind the right to environment.

For urban consumers, environment means parks, gardens, and deteriorating air and water quality. Most urban areas are bereft of any wildlife and people are unaware of the biodiversity around them. On the other hand, rural consumers rely on their environment for fulfillment of their basic needs. The need for environmental conservation is seen as a necessary defense against deteriorating quality of life world-wide. We are all victims of contaminated food and water supply, pesticide-ridden food, adulterated milk and choking exhaust fumes emitting from vehicles (Anderson, 1998).

According to a World Bank report, India is being pushed back due to its high environmental costs. We lose around Rs 24,500 crore every year in terms of air and water pollution alone. If one lives in a city, he must have experienced air and water pollution at some point of time. Children often fall ill due to polluted environments, it leads to increased health costs and discomfort for consumers. Valuable resources and man-days are lost due to polluted environment and living conditions. Consumers need to understand that only a safe environment can ensure the fulfillment of their consumer rights (Anderson, 1998).

Consumers International (a nodal agency of consumer organizations from all over the world) has made certain guidelines for ensuring consumers' right to safe environment. Consumers should be protected from environmental pollution by:

1 Promoting the use of products which are environmentally sustainable.
2 Encouraging recycling.
3 Requiring environmentally dangerous products to carry appropriate warnings and instructions for safe use and disposal.
4 Promote the use of non-toxic products.
5 Raising consumer awareness of alternatives to toxic products.
6 Establishing procedures to ensure that products banned overseas do not enter national markets.
7 Ensure that the social impacts of pollution are minimized.
8 Promote ethical, socially and environmentally responsible practices by producers and suppliers of goods and services.

Rural consumers are invariably closer to their environment than urban consumers. Their livelihoods and way of life depend on the environment around them. Their firewood and sources of energy come from trees, manure for fields comes from livestock, water is procured either from underground water supply or from rivers, the crops heavily depend on annual rainfall, even pesticides for safeguarding of crops and storage also come from trees like neem. In short, the rural life revolves around natural resources. For them, this dependence on the environment is complete and they have a stake in its preservation, whether it is for building their houses, fodder for their cattle etc.

The quantitative and qualitative complexities of the discipline of environment have had their own impact on the legal framework in India. Article 21 of the Constitution of India requires the State to protect life, which includes the right to have a healthy and safe environment. Article 48A of the Directive Principles of State Policy directs the state to endeavor to protect and improve the environment, forest and wild life. Besides these provisions, Article 51A (g) imposes a Fundamental Duty on the citizens to protect the environment (Ministry of Environment and Forest Department, 2007).

The legislative measures of Government of India aims at protecting the environment in all possible ways. With this view, the term environment has given the widest meaning and complex administrative machinery is geared for this purpose. The laws relating to environment in India have been collected from a number of sources (codified and un-codified). The Statutory laws comprise Central Acts as well as a few States' Acts. The Central Acts cover general enactments such as Indian Penal Code (certain sections), the Code of Criminal Procedure (certain Provisions) and the Code of Civil Procedure (certain sections). Along with these, the Statute Book contains certain specific and comparatively recent Central Acts, dealing with specific areas of environmental law, or addressed comprehensively to environmental law. The Indian legal system recognizes the doctrine of Precedent' and it has led to the recognition of 'Case law' as a source of law. The principle of absolute liability on the civil side, for the harm caused by an environmental wrong, through hazardous substances, has come to the established by judicial decisions (Acharya, 2005).

Several Acts relevant to environmental protection have been enacted in India. These are, The Water (Prevention and Control of Pollution) Act, 1974. The Forest Conservation Act, 1980, The Air (Prevention and Control of Pollution) Act, 1981, The Environment Protection Act, 1986, The Public Liability Insurance Act, 1991, The National Environmental Tribunal Act, 1995 and The National Environmental Appellate Authority Act, 1997. Among these various Acts, Environmental Protection Act, 1986, is the most far-reaching measure. A good deal of subordinate legislation has been issued under this Act, including various rules and notification relating to hazardous chemicals and toxic waste. The main Act in India relating to pesticides is the Insecticides Act, 1968. The Insecticides Act provides for the regulation of import, manufacture, sale, transport, distribution and used of insecticides with a view to preventing risk to human beings or animals connected therewith. The manufacture and distribution of insecticides is regulated through registration and licensing.

The legal framework in India relating to the environment is fairly complex. The varieties of agencies administering segments of the relevant legislations have been given rise to the possibility of a large number of statutory and non-statutory instruments being issued by various agencies concerned. Multiplicity of law leads to complexity, thereby rendering difficulties for the citizens, as well as the bureaucracy, agencies and personnel concerned with adjudication and enforcement. The avenues available for redressal for environmental wrongs are many. The remedies are available under the Constitution (through writ petitions under Articles 32 and 226), the Code of Civil Procedure, 1908 (Section 91), the Code of Criminal Procedure, 1973 (Section 133 to 144), Prosecutions under the Indian Penal Code, Prosecution under the Specific Act, Suit by an individual who has suffered special damage (in tort) and Suit for compensation under the Public Liability Insurance Act, 1991 and the National Environmental Tribunals Act, 1995.

The variety of agencies administering segments of the relevant legislation has given rise to the possibility of a large number of statutory and non-statutory instruments being issued by the agency concerned. Some are statutory as these are issued under the formal designation of rules and some are non-statutory due to being issued as executive instructions. At the Union level, the Ministries mainly concerned with environment issues are: Ministry of Environment & Environment & Forest, is concerned with the Environment Protection Act, 1986; the Forest Conservation Act, 1980 and the Insecticides Act, 1968 (Protection of environment part only); Ministry of Agriculture, is concerned with the Insecticides Act, 1968 (the Registration Authority, and the State Department of Agriculture implements the law); Ministry of Chemicals & Fertilizers, is concerned with the Insecticides Act, 1968 (import and manufacture of pesticides, at the national and state levels as the case may be); Ministry of Health and Family Welfare (through the Controller of Drugs) is concerned with the Poisons Act, 1918, and the Insecticides Act, 1968 (regarding the aspect of pesticide residues in food and their health implications) and the enforcing authority is the Food and Drug Administration of each state; The Ministry of Labour, the Director General and the Chief Inspector of Factories in the respective states are concerned with the Factories Act, 1948; Ministry of Surface Transport is concerned with the Motor Vehicles Act, 1988. The Ministry of Environment and Forests, is also concerned with the following enactments: National Environmental Tribunal Act, 1995 and National Environmental Appellate Authority Act, 1997 (Leelakrishan, 1984).

The following are the principal Boards constituted for the enforcement of some of the important laws relating to environment: Central Pollution Control Board (CPCB), State Pollution Control Board (SPCB), Joint Pollution Control Board and Pollution Control Committees (these can be vested with certain functions in areas for which no Statutory Board, as such, has been constituted). The Boards stated above were initially envisaged by the Water (Prevention and Control of Pollution) Act, 1974, but later their functions were widene d to cover control of other kinds of hazards to the environment. The Central Board is the most important amongst all the agencies mentioned above, not only because its role in the formation and implementation of policy is crucial, but also because it has statutory powers to issue certain directions to the State Boards. The Central Board can constitute committees for various purposes (Section 4, Water Act; Section 6 Air Act) and has accordingly delegated powers to committees for Union Territories (Selvadas, 1998).

The environment laws in India, when studied along with the administrative network evolved for implementing the same is found to be high complex. It is seen that the multiplicity of laws has led to a multiplicity of administrative mechanisms. A single legislative measure may sometimes involve different administrative departments making the implementation of the law virtually difficult and the ultimate sufferers are consumers.

1.5.ii.(f)   Right to Safety

Consumer right to safety is as vast in its purview as the market reach itself. It applies to all possible consumption patterns and to all goods and services. In the context of the new market economy and rapid technological advances affecting the market, the right to safety has become a pre-requisite quality in all products and services. For e.g. some Indian products carry the ISI mark which is a symbol of satisfactory quality of a product. Similarly, the FPO and AGMARK symbolize standard quality of food products. The market has for long made consumers believe that by consuming packaged food or mineral water, consumers can safeguard their health. This notion has been proved wrong time and again due to rampant food adulteration in market products. Right to food safety is an important consumer right since it directly affects the health and quality of life of consumers.

Earlier, the interpretation of the right to safety was limited to electronic products and other such products. Now, its definition has expanded a lot to include safety aspects of new technologies like GM (Genetically Modified) food, food labeling, chemical ingredients in food products etc. In today's scenario of globalization, consumers have no control over where the products or commodities they use come from. For instance, the chocolates or syrups we consume may be manufactured in countries as far as the U.S. or Australia. Consumers in India would have no control over or knowledge of the manufacturing practices of those countries and will have to rely completely on import regulations of the Indian government and food labeling. This makes the consumer right to safety a very important and critical issue for consumers (Muraliand and Kulkerni, 1990).

Earlier, right to safety meant that a consumer should be protected from health risks of using electronic products like irons, plugs, or other such things. Technological changes have however widened the ambit of this consumer right. The right to safety has now expanded in purview to include GM food. GM food can be Food safety should ensure that consumer has no short-term or long-term adverse health effects due to consumption of GM food. Genetically Modified organisms can be defined as 'organisms produced as a result of Biotechnological changes or genetic engineering'. GM technology is suspect because making changes in the genetic code alters the entire sequence of the material and that might lead to unintended development of many undesirable traits. For e.g. A virus while in contact with a gene resistant plant may acquire the genetic material (disease resistant quality) and may become even more dangerous. If any such virus becomes virulent, it may destroy desirable plant species and create serious imbalance in the given eco-system. Also, if a consumer eats GM food products, s/he may develop resistance to anti-biotic or allergies in certain cases.

Safety of natural food products is also a problem of growing concern since due to increased chemical inputs in farms, our food supply is being contaminated with pesticides and chemicals. This poses a grave danger to consumer health. For non-vegetarians, the problem is even more serious since food animals are being fed anti-biotic to fight diseases among animals and boost their growth. This can have serious repercussions on consumer health. The consumer safety is related to consumer products. Consumers have the right to purchase goods and services that are safe and have good quality. In developing countries like India, products that are of poor quality or even hazardous to health can enter the market because of doubtful our widespread practice like dumping, planned obsolescence and outright fraud. Thus the right to safety means the right to protection against products, production processes and services, which are hazardous to health or life. It includes concern for the long-term interests of consumers as well as their immediate requirements (Sarkar, 1989).

In India, the right to safety is not spelt out directly in the Constitution. However, certain provisions under the Chapters on Fundamental Rights and the Directive Principles of State Policy are related to this right. Article 21 of Concerned with prohibition of employment in factories or engagement in any hazardous employment of children below the age of 14 years. According to Article 39 (e) of the Directive Principles of State Policy, the State required to direct its policy towards securing the health and strength of workers, men and women, prevention of child abuse and employment of citizens in vocations unsuited to their age or strength.

In India safety measures are implemented through various Acts passed by the Parliament from time to time. Standards form the reference, detailing the characteristics of products or services and have a bearing on providing satisfaction and safety to the user of the product. The Indian Standards Institution (ISI) was established in 1947, with the objectives of preparing and promoting the general adoption of standards on a national and international basis relating to structures, commodities, materials, practices, operations etc. It coordinates the efforts of producers and users for the improvement of materials, products appliances, processes and methods and provides the registration of certification marks applicable to products, commodities etc.

The constitution of ISI required that Standards Formulating Committee should have representation from all interests with predominance of consumer interests. In the mid-1990s a new Advisory Committee for Consumers Affairs was set up to consider, among other things, the stipulation of safety / health parameters and grades in Indian standards. They cover item like building materials, building hardware, medical equipments and instruments, domestic refrigerators, LPG stoves, oil pressure stoves, hurricane lanterns, gas cylinders and valves, domestic electrical appliances, GLS lamps, electrical switches and sockets etc. In India right from 1956, a number of Indian standards of interest to the consumers in the areas of quality and safety have been implemented through ISI Certification Mark Scheme voluntarily adopted by manufacturers in the case of biscuits, refrigerators, pressure cookers etc. The ISI Certification Mark Scheme made mandatory through various Acts, Rules Regulations in the case of food additives, cement, LPG Cylinders, oil pressure stoves, electric irons, plugs and sockets etc. The Government of India has passed a few legislations making the use of ISI Mark mandatory on consumer products. These legislations are Prevention of Food Adulteration (PFA) Act, 1954; Essential Commodities Act, 1955, Electrical Appliances Quality Control Order, 1987 and Gas Cylinder Rules 1981 (Chaturvedi and Hirani, 1986).

The Bureau of Indian Standards (BIS) Act was passed in 1986 by which to ISI was converted into BIS, which virtually became a department of the Central Government, answerable to the Ministry of Food & Civil Supplies for its operations Basically standardization is a voluntary act. It is up to the producer to decide whether to opt for conformity with standards or to obtain certification marks or not. The safe to use taking the gravity of the situation of inflow of unsafe products into the market the need for fixing certain standards for composition, contest, design etc. has become a necessity leading to standardization, marking and quality certification of good (Natarajan, 1990). Thus the BIS Act, 1986 provides that the Central Government, in consultation with the BIS may notify any article or process to conform to Indian Standards and direct the use of standard mark under license as compulsory on such an article/ process (Section 14 of the BIS Act). The voluntary character standards, and direct the use of standard mark under license as compulsory on such an article/process (Section 14 of the BIS Act). The voluntary character of standardization has exceptions where products are for mass consumption or where the issue of health-hazards is concerned. In such cases standards have been made statutory and certification has been made compulsory.

In order to carry out tests as per Indian Standards, there are a number of recognized laboratories in India, both in private and public sectors. The BIS also has a chain of laboratories at its regional and branch offices, primarily to test products connected with the ISI Certification Scheme. Regarding the standards for services, the International Standards pertaining to the management of services IS/ISO 9004-2:1994 Quality Management and Quality System Elements (Part 2, Guidelines for Services). Makes it clear that the requirements of a service need to be clearly defined in terms of characteristics that are observable and subject to customer evaluation.

With respect to health care goods and facilities, various laws have been passed to regulate their production, supply and distribution. The legislations in this field are: The Drugs and Cosmetics Act, 1940; the Drug (Control) Act, 1950; the Dangerous Drugs Act 1930 and Cosmetics Act, 1940 covers Allopathic. Homeopathic and Indigenous systems and Ayurvedic and Unani Medicine. In this act, Standards of quality for drugs are elaborated and importing of misbrand, spurious and adulterated drugs are prohibited. Under the Act, a Drug Consultation Committee has been formed which advises the Central Government, State Government and the Drug Technical Advisory Board. Indian Medical Council Act, 1956 and Medical Degree Act are the basic laws in India Governing the conduct of medical practitioners and include provisions for the safety of patients. Provisions of these Acts have been invoked through the State Medical Council to prevent advertisement by doctors. Professional misconduct and use of unrecognized or fake degrees by doctors (Natarajan, 1990).

The Dangerous Machines (Regulation) Act was passed 1983. This Act provides for the regulation of trade and commerce in the production. Supply. Distribution and use of the product of any commerce in the production, supply, distribution and use of the product of any industry producing dangerous machines, with view to securing the welfare of the labour operating any such machine, and for payment of compensation for the death or bodily injury suffered by the worker while operating any such machine, and for matters connected therewith or incidental there to (Natarajan, 1990).

The Radiation Safety in the use of radiation generating plants is governed by section 17 of the Atomic Energy Act. 1962. On the basis of this Act, the Central Government had promulgated the Radiation Protection Rules. 1971, which stipulate the basic safety standards for all type, of radiation application in medicine, industry, research etc. In November 1983, the Government of India constituted the Atomic Energy Regulation Board (AERB), and entrusted it with the responsibility of developing and implementing appropriate regulatory measures aimed at ensuring radiation safety in all applications involving ionizing radiation (Food and Civil Supply Department, 2007).

The Indian Electricity Rules were framed in 1956 under the Indian Electricity Act, 1910 for incorporating the provisions relating to the safety of consumers. In 1987 the Government of India notified Electrical Appliances Quality Control Order under the Bureau of Indian Standard Act for furthering the consumers' safety. The Indian Railways Act, 1989 deals with various provisions relating to consumer safety. The railway authority has the power to refuse to carry a person suffering from an infectious disease for the safety of the rest of the passengers. For the safety of the female passengers traveling alone, an exclusive compartment or adequate number of births according to requirements have been provided in every train. The Act prohibits the carrying of dangerous or offensive goods without notice.

Despite making it mandatory for certain products to a adhere to the ISI norms, many products can be found in the markets without ISI specification/marks. Even the ISI marked products in certain cases are found not be adhering to the specifications thus making the ISI certification a mockery. Besides, the rampant corruption in the system makes the law ineffective in many cases thus making the consumers deprived of justice.

1.5.ii.(g) Right to Information

Right to information means the right to be given the facts needed to make an informed choice or decision about factors like quality, quantity, potency, purity standards and price of product or service. The right to information now goes beyond avoiding deception and protection against misleading advertising, improper labeling and other practices. For e.g. when one buys a product or utilize a service, one should be informed about a) how to consume a product b) the adverse health effects of its consumption c) Whether the ingredients used are environment- friendly or not etc. Due to the ever-increasing influence of the market and the ever-changing scene with price wars and hard-sell techniques, the consumer's right to information becomes even more important (Promod, 1986). The right to information means much more than simple disclosure of the product's weight or price. A consumer has the right to know how the product has been prepared, whether it has been tested or animals or not, if environmentally-sound techniques and resources have been used in its production processes, what kinds of chemicals are used into its manufacturing and what could be their impact on consumer health. Clearly, a consumer has to consider a lot of factors before s/he buys a product.

Ideally, a consumer should have knowledge of the entire 'cradle to grave' journey of the product to determine whether it's safe and beneficial for use or no. The 'cradle to grave journey' refers to the processes a product goes through- from the time of it being made out of raw material, the processes of its molding into its final shape, transportation, labour, ingredients used, to the form in which it ends up on market shelves. It is only when a consumer is aware of the history of the product that he can make informed choices. An example of this is the GM food controversy. GM food is promoted as the answer to world's hunger and malnutrition but its safety for consumers and the environment is yet to be proved. Despite strong lobbying by pro-GM groups and the market, consumers in Europe have campaigned effectively against the entry of GM food into their food chain and markets. There are information and publicity campaigns that have made consumers rally behind a common consumer stand against GM food (Ramchander, 1988). As a result, the governments and the European Union have placed strict restrictions on the trial uses of GM technology in the market or in agriculture.

Recently, it has come to light that most cosmetics like lipsticks, Kajaland mascara are tested on animals in laboratories to see whether they have any adverse effects on them or no. There was also a controversy about how Nike shoe company was using sweat labour in South Asian countries, paying its workers abysmally low wages for manufacturing shoes. Similarly, there was a 'McLibel' case against McDonald's alleging that Mc Donald's generated a lot of unwanted waste due to its excessive packaging and harmed the environment.

The advertising techniques of many products, directly targeting and featuring children have also been questioned. Many parents don't even know that their children are being targeted by market surveyors to determine their consumption habits by collecting data through surveys, interviews and by offering free samples of products (Narayan, 1989).

It is not just the consumers who use information gathering or disseminating techniques and tools to protect their consumer rights. Information dissemination is also used very extensively by advertisers and the market to get their message across to the consumer. Tools and agencies of information like newspapers, print media, television and the Internet are utilized by marketing of consumer products and services. This has made advertising a multi-million dollar industry in India and also world-wide. Information is a precondition for real choice, one can make choices, but if one lacks information about alternatives such as their pros and cons, uses, side effects and dysfunctions, the result of those choices can range from inadequate to catastrophe. Information can also create choices or guided choices concealing rather than elucidating the full range of options. Here the right of consumers to information is assuming paramount importance from standpoint of consumption (Neeraja, 2005). Thus the right to be informed means the right to be given the facts needed to make an informed choice or decision.

A developing country like India where asymmetric information is the order of the day, a large number of consumers are not able to exercise their choice of goods and services due to lack of correct and reliable information about the quality, quantity and potency of the products. The consumers shall be provided with true and adequate information to act wisely and responsibly. They must also be protected from misleading or inaccurate publicity material, whether included in advertising, labeling, packaging or otherwise. Thus, the business organizations, consumer organizations and the government all have a role in informing consumers. The most importance aspect of the role of business is the disclosure of information about specific goods and services because in most cases it is beyond the ability of an average consumer to use the information provided by business in a correct and coherent manner.

The vast masses of consumers in the country are not aware of the rights, protection and remedies available to them. Media can play an effective role here. A product reaches the market through advertisements. If there is distortion at that stage, the final victim is the consumer. Therefore, independent initiative should be taken by the media to verify the claims of the advertisements. The Constitution of India has come provisions relating to the right to information. Though Article 19(1) of the constitution empowers the fundamental rights of expression and speech, which included the freedom of the press. Article 19(2) laid down restrictions on it. Article 19 of the Indian Constitution deals with the Article, but it is assumed to flow from the freedom of speech and expression, which is guaranteed to all citizens. Freedom of press is very important to the consumer as it acts as a vehicle for the free flow of information useful to the consumers. But it should be noted that the press is not immune from the general law of liability for deformation (Uppal and Kaur, 2007).

It has been provided in the Agricultural Produce (Grading and Marketing) Act, 1937 that AGMARK labels, carrying the appropriate grade designation mark, should be affixed to the packages containing the graded agricultural produce to enable consumers to ensure that the agricultural produce is of good quality as per the prescribed grade and standard. The Drugs and Cosmetics Act 1940 aims at prohibiting the production, trade distribution. Import and export of drugs and cosmetics that do not conform to the prescribed standards or are being sold under false brands. The Act has made it obligatory on the part of the manufacturers to give information relating to name of the medicine, name and address of the manufacturers, batch number and date of manufacture, date of expiry of the medicine, detailed composition of the medicine and the precautions regarding harmful effects or side effects of the medicine. The Drugs & Magical Remedies (Objectionable Advertisement) Act, 1954 has its objective of controlling advertisements of drugs and prohibits advertisements of remedies for diseases for which no cure is normally possible. It also prohibits advertisements of remedies that are supposed to be marginal cure (Krishnam, 1983).

Under Sections 14 of the Prevention of Food Adulteration Act (PFA), 1954 the manufacturer, distributor / dealer in the sale of food/ food products shall not sell any food unless they give a warranty in writing about the nature and quality of the product sold. Similarly, Section 9 of the PFA Act empowers the State governments to issue notifications for information to the public about persons appointed as food inspectors in local areas, where they would exercise their powers to take samples for analysis of food, and take action as per law when samples are found to be adulterated. The Fruits Products Order, 1955, makes it mandatory for the manufacturers of fruit and vegetable products to obtain a license and to ensure minimum standards for quality, packing and sanitary conditions.

Section 10 (b) of the Essential Commodities Act, 1955 deals with the publication of information when any company is convicted under this Act. All Occurrences of food poisoning are required to be notified by the medical practitioners in the specified local area to such officers as may be specified in the government notification (Section 15 of the Act). The Trade and Merchandise Marks Act, 1958 provides for the registration of trademarks of manufactured goods to protect the consumers from being cheated due to non-identifiable products (Krishnam, 1983). The Act also provides for action against the trader or shopkeeper who sells spurious goods as well as the person who affixes the trademark in a duplicate manner. The Insecticides Act, 1968, contains provisions relating to safety information, dosages and applications that are to be given to users.

The 'Unfair Trade Practices' under the MRTP Act, 1969 is related to false information given to consumers, baiting them through wrong advertisements and such other issues. The activities that constitute unfair trade practices are in their very nature infringement of consumers' right to information. The merchants and manufacturers are adopting unfair trade practices for promoting the sale of goods or boosting the use of certain services and the consumers who are not well informed are the sufferers. The unfair trade practices are further divided into misleading advertisements and false representations, bait advertising and switch selling which entails fooling the buyer with false pretenses, gift offers and promotional contests whereby a false claim of offering certain goods or services free of cost is made to the consumers, when the cost of supplying it is fully or partially covered by the amount charged in the transaction as a whole (Krishnam, 1983).

The Water (Prevention and Control of Pollution) Act 1974 and the Air (Prevention and Control of Pollution) Act, 1981 contain provisions which enables the court of law to publish the offender's name place of residence, the offence and penalty imposed, at the offender's expense. The Standards of Weights and Measures Act, 1976, and the Standards of Weights & Measures (Packaged Commodities) Rules, 1977, deal with information about weights, number, measure, sale price, date of manufacture, name and address and other descriptions of the manufacturers to be printed on the packaged products. The 1986 amendment to the Act empowers any aggrieved consumer or registered voluntary consumer organization to file a complaint in a court.

Rule 38 of the Standards of Weights & Measures (Packaged commodities) Rules, 1977, provides that the Director of Weights and Measures shall compile a state wise list of manufacturers registered by him and circulate such list to the controllers in the states so that they may take samples and test the materials. Rule 6 of the Standards of Weights and Measures (Packaged Commodities) Rules, 1977, makes it compulsory on the part of manufacturer/packer to put a label on every package, and to fix it securely on the package, and the label should contain information about the name and address of the manufacturer and also of the packer, common or generic names of the commodity and other information as prescribed.

Household Electrical Appliances (Quality Control) Orders, 1981 & 1988 prohibit the manufacture, storage and sale of 40 household electrical appliances unless these conform to the specifications of the Bureau of Indian Standards. With respect to the right to information, the greatest drawback of the existing system is the inadequate implementation of existing laws. A law can be judged as good only when its implementation is done in proper manner. In a country like India where the literacy rate is very low, the written word is often the least effective way to convey information. In India effective institutional mechanism for dissemination of information is not available and the consumers are in a disadvantaged position with regards to their right to information (Agarwal, 1989).

1.5.ii.(h)   Right to Choice

Different interests can interpret the right to choice in different ways. For the developed world consumers, right to choice translates into more and a variety of products to choose from. For e.g. American consumers can choose from 25,000 super market items, 200 kinds of cereals, and read 11,092 magazines. This kind of choice often gives consumers a sense of well-being and safety and encourages them to believe that abundance leads to good living. The market also perpetuates this line of thought by advertising and promotion gimmicks. The right to choice has a very different definition in developing countries. For a population dependent on the environment for livelihood, the right to choice and other consumer rights need a shift in focus. The focus needs to be on choice of good practices like organic farming and conservation of natural heritage. In cities, people should be able to choose cleaner and safer ways of transportation over polluting ones (Neeraja 2005). Similarly, healthy and fresh food should be chosen over junk food. The right to choose must essentially be a consumer's right to choose a safe and healthy product of good quality over an unsafe or defective product. This can give a consumer immense leverage not just to choose products that are safe but also to influence the practices adopted by the market.

Misinterpretation of choice by market forces has systematically weakened the consumer's position vis-à-vis the market. The market has exploited this situation by interpreting the right to confuse and exploit the consumer. The consumer has been made to believe that more varieties of the same product on the market shelves give him or her right to choose what s/he wants. In reality, more varieties of the same product just encourage false advertising claims and give the consumer a false sense of choice. Various kinds of shampoos, soaps, and other cosmetics differ merely in colour, smell and brand image. Each one of them claims one-upmanship over the other but gives the consumer very little value for money or a better-quality product.

Ever since trade liberalization in India started taking place, the consumer world has been witnessing increased availability of exotic fruits, vegetables and imported food items. These days, one can buy imported apples that cost Rs. 200 a kilo and syrups, jams, sauces, drinks that are manufactured overseas. However, neither the market nor the consumers pay any attention to the over-consumption of resources as a result and its environmental impact. When products are manufactured in distant lands, they have to be packaged and preserved in a special way to last longer. A lot of resources go into its packaging and transportation. All these facts and their impact are often not made known to consumers and they end up harming the environment and paying an exorbitant price for their consumption choices.

Choice is something one gets used to. It is inextricably linked up with morality, notions of right and wrong, good and evil. However, choice by itself does not mean anything and it needs to be accompanied by several other things to make it meaningful. Choice without information is not a real choice. What sort of information's is appropriate? How much and given by whom, are crucial questions. Choice that is limited only to those with resources undermines the advantages of choice for all. The globalization and liberalization polices in the last ten years have changed the contours of consumer demand for goods and services. The consumer now expects the domestic producers to supply him/her quality goods and services at globally competitive prices (Leelakrishan, 1983).

The right to choice lies at the centre of the idea of consumption and it has become a very sensitive issue and it is nothing but an assurance, wherever possible of a availability, ability and access to variety of good and services at competitive prices and to consume them in a sustainable manner. The right to choice is also important with respect to the provision of commodities and services where competition is not possible, and government regulation is supreme. In this case right to choice means assurance of satisfactory quality, and at fair prices. In strict economic terms, the right to choice is justified by equity principle and related to the efficiency principle. Unless there are efficient production and distribution systems consumer will have little or no access to choose between alternatives. The right to choice inherently relates to secure and protect the welfare of the people (Consumers) as very often development is also referred to as enlarging People's choice (Giordan, 1980). Thus this right is one of the basic pillars of a democratic country.

The preamble to the Indian Constitution adopts, enacts and promises to secure for all its citizens social, economic and political justice and also liberty of thought and expression. The right to choice cannot be maintained unless there are justice and liberty, i.e. the adherence to norms and regulations. According to Article 38 (Directive Principles of State Policy). It is the duty of the state of promote the welfare of the people by securing and protecting as effectively as it can, a social order in which justice shall govern all the institutions of national life.

Certain Acts have been passed by the Union government to secure, protect and enable consumers to exercise their right to choice. The Essential Commodities Act (CA), 1955, primarily controls production, supply and distribution of essential commodities and further endows the concerned authorities with the power of confiscation and acquisition. A corollary of the ECA 1955 is the Prevention of Black Marketing and Maintenance of Essential Commodities ACT, 1980. This Act empowers the Union Government and the State Governments to issue permits and licenses for supply and distribution of essential commodities and for further control of prices. This Act provides access to essential commodities to the disadvantaged consumers, and also plays the role of checks and balances on marketing of essential commodities. Special courts have been constituted to prosecute offenders violating provisions of this Act. The Monopolies and Restrictive Trade Practices Act, 1969 (MRTP Act), restricts monopoly of industries and ensures fair competition among industries. The Act prohibits practices that tend to restrict competition and deprive consumers of their right to choice. This Act prescribes imprisonment and fines for offenders (Shah, 1987). The Government has omitted sections 20 to 26 of the MRTP ACT vide an ordinance on 27th September 1991. These sections dealt with dominant market power and merger, amalgamation and takeovers.

The Standards of Weights and Measures Act, 1976, stipulated that all goods produced in the country can be sold only in standard weights and measures, which are annually stamped by the authorities. This Act ensures that certain commodities can be sold only in certain measures on weights. Rules regarding the sale of packaged commodities are also stipulated in the Act. The Bureau of Indian Standards Act, 1986 deals with the setting up of a benchmark of high quality supported by a visible presentation. The purpose behind this is, enabling the consumers to take an informed choice. Stipulations on information about commodities like quality, Quantity and maximum retail price are made in the Act and in the appended rules. The authorities are empowered to seize, confiscate and pass orders of cease, desist and fine. Thus, these Acts ensure a clear flow of information to consumers to help them choose between goods of different quality and different prices (Giri, 1987).

Thus, it shows that, in India, the Government is sincere in ensuring the consumers' right choice, but the proper implementation of the regulations remains a serious issue. Similarly, the new economic policy has opened a floodgate of consumer products in the market without an effective regulatory mechanism. The deficiency of quick and true information regarding the products makes the consumers facing the problem of choosing between too many products with too less information.

1.5.ii.(i)   Right to be Heard

The right to be heard means that consumers should be allowed to voice their opinions and grievances at appropriate fora. For e.g. if someone has been cheated in the market place or deprived of the right quality of service, his complaint should be heard and given due attention by the authorities. Consumers should also have a right to voice their opinion when rules and regulations pertaining to them are being formulated, like the recent amendments in the Consumer Protection Act. The right to be heard holds special significance in the Indian context because Indian consumers are largely unaware of their rights and passively accept their violation. Even when they have legal recourse, they prefer not to use it for fear of getting embroiled in legal complexities. To allay consumer fears and to allow them to express their views and grievances, consumer forums have been in existence in India for a long time. Consumers have been approaching these forums and consumer NGOs regarding their problems and complaints(Jha, 2003).

1.5.ii.(j)   Right to Redress

Competition is the by-product of the market economy. Everyday, manufacturers are discovering newer ways of cheating and duping consumers. Unscrupulous market practices are finding their way into consumer homes, violating consumer rights and jeopardizing their safety. It is to protect consumer interests that consumers have been given the right to obtain redress. India has a redress machinery called Consumer Courts constituted under the Consumer Protection Act (1986), functioning at national state and district levels. But it has not been made complete use of under due to lack of awareness of basic consumer rights among consumers themselves.

While in the developed world, right to redress is perhaps the most commonly exercised consumer right, in developing countries, consumers are still wary of getting involved in legal redress system. There are consumer courts in India where any consumer can lodge a case if s/he thinks he or she has been cheated. The details of how to lodge a complaint have been explained elsewhere in the manual.

In India, until the Consumer Protection Act, 1986 was enacted, the consumers had to rely on a number of diverse legislation, none of which provided an effective remedy against the violation of consumers' rights. A welfare state must provide adequate and effective means of dispute resolution to every citizen, and at reasonable cost. To ensure justice, effective dispute resolution is very essential. The importance of the right to redress lies in addressing and securing justice. The entire system of administration of justice is based up on equal access to justice to all people.

The objective of the right to redressal is based on the principle of making justice feasible as well as approachable in order to enable the consumers to take advantage of the judicial system. The right to redressal means a fair settlement of just claims, not only economic but also social and political. The socio-political dimension of the issue stems from the facts that, in a stratified society like India, vulnerable sections may not have real access to justice. In India the poor progress of consumer interests and protection is due to poverty of the consumer due to which real access to justice is denied. The hungry consumers do not differentiate between adulterated and unadulterated food. They accept without protest whatever they are supplied with Inadequate organization of consumers adds fuel to this problem and poor implementation of laws makes the problem acute (Subhojyoti, 2005).

The Consumer Protection Act, 1986 was passed with the specific purpose of protecting consumers' rights and providing a simple quasi-judicial dispute resolution system for resolving complaints. The consumer Protection Act, 1986, incorporates the right to redressal, the rational of the Act is to take the system of redressal to people's doorstep and it envisages a supply side approach to the issue of consumer protection. The consumer Protection Act, 1986, envisages establishment of Consumer Protection Council at the Centre and in the States, whose main objectives are to promote and protect the rights of consumers. In India an aggrieved consumer has various external channels open to him/her to redress his/her grievances. But it is petty to note that the internal redressal system in business organizations, companies and public utilities etc., for resolving consumer disputes expeditiously and inexpensively, are either non-existent or ineffective (Gulshan, 2007).

The right to seek redressal is set out in the Preamble to the constitution of India, where it has been declared that the people will strive for justice, social, economic and political and equality of opportunity. As per Article 39A of the Directive Principles of State Policy, the state shall secure the operation of the legal system, which promotes justice on the basis of equal opportunity, and shall provide free legal aid, by suitable legislation or schemes or in any other way. It should ensure that, opportunity for securing justice are not denied to any citizen by reason of economic or other disabilities. The Constitution guarantees specific enforceable Fundamental Rights. It also ensures non-justifiable rights in the form of Directive Principles of State

Policy. Article 32 and Article 226 of the Constitution confer a unique and extraordinary jurisdiction on the Supreme Court to issue directions, orders or writs for the enforcement of fundamental rights. Among the writs encompassed in Articles 32 and 226, the writ of Mandamus, writ of Certiorari, Writ of Prohibition and writ of Quo-warranto are related to the right to redressal. On the basis of the proceedings, courts may be classified as judicial or quasi-judicial and Consumer Disputes Redressal Forums are quasi-judicial courts.

The Consumer Protection Act, 1986, is one of the most progressive and comprehensive pieces of legislation enacted for the protection of consumers. It applies to all goods and services unless specifically exempted by the Union Government. It covers all the section, whether private public or co-operative. This Act gives consumers an additional remedy besides those, which may be available to her/him under the provisions of other existing laws, and she/he is free to choose any remedy at her/his discretion. This Act enshrines the consumers rights related to safety, information, choice, representation, redressal and consumer education As per the Act, Consumers, Voluntary Consumer Organization and Government can file a complaint. With a view to provide locus standi to registered consumer associations, the Prevention of Food Adulteration Act, 1940; the Drugs and cosmetics Act 1940; the Standards of Weights & Measures Act, 1956; the Essential Commodities Act, 1955 and the MRTP Act, 1969 were amended in 1986 (Antony, 1991).

To provide simple, speedy and inexpensive redressal of consumer grievance, the consumer Protection Act, 1986, envisages three-tier quasi-judicial machinery at the National, State and District levels. At National level the Consumer Disputes Redressal Mechanism is known as "National Commission", at State level it is known as "State Commission" and at District level it is known is "District Consumer Forums". These quasi-judicial bodies are required to dispose of complaints within a prescribed time frame. District Forums have original jurisdiction, but State and National Commissions have been vested with original, appellate and revisional jurisdictions.

The Monopolies and Restrictive Trade Practices (MRTP) Act, 1969, entitles any aggrieved consumer to seek redressal against unfair and restrictive trade practices by filing a complaint before the MRTP Commission. The Commission is a quasi-judicial body enjoying all the powers of a Civil Court while trying a suit.

The transformation of a laissez-fare state into a welfare state led to the establishment of tribunals for adjudication disputes between public and individuals. The tribunals are established under a statute with the objective of providing cheap, accessible, simple and flexible remedies to the individuals. Its members have greater insight due to regular handling of related matters. Arbitration as a mode of resolution of disputes is ingrained in the justice delivery system of India.

The popular practice of referring disputes and conflicts to a group of respected and wise persons of the villages called the "Panchayath" was very popular in the past and the system was informat, cheap, expeditious and binding upon the parties in the dispute. Following its footsteps, the Indian Arbitration Act, 1940, was passed. The purpose behind this Act was to refer matters of dispute, both present and future, to arbitration without the intervention of courts of law, ensuring speedy justice to some extent. Due to cumbersome procedures, legal technicalities and challenging of awards granted by arbitrators without any exception, the dispute redressal through arbitration became unpopular and the Parliament has repealed the Indian Arbitration Act, 1940 and enacted a new legislation known as the Arbitration & Conciliation Act, 1996, to make the redressal of disputes less costly and more effective. Apart from the Indian Arbitration Act, 1940, the new Act takes in to consideration the arbitration (Protocol and Convention) Act, 1934 and the Foreign Awards (Recognition & Enforcement) Act, 1961 (Karnik, 1995).

A number of associations have set up their own codes of ethics and business practices for redressal of consumer grievances. The Council for Fair Business Practices established in 1996. Advertising Standards Council of India established in 1985, Associated Chambers of Commerce and Industry, Confederation of Indian Industry, Confederation of Indian Food Trade and Industry are safe guarding the interests of the consumers in an institutional manner and thereby helps to elevate the public image of business.

Even though the purpose of the Consumer Protection Act, 1986 is to take the system of redressal to the people's doorsteps, it did not yield the expected results. Most state governments do not evince the requisite enthusiasm and attention in promptly implementing the provisions of Consumer protection Act,1986 by carrying out their mandatory obligations of establishing District Forums and State Commission (Ghatak, 1991). The justice delivery system through other media is also plagued by systematic problems resulting in inordinate delays to consumers and delayed justice is, justice denied to consumers.

1.5.ii.(k)   Right to Consumer Education

Consumer education empowers consumers to exercise their consumer rights. It is perhaps the single most powerful tool that can take consumers from their present disadvantageous position to one of strength in the marketplace. Consumer education is dynamic, participatory and is mostly acquired by hands-on and practical experience. For instance, a woman who makes purchase decisions for the household and does the actual buying in the marketplace would be more educated about market conditions and 'best buys' than a person who educates himself about the market with the help of newspapers or television (Singh, 1987). Also, today, it is not just the market or products that a consumer needs to educate himself about but s/he also needs to know about company profile, government policies and introduction of new technology.

Market influences have grown so much that not just wholesale and retail sellers but even medical practitioners are falling prey to their pressures. The pharmaceutical industry is one such example. India, with its 1 billion population and largely uneducated consumers, is a very lucrative market for this industry. The pharmaceutical industry, to boost its sales, offers free samples of medicines, freebies, and even free luxury holidays to physicians to influence them to use their brands and give them preference over other brand names. There have been many instances when drugs banned in countries like US, have been prescribed to Indian consumers and are readily available as over-the-counter drugs. It is a sad example of gross violation of consumer trust by medical practitioners (Selvadas, 1998). This situation is rampant not just in rural areas but also among educated urban consumers.

The reason why the market, in connivance with physicians, is able to exploit consumers is that Indian consumers are not aware of the prevailing situation and do not keep themselves abreast with latest developments taking place around them. Consumer education can play a crucial role in protecting consumers against such dangers.In the Indian context, sustainability and traditional knowledge can play a vital role in empowering consumers but consumers are unable to connect to their knowledge base. Consumer education can rejoin the broken link and make traditional knowledge accessible to consumers again. Some sources of consumer education are past experiences of consumers, information dissemination by government agencies and NGOs, classroom teaching by teachers and informal lessons by parents.

The right to consumer education means the right to acquire the knowledge and skills to be an informed consumer throughout one's life. The right to consumer education incorporates the right to knowledge and skills needed for taking actions to influence the factors, which affect consumer decisions. India is one of the few countries where consumer education has already been introduced in school curricula. The adult community consumer education has already been introduced in school curricula. The adult community consumer education in important to build a society of critically aware consumer. The department of consumer affairs, under the Ministry of Consumer Affairs & Public Distribution, is conducting training programmes in the field of consumer protection to educate consumer organizations and other sections of society. Besides these, publicity measures through documentaries like "Mubarak Kadam" and "misleading Advertisements" have been prepared and were telecasted on Doordarshan. A 12 part serial in Hindi on consumer related matters, entitled "Grahak Dost" was produced and began it's telecast in June 1998. For the benefit of the consumers all over

India, this is now being produced in regional languages (Ramachander, 1988).

For providing more insight to the consumers with regard to 'Right to consumer Education's the Department of Consumer Affairs has also brought out Brochures entitled "Salient Features of Consumer Protection Act, 1986", "Right of Consumers", "Consumer Protection Act and You", Booklets entitled" Help Prevent Adulteration", "Consumer Protection & Weights & Measures" and " Directory Addresses of Redressal Agencies'" quarterly journal entitled "Upabhokta Jagaran" etc. These are provided to the consumers and the consumer organizations at free of cost. The Consumer Co-ordinations council (an apex body of consumer organizations of India) has been conducting several programmes on consumer education for activists and others.

It has published training materials covering the Consumer Protection Act, 1986; water, food and public distribution system; health, drugs and cosmetics and road transport and railways. Since the enactment of Consumer Protection Act, 1986 and even before that, newspapers and magazines have been responding to the needs of consumers in more than one way. Apart from publishing articles, columns etc. newspapers have also tried to come to the rescue of harassed consumers. This shows the reflections of the role of the press in educating the consumers with regard to their right to consumer's education. The role of Universities in imparting consumer education requires special mention in this context. The Kakatiya University in Warangal, Maharashtra Open University in Pune and Indira Gandhi National Open University are the forerunners in consumer education.

The Consumer education in India faces the universal problem of matching limited resources against an infinite need. The problem acquires a larger dimension due to vastness of the country and multiplicity of languages. Apart from the problem of resources, there is also lack of planning in developing a comprehensive curriculum for consumer education. Thus, majority of the consumers are still not fully aware of all the consumer protection legislation and its implementation mechanisms.

1.5.ii.(l)   Consumers' Right to Representation

The consumers' right to representation is nothing but the right to be heard of. It is the right to advocate consumers' interest with a view to receiving full and sympathetic consideration in the formulation and execution of public policies. This right includes the right to represent the views pertaining to consumer welfare in the government and in other policy-making bodies (Ministry of Environment and Forest Department, 2006). The right to representation is one of the important aspects that provide opportunities for consumer bodies to present their views on the decision-making processes and policy matters affecting consumers at large. This right enables the consumers to put forward their views on appropriate platform.

In India the right to representation is being implemented through a set of administrative as well as organizational instruments involving the Government and Consumer Organizations. In order to facilitate the process of representation, the government has set up different Parliamentary Committees as well as representation mechanisms in various Departments. Both the Houses of Parliament have 'Petitions Committees' and petition on public issues can be presented to each or any one of them. The Committee also considers representation, including letters and telegrams from individuals and associations, which are not covered by the Rules, in relation to the petitions and then gives directions for disposal. A second important representation mechanism is that of complaints to the Government Departments. The Directorate of Public Grievances handles complaints that are addressed to the Central Government. Thirdly, any individual or association can seek remedies through representation by filing writ petitions in the Supreme Court or in the High Court. In order to have representation through consumer organizations, the Government has set up the Central Consumer Protection Council and The State Consumer Protection Council as per Consumer Protection Act, 1986.

Despite the existence of a number of administrative as well as organizational tools, the implementation of consumers' right to representation faces several drawbacks. One of the major drawbacks is that the consumer movement in the country has not developed to the size and reach required for serving the vast country and its huge population. The government has done little to facilitate the growth and development of independent consumer organizations. There is lack of effective coordination among different consumer organizations to ensure proper representation. As they are not able to penetrate deep into society where the poor, low income and disadvantaged consumers live, the representation still a far cry.

1.6. Consumer's Responsibility

While we all like to know about our rights and exercise them, we hardly ever accord the same importance and urgency to our consumer responsibilities. Consumer rights and responsibilities are intertwined together and without sharing consumer responsibility, consumers will find it very difficult to enjoy their rights on a long-term basis.

Consumers need to tread cautiously in the market place. While buying a product, ask yourself these questions:

- Do you really need this product?
- For how long would you like to use it?
- Will it last as long as you would like it to?
- What are the health fallout of that product?
- If it is a food product, does it give you any health benefits?

- Check the labelling of the product to see the nutritional chart of the product.

You can also empower yourself by knowing the law. For e.g., did you know that ISI mark on bottled mineral water has been made mandatory by the government and now labelling of non-vegetarian ingredient in food products will also mandatory for the industry?

Consumer responsibility can play a very important role in not only checking the market but also in restricting unnecessary consumption. It is not the sole responsibility of the market or of the government to provide consumers with detailed information. A consumer, on his part, must make every effort to inform himself of the product or service. For example, if a consumer consumes a health product, he must make efforts to inform himself beforehand about its possible side-effects, and must also exercise caution regarding his eating habits, diet and physical exercise, to take full advantage of the product.

Consumer responsibility is based on ethics and rationale. There are no definitive set of consumer responsibilities and a consumer must exercise restraint in consumption to consume responsibly (Nicouland, 1987). For example, conservation of the environment cannot be forced upon consumers but a consumer must make a conscious effort to reduce consumption, choose environment-friendly alternatives and conserve energy.

Consumer responsibility needs to be shouldered by different consumer segments. Every segment has its own special consumer profile and consumption patterns. These patterns define the kind of consumer responsibility that a segment must discharge.

1.6.i. Responsibility towards safe waste disposal

Most often we consume without sparing any thought for what's going to be left behind as waste. More and more percentage of waste generated in urban areas today consists of non-biodegradable waste. Urban consumers are making use of plastic, paper and cardboard packaging, disposables batteries, plastic throw-away pens, use and throw nappies, empty cans etc. are becoming a common feature of an urban dustbin. India's urban population is around 300 million. By 2011, the total quantity of solid waste generated in urban areas is expected to cross 56 million tonnes, creating a waste management crisis for urban India. Consumers need to become accountable for their consumption patterns and their serious environmental and economic implications. The 4 Rs of consumption (Reduce, Recycle, Refuse and Reuse) are not just a consumer's prerogative but also his consumer responsibility.

1.6.ii. Responsibility to endorse safer products Ecolabelling

Eco-friendliness is an important criterion in judging a product's feasibility.

It is a way of assessing how much damage a product has caused to the environment. 'Eco-mark' is one way of knowing which products conform to environmental standards and are more environment-friendly than others. Ecolabelling is a methodology practised by many countries in the world, including India. The Indian government has formulated a scheme whereby some categories of products are awarded the 'Ecomark' if they conform to certain standards set by the Ministry of Environment and Forests. Unfortunately, in India, the scheme has not taken off due to consumer apathy and lack of response. The market has manipulated this situation to lobby with the government to make ecolabelling a voluntary scheme, which will allow manufacturers to disclose and cover information at will.

1.6.iii. Consumer Bonding

The consumer movement needs active participation of consumers to lobby with the government, pressure the market to deliver better quality, and to support consumer rights campaigns. Empowerment of consumers by NGOs and public campaigns is a two-way process and without continuing consumer support, no campaign can flourish (Shourie, 1998).

1.6.iv. Young Consumers and Consumer Responsibility

Children, teenagers and youth constitute a very important consumer segment for the market. Their consumption habits are unique and their purchase decisions are based on popular trends, brand image, use of new technology, flavour of food products, and style. The market also realises that young consumers have a propensity to consumer junk food and prefer them over traditional forms of food. This characteristic is exploited by the market by associating convenience and a brand image with junk food like colas, pizzas, and fast-food joints.

There are three major brands of toothpaste in India, viz. Colgate, Pepsodent and Close Up. All three of them compete with each other to capture maximum market share. In order to achieve this, they not only target children as consumers but also feature them in their advertisements to attract other young consumers. Colgate, for e.g., targets young children in the age group of 5 to 12 and offers free cartoon booklets along with toothpastes. Pepsodent vies for the same consumer segment and depicts some children relishing snacks, confectionery and sweets, while others are scolded by their mothers for having done the same thing. This advertisement makes children believe that consumers who use Pepsodent are immune to any tooth decay because of the superior quality of the product. This claim is unauthenticated and attempts to mislead children.

Close Up, on the other hand, does not perceive children as its target audience. Instead, it targets teenagers and the youth. It creates a brand image of confidence and popularity for young consumers between the age group of

16-30. Its advertisements constantly feature successful friendships and romances between Close-Up users (Mitchel, 2000).

Millions of rupees are spent on advertising a product which costs as little as Rs. 30 and is considered ordinary by most consumers. From pushing toothpaste on neem sticks to advertising in the Kumbhmela, the market can go to any extent to boost its sales. After a point, the sales tend to stagnate. This negative development is offset by constantly repackaging the present product and introducing new products.

Sum up

The description shows that consumers have different kinds of rights and responsibilities. Even after having various rights, they are facing various kinds of problems. The necessity of adopting measures to protect the interest of consumers arises mainly due to their helpless position and the unfair business practices. No doubt consumers have the basic right to be protected from the loss or injury caused on account of defective goods and deficiency of services. However, consumers are unable to make use of their rights due to lack of awareness and ignorance.

References

M.J. Selvasdas (1998), *"A Study on the Consumer Protection Movement in Kerala,"* Ph.D. Thesis, University of Kerala, p.321, 328, 349, 245-250, 301, 329.

Subhojyoti Acharya (2007), *Consumer Protection & Law - A General Study from India's Perspective*, New India Publications, Delhi, p. 365, 359.

Abbokar Siddiq (2009). "Consumer Protection in India: Some Reflections" *Southern Economist*, Feb. 15.

Erdener Kaynak (1982*), "Consumerism: A Neglected Aspect of Marketing Planning in Developing Economics,"* in Vinay Kothari (ed.) Developing in Marketing Science, pp. 607-610.

G. Padma (1990), *Media and Consumer Protection– A Manual*, Consumer Education and Research Centre, Ahmedabad, p. 97.

A.C. Fernando (2009), *Business Ethics: An Indian Perspective*, Pearson Education India, New Delhi, p. 45.

J.P. Chandra (2004), *Rights of Consumers*, Jag Parvesh Chandra, New Delhi, p. 104.

P. Leela Krishan, (2002), *Consumer Protection and Legal Control*, Eastern Book Co., Lucknow, p. 337.

S. Joseph (2004), "Rational Approach to Consumer-Directed Health Care Engaging Consumer and Providers in Controlling Health Care Costs." *Compensation Benefits Review*, Vol. 36, p. 40.

Robert O. Herrmann (1980), "Consumer Protection: Yesterday, Today and Tomorrow", *Current History* 78 (May), pp.193-196, 226-227.

M. K. Ramesh (1989), "Consumer Interest in Legal Profession-Problems and perspectives", *Cochin University Law Review*, Vol.13, December 4, pp. 405-407, 413, 405.

Peter Drucker (1987), "Consumerism and A Shame of Modern Marketing", *Journal of Marketing*, Vol.25 (Sep), p. 19.

Kotler Philip (1972), "What Consumerism Means for Marketers", *Harvard Business Review*, Vol. 50 (May-June), pp. 57-59.

Hans B. Thorelli (1988), *"Consumer Problems: Developed and Less Developed Countries"*, in the Frontier of Research in the Consumer Interest, E. Scott Maynes (ed.), Columbia, MO: American Council on Consumer Interest; p. 523, 527.

D.N. Saraf (1990), *"Law of Consumer Protection in India"*, N.M. Tripati Bombay, p. 259.

A.C. Fernando (2009), *Business Ethics: An Indian Perspective*, Pearson Education India, New Delhi, p.47.

O. Daniel (1988), *"Report of the National Conference on Weights and Measures United States"*, Bureau of Standards, National Institute of Standards of Technology (U.S.), p.89.

S.M. Shah (1990), "Confused Customer Diffused Movement", *Times of India*, March 28.

J. Sing (1990), *"Consumer and Safety",Journal of Marketing*, March 25, p. 103.

Pritee Shah (1987), *Shome Safety*, Consumer Education and Research Centre, Ahmadabad p. 42, 32.

Siddiq Abbokar (2009), *"Consumer Protection in India: Some Reflections"*, *Southern Economist*, Feb 15, p. 19, 23, 24.

A. Sarkar (1989), *Problems of Consumers in Modern India*, Discovery Publishing House, Delhi, p. 26.

C. Adamson (1982), *Consumer in Business*, National Consumer Council, London, p. 42.

M.M. Nicouland Brigittee (1987), "Consumerism and Marketing Management's Responsibility", *European Journal of Marketing*, Vol . 21 (3), p. 7.

Sanjay Gupta and Anurag (1989), *"Business Callous to Consumer Interest"*, *Consumer Confrontation* Vol. 9 (1) Jan-Feb, p.17.

F. Fetterman and M.K. Schiller (1978), *Let the Buyer Be Aware; Consumer Rights and Responsibilities*, Fairchild Publication, New York, p.217.

Sanjay Gupta & Anurag (1988), "Business ethics and consumer interest", *Consumer Confrontation* Vol.8 (5) May-June, p. 13.

S. Sivazaman (1991), *"Government and Consumer Exploitation"*, *Economic Times*, August 20.

Riswadkar Shobhana (1983), *Unfair Price Shops*, Consumer Education and Research Centre, Ahmedabad, p.10, 16.

E.A. Lizzy (1996), *Women and Consumer Protection*, Ph.D Thesis, Cochin University. p. 321.

Karmatala (1976), *Consumer Service Society India: Some Tips to Remember*, Karnataka Consumer Society Bangalore (India) pp. 35-37.

J.P. Chandra (2004), *Rights of Consumers,* Jag Pradesh Chandra, New Delhi, p.104.

Easther Peterson (1987), *The United Nations and Consumer Guidelines,* T. Wheelwrd (Ed.) Consumer Transnational Corp. and Development Sydney. Transnational Corp. Research Project, University of Sydney, pp. 343-351.

David Harland (1988), "The United Nations Guidelines for Consumer Protection, Reply to the Comment by Weidenbaum", in JCP (1987), 10:4, *Journal of Consumer Policy,* 11 (March): pp. 111-115.

Ashok K. Jha (2003), Consumer Protection, Consumer rights, *Bihar Samachar,* March 15.

J.P. Chandra, (2004), *Rights of Consumers,* Jag Parvesh Chandra, New Delhi. p.109.

L.P. Singh (1978), "Consumer Problems in India", *Indian Journal of Commerce,* Vol. 21 (115), Part-I, p. 49.

O.P. Garg (1990), *Consumer Protection Act, 1986*, Vinod Publishing House, Delhi, p. 354.

V.K. Agarwal (1989), *Consumer protection in India,* Deep & Deep Publication, New Delhi, p. 257.

Gordon Borrie (1984), *The Development of Consumer Law and Policy,* Bold Spirits and Timorous Soul, p. 3.

E. Fetterman, and M.K. Schiller (1978), *Let the Buyer Be Aware; Consumer Rights and Responsibilities,* Fairchild Publication, New York, 1978, p. 217.

Ministry of Information & Broadcasting (1990), *India* ,A Reference Annual Research & Reference Division (Govt. of India), Publications Division, New Delhi.

Ministry of Food & Civil Supply Department, *Annual Report (1989-1990),* Government of India, New Delhi, p. 49.

Ministry of Food & Civil Supply Department, *Annual Report (2003-2004),* Government of India, New Delhi pp. 73-74.

Riswadkar Shobhana (1983), *Unfair Price Shops,* Consumer Education and Research Centre, Ahmedabad, p.16.

Ministry of Food & Civil Supply Department, *Annual Report (2006-2007),* Government of India, New Delhi, pp. 140-143.

Annual Report of the Public Accounts Committee (PAC) of Union Parliament (2000) Delhi.

J. M. Anderson, (1998), *For the People; A Consumer Action Handbook,* Addison-Wesky Publishing Co., California, p. 379, 345-351.

Annual Report of World Bank 2006.

Ministry of Environment and Forest Department, (2007), *Annual Report,* Government of India, New Delhi.

Subhojyoti Acharya (2005), *Consumer Protection. Protection and Law: A General Study from India's Perspective*, new India Publications Delhi, p. 365.

P. Leelakrishan, (1984), *Consumer Protection and Legal Control*, Eastern Book Co, Lucknow, pp. 332-339.

D. Muraliand M.S. Kulkerni, (1990), "Awareness of Housewives Regarding Food Adulteration", *Indian Journal of Marketing*, Vol. No. 20 (5) Jan., pp. 27-28.

A. Sarkar (1989), *The Problem of Consumer in Modern India*, Discovery Publication House Delhi, (1st Ed.), p.105.

Leena Chaturvedi and J.A. Hirani (1986), *Ensure LPG Consumer Safety*, A Report CERC, Ahmedabad.

K. Natarajan (1990), "Consumer Awareness Towards ISI Mark", *Indian Journal of Marketing*, Vol. XX (7), p. 35, 290, 285.

Food and Civil Supply Department (2007), Annual Report of Ministry 2006-2007, Government of India, New Delhi pp. 156-159.

Kulkarni Promod (1986), *Inadequate Information on Lebal of Product*, An Annual Report of CERC (Ahmedabad).

S. Ramchander (1988), "Consumer Behaviour and Marketing Towards on Indian Approach", *Economic and Political Weekly*, Feb 27, Mumbai, p.122.

R. Narayan (1989), *Consumer Awareness and Business ethics*, An Annual Report of CERC (Ahmedabad), pp.97-101.

Rashmi Neeraja (2005), "Consumer Awareness Rights and Responsibilities", *MCM* College Magzine, Chandigarh.

R.K. Uppal and Rimpi Kaur (2007), *Consumer Protection through Mass Awareness:New Challenges and Opportunities*, New Delhi, Mahamaya Publication 2007 XVI, p.392.

P. Leela Krishnam (1983*), Consumer Protection and Legal Control*, Eastern Book Co. Lucknow, p.371, 315, 325-327, 332.

V. K. Agarwal, (1989), *Consumer protection in India*, Deep & Deep Publications, New Delhi,p. 248.

Rashmi Neeraja (2005), "Consumer Awareness Rights and Responsibilities", *MCM* College Magzine, Chandigarh.

M. Giordan (1980), *Consumer Education; A Hand Book for Teachers*, Methuen & Co. Ltd. London, p. 85.

H.N. Giri (1987), *Consumer Crimes and Law*, Ashish Publishing House, New Delhi.p. 349.

Ashok K. Jha (2003), *Consumer Protection, Consumer Rights", and Consumer Disputes* Redressal Commission in India.

Acharya Subhojyoti (2005) *Consumer Protection and Law: A General Study from India's Perspective*, New India Publications Delhi, p. 259.

S.S. Gulshan (2007), *Consumer Protection and Satisfaction*, Deep and Deep Publishing House, New Delhi.

M.J. Antony (1991), *Consumer Rights*, Clarion Books, New Delhi, p. 132.

Sunil Karnik (1995), *Consumer and Law*, Consumer Education and Research Centre, Ahmedabad.

A. Ghatak (1991), *Consumerism in India: An General Study*, Naurang Rai, New Delhi, pp. 363-367.

S.N. Singh (1987), "Consumer Protection Legiclation-A Critipe", *Journal of the Indian Law Institute*, July 90, 29(3), pp. 380-387.

S. Ramachander (1988), "Consumer Behaviour and Marketing towards on Indian Approach", *Economic and Political Weekly*, Feb 27, pp. 122-125.

Ministry of Environment and Forest Department (2006), *Annual Report 2005-2006*, Government of India, New Delhi, pp. 139-142.

Brigitte, M.M. Nicouland (1987) "Consumerism and Marketing Management's Responsibilities", *European Journal of Marketing*, 21(3): 7-16.

H. D. Shourie, (1998), "Consumer Protection – Pass Lows and Sleep". *Hindustan Times*, August 10, 1989.

Alan Mitchel (2000), "Invited presentation: Global brands or global blands?" *Journal of Consumer Studies & Home Economics*; vol.24 (2), pp. 85-93.

CHAPTER – 2
REVIEW OF LITERATURE AND RESEARCH DESIGN

Two important activities in the research are review of literature and preparation of research design. In the present chapter, an attempt has been made to review the literature concerning the problem in hand to find out research gap. In addition, the chapter also presents a picture of research design formulated for the present research work. Accordingly, the present chapter has been divided into two sections, namely, Section – A and Section – B. Section – A deals with the Review of Literature and Section – B deals with the Research Design.

Section – A

In this section an attempt has been made to review the existing literature having direct or indirect bearing on the problem in hand.

2.A.1. Review of Literature

A literature review is a body of text that aims to review the critical points of current knowledge including substantive findings as well as theoretical and methodological contributions to a particular topic. Knowledge of existing and up-to date relevant literature related to the studies and their critical and comprehensive review helps a researcher to formulate research project on scientific lines. It guides the investigator to solve the researchable issues of the study. Literature review acts as a searchlight to guide the course of prospective research activity. Keeping in view this logical thinking, here an effort has been made to make analytical review of the relevant literature. The literature on consumer protection has been reviewed under two headings, namely, Worldwide Studies and Studies in India.

2.A.1.a Worldwide Studies

Many scholars and researchers have conducted research studies to in field of consumer protection, consumer rights and consumer awareness worldwide. Here an attempt has been made to review the worldwide studies.

Katona (1960) in his book entitled 'Powerful Consumer: Psychological studies of American Economy' reports the findings of the "Research Studies in Economic Psychology" by the survey research centre, University of Michigan. This study has shown marked economic fluctuations, which is attributed to the diverse behaviour of buyers, business, and the government and effects are reflected in the outcome of an increased income and willingness to buy goods. The latter is a sum of psychological factors like motives, attitudes, aspirations, expectations, group belonging etc. of the decision-making unit. The analysis reveals that the consumer is powerful and is the major cause prosperity, stagnation, inflation, recession, progress or downfall in an economy, Hence, a continuous understanding of consumers as a group is of supreme significance for the very development of the economy.

Nadel (1971) in his study 'Politics of Consumer Protection' presents an analysis of formulation of consumer protection polices in the Federal Government. According to him consumer protection is one form of government regulation of economic activities. Public opinion played an important role in the success of this type of legislation. He gives a brief sketch of the development of consumer protection to the present time. The author explains the factors associated with the emergence of consumer protection for making it a current political issue.

David (1975) in his book entitled 'Reference Guide to Consumers' has given consumer information from various sources such as Books, pamphlets, magazines, Films, newspapers, organizations etc., Its main purpose is to aid consumers in the U.S. and Canada in their purchasing decisions. These materials relate to the period 1960 to 1974. Part I is on" multimedia materials," Part II is on "organizations" and Part III is on "newspapers".

Berger (1975) in his book entitled 'Consumer Protection Labs' describes an informal visit to consumer protection labs. He explains how scientists check, survey, and compares different consumer durables form the point of view of performance, safety, convenience and economy. He describes the government Food lab and the important contributions of inspectors, scientists, and researchers towards the deliverance of safe and wholesome food products.

Painter (1978) in his book entitled 'Guide to Consumer Protection Law' gives a vivid description of the Criminal and Acts related to consumer protection in the United Kingdom. It emphasized the need for registration and licensing and stamping of goods and services and it special reference with regard to explosives and positions are also given. It gives information a about the price control methods, price check schemes, offences of government and private traders and precautionary steps to be taken by consumers.

Anderson (1978) in his book entitled 'For the People: A consumer action Handbook' helps the exploited consumer to back up his grievances with constructive action and to overpower commercial abuses. Introduced by Ralph Nader, the pioneer of consumer rights, it carries consumer action projects developed by Nader's colleagues. The book covers significant issues like how patients in nursing homes can be assured of their rights, finding and eliminating energy waste, fighting for lower utility bills, comparative growing prices, finding the best buying products, working effectively with the media and changing the laws by lobbying.

Fetterman and Schiller (1978) in their book 'Let the Buyer Be Aware; Consumer Rights and Responsibilities' explain how the consumer can avoid problems through better buying techniques and careful planning. They stress the need for knowing by the Consumers about their rights in the market place and accepting fully their responsibilities to improve the choice among alternatives. According to them the consumer must be able to identify the merchants who are using false or misleading advertisements and it is his duty to reports such practice to the authorities.The book contains the names of a variety of government agencies that work in the field of consumer protection along with the relevant points, which the buyer should keep in mind for avoiding the problems.

National Consumer Council U.K. in its book (1979) entitled 'Consumer and State: Getting Value for Public Money' examines the structure and problems of the public sector, public spending and taxation. The book analyses the consumers' movement by highlighting the economic troubles in U.K. and discusses the role of consumers in a mixed economy and the needs of a healthy economy, which are essential for balanced economic development.

Epstein and Nickles (1980) in their book entitled 'Consumer Law' discuss major issues related to consumer law in U.S.A. It highlights the procedure, enforcement, private action and administrative actions for the law through its transactions and dealings. The book explains lease agreements, the need for credit terms, disclosure, status of debtors and other details of credit transactions as stated in leading Act. The legal and historical background of the laws related to regulation of rates in credit, needs and problem against creditors are given.

International Organization of Consumer Union Japan(1980) in its collection of background reading entitled 'Law and the Consumer: Background Readings' presented at the 63rd session of the Union Nation's

Economic and Social Council on consumer protection defines the problems and measures for individual protection and provides a review of the activates of United Nations and international assistance. Working of the agencies like United Nations Educational, Scientific and Cultural Organization (UNESCO), Food and Agriculture Organization (FAO), United Nations Children's Fund (UNICEF), in the areas of marketing, prices, consumers' representation etcare analyzed. It looks into defensive remedy through consumer education, consumer protection law etc. suggested by the different nations. It recommended government regulation and action by restricting under unfair trade practices, anti-inflationary measures and providing financial assistance to consumers' organizations. The activities of the privately run consumer originations are outlined. Consumer Protection law of Japan and the Consumer protection Act of Finland are also mentioned.

Giordan (1980) in his handbook entitled 'Consumer Education: A Handbook for Teachers' highlights the key elements relevant to consumer education. According to the author Consumer Education has come to be greatly recognised because of the progressively growing global concern for consumer affairs. The situation warrants suitable corresponding development of instructors, course materials and general environment. The potential for incorporating topic for consumer interest in the syllabi of home economics, commerce and business courses, environment communication, family and community studies, pre-retirement programmes and other curricula is discussed.

Lowe and Woodroffe (1980) in their book entitled 'Consumer Law and Practice' concentrates on the problems faced by a person who orders goods or services form a suppler and the remedies available to these problems. It is of much help to those individuals who are called upon the advice on consumer problems. The book has four parts: the consumer and the civil law, the consumer and the criminal law, administration control and special protection in credit transactions. It also deals with issues like trade descriptions, consumers' safety, crime and compensation.

International Organization of Consumer Unions (IOCU) Malaysia(1981) in its book entitled 'Malaysia Guide To Consumer Lawyers' provides the names of 45 Lawyers belonging to 33 consumer organizations of different nations of the world namely NCC U.K. Consumer Association Oreland, PAC Malaysia: Indian federation of consumer organizations, India; Karnataka Consumer service society, India and others. It also states the names of the persons, organizations names, addresses, languages used and main areas of work like legal advice, representing consumers in courts etc.

Silber (1983) in his book entitled 'Test and Protest; the influence of Consumers Union' narrates the beginning of the modern consumer movement, the circumstances under which consumerism and environmental concerns blend, the evolution of the consumer advocacy profession etc. The book has been divided into six chapters dealing with the consumer reform as a science, consumer protest tradition, health hazards connected with smoking, casualties caused by defective automotive design, environmental commendation and science and reform. The author gives special emphasis on issues like the unreliability of sellers, scarcity, ethical consumption, consumer's research and consumers union.

Groeneveld (1984) in his book 'Simple Tests Manual' explains various tests conducted on consumer products. The introductory part of the book discusses the kinds of tests, the place where certain tests should be conducted, the person who should conduct the test, equipment and chemicals used for conducting tests and information about basic maintenances of the laboratory. The book gives the reader a very good insight about the methods and procedures to be followed while conducting tests. A list of reagents used and names of the chemicals, chemical formulae and other relevant particulars are included in the appendices.

Grada (1985) in his booklet entitled 'Promoting Consumer Education in Schools' dwells up on areas common to most of the education systems the world over. It constitutes a resource for individuals in consumer organizations to be consumer educator. Consumer education has the objects like imparting knowledge (of consumer rights, law etc,) ; understanding of society-consumer relationships; development skills (drafting complaints, pinpointing deceit/fraud); and inculcating a sense of the importance of being and acting as an enlightened/discerning consumer, introducing consumer education in schools, hurdles in the promotion of the concept, syllabus, training of educators and resources are discusses.

Cooper (1986) in his book 'Consumer Education' discusses in depth important areas of home economics and deals with problems that a consumer might experience. It covers subjects like how to make a wise choice while buying goods or services, care to be taken in receiving unsolicited and dangerous goods, paints to be remembered while buying goods in credit, remedies against unfair contract terms, advertising standards, food or drink for human consumption and legal aspects of borrowing money for buying a house.

Stanesby (1986) in his book 'Consumers Rights Handbook' analyses the Rights of consumers and the Acts protecting them in the United Kingdom. It explains legal terms and principles like damages, warranty etc. It narrates the responsibilities and duties of the traders and shopkeepers. The offences committed by sellers of all types of goods including door – to – door salesmen and mail order sales are listed along with precautions to be taken to avoid them.

Wells and Sim (1987) in their book entitled 'Till they have Faces; women as consumers' discuss the role of women as consumers and describes how they have become the worst victims of injustice. The authors deal with issues like housing, medicine, food, health, water, technology, fuel and transport, hazardous products, and credit, and it brings out the important role played by women as consumers of all these items and how they are neglected. With the help of case studies the authors illustrate how women consumers have organized and created a better situation for themselves. They enumerate the reasons why women are held back as consumers. The book suggests how community organizers, development workers, intermediaries. Or agents can play an important part in bringing women together to talk about problems they face, helping them recognize the reason and work out solutions.

Daniel (1988) in his article 'How the Federal Trade Commission Serves the Consumer' throws light on the FTC's usefulness to consumers. He describes the commissions key functions (anti-trust action, consumer protection and consumer advocacy) and singles out its mission as "preserving the free market", because, only competition seems to provide consumers the best protection. Striking at some of the United States Government polices he substantiate his stance with cases. The FTC chief reiterates his mission of fostering fee markets and thus strengthening the consumers' own resistance.

Grant (1989) in his article entitled 'Indian Consumer Must Shake off his Apathy' encourages Indian consumers to fight for their rights. According to him Personal initiative and effort are necessary to accelerate the pace of the consumer movement and make the consumer protection laws a success.

International Organization of Consumer Unions Netherlands(1989) in its book entitled 'International Consumer Directory 1989' is meant to provide information about 300 worldwide consumer organizations in terms of their names, Address - telephone - telex – fax, officers, own membership details, stiff, affiliations, principal areas of work, sources of funds, publications, year of establishment, and IOCU- membership category. It is an annual publication of IOCU.

Rebellow (1989) in his article 'American's View of consumer Protection' make a picture of Indian consumerism as perceived by an American Lawyer, Mr. David Averbuck. Though the consumer movement is stated to be retarded, it contains some impressive features. The interview with Averbuck points out the merits of the consumer protection Act 1986 and expedient settlement of disputer in consumer forums. He states the deficiencies and suggests remedial measures.

Wilcox's (1989) book entitled 'Educated Consumers; an analysis of curriculum needs in consumer education' is collection of papers which discusses and analyses consumer education programme in the United States. It discusses about consumer education resource network consumer action learner societal and consumer needs in consumer education, the philosophy of consumer education, concepts related to the basic definition of consumer education, consumer citizenship and the environment of consumer occasions, development and implementation of consumer education, consumer identity, socio-political context of consumption etc.

Rebellow (1989) in his article 'Long wait for redress panels' discloses the slackness and ignorance of the Government Officials and the State Legal Department in implementing decisions of the consumer redressal forums and commissions. The constant refusal of the capable judges and personnel to accept public service worsens the plight of the consumers who are left with no other choice in ventilating their grievances.

Sing (1989) in his article 'Consumer Complaint Intentions and Behaviour; definitional and issues' draws attention to the Consumer Compliant Behaviour concept examining questions on its nature, structure and taxonomy. He analyses consumer intention and behaviour in four different situations (medical care, grocery, repair and bank) in the form of responses or attitudes like immediate action, voice etc. The concept is said to be of help to marketers and theory formulators of consumer complaint behavior. He is bringing out the importance and application of consumer behaviour concept with the help of a study conducted among common households in Texas.

Rebellow (1990) in his article entitled 'Is service sector any the better' pointed out the pathetic state of the service sector in India. Be it a bank, railway, or airlines, the services are known to have taken the consumers for granted. There is need for an organized initiative and action from consumers to change the trend. The article calls up on the Indian consumers to raise their voices against exploiters in the government and private sector service sellers, to make the movement successful.

Saraf (1990) in his book 'Law of Consumer Protection in India' narrates the evolution of consumer law and depicts its development in USA, U.K. and India. It gives a profile of Indian consumers and highlights major consumer problems arising out of operation of public utility services (Railways, Road Transport, Air Transport, Telephones, Banking Service and Insurance) which are peculiar to India due to monopolization of production, distribution and control of some essential goods and services by the state. He critically examines utility of certain doctrines like the doctrine of 'caveat emptor'. He goes in to the safeguards contains in Sale of Goods Act like conditions and warranties, implied undertakings as to title, implied conditions implied conditions relating to descriptions, implied conditions as to merchantable quality and fitness of purpose and suggests some reforms for protection of consumer particularly in relation to exclusion of liability in contracts. It contains a table of cases and an index. As pioneering work on consumer protection, it has been found useful by consumer activists.

The WTO Centre for international Trade, Economics and Environment, (2001) under CUTS International conferences on competition policy published an article for the purpose of helping consumers to generate minimum awareness on anti-competitive behaviours in the market. So that consumers can alert the government as well as competition authority in the implementation of competition legislations. Furthermore the article raise emphasis that, consumers gain a lot from healthy competition in the market, due to the fact that competition enables undertakings to function efficiently. Also competition presents to consumers a greater choice of products at lower prices. The article purports that developing countries should design their competition structure based on their economic, social and historical factor not based on the developed nations.

Judit (2005) has identified the relationship between competition law and consumer protection. Competition law make certain that market remains competitive by cheering new market entrants at the same time it creates incentive for innovation, therefore competitive prices will be promoted at the same time it increase product choices. Cseres has attempted to fill the gap, of how competition law benefits consumers and how consumer protection benefits the whole process of competition in the market. The author has shown to what extent consumer protection law will exist on a market where effective competition rule operate. In some other circumstance there is no need of enacting ineffective law which it aim is already covered by another legislation, this results into wastage of tax payers money and government time. This research paper has gone further to research whether competition law is effective tool to protect consumers. The study has taken into account the developed jurisprudence of competition law that is US and EC, with the developing jurisprudence of competition law that is Tanzania.

Kahyarara (2004) has examined different competition policy, regulations and upcoming institution that regulate the activities of dominant firms to avoid monopoly through mergers and anticompetitive behaviours in Tanzania. His research was part of the initiative taken by the United National Conference on trade and development. He has extensively surveyed the results of monopoly through mergers and anticompetitive behaviours in Tanzania. That consumer will be limited in terms of choices and prices, this robes consumer's utility, as they will buy products unwillingly. This research paper will go further to study how the Fair Competition Act of Tanzania protects consumers.

Vedder (2006) in order to identify the relationship between competition law and consumer protection, he has first and foremost defined what is the objective of competition law as an economic phenomena. He comes to the conclusion that, the link between competition law and consumer protection is limited to the restriction of competition regulations that have some consumer protection objective. However, one can criticise Hans Vedder on the point of view that the main objective of competition rules and regulation is economic effectiveness, when defining the word economic effectiveness it includes consumers' welfare, if consumers lack competitive prices and arena for choices that means the economy is not effective.

Micklitz (2006) the author has discussed on the relationship between antitrust law and consumer law in the European Commission (EC), the EC has formed several directives that relates to the consumer protection in EC.The coming into force of these directives have reaffirmed the relationship between antitrust and consumer law. Hans W Micklitz has raised an emphasis that, private enforcements are of vital importance for the development of competition law and consumer protection relations. This dissertation paper will go further to study the relationship of competition law and consumer protection in US, EC, South Africa and evaluate what lessons Tanzania can learn from these countries.

OECD (2009), discussed on how competition policy and consumer protection share common goals and how they complement each other. The two policies share a common goal that is both aim at the welfare of consumer, they both speak the same language with the same goal. In this case this research paper will research if there is a need of having two legislations with the same aim, the paper will evaluate if competition law is effective tool to protect consumers or there are some consumers' problems that cannot be protected under competition legislations.

2.A.1.b Studies in India

Here an attempt has been made to review the studies conducted by various scholars and researchers at the national level in India.

Mathews' (1975) findings on awareness of housewives towards food adulteration in Udaipur city revealed that majority of food available in the market were adulterated but small section of population knew about its ill effects. However, majority of housewives preferred homemade articles because of their wholesomeness, freshness, better flavor and color. They did not favor the purchase of commercially prepared food items because of inferior quality and adulteration.

Karnataka Consumer Services Society India (1976) in its booklet 'Some Tips to Remember' explains and guides the consumer on how to buy various products. The booklet enumerates tricks used by sellers and advises consumers on protecting themselves against such malpractices. The Booklet contains information on simple test, which can be carried out by consumers themselves to detect adulteration. A few suggestions to lesson environmental problems are also included in the booklet.

Shah's (1981) 'Public Interest Groups and Developmental Journalism' is a booklet containing the text of the speech given by himself. According to him public interest groups help the common man to bring to the notice of the concerned authorities, the problems faced by him. He opines that the right to information and the right to expression are practiced very weakly in India. The booklet also contains a list of Consumer Education and Research Center's research publications.

Subramanyam (1981) conducted study in Guntur revealed that 52 per cent of the respondents stated that the ineffective supervision of the government was responsible for the high prices of consumer goods in the economy. More than 3/4th of them complained that the display of prices (83%) was not observed by the traders and 93 per cent of them accepted that local taxes were not made known to the buyers by the concerned departments who took such taxes on the products.

ShobhanaRiswadkar (1983) in the study entitled 'Unfair Fair Price Shops' assesses the effectiveness of Fair Price Shops (FPS) in providing adequate services to the people in the villages of Gujarat tribal areas. The study brings out the problems faced by the Fair Price Shop users and the various instances of malpractices prevailing *in the Fair* Price Shop System. The booklet includes few tables which inform about: - (1) the status of FPS operates within the village and outside the village (2) list of complaints against FPS and (3) cases of false billing.

Leela's (1984) book entitled 'Consumer Protection and Legal Control' is a compilation of papers on the problem of consumer exploitation in India presented and discussed at a 'National Seminar on Consumer Protection and Legal Control' held at Cochin (India) in 1981. It throws light on the general problems of consumers and various aspects of consumerism. The fundamental Rights available to Indian consumers and the principles that are followed by the state are analysed. The means to justice, Public interest litigation and the role of legal authorities in protecting consumer's interests are enlisted in it.

Chandra (1984) in his book 'Rights of Consumers' depicts the disappointments and frustrations of the dissatisfied consumer. It is an attempt to create better understanding between the merchants and consumers. Merchants must understand and accept the concept of consumerism; consumer's rights, tricks of traders etc. are enumerated. The government should be more active in ensuring legal support to consumers and abolish unfair trade practices. Promotion of business and consumerism through co-operative steps is suggested. There is a request to the press to help the consumer movement by providing coverage and reproducing the grievances of consumers. The book suggests the setting up of a Consumer Affairs Centre exclusively for treating consumer related matters.

Dave (1987) in the research study entitled 'Speeding towards road safety' gives a comprehensive account of road accidents, their causative factors and also spells out future action plans to prevent such unnecessary mishaps. The report states that in India in every four minutes one accident occurs killing or injuring one person one an average. The report points out the alarming rate of increase in the number of accidents in India. It states that though India possesses hardly one percentage of all vehicles in the world, it accounts for nearly 6 percent of all accidents. It should be noted that though only 25 percent of the Indian population is housed in cities, 75 per cent of the road accidents are occurring in cities and the drivers are found to be responsible for more the 70 per cent of the accidents. The research findings are tabulated in 12 different categories and annexure are divided into 7 sub chapters.

Kamath (1987) in his book 'Servants, Not Masters' narrates the author's bizarre ordeals with the bureaucrats, the police force and other public servants. Drawing heavily on Gandhian philosophy, the book explains the lessons for consumer activists outlining the teething troubles, pitfalls, possible remedies, basic formalities, guiding principle, strategies, tactics, efficient and effective use of media, legal and other forces, cases, episode, references and a draft consumers' Bill of Rights all effectively included to provide a wide perspective.

Shah (1987) in the study paper entitle 'Home Safety' presented at the International Congress on Safety, Health Environment held at New Delhi in February 1987, organized by National Safety Council Bombay, explains the causes of accidents in the home namely, electricity hazards, explosion, construction failures, fire, faulty lighting, building design and interior design. The paper points out that the safety of the health of the residents is also an issue of home safety and hence suggests the selection of location away from chemical factory, river sites and noise pollution.

Giri (1987) in his book entitled 'Crimes and the Law' gives stress on protecting the Indian consumer with extensive case analysis, references to development in western countries and remedy to protect the interests of consumers in India. It narrates the current state of the law relating to the problems of false and fraudulent trade practise of manufactures or dealers in food and drugs. He concentrates on the evaluation of the effectiveness of the existing legal mechanism in the light of current knowledge of the causes and treatment of disorder. He studies and interprets factors that contribute to the perpetration of such offences and considers the role of judiciary in executive control over these evils.

Agrawal (1989) in his book 'Consumer Protection in India' analyses the legal protection available to the consumers in India. He evaluates the MRTP Act and Consumer Protection Act, in the context of restrictive/unfair trade practices and rights of consumers. Presented in six parts the text summarizes various sections of the above said Acts. The introductory part contains the historical background of the Acts in India and similar legislations in different nations of the world like Germany, Belgium, and U. K. etc. He explains the scope, provisions and penalties under the MRTP Act. The activities, powers and penalties imposed by the District Forums, State and National Commissions are discussed.

Bakshi (1989) in his article titled 'Consumer Law and Voluntary Agencies' explains the activities and role of voluntary consumer organizations. The legal issues such as legal advice and aid to consumers and society are stressed in the article. The organizations are praised for taking initiative and lodging complaints or suits, attending court proceedings, public litigation etc. The sections of Indian Penal Code enhancing consumer's rights are highlighted. The need for legal literacy and guidance is pointed out in the context of the activities of the organizations.

Dixit (1989) in his article entitled 'Consumers don't Take Things Lying Down' requests earnestly the Indian consumers to rise, realize and adopt their rights as consumers to fight back explications and clever business tactics. He depicts a picture of the consumer as exploited and taken for granted in spite of his so-called importance in the economy. He encourages the consumers to learn about their rights thought voluntary consumer organizations and government agencies. He calls up on the consumers to rise to occasion to encourage public interest litigation to seek what they deserve.

Imam (1989) in his article 'Consumer not the King' points out that despite the enactment of the consumer Protection Act 1986 and over 30 other laws stipulating standards or a affording relief, poor awareness and lack of organizational skills on the consumers' part impede their desirable impact in India. The situation has become worse due to the failure of a large number of States to set up the enforcement machinery. This situation necessitated the Supreme Court to order the States to set up the machinery with six weeks. The article pronouns confidence in the consumer movement gaining momentum and stresses the need for independent product testing laboratories, comparative reporting of products/services and educating the consumers with regard to environmental hazardous matters.

Narayan (1989) in his article 'Hope for harried consumers' analyses the role and activities of the Consumer Grievance Forums in India. According to him the powers of the Forum have expanded resulting in the co-operative attitude of many companies thereby following fair practices. He points out that, though the Forums are growing in importance and power but are facing problems with government organizations.

Ramesh (1989) in his paper 'Consumer Interest in Legal Profession-Problems and Perspectives' presented at the national seminar on consumer protection held form March 16-18, 1989 at the Cochin University of Science and Technology, introduced the reader to the deterioration economic system and the adverse impact of trade on the consumers. The pathetic condition of the innocent consumers is brought to light in the wake of lack of knowledge and confidence. He points out that the best solution to escape from this helpless situation is creating awareness through education among consumers of consumers, the attitude of lawyers and drawback of the legal profession as reflected under the Consumer Protection Act, 1986. He narrates the duties of lawyers and the need for rules and control through the Bar Council of India. He has invited the attention of the readers to the malpractices of lawyers such as charging exorbitant fees and making their services inaccessible to common man. The paper ends with suggestions for improvements such as peer group adjudication, strict liability under Consumer Protection Act, 1986 and penalty for offence to professionals.

Shah (1989) in his article 'Confused Consumer Diffused Movement' narrates how the plethora of consumer legislations in India, by virtue of their complex and all-encompassing characteristics, has rendered the consumer utterly bewildered and cornered into a pitiable state. The author questions whether these laws have deterred business from explanting the consumer through malpractices and whether GrahakSurakshaMandls with their narrow vision and conservative approach can make any worthwhile contribution to consumer protection. He also observes that the spate of spurious goods and poor services are continued unabated.

Shah (1989) in his article entitled 'Consumer and Clothing' highlights the inadequacy of textile production, factors responsible thereof and unfair trade practices followed by the textile mills. The matters such as pricing, quality, safety and legal remedies which are of much concern to the consumers are looked in to. The article appeals to the industry to practice discipline and to discontinue all marketing and stamping, which are defrauding, misleading and confusing to the consumer. The article concludes with a suggestion that all relevant information that will enable a consumer to purchase and use the fabric and the garment must be clearly and unambiguously set on them.

Sivaranam (1989) in his article 'Combating Consumer Exploitation' narrates the working of the consumer action group Madras, whose objectives is strengthening the consumer lobby as an economic force to be reckoned with. He explains consumer action group's stricture and how public interest issues are handled by it. He also gives an account of various cases that Consumer Action Group has successfully resolved.

Sarkar (1989) in his book entitled 'Problems of Consumers in Modern India' deals with major problems of consumers such as price-rise, inflation, population explosion, adulteration of food, substandard goods such as drugs, cosmetics, utensils, pesticides and insecticides. Problems like short weights and measures, inadequacies in transport services, communication, sanitation, housing, drinking water and electricity are also examined. According to him government and voluntary consumer organizations have attempted to mitigate all these problems by introducing various legislative and administrative measures. The book contains information about the consumer co-operative movement and the role played by various consumer organizations.

Shourie (1989) in his article 'Consumer Protection – pass lows and sleep' points out the failure of the Consumer Protection Act, 1986 to implement or materialize its rules and provisions. According to him the passing of the Act is victory for consumers but the delay of failure in setting up the required three – tier structure of District Forums, State Commission and Central

61

Councils has lowered the very progress of consumer grievance redressal. The success and growth of these Forums has further been affected by the dispute in between the Central Government and the State Governments in providing funds.

Thanulingum and Kochadai (1989) conducted a study in Madhurai city and results revealed that majority of the consumers were aware of the importance of food labels, trademarks so on. But very few consumers knew the procedure of lodging complaints about adulterated products. Apart from the legal and other aids that are available for the protection of consumer interests, the most significant development in recent years has been the provision of redressal machinery for dealing with genuine consumer grievances.

Bijlani (1990) in the dissertation entitled 'Role of Mass Media in Consumer Education' measures the potential of mass media and their limitations. The author defines consumer education and explains its significance, spells out the customer rights and responsibilities, discusses consumer movements abroad and in India and deliberates on the use of mass media for consumer purposes and explores the possible constraints in the process. It points out the need for the consumer groups to maintain close liaison with media and providing factual, unbiased information for public interest and taking advantage of public service adverting over AIR and TV. The author asserts that the consumer groups and the mass media must work hand – in hand, appreciating their common interests and respective constraints.

Garg (1990) in his book 'Consumer Protection Act, 1986' gives procedures for handling different types of comments on drugs, trade practise, and advertising etc. An idea about the activities of the voluntary consumer organizations. Consumer protection council, international agencies, their procedures, founds and members is provides. The procedure of appealing in courts and tribunals is discussed along with the ways of enforcing orders. Expansions of the meaning and scope of the terms used in the Act is also given. The Rights of Consumers' are discussed including the services of banks, insurance companies, etc.

Joshi (1990) in his article entitled 'Creating Consumerism' shows the overall scenario of the consumer movement in India in 1989, as it emerged during a panel discussion on 'Consumer Protection: "Myth or Reality", held in New in April 1989. Although the movement became stronger and the overall climate became conducive as progressive laws were enacted, major impediments like consumers' callous attitude towards their rights and laxity and corruption in the law enforcement machinery prevented its consolidation and success.

Kumar and Batra (1990) have studied Consumer awareness about rights and responsibilities in small town of Haryana. Study revealed that, majority of respondents were aware of their rights like right to product safety (94%), right for information (92%), right to be heard (93%) and right to healthy environment (95%). Because the town was well connected with radio and television networks. Further, it was reported by 73 per cent of the respondents that they were not having option to choose the products because of lack of variety of goods in small town. In case of right to product safety, majority (60%) of respondents took no action against defective packaging. Those who took action limited to complaining to the seller about defect. The survey indicated that consumers were well aware of their rights but very few of them were excising them because of unsatisfactory response of their voice, and they received unsatisfactory and discouraging response.

Mehta (1990) in his article 'Blow for the consumer' explains the salient features of the Consumer Protection Act, 1986 The three tier enforcement machinery, the monetary and territorial jurisdiction and time horizon for disposal of cases are explained along with some of the achievements and failures. He points out that the law has generated a consumer revolution capable of gaining momentum over time.

Murali and Kulkarni (1990) conducted a study about awareness about food adulteration among housewives of Parbhani city. The study revealed that, higher percentages of housewives were aware of food adulteration. All the selected housewives were using homemade food items for its freshness, better flavor and taste. Though majority of the housewives expressed their awareness regarding food adulteration but they were not aware of harmful effects of adulteration on health and government actions to prevent food adulteration.

Natarajan (1990) has studied Consumer awareness about ISI mark in Madhurai city. The results indicated that consumers had better awareness about ISI mark and its benefits. Consumers had favourable attitude towards quality, performance and dependability of ISI mark goods. The consumers view that the price of ISI mark goods were high and inferior goods were available with ISI mark. Consumers opinion that more number of goods should be brought under ISI certificate scheme.

Padma (1990) in the manual entitled 'Media and Consumer Protection' aims at helping consumer activists to use media effectively and to help media personnel to get some idea of the consumer movement. The manual is organized in two parts. Part I is aimed at helping consumer groups and activists to understand the needs and concerns of the media in terms of what makes news. Part II concentrates on familiarizing media personnel with the consumer movement; the history and growth of consumer groups in India and abroad, laws relating to it etc. Names and addresses of various research institutions in India and abroad are included in the manual.

Padma and Karnik (1990) in their book entitled 'Complaints Handling' target those people of consumer protection groups who deal with complaints. The authors explain the entire process of Complaint Handling in a simple effective language using actual complaints handling by consumer Education and Research centre as examples. They stress the need for scientific approach to complaints handling. The broad areas covered in this book are process, follow-up and analysis of complaints and setting up a complaints service. The authors make it clear that the main objective of a consumer protection group is bringing about a just and fair solution to any complaint lodged with them by the consumer. According to them when complaints throw light on the paucity of laws in a particular area, the consumer protection groups can lobby for new laws or amendments in existing law.

Parigi (1990) in his article 'Safer Products for the Consumer' Quoting some statistics about accidental casualties in and around homes attributed to unsafe/hazardous products pronounces concern for general safety because injury/death cases outnumbers those owing to traffic or work reasons. He has highlighted the need and necessity for a Consumer Protection Safety Commission to examine product designs, manufacturing process, materials and performance. The relevance and significance of voluntary self-regulation by business and industry are emphasized drawing on the example of Sweden.

Antony (1991) in his book 'Consumer Rights' explains the nature and extent of consumer protection in India. He discusses its impact on the government, legislation, consumers, business and society, According to him, a welcome development in the field of consumer protection in the Indian legal context is that many legislative measures, which were available in the earlier days, have been reinforced by suitable modifications or fresh enactions.

Jayadevan (1993) in his dissertation work entitled 'Banking Service and Consumer Protection' describes the banker's liability for deficiency in dealing with his depositors, deficiency of service in providing loans and defects in subsidiary services. The author suggests that business self-regulation is best for protecting the interests of banking consumers.

Sreevidya (1993) in her dissertation work entitled 'Consumer Justice and Public Utility Services' assesses the working formula under the Consumer Protection Act, 1986 for rendering justice to the public utility Services.

Lizzy (1996) in her Ph.D thesis entitled 'Women and Consumer Protection' highlights the role of women in promoting consumerism in Kerala. She also suggests various measures for the speedy functioning of the consumer disputes redressal agencies in Kerala.

Sawarkar and Giram (1996) conducted a study on consumer awareness about consumer protection act in Marathwada region. Study revealed that 48.63 per cent of respondents were aware of consumer protection act in which maximum of them belonged to the age group of 20-30 years (24.13%). Awareness was more among graduate respondents (26.93%) than among non-graduates (21.73%). Further findings of the same author on college teachers in Marathwada region revealed that awareness of consumer protection act among college teacher was 84.21 per cent and half of the respondents were aware of the redressal machinery established under the consumer protection act, but majority were not knowing the procedure of complaint lodging.

Hasalkar and Ashalatha (1998) conducted study on awareness of homemakers about Indian Standard Mark on consumer goods in Dharwad city. Results showed that maximum number of employed homemakers were aware of the ISI mark (71%) and Agmark (30%). Higher percentages of employed homemakers have purchased the ISI mark bearing household equipments than the unemployed homemakers. Highest percentage of respondents both from employed and unemployed class (99% and 92% respectively) expressed the need for consumer education. As high as 95 per cent of employed and 91 per cent of unemployed homemakers said that they insist on the guarantee card for the equipment while purchasing.

Reddy and Ramesh (1998) conducted a study on the role of an independent agency to protect the consumer interest in twin cities of Hyderabad and Secundrabad. Hyderabad forum received 12,116 cases since its inception, of which 8,051 (66%) have been dispensed of and 4,065 (34%) cases were pending. Study also reported that only 19 per cent of them were fully aware of the Consumer Protection Acts and more than half of the respondents were partially aware of the consumer rights and 30 per cent were not aware of it. Awareness of consumer protection was more among men than the women. From the above studies reviewed it was clear that maximum number of respondents were aware of consumer welfare programmes i.e., Consumer Protection Act but very few consumers utilized the facilities.

Hasalkar and Ashalata (1998) conducted a study in Dharwad city. According to their findings majority (91%) of employed and 82 per cent of unemployed homemakers agreed that they read instructions on the label and acted accordingly. More than 82 per cent of both the groups had come across the adulterated foods while purchasing. But method of detection of adulteration was known only to 55 per cent of employed and 45 per cent of unemployed homemakers. Negligible number of homemakers of both employed and unemployed homemakers had approached the consumer forum for justice. It could be inferred from the reviews collected that almost all the articles were adulterated and high percentage of housewives were aware of it, but no action was taken.

Selvadas (1998) in his Ph.D thesis entitled 'A Study on the Consumer Protection Movement in Kerala' evaluates how for the Consumer Protection Act, 1986 has been effective in Kerala since its enactment. This general study about the consumer movement in Kerala mentions about voluntary consumer organizations in Kerala, perception of consumers and business community with regard to Consumer Protection Act, 1986 and the working of consumer disputes Redressal agencies in Kerala.

Gambhir (2002) conducted a study in Chandigarh revealed that 54 per cent of the respondents were aware of the ISI mark and 46 per cent of the respondents were not aware of it. Further out of 54 per cent of respondents only 30 per cent bought products that had ISI mark. It can be concluded from the reviews presented that consumers had better awareness about ISI mark and they bought the ISI mark bearing household equipment.

Gupta and Agarwal (2003), look at the three major drivers of growth in consumer finance: auto finance, housing finance and consumer durable finance in view of this changing landscape. They discuss the trends in each of these areas as well as the shortcomings which are slowing down growth. They present some of the innovative product ideas which have appeared in the market recently and others which have the potential and can pick up provided adequate attention is paid. These include customer financing by large retail outlets, range of credit card offerings, innovations in education finance, rural finance, etc. The role of risk management has also been discussed as far as containing delinquencies and losses in repayment of loans are concerned. The mortgage portfolio performance will get affected by a sharp drop in real estate prices, drop in rents, changes in the tax laws removing exemptions for mortgage repayments. The Auto loans portfolio can get affected by the drop in re-sale values of cars, decrease in car prices, exchange rates, etc. Unsecured products like personal loans and credit cards can get affected by macro-economic factors like employment rates, inflation, interest rates etc. We therefore provide an overview of the risk mitigation strategies which are available to lenders and progress made in this direction so far.

Nisa (2007) is of the opinion that India is one of the largest emerging markets, with a population of over one billion. India is one of the largest economies in the world in terms of purchasing power and has a strong middle class base of 300 million. Around 70 per cent of the total households in India (188 million) reside in the rural areas, where mostly traditional retail outlets, commonly called kirana stores exist. These are unorganized, operated by single person and runs on the basis of consumer familiarity with the owner. However, recently organized retailing has become more popular in big cities in India and most of the metropolitan cities and other big cities are flooded by modern organized retail stores. Many semi-urban areas also witnesses entry of such organized retail outlets. Till now, entry of foreign retailers was restricted in Indian retail market because of the ban on Foreign Direct Investment in Indian Retail Sector. But recently, as government has changed its policy and the cabinet has allowed 51 per cent FDI in single-brand retail, the prospects of foreign players entering India became high.

Gupta (2008) opines that Internet banking has attracted the attention of banks, securities trading firms, brokerage houses, insurance companies, regulators and lawmakers in developing nations since the late 1990s. With the rapid and significant growth in electronic commerce, it is obvious that electronic (Internet) banking and payments are likely to advance. Researches show that impact of Internet banking on cost savings, revenue growth and increased customer satisfaction on Industry is tremendous and can be a potential tool for building a sound strategy. However, it has raised many public policy issues before the banking regulators and government agencies. Interestingly, reliable and systematic information on the scope of Internet banking in Indian context is still not sufficient, particularly what it means to the consumers and the bankers. The paper fills significant gaps in knowledge about the consumer's perspective of Internet banking, trace its present growth and project the likely scenario. The paper presents the data, drawn from a survey of Internet banking consumers and the services providers (banks) that offer Internet banking and develops a functional model for maximizing value to the consumers, which the banks may choose to adopt Internet banking strategically. The paper identifies the weaknesses of conventional banking and explores the consumer awareness, use patterns, satisfaction and preferences for Internet banking vis-à-vis conventional form of banking and also highlights the factors that may affect the bank's strategy to adopt Internet banking. It also addresses the regulatory and supervisory concerns of Internet banking.

Chatterjee et al. (2009) attempts to explore and identify consumer awareness regarding consumer, responsibilities and Consumer Protection Act, 1986. It is patently obvious that consumers are not only the largest economic group but also the pivots of all the economic activities. It is also true that the very consumers are the most unaware or voiceless group in most of the countries of the world. There are plethora of laws and other mechanism to ensure the welfare of consumers, yet they have no power to order where he can make his purchase at will. They suggest that consumer should organize together to develop the strength and influence to promote and protect their own interest. Government should make and implement rules of punishment more harsh so that manufacturer and shopkeeper think twice before adopting fraudulent practices. A campaign should be set in motion to involve each and every consumer for making them more conscious and aware of their right and responsibilities. Government and other consumer agencies should make efforts in the direction of propaganda and publicity of district forum, state and national judiciary established for consumer protection so as to make more and more consumer aware about machinery for their greater involvement and to seek justice in case of grievances. And finally, redress procedure should be made more logical, easy enough to be understood by a large number of consumers. Further procedures shall so designed as to have easy handling and quick disposal of cases.

Choudary, (2010) worked on study entitled "A Study on the consumer preference on various mobile connections and buyer behavior" was conducted in Chennai with special reference to RELIANCE INFOCOMM. The study was undertaken to know the preference level of consumers towards various mobile connections. The study covers various brands like Airtel, Aircel, BSNL, Tata Indicom, and RIM in relation to various aspects. The survey was conducted by collection from various consumers (Mobile Users). The expectations of the consumers are quite high. Many expect high performance, Zero error in billing and in need of more collection centers. The experience of the consumers and their rating of the mobile are moderate, proper awareness should be given importance. As the study was limited to Chennai town only, it was possible to understand the demographic profile and consumer preference. The preference of individual consumers depends mainly on annual income and actual performance of the product as well as external influencing factors like society and etc., consumers prefer the advice of others also. Consistency in performance, level of satisfaction has a major impact. The study of consumer preference towards mobile users gives an idea of individual preference towards the product based on various influencing factors like Price, group influences, social influences and psychological influences. It also gives an idea on rating of product done by the consumers generally etc., particularly relating to Chennai.

Suresh (2010), opines that in the world of changing business scenario, consumers interest towards protection of environment are raising dramatically and their consumption also getting change noticeably towards the protection of environment. It is evident from a study, In India around 25 percentages of the consumers prefer environmental-friendly products, and around 28 percentages may be considered as healthy conscious. The increasing awareness among the consumers towards environmental friendly-products ensures the industry to produce environmental friendly products rather than environmental harmful products. In advertising itself, there are some firms emphasizing the features of green products, for instance, surf excel advertisement for water saving, Idea m obile for tree protection through saving of paper and recently Aircel for save the tiger. In connection with these, what will be the attitude of consumers to select green products? In other words, what will be the impact of green advertisement on consumer buying behavior. With the object of identifying the solution to this problem, the study has been conducted based on the survey of 200 randomly select respondents in Tamil Nadu. The study reveals that 60 percentages of the respondents are friendly to green products, further it reveals that there is no impact of green advertisement on the consumer buying behaviour.

Dahat (2010) feels that public awareness of medical negligence in India is growing. Hospital managements are increasingly facing complaints regarding the facilities, standards of professional competence, and the appropriateness of their therapeutic and diagnostic methods. After the Consumer Protection Act, 1986, has come into force some patients have filed legal cases against doctors, have established that the doctors were negligent in their medical service, and have claimed and received compensation. As a result, a number of legal decisions have been made on what constitutes negligence and what is required to prove it. Negligence is the breach of a legal duty to care. It means carelessness in a matter in which the law mandates carefulness. A breach of this duty gives a patient the right to initiate action against negligence. Persons who offer medical advice and treatment implicitly state that they have the skill and knowledge to do so, that they have the skill to decide whether to take a case, to decide the treatment, and to administer that treatment. This is known as an "implied undertaking" on the part of a medical professional.

Kumar (2011) focuses on examining the perception of Indian consumers about celebrity endorsements, examining the celebrity attributes likely to influence consumer purchase intentions and finally the impact of celebrity endorsements on their purchase intention. This project begins with the review of existing literature available on celebrity endorsements, which provides an insight into the research topic and clarifies many important aspects related to the subject. A quantitative method is used for this research project to investigate the perceptions of the consumer, attributes and its subsequent impact on purchase intention. The data is collected through a questionnaire and later analysed using the data analysis software program SPSS. It was proven in this research that consumers find celebrity endorsements more attractive and influential as compared to non-celebrity endorsements. Moreover, the tested attributes show positive relationship with purchase intention. In other terms, celebrity attributes do impact the purchase intention of consumers. Finally, the results of the study prove that celebrity endorsements positively impact the purchase intention of the consumers.

Roy(2011) includes growth of retail sector in India, strategies, strength and opportunities of retail stores, retail format in India, recent trends, and opportunities and challenges. This paper concludes with the likely impact of the entry of global players into the Indian retailing industry. It also highlights the challenges faced by the industry in near future. This paper provides detailed information about the growth of retailing industry in India. It examines the growing awareness and brand consciousness among people across different socio-economic classes in India and how the urban and semi-urban retail markets are witnessing significant growth.

The review of literature reveals that many scholars have studied the consumer awareness, consumer protection and consumer rights at the national and international level. The major finding emerging from the review of relevant studies on the subject is that there is hardly any research work, which has been undertaken to study the consumer awareness in Himachal Pradesh. The present study would fill this gap. As the consumer awareness about their rights is important to protect them from the unfair business practices, it is important to study consumer's alertness and awareness level. It is in this background that the present study was conducted.

Section – B

This section discusses the research design, objectives of study, hypotheses, need of study, data collection and analysis methods etc.

2.B.1. Research Design

The formidable problem that follows the task of defining the research problem is the preparation of the design of the research project, popularly known as the research design. Decision regarding what, where, when, how much, and by what means concerning an inquiry or a research study constitute a research design. Research design has been defined by different social scientists in different terms. All these definitions emphasize systematic methodology in collecting accurate information for interpretation with economy in procedure.

Stated in a simple language, a research design is a plan of action, a plan for collecting and analyzing data in an economic, efficient and relevant manner. A research design could be constructed either to test a hypothesis or to give a cause-effect relationship to a situation. Thus, a research design is a plan of action to be carried out in connection with a research project. It is the conceptual structure within which research is conducted and it constitutes the blue print for the collection, measurement and analysis of data.

Therefore, here an attempt has been made to present a clear picture about the research design formulated for the present study. This include need and importance of the study, objectives of the study, hypotheses of the study, scope of the study, research methodology, sampling procedures, tools and techniques for analysis and interpretation of data and limitations of the present study.

2.B.1.a. Selection of Problem

Though government is playing its role in protecting rights of the customers, but as long as the customer is not made aware, the problem cannot be addressed. Making laws would help but that is not the solution if the customer is not aware. Education and awareness is the most powerful means for the growth of the country and an educated individual is able to make rationale choice as a consumer.

Consumer Protection Act was enacted in 1986 and has been recognised as one of the finest foundation of legislation enacted in any part of the world and India can boast of being only country having such specialized legislation for consumer protection. However, only consumers aware of this legislation can make use of it. Hence, awareness of this legislation has been an aspect of this study.

Role of academic and consumer organizations as well as the NGOs is very important in educating and involving the consumers in the movement. Another area, which relates to consumer protection, is the implementation of weights and measures laws. In helping the consumer exercise their rights, quality and standards have a crucial role to play.

In order to promote and protect the rights and interests of consumers, quasi-judicial machinery is sought to be set up at district, state and central levels. These quasi-judicial bodies have to observe the principles of natural justice and have been empowered to give reliefs, of specific nature and to impose penalties for non-compliance of the orders given by such bodies. The main object of these bodies is to provide speedy and simple redressal to consumer disputes. It is one of the benevolent pieces of legislation intended to protect the consumers at large from exploitation. However, a study has been required to examine if the redressal system has been speedily resolving disputes or not. Hence, this study has covered this aspect also. Keeping in mind, all the points mentioned above, this study has been undertaken.

2.B.1.b. Importance of the study

In today's market economy, it is important to protect consumers from the unfair business practices. No, doubt consumers have the basic right to be protected from the loss or injury caused on account of defective goods and deficiency of services. The protection of consumer's rights largely depends on their awareness and the proper implementation of consumer protection laws and regulations. It is in this direction that the present study was conducted. The following points illustrate the importance of present study:
It will contribute, theoretically and empirically, to a better understanding of the issues involved in consumer's rights and protection.

It would be critical in designing not only appropriate laws and regulations for consumer protection but also for their awareness.

This study would be a great help to law makers and implementing authorities in making efforts to streamline the process of implementation of various consumer protection laws and regulations.

This study would also help the students and researchers to understand the complex dynamics of the phenomenon of consumerism, consumer rights and consumer protection.

The study would also have an added significance from the academic point of view, as not much has been done earlier in this direction in Himachal

Pradesh.

2.B.1.c. Scope of the Study

The study has covered the consumer protection legislation in India. It has mainly focused on working of consumer protection agencies in Himachal Pradesh. Besides, it has also analyzed the degree of alertness in consumers of Himachal Pradesh, level of awareness of consumer protection legislation. Finally, the study has covered an examination of various sources of information for consumer protection.

2.B.1.d. Objectives of the Study

The present study was undertaken to achieve some objectives. These objectives were as follows:

1. To examine critically various laws and regulations for consumer protection in India.

2. To understand the functioning of Consumer Organizations in Himachal Pradesh.

3. To examine the level of alertness among consumers of Himachal Pradesh.

4. To examine the level of awareness among consumers of Himachal Pradesh with regards to consumer protection laws, consumer rights and general consumer protection scenario.

5. To examine the variation in alertness and awareness among the consumers in Himachal Pradesh with respect to demographic attributes like gender, age, occupation and educational qualification.

6. To suggest measures that would help in enhancing consumer alertness and awareness and streamlining the implementation process of consumer protection laws and regulations.

2.B.1.e. Hypotheses of the Study

At the time of conducting research, one cannot proceed in complete ignorance. Research must have some idea as to new aspects that are likely to be discovered. In the absence of any proper or suitable hypothesis, a lot of time and labour is wasted in fruitless research. A hypothesis in statistics is simply a tentative statement about the population. Therefore, on the basis of aforementioned objectives, following null hypotheses have been developed and tested during the study

1. There is no significant difference of alertness in males and females.

2. There is no significant difference of alertness in respondents belonging to different age groups.

3. There is no significant difference of alertness in respondents belonging to different occupations.

4. There is no significant difference of alertness in respondents belonging to different educational qualifications.

5. There is no significant difference of awareness in males and females.

6. There is no significant difference of awareness in respondents belonging to different age groups.

7. There is no significant difference of awareness in respondents belonging to different occupations.

8. There is no significant difference of awareness in respondents belonging to different educational qualifications.

2.B.2.   Research Methodology

The application of appropriate methods and adoption of scientific form of mind is an essential requirement for any systematic study. Keeping in view the set assumptions and objectives, methodology of data collection, procedure of sample selection, and analysis of data has been discussed in the following paragraphs.

2.B.2.i   Methodology of Data Collection

With a view to achieving the objectives and testing the hypotheses, the present study was based on the primary as well as secondary data. The methodology of data collection has been discussed as under:

(a) Collection of Secondary Data

The secondary information has been collected to have in depth understanding of consumer's rights and protection and to examine the working of consumer protection agencies in Himachal Pradesh. In the present study, secondary data was obtained from the office records of the Department of Food & Civil Supplies and Consumer Affairs. To obtained secondary data Right to Information has also been used. The secondary data have also been collected from the various books, research papers, journals and internet sites.

(b) Collection of Primary Data

In the present study, primary data was collected through a sample survey by administering the questionnaire. For this, well-designed questionnaire have been administered to the respondents selected through sampling method. Discussion and observational method was also used to elicit the first hand information from the respondents.

2.B.2.ii   Universe & Sample

Consumer alertness and consumer awareness related to all the people in the society. The universe for the present study comprised of all the residents of Himachal Pradesh. It was not easy to use census method as the universe was too large. Hence, sampling was used for the selection of sample respondents. In sampling technique, information is collected from a representative part of the universe and the conclusions are drawn on that basis for the entire universe. Two stage purposive-cum-convenient sampling method was used to collect data from the respondents.

At the first stage, out of total 12 districts of Himachal Pradesh, five districts, namely, Kangra, Kullu, Shimla, Solan and Una were selected. These districts were selected after taking into consideration the population and markets in these districts.

At the second stage, sample of respondents was selected. The size of sample denotes the number of elements selected for the study. The size of sample should be adequate to draw conclusions and inferences. Hence, 1250 respondents (250 from each district) were selected conveniently. All the respondents were the consumers of one or another goods. These respondents were selected after visiting the main markets of the selected district. As the present study was focused on the consumer alertness and consumer awareness regarding the consumer protection, the respondents were personally contacted alongwith schedule. In all, consumer visiting medical stores, grocery stores, electrical/electronic shops and malls were contacted. The consumers, after brief introduction to the research and having consent from consumers, were requested to fill the scheduled prepared for the present study.

2.B.2.iii   Tools and Techniques applied for Analysis and Interpretation of Data

The data collected from the primary and secondary sources have been properly arranged and tabulated for the analysis and interpretations. Data analysis and processing are the logical steps. Analytical skills and statistical tools provide the sophistication that is needed to draw meaningful conclusions. The analysis and interpretation of tabulated data has been carried out with the help of mathematical methods, statistical tools and graphical methods. These tools and techniques have been discussed as follows:

To examine the working of consumer forums in Himachal Pradesh, analysis represents use of percentages to find the quantum of cases admitted and resolved. Level of alertness while making purchases and level of awareness of consumer protection has initially been examined individually using frequency tables. Pie diagrams have been used to examine individual variables. Thereafter, arithmetic mean and standard deviation have been used to find the comparative position of various activities or provisions of consumer protection and other related aspects. Arithmetic Mean, often simply known as mean or average is one of the most commonly used statistics. It is used for getting an estimate of the central value of a series. The formula for calculating the arithmetic mean is:

$$\left(\frac{1}{n}\right) \cdot \sum_{i}^{n} x_i$$

where X_i is the ith element of the series.

The mean is thus the sum of all elements of the series divided by the number of elements in the series.

Standard deviation (S.D) or sigma is the measure of the spread of a series from its mean value. S.D. indicates the differences and variability, which a set of number has. S.D. is mathematically the square root of variance, which is defined as the mean of the square of the differences between the elements and their mean. It is calculated as follows.

$$\sigma = \sqrt{Variance} = \sqrt{\frac{\sum_{i}^{n}\left(x_i - mean\right)^2}{n}}$$

ANOVA

For the testing of hypotheses, analysis of variance (ANOVA) has been used whereby demographic variables have been treated as grouping variables, while variables related to level of alertness and awareness have been used as dependent variables. ANOVA is an important technique for analyzing the effect of categorical factors on a response is to perform an Analysis of Variance. An ANOVA decomposes the variability in the response variable amongst the different factors. Depending upon the type of analysis, it may be important to determine: (a) which factors have a significant effect on the response, and/or (b) how much of the variability in the response variable is attributable to each factor. What ANOVA looks at is the way groups differ internally versus what the difference is between them. It is calculated in the following steps.

1. ANOVA calculates the mean for each of the final groups.

2. It calculates the mean for all the groups combined - the Overall Mean.

3. Then it calculates, within each group, the total deviation of each individual's score from the Group Mean - Within Group Variation.

4. Next, it calculates the deviation of each Group Mean from the Overall Mean - Between Group Variation.

5. Finally, ANOVA produces the F statistic, which is the ratio Between Group Variation to the Within Group Variation.

If the Between Group Variation is significantly greater than the Within Group Variation, then it is likely that there is a statistically significant difference between the groups.

2.B.3. Limitations of the Study

The present study was conducted with best efforts to examine and analyze all aspects set as per objectives and need of the study. Despite this, there were some limitations which have been discussed as under:

1. The sample size of respondents has been fixed at 1250, taken as 250 respondents each from five districts of Himachal Pradesh. As the consumer population of Himachal Pradesh, the sample may not be adequately representing the level of overall consumer population.

2. This sample has been collected by selecting respondents from five districts of Himachal Pradesh, viz. Una, Shimla, Solan, Kangra, and Kullu. Due to paucity of time and other resources, other districts of Himachal Pradesh have not been covered in this study.

3. This study is based on working of consumer organizations in Himachal Pradesh. Hence, the results are restricted to Himachal Pradesh only. These results cannot be generalized for the population of India.

4. Results obtained from the primary survey are based on the opinions and responses of the respondents. Hence, possibility of any casual response,

lack of interest, or hidden information on the part of respondents cannot be ruled out.

References

G. Katona (1960), *Powerful Consumer; Psychological Studies of American Economy*, McGraw Hill Book Co. New York, pp. 276-283.

M. V. Nadel (1971), *Policies of Consumer Protection*, Babbs-Merril Educational Publishing Indianapolis, pp. 257-274.

N. David (1975), *Reference Guide to Consumers*, R. R. Broker Co, New York, pp. 327-336.

M. Berger (1975), *Consumer Protection Labs*, The John Day Company, New York, pp. 135-39.

A. A. Painter (1978), *Guide to Consumer Protection Law*, Barry Rose (Publishers) Ltd., London, pp. 173-196.

J. M. Anderson (1978) *For the People; A Consumer Action Handbook*, Addison-Wesky Publishing Co., California, pp. 379-382.

E. Fetterman and M. K. Schiller (1978), *Let the Buyer Be Aware; consumer Rights and Responsibilities,* Fairchild Publications, New York, pp. 217-245.

National Consumer Council (1979), *U.K., Consumer and State; Getting Value for Public Money*, National Consumer Council, London, pp. 22-45.

D. G. Epstein and S. H. Nickles (1980), *Consumer Law,* West Publishing Co, U. S. A., pp. 418-424.

IOCU (1980), *Japan, Law and the Consumer; Background readings*, IOCU, Hong Kong, pp. 100-115.

M. Giordan (1980), *Consumer Education; A Handbook for Teachers*, Methuen & Co. Ltd, London, pp. 81-95.

R. Lowe and G. Woodroffe (1980), *Consumer – Law and Practice*, Sweet & Maxwell ltd, London, pp. 368-396.

IOCU, (1981), *Malaysia Guide to Consumer Lawyers*, IOCU, Penang, pp. 47-74.

N. I. Silber (1983), *Test and protest; The influence of Consumers Union*, Holmes & Meier Publishers, London, pp. 172-196.

J. Groeneveld (1984), *Simple Tests Manual,* IOCU, Penang, pp.118-138.

H. T. Grada (1985), *Promoting Consumer Education in Schools*, IOCU, Penang, pp. 76-95.

I. Cooper (1986), *Consumer Education*, Oxford University Press, Oxford, pp. 64-86.

A. Stanesby (1986), *Consumer Rights Handbook*, Pluto Press ltd. London, p.235.

T. Wells and E. G. Sim (1987), *Till they have Faces; Women as Consumers,* International Organization of Consumers Union, Penang, pp. 142-174.

O. Daniel (1988), "How the FTC Serves the Consumer", *Consumer Research*, August, pp. 18-20.

N. B. Grant (1989), "Indian Consumer Must Shake off His Apathy", *Times of India*, May 22.

IOCU (1989) *International Consumer Directory 1989*, Longman Group, Essex, Netherlands, pp. 201-206.

A. J. Rebellow (1989), "American's View of Consumer Protection", *Indian Express*, August 26.

S. D. Wilcox (1989), "Educated Consumers; An Analysis of Curriculum Needs in Consumer Education", *Michigan Consumer Education Centre*, Michigan, pp. 116-146.

A. J. Rebellow (1989), "Long wait for Redress panels", *Indian Express*, November 6.

J. Sing (1989), "Consumer Complaint Interion and Behavior; Definitional and Issues", *Journal of marketing*, January 25, pp. 93-107.

A. J. Rebellow (1990), "Is service sector any the better", *Indian Express*, April 11.

D. N. Saraf (1990), "Law of Consumer Protection in India", *Tripati, Bombay*, pp. 259-278.

CUTS, (2001), *Competition policy & law made easy, monographs on investment and competition policy, no. 8*, CUTS centre for international trade, economics and environment pp. 1-20

Cseres Katalin Judit (2005), *Competition Law and Consumer protection*, Kluwer Law International, pp. 403-419.

Godius Kahyarara (2004) "Competition policy, manufacturing exports, investment and productivity: Firm-level evidence from Tanzania manufacturing enterprises," *Competition, Competitiveness and Development: Lessons from Developing Countries*, pp. 39-46.

Hans Vedder (2006), "Competition law and consumer protection: How competition Law can be used to protect consumers even better- or not" *European Business Law Review*, Volume 17, Issue 1, pp. 83-95.

W Micklitz Hans (2006), "Consumers and competition – Access and compensation under the EC law" *European Business Law Review*, Volume 17, Issue 1, pp. 69-75.

OECD, global forum on competition, interference between competition law and consumer welfare, DAG/COMP/GF/2008 at http://www.oecd.org/competition 01/07/2009,

S. Mathew (1975), "Awareness of housewives towards food adulteration and the extent of adulterated foods sold in the local markets of Udaipur city". *Indian Journal of Home Science*, 9 (3), pp. 81-85.

Karmatala Consumer Service Society India, (1976), *Some Tips to Remember*, Karnataka Consumer Society, Bangalore (India), pp. 35-37.

Manubhai Shah (1981), *Public Interest Groups and Development Journalism*, Consumer Education and research Centre, Ahmedabad. pp .6-9.

D.A.R. Subramanyam, (1981), "Need for Consumer Organizations". *Indian Journal of Marketing*, pp. 17-20.

Shobhana Riswadkar (1983), *Unfair Fair Price Shops*, Consumer Education and Research Centre, Ahmedabad, pp. 16-26.

P. Leela Krishan (1984), *Consumer Protection and Legal Control*, Eastern Book Co, Lucknow, pp. 332-339.

J. P. Chandra (1984), *Right of Consumers*, Jag Parvesh Chandra, New Delhi, pp. 104-105.

Niharika Dave (1987), *Speeding towards road safety*, Consumer Education and Research Centre, Ahmedabad, pp. 80-95.

K. P. S. Kamath (1987*), Servants, Not Masters, Consumers' Forum*, Udupi (Karnataka), pp. 128-135.

Pritee Shah (1987), Shome Safety, Consume Education and Research Centre, Ahmadbad, pp. 19-26.

H. N. Giri (1987), *Consumers Crimes and the Law*, Ashish Pub. House, New Delhi, pp. 349-359.

V. K. Agarwal (1989), *Consumer protection in India*, Deep & Deep Publications, New Delhi. pp. 43-64.

P. M. Bakshi (1989), "Consumer Law and Voluntary Agencies", *Financial Express*, May 24.

V. C. Dixit (1989), "Consumers Don't Take Things Down", *Social Welfare*, May 25.

Z. Imam (1989), "Consumer not the King", *Hindustan Times*, October 18.

R. Narayan (1989), "Hope for Harried Consumers", Indian Express, November 25.

M. K. Ramesh (1989), "Consumer Interest in Legal Profession-Problems and Perspectives", *Cochin University Law Review*, Vol. No. 13 December 4, pp. 405-425.

S. M. Shah (1989), "Confused Customer Diffused Movement", *Times of India*, March 22.

Munubhai Shah (1989), *Consumer and Clothing*, Consumer Education and Research Centre, Ahmedabad, pp.11-34.

S. Sivaraman (1989), "Combating Consumer Exploitation", *Economic Times*, March 19.

A. Sarkar, (1989), *Problems of Consumers in Modern India*, Discovery Publishing House, Delhi, pp. 264-274.

H. D. Shourie (1989), "Consumer Protection – Pass Lows and Sleep". *Hindustan Times*, August 10.

N. Thanulingam, and M. Kochadai, 1989, "An evaluation of consumer awareness". *Indian Journal of Marketing*, 19 (8) pp. 3-8.

D. Bijlani (1990), *Role of Mass Media in Consumer Education,* Centre for Development Communication, Gujrat University, Ahmedabad, pp. 70-83.

O. P. Garg (1990), *Consumer Protection Act,*Vinod Publishing House, Delhi, 1990, pp. 354-396.

N. Joshi (1990), "Creating Consumerism", *Financial Express*, December 21.

N. Kumar and N. Batra (1990), "Consumer rights – awareness and action". *Indian Journal Marketing*, 21(4) : pp. 21-23.

P. S. Mehta (1990), "Blow for the Consumer", *Indian Express*, January 22.

M.S. Kulkarni and D. Murali (1990), "Study on purchasing practices of consumers of Parbhani Town". *Indian Journal of Marketing*, 26, pp. 3-7.

K. Natarajan (1990), "Consumer awareness towards ISI Mark". *Indian Journal of Marketing*, 20 (6), pp. 16-19.

G. Padma (1990), *Media and Consumer Protection, a manual,* Consumer Education and Research Centre, Ahmedabad, pp. 97-104.

G. Padma and SunilKarnik (1990), *Complaints handling*, consumer Education and Research Centre, Ahmedabad, pp.32-39.

V. K. Parigi (1990), "Safer Products for the Consumer", *The Hindu*, March 20.

M. J. Antony (1991), *Consumer Rights,* Clarion Books, New Delhi, pp. 126-129.

R. Jayadevan (1993), *Banking Service and Consumer Protection*, Dissertation Work, Law Department, Cochin University, pp. 97-103.

K. Sreevidya (1993), Consumer Justice and Public Utility Services, Dissertation work, Law Department, Cochin University, pp. 88-95.

E. A. Lizzy (1996), *Women and Consumer Protection*, Ph. D Thesis, Cochin University, pp. 352-385.

J.G. Sawarkar and S.J. Giram (1996), "Consumer awareness: A survey analysis". *Indian Journal of Marketing*, 25 : pp. 13-21.

S. Hasalkar and K.V. Ashalatha (1998), "Awareness of home-makers about Indian Standard Marks on consumer goods". *Karnataka Journal of agricultural. Science*, 11(4): pp. 1148-1151.

N.P. Reddy and A.N. Ramesh (1998), "The role of an independent agency to protect the consumer interest on empirical study", *Indian Journal of Marketing*, 28, pp. 2-11.

S. Hasalkar and K.V. Ashalatha (1998), "Awareness of home-makers about Indian Standard Marks on consumer goods". *Karnataka Journal of agricultural. Science*. 11(4), pp. 1148-1151.

M. J. Selvadas (1998), *A Study on the consumer Protection Movement in Kerala*, Ph. D. Thesis, University of Kerala, pp. 321-329.

C. Gambhir (2002), "Consumer protection: Law and Practice". *Indian Journal of Marketing* 32: pp. 17-20.

Akash Gupta and Rahul Agarwal (2003), 'The Consumer Financing Business in India'-Building Blocks for the Future. Available at SSRN: http://ssrn.com/abstract=619721

Nisa Syeedun (2007), FDI in Indian Retail Industry. Available at SSRN: http://ssrn.com/abstract=983711

Pankaj Kumar Gupta (2008), "Internet Banking in India – Consumer Concerns and Bank Strategies", *Global Journal of Business Research*, Vol. 2, No. 1, pp.43-51.

Sheetal Sahoo and Aman Chatterjee (2009), "Consumer Protection - Problems and Prospects". Available at SSRN: http://ssrn.com/abstract=1452526

Y. Lokeswara Choudary (2010), "Consumer Preference on Mobile Connections and Buyer Behaviour towards Relience Mobile in Chennai City" (January 10, 2010). Available at SSRN: http://ssrn.com/abstract=1623429

G. Suresh (2010), "Consumers Attitude and Green Advertisement: An Evaluation", Available at SSRN: http://ssrn.com/abstract=1640006

Prashant R. Dahat (2010), "Medical Negligence and Consumer Protection Law" (April 14, 2010). Available at SSRN: http://ssrn.com/abstract=1589192

Amit Kumar (2011), Celebrity Endorsements and Its Impact on Consumer Buying Behaviour (April 4, 2011). Available at SSRN: http://ssrn.com/abstract=1802531

Satyajit Roy (2011), An Overview of Retail Industry in India: Its Growth, Challenges and Opportunities (January 29, 2011). Available at SSRN: http://ssrn.com/abstract=175079

CHAPTER – 3
CONSUMER PROTECTION MOVEMENT AT INTERNATIONAL AND NATIONAL LEVEL

The needs of the human beings in the primitive stage were limited. They lived in forests and caves and continued to lead a life governed by the law of the jungle. With the passage of time people learned to form social groups. Initially every family had to provide its own food and shelter and the people started different occupations. The farmers started cultivating wheat while weavers started weaving cloth and the blacksmith or carpenter started making tools of agriculture and husbandry. This gave rise to the barter system whereby direct exchange or trade took place for goods produced by one person with the goods required which some other person could spare.

But the barter system was faced with many difficulties due to increase in the volume of trade and the production. It was found that the exchange of goods and services could not take place unless and until a person required the same thing which the other person could spare and could himself spare the same article which the other person demanded. It was difficult to store the goods and to provide services for a long period and it was also difficult to calculate the exact value of goods and services to be exchanged. Thus The barter system, being inconvenient, gave place to the commonly accepted commodity known as money or currency to buy and sell the goods and services (Myrlie, 1983).

The present chapter is an attempt to discuss consumerism and consumer protection movements at the international and national level.

3.1. Consumerism

The term 'Consumerism' came into existence in the early 1960s when it was coined by the business community in the western world particularly in

America. It is the social force designed to protect the interest of consumer by organizing the consumer to bring pressure on business community to heed to their say.

Consumerism is a social force designed to protect consumer interests in the market place by organizing consumer pressures on business houses. Consumer organizations could provide united and organized efforts to fight against unfair marketing practices and to achieve consumer protection. The balance of the power in the market normally rests with the seller. Consumerism is society's efforts to set right this imbalance in the exchange of goods and services between seller and buyers.

The reflections of consumer protection could be seen in the early civilization itself. As remarked by H. Virginia Knauer, the early Mosaic (Biblical) and Egyptian laws governed the handling of meat from traders to consumers. Similarly, the Greek and Roman laws prohibited the adulteration of wine with water. The Lex Julia de Annona enacted in 50BC, by the Romans was to protect the corn trade against unnatural rise in the price of corn. In A.D. 301, a special rule was passed by the Roman Emperor to bring down the prices of goods in day-to-day use. Another important development in the Roman law was the promulgation of the constitution of Zeno in A.D. 483. This constitution was intended to protect the consumers against the artificial increase in the price of food-stuffs and other commodities of daily use (Barker, 1987).

Consumerism describes the shift in American culture from a producer-oriented society in the nineteenth century to a "consumerist" society in the twentieth century. Changes in domestic demographics and advances in industrialization, manufacturing, transportation, and communication all contributed to the change. Consumerism also contributed greatly to the liberal thrust of the Progressive Era and spawned a long-running trend of consumer advocacy and consumer protection legislation (Ryans, John, Samiee, and Wills, 1985).

Consumerism is a social and economic order that is based on the systematic creation and fostering of a desire to purchase goods and services in ever greater amounts. The term is often associated with criticisms of consumption starting with Thorstein Veblen or, more recently by a movement called Enoughism. Veblen's subject of examination, the newly emergent middle class arising at the turn of the twentieth century, comes to full fruition by the end of the twentieth century through the process of globalization (Scherhorn, 1988).

The term "consumerism" is also used to refer to the consumerist movement or consumer activism, which seeks to protect and inform consumers by requiring such practices as honest packaging and advertising, product guarantees, and improved safety standards. In this sense it is a movement or a set of policies aimed at regulating the products, services, methods, and standards of manufacturers, sellers, and advertisers in the interests of the buyer (Onah, 1979). In economics, consumerism refers to economic policies placing emphasis on consumption. In an abstract sense, it is the belief that the free choice of consumers should dictate the economic structure of a society. The term "consumerism" was first used in 1915 to refer to "advocacy of the rights and interests of consumers" but the term "consumerism" refers to the sense first used in 1960, "emphasis on or preoccupation with the acquisition of consumer goods".

In short, consumerism refers to the efforts organised by consumer groups to remedy their frustration in realising their standard of living caused by products not conforming to their expectations. Consumer orientation can thus lead to helping the consumer fulfill his needs by offering appropriate products at reasonable prices. A part from helping the consumer, it is the long-term interest of the manufacturer to protect the interest of the consumer. If he does so, as in countries like the U.S.A. the consumerism movement will gain extra momentum.

Thus, consumerism can be explained as, 'lets us the seller beware.' It is the social force for the protection of consumer and aiding the consumer, it is engaging in actions intending to stir public opinion and generate public pressure.

In other words, it is an organised effort to fight against the unfair marketing practices with a view to secure the consumer protection. Consumerism is the society's attempt to bring back the balance in the exchange between the buyers and sellers as the strength of power is normally in favour of sellers rather than buyers.

3.1.1. Aim of Consumerism

The consume movement stands for the organized efforts of consumers seeking to redress, restitute and remedy for the dissatisfaction of the standard of living. It is a social movement seeking to challenge the rights and powers of the buyers in relation to those of sellers. Consumerism, like democracy, is a movement by the people and for the people where the role of common man is uncommon.

Consumerism includes two basic areas which are as under:
1. To remove discontent and dissatisfaction created in the business relations between the buyers and sellers in market.
2. To protect the consumers against the prejudices caused in the exchange relations.

Though these are the two major aspects of consumerism, the modern concept of consumerism states yet another important aspects namely consumer interests in environmental forces influencing their quality of life (Scherhorn, 1988).

Thus, consumerism is the social demand of the refinement in marketing practices by revamping them to be more truthful, efficient, informative, responsive, sincere and making the business house more concerned about the quality of life.

3.2. Origin of Consumerism at International Level

Consumerism has weak links with the Western world, but is in fact an international phenomenon. People purchasing goods and consuming materials in excess of their basic needs is as old as the first civilizations (e.g. Ancient Egypt, Babylon and Ancient Rome). A great turn in consumerism arrived just before the Industrial Revolution. In the nineteenth century, capitalist development and the industrial revolution were primarily focused on the capital goods sector and industrial infrastructure (i.e., mining, steel, oil, transportation networks, communications networks, industrial cities, financial centers, etc.) (McGregor and MacDonald, 1997). At that time, agricultural commodities, essential consumer goods, and commercial activities had developed to an extent, but not to the same extent as other sectors. Members of the working classes worked long hours for low wages – as much as 16 hours per day, 6 days per week. Little time or money was left for consumer activities.

Further, capital goods and infrastructure were quite durable and took a long time to be used up. Henry Ford and other leaders of industry understood that mass production presupposed mass consumption (Maynes, 1990). After observing the assembly lines in the meat packing industry, Frederick Winslow Taylor brought his theory of scientific management to the organization of the assembly line in other industries; this unleashed incredible productivity and reduced the costs of all commodities produced on assembly lines. While previously the norm had been the scarcity of resources, the Industrial Revolution created an unusual economic situation. For the first time in history products were available in outstanding quantities, at outstandingly low prices, being thus available to virtually everyone. So, began the era of mass consumption, the only era where the concept of consumerism is applicable.

Consumerism has long had intentional underpinnings, rather than just developing out of capitalism. As an example, Earnest Elmo Calkins noted to fellow advertising executives in 1932 that "consumer engineering must see to it that we use up the kind of goods we now merely use", while the domestic theorist Christine Frederick observed in 1929 that "the way to break the vicious deadlock of a low standard of living is to spend freely, and even waste creatively". The older term and concept of "conspicuous consumption" originated at the turn of the 20th century in the writings of sociologist and economist, Thorstein Veblen (MacDonald, 1998). The term describes an apparently irrational and confounding form of economic behaviour. Veblen's scathing proposal that this unnecessary consumption is a form of status display is made in darkly humorous observations like the following:

It is true of dress in even a higher degree than of most other items of consumption, that people will undergo a very considerable degree of privation in the comforts or the necessaries of life in order to afford what is considered a decent amount of wasteful consumption; so that it is by no means an uncommon occurrence, in an inclement climate, for people to go ill clad in order to appear well dressed (McIlhenny, 1990).

The term "conspicuous consumption" spread to describe consumerism in the United States in the 1960s, but was soon linked to debates about media theory, culture jamming, and its corollary productivism.

3.2.1. Industrial Revolution and Consumer Protection and Guidance

The industrial revolution and the development in the international trade and commerce has led to the vast expansion of the business and trade, as a result of which variety of consumer goods have appeared in the market to cater the needs of the consumers and a host of services have been made available to the consumers like insurance, transport, electricity, housing, entertainment, finance and banking. A well-organized sector of manufacturers and traders with better knowledge of markets has come into existence thereby affecting the relationship between the traders and the consumers making the principle of consumer sovereignty almost inapplicable in the second half of the twentieth century. The advertisements of the goods and services in the television, radios, newspapers, cinema and magazines influenced the demand of the consumers although there may be manufacturing defect or imperfection or shortcoming the quality, quantity and purity of the goods or there may be deficiency in the services rendered (Silber, 1983).

Due to the international character of trade and industry having well organized and highly professionalized producers and traders on one side and illiterate and unorganized consumers with little time on the other, the exploitation of the consumers is common. The exploitation of the consumers cannot be avoided without the development of international consumer protection movement. Various international organizations like the International Labour Organization (ILO), the World Health Organization (WHO), the Economic and Social Council of the United National (UNESCO), United National Conference on Trade and Development (UNCTAD) and United Nation International Children Emergency Fund (UNICEF), have contributed a lot for the protection of the rights of the consumers in the international sphere. In addition, the world Industrial Property Organization, International Organization of Consumer Union and the Inter-Scandinavian Committee on Consumer Matters are also busy in protecting the interests of the consumers at the international level.

3.2.2. Marketing Development and Consumer Protection and Guidance

With the evolution of mankind from stone age to the present day social welfare stage, the relationship between the suppliers of goods and services and the consumers has undergone radical change. The present-day market system is most complex which is not only confined to the national level but has assumed international character. The 'Caveat Emptor' (buyer beware) principle is not applicable to the full extent in the recent day market system. Human wants for the goods and services are unlimited. The resources for the production of these goods and services are scarce and, therefore, the economic theory has to decide how to use the scarce resources or means for obtaining the maximum satisfaction or utility for the members of the society. The concept of consumer protection and guidance can be traced back to Adam Smith. In his classical work 'Wealth of Nations' Smith pointed out the flaws in capitalism. According to him it is a way to regulate the selfish passions instead of welfare of consumers, it is welfare among producers and which entails heavy costs and mounting wastage of competition, which have fuelled the fire for today's quest for consumer rights.

Peter Kotler stated three alternative concepts in marketing activities. They are the product-oriented concept, the sales-oriented concept and the consumer-oriented concept. The product-oriented concept maintained that the production was meant for consumption purpose and product differentiation and technicalities were absent. If the product-consumer response is favourable, very little promotional efforts are necessary from the marketers. This was the marketing philosophy till 1930. The sales-oriented concept which continued in 1940s realized that there cannot be enough consumers response without promotional efforts. In 1950s marketing experienced the complete reversal of its orientation and the market became slowly consumer oriented. The consumer-oriented concept points out that the primary task of business enterprises is to study the needs, desires and values of the potential consumers. The period of 1960s and 1970s witnessed rapidly changing expectations with respect to the performance of business and other institutions (Nicouland, 1987). By 1990s marketing has become broader in the function and scope by giving more concern to public welfare, better living environment and quality of life. As social welfare is the order of the day, the present trend in marketing is, adopting socially responsible marketing policies aiming at consumer welfare thus making a dramatic change from mere product-oriented marketing to a social-oriented one, where consumer satisfaction is the prime responsibility of marketers.

3.2.3. U.S. Reflections on Consumer Protection and Guidance

The present consumer protection and guidance movement of America is largely accredited to the farming community and honest businesses. The impetus behind the movement for the earliest legislation gathered strength during the 1870s and 1880s. The farmers noticed the contrast between the rapidly falling prices, which they received for their produce, and the relatively high prices of the goods, which they needed to buy. The price, which the farmer received for the commodities sold by him, seemed to him, have been fixed by the buyers and the price of the goods bought by him, have been fixed by the sellers. Thus the farmers lost both as buyers as well as sellers. The main reason for this situation was the presence of trust and monopolies (Harland, 1987). As farmers were better endowed with the political influence at that time, they influenced the Congress and consequently in 1889 the Sherman Act was passed. This Act, declared such trusts unlawful. Although the Sherman Act, 1889 to a great extent curbed the formation of trusts, there were several monopolies and restrictive trade practices to which the Act did not reach. In order to remove these infirmities, Clayton Act, 1914 was passed. This Act declared, price discrimination, exclusive dealing, and trying agreements, acquisition of completing companies, and interlocking directions illegal. However, there was no provision to deal with the unfair trade practices (Harland, 1988).

The US Supreme Court in Standard Oil Co. Vs. United States confined the role of Sherman Act by holding that, only unreasonable contract in restraint of trade, would be held unlawful. Within no time, Senator Frances G. Newlands proposed that Congress should constitute an administrative tribunal similar to that of Interstate Commerce Commission. Thus the Federal Trade Commission Act, 1914 was passed. The Federal Trade Commission was armed with more powers by the enactment of the Magnusm-Moss Warranty-Federal Trade Commission Improvement Act. This amendment popularly known as FTC Improvement Act has expanded jurisdictional each of the Commission to matters in or affecting commerce. It confirmed the Commission's authority to promulgate trade regulations, rules defining unfair or deceptive acts or practices (Harland, 1987). It gave the Commission an authority to represent itself in court proceedings and made clear that the Commission's investigative authority extended to persons, partnerships and corporations, instead of only corporations as in the past.

In the United States, three distinct consumer movements being early 1900s mid 1930s and mid 1960s have shaken business scene. Until mid1920s, the consumer movement consisted mainly of sporadic local activities. The second phase of American consumer movement in the mid 1930s was triggered by various factors. The major among them were the contribution of writers such as R.H. Townie (Acquisitive Society), T. Vebtin (Theory of the leisured Class), and the joint work of Stuart Chase and F.J. Flinch (Your money's worth). The third wave of consumerism was started in 1960s. E.B. Weiss observed that this period has attributed consumer unrest to rising public standards of business conduct and social responsibility brought about by the education and sophistication. In addition, books such as Galbraith's "The Affluent Society" stating the interaction of consumer unrest also fuelled the consumer movement (Hendon, 1975).

The U.S. consumer movement that came to blossom in the 1960s had its foundation in the development of the Common law. A new and significant legal doctrine known as 'Product Liability' in cases of personal injury caused by defective products was accepted in 1950. Accordingly, when mass produced goods are used in normal fashion and failure to perform as expected or when they are designed in such a fashion as to be unreasonably dangerous, an injured person need not prove that, the seller was negligent, but instead can hold the seller and manufacturer legally responsible upon a showing that the defective product caused his injury. This legal development was a giant leap forward for the average consumer who totally relies on manufacturers for a wide range of consumer movement was further developed (Herrmann, 1970). The late 1960s also saw the rise of a charismatic consumer champion Ralph Nader. Mr. Nader's training as a lawyer and his enunciation of consumer clearly set forth the common law legal standard that marked safety and health policies underlying the death and injury caused by defective products. It is this expanded definition of consumerism, well beyond a strict economic value, which includes considerations of health and safety that has become the backbone of consumerism today.

In 1962, President John F, Kennedy declared four basic consumer rights, which institutionalized and expanded consumer expectations in the United States. These rights were the right of safety, the right to be informed, the right to choose and the right to be heard. While this is clearly a benchmark in the consumer movement, it was the consumer activists official role in government as consumer counsel that allowed the consumer movement to have a legitimate voice and a modern identity (Herrmann, 1980). The American consumer movement is intensified now a days due to four elements such as the existence of private lawyers to take up consumer issue on contingency basis, the government control on consumer issues, the involvement of press and the services of voluntary consumer organizations.

From the colonial era until the late nineteenth century, the United States was a producer-oriented nation. Simply, most Americans produced what they needed, generating only what their immediate families or villages could use. Farmers-sometimes inaccurately called "subsistence farmers"-grew a variety of crops and vegetables on small acreages, stored what their families could use, and peddled whatever surplus there might be in the nearest town. The raising of livestock usually centred on one or two family dairy cows and some swine and fowl for slaughter. Few large commercial herds existed.

In villages and towns, artisans produced durable goods-such as furniture, clothing, tools, and firearms, but on a piece-by-piece basis. No mass production existed, and while artisans strove for uniformity, every chair, musket, or watch had to be handmade. Of course, exceptions existed. In New England, American shipbuilders, exploiting an abundance of timber, made ships and boats that, through the British mercantile system, ultimately serviced much of Europe and the New World (Cooper, 1986). In the South, where open fields were plentiful and lent themselves to plantations, agrarians created world markets for tobacco, rice, sugar, indigo, and later, cotton. None other than George Washington created a seaboard market for fish that his slaves and workers seined out of the Potomac River. But in the main, most Americans produced only what they could use or sell close by, and bought only what their neighbours had to offer. The market was one of scarcity.

The producer-oriented dynamic gave Americans an advantage as they sparred with England over issues of taxation and representation prior to the American Revolution. As Parliament levied tax after tax on goods that British merchants sold to American buyers, the Yankees protested with a "non-consumption" movement, choosing not to buy taxed goods but instead to make them at home. American women, who had to fill the gaps non-consumption left by spinning thread and making extra candles or garments, proved to be the backbone of the movement (IOCU, 1980).

In the early days of the republic, however, some American leaders urged a broadening of the American economy. Alexander Hamilton, President Washington's secretary of the Treasury, and most members of the New England–based Federalist Party believed that for the United States to become fiscally sound it needed to sell products to the rest of the world. Hamilton's "Report on Manufactures" (1791) advocated larger, consumer-oriented businesses that could carve niches in world markets (Harland, 1988). External trade, of course, was Hamilton's impetus, but the mechanisms that Americans would create to achieve larger world markets would also change domestic buying. Hamilton's stance caused the rise of the first American party system. Believing that agrarian, producer-oriented independence was essential for a strong republic and democracy, Thomas Jefferson and his followers in the Democratic-Republican Party opposed Hamilton's bid to strengthen business. Ultimately, Americans would balance both ideas for more than a century.

3.2.4. Key Elements in the Development of Consumerism

Many factors and elements are responsible for the development of consumerism. Key elements in the development of consumerism have been discussed as below:

3.2.4.i. Improvements in Manufacturing

One of the key elements in the development of a consumerist nation would be uniformity and speed in manufacturing. By 1798, thanks to the brainchild of Eli Whitney, that element was taking hold. Whitney, best known for creating the cotton gin (which made southern cotton profitable and renewed southern dependence on slavery), also developed the idea of interchangeable parts (Nelson, 1979). Whitney realized that artisans could speed their work and double, perhaps triple, their output if they did not have to hand-craft every part of whatever they built. For instance, why hands make every lock mechanism for a musket? Instead, create a machine that could uniformly stamp each, trigger, pan, and so on. The benefits would be manifold: artisans or manufacturers could more rapidly turn out individual pieces; prices for the pieces would drop, making them more accessible to consumers; and the items would become more durable. Instead of requiring a whole new item if a component part broke, the owner could simply get a cheap replacement part. Manufacturing soon adopted the idea of interchangeable parts. One of the first to do so was textile mills and clothing makers. With sewing machines now cheaper to operate, the entrepreneur Francis Cabot Lowell saw an opportunity. He collected hundreds of sewing machines into a manufactory at Waltham, Massachusetts, between 1812 and 1814, and then he sought seamstresses to operate them (Harland, 1988). Lowell encouraged young women to leave their family farms and live in dormitories he built at Waltham. They would work during the day, and they could attend Lowell sponsored education classes by night. At Waltham, Lowell created a "company town," and he encouraged one of the first farm-to-city migrations in the nation's history. Other manufacturers followed suit, and a cycle began: Americans gradually began leaving family farms to work at industrial, née urban, centers, quickly making cheaper goods that other Americans could afford.

3.2.4.ii. Transport and Territorial Expansion

Another factor also stimulated growth: American expansion and transportation. Even before the American Revolution, Americans were taking territory west of the Appalachian Mountains. With American victory in the Revolution, the nation had control of the land south of the Great Lakes and west to the Mississippi River (Douglas, and Craig, 1983). Settlers quickly spread into those regions. Open acreages were conducive to commercial agriculture, but the agrarians discovered that it was difficult to get their produce back over the Appalachians to eastern markets. The quickest route was to float goods down the Ohio River, onto the Mississippi River, and out the Gulf of Mexico, around Spanish Florida, and up the Atlantic coast to

New York. Such a trip was cumbersome and fraught with the potential for financial loss.

The arrival of steamships (whose engines could be efficiently built with interchangeable parts) revolutionized market shipping. Now boat captains could go upriver instead of only downriver. And if rivers did not exist from one place to a convenient market, Americans simply created a waterway with the advent of the "Canal Era. "Americans hesitated little to mold the land to their needs. They built canals from city to city throughout the East and in some portions of the South. The most famous was the Erie Canal. Completed in 1825, it connected the Great Lakes with the Hudson River in New York, and the Atlantic Ocean (Bloom and Greyser, 1981). Thus, the American West was connected with the sea.

Steam-powered locomotives and railroads, however, soon supplanted the canals. Canals were prone to stagnation in summer months. Also, towing animals often fell in them and drowned; and sediment deposits forced frequent dredging. Railroads had none of those problems-one could simply lay down some tracks and run a locomotive over them. By the 1840s, most areas of the Northeast and North were becoming linked to the west by rails. In short, manufacturing and transportation were coming together to make products cheaper and more accessible to Americans. Railroads continued to boom for the next two decades, and in 1862, during the Civil War, the United States Congress passed the Pacific Railroad Act that authorized a transcontinental railroad to link the East with the far West (Johnston, 1985). That same year, Congress passed the Homestead Act, which promised settlers free land in the West for simply occupying and improving the land. Both measures did much to help the United States utilize the land it had claimed by treaty and war in the early nineteenth century. They also did much to speed consumerism. Railroads made more money carrying freight than they did carrying passengers. With the first transcontinental railroad completed in 1869 and others soon to follow, railroad managers realized that for the western lines to remain profitable they had to find a way to carry goods to the settlers in the West and their produce or manufactured items back to the East. That certainly would not work if the settlers remained in a producer-oriented, subsistence cycle. Gradually railroad agents and grain brokers convinced western farmers that the open expanses of the West were ideal for commercial farming. That is, the farmers could concentrate vast acreages in one or two crops, ship the produce to the East, and use their profits to buy supplies and other food that the railroads shipped in from the East. Railroads did the same for livestock. In 1866, Texans and other southerners looking for opportunities after the Civil War began rounding up wild longhorn cattle in south Texas and driving them to northern markets. Instead of driving them all the way to Chicago, however, the first drivers took herds to a railhead at Sedalia, Missouri (Blake and Walters, 1987). Later they drove cattle to more westerly railheads at Kansas towns like Abilene, Caldwell, and Dodge City. The expanding rail network then took the cattle to stock-yards, most notably in Chicago but later, as railroads spread across the South, in Fort Worth as well.

3.2.4.iii. Technology and Consumerism

Technology has increasingly impacted consumerism. Compact computers designed to help astronauts fly to the moon in the 1960s became the basis for the first handheld calculators of the 1970s. Both are the forerunners of today's personal computers and Macs. The obsolescence curve of computer equipment ensures a continually fresh curve of computer consumers. The appearance of videocassette recording technology in the late 1970s gave American television viewers more latitude in their viewing habits. No longer were they slaves to television schedules; they could record one program while watching another (Douglas and Craig, 1983). Videocassette recorders also gave rise to the entirely new video rental industry, in the 1980s. As the new millennium began, digitally recorded movie discs – DVDs - were pushing videocassettes aside. In music, the rapid public acceptance of compact discs - CDs - in 1986 made vinyl records obsolete. Suddenly a new market opened up, as millions of baby-boom rock 'n' rollers strove to replace their vinyl record collections with new digital ones (The Nordic Council of Ministers, 1999).

A postwar boom in technology sped the transportation of goods. With a device called a steam brake, George Westinghouse invented a safer, easier way to stop trains; also, advances in telegraphy made it easier for railroad headquarters to coordinate schedules. After inventor Alexander Graham Bell perfected a telephone in 1879, railroads could do the same thing by voice. Refrigerated cars enabled railroads to carry perishable goods safely across the country. Railroads themselves became more durable. American industrialist Andrew Carnegie imported from Great Britain the "Bessemer Process" for making steel. Stronger than iron, steel was perfect for rails and the running gear on locomotives and cars. It made Carnegie millions of dollars, and it provided another step in the dominance of rail transportation (Cattell, 1978). The same technological boom affected other areas of the economy. Industrial workplaces boomed. Plants made steel, locomotives, rail cars, trolleys, wagons, textiles, clothing, furniture, and new electrified appliances such as the first American refrigerators and washing machines. Inventor Thomas Alva Edison's electric light bulb made it possible for industrial employees to work before sunrise and after sunset, the traditional agrarian limits of work. Industrial areas became centralized, largely in the Northeast and North, and created urban centers as they grew. After financial panics—the early-day equivalent of depressions—in 1837, 1857, and 1873, more and more farmers and farm families gave up on the vagaries of weather, drought, and crops to move to cities and take steady, if grueling, work in industry (Kaynak and Wikstrom, 1985). As those new industrial workers gave up traditional reliance on the land, they became dependent on the growing commercial and transportation system. Cities and urban areas grew around industrial centers; grocery and general stores, drugstores, doctors' offices, and municipal water, gas, and electrical supply grew to support the industrial workers and their families (McGregor and MacDonald, 1997). At the same time, industry created more efficient ways for the decreasing number of American farmers to feed more and more people.

3.2.4.iv.   A New Society

Most historians point to 1880 as the start of the American consumerist movement, not because of any one event, but because by that year the essential elements of a consumerist society were in place. Industrial centres supported agricultural regions; agricultural regions fed industrial centres. People in both consumed what the other produced. Service industries sprang up around both. And in the middle, rapid communication and transportation linked the two (Onah, 1979). The social transformation was not easy, and it bore heavily on those at the bottom arc of the cycle—the workers, both industrial and agricultural. On the farms, growers soon felt enslaved by the railroads. They were bound to pay whatever freight rate the railroads demanded, and there was little competition to mitigate those rates. If upstart railroads started competing against older lines, the more established company would start a rate war, slashing its rates until the new company went out of business. Then the older company would raise prices even higher simply because it could. Railroads might also alter schedules to remote areas, forcing farmers to store their grain—at exorbitant prices—in railroad-owned storage silos. It did not take long for growers to realize that grain brokers, who sold their grain in eastern markets, were making more off the crops than the farmers were (Lee, 2000). In the industrial workplace, employees faced long hours—often twelve or more per day—in sweaty, dangerous conditions. Pay was low, and employees had little recourse against employers, who protected their own pocketbooks rather than their workers. Industry owners felt no obligation to recompense employers injured on the job or the families of workers killed in workplace accidents.

Urban centers that grew around the industrial centers also attracted foreign immigrants, many fleeing famine and political unrest in Europe. Political "boss machines"—usually corrupt systems for maintaining order in the chaotic urban areas—found ways to fit immigrants into the complex cities, usually by giving them jobs in exchange for votes on election day. Nevertheless, cities became crowded, polluted, infested, and malignant. Yet the cities thrived, as the rest of the nation, now consumerist, devoured their products (Thorelli, 1990).

As production soared, businessmen had to continually create markets. They did so with mass advertising. Newspapers and magazines began carrying ads for everything from corsets to constipation remedies. As homes gradually became electrified, industrialists advertised electrical products such as irons, washing machines (essentially the same old wash tub with electric rollers fitted to it), and home-permanent devices for women, something that, when in use, made the user look like an electrified Medusa. Coca-Cola, based in Atlanta, Georgia, and Dr. Pepper, from Waco, Texas, entered the American vernacular through advertising. So did patent medicines like Lydia E. Pinkham's elixir for all women's problems. Buyers would later rebel when they discovered that most patent medicines contained 20 percent or more of opiates and alcohol (Kerton, 1988).

3.2.4.v.   Consumer   Protection   Movements   and Government

Midwestern and Western farmers were the first to push for significant consumer protection from the mighty railroads. Banding together in the late 1870s as the Patrons of Husbandry—more popularly known as the Grangers—they sought government intervention into the malevolent rate practices of the railroads. That farmers would ever seek such intervention from the government was in itself a watershed, for Americans had traditionally wanted a laissez-faire government, one that handled foreign relations, wars, the coinage of money, and tariffs but kept its nose out of the affairs of private individuals and businesses (Ramesh, 1989).

The efforts of the Grangers coalesced into the Populist Party in the 1880s and bore fruit in 1887 when Populists convinced Congress to pass the Interstate Commerce Act. The act created the Interstate Commerce Commission, designed to watch over the practices of the railroads. It was the first such interventionist act in American history.

By the elections of 1896, the mainstream Democratic Party had co-opted the Populist platform, and populism itself melded into a new era known as progressivism. Like populism, progressivism sought consumer protections, but also protections for the industrial, urban working classes that fueled consumerism. Progressivism would ultimately see a variety of acts strengthen the Interstate Commerce Act: eight-hour workdays established, fire safety mandated in workplaces, child labour abolished, and monopolies attacked.

One of the biggest breaks for consumers came in the administration of President Theodore Roosevelt (1901–1909) when Congress passed legislation to guard the purity of prepared foods and drugs. Consumer advocates had known for some time that packing companies used additives such as formaldehyde and other chemicals to preserve food, and Congress considered bills in 1892 and 1902 to protect buyers from harmful ingredients. Republicans, many of whom had interests in or connections to meatpacking, defeated the measures (Thorelli, 1990).

By 1906, however, the political climate was changing. Muckrakers—journalists who used often sensational investigative reporting to expose graft, corruption, and wrongdoing in a variety of business arenas—began targeting food preparation. One of them, Upton Sinclair, a socialist who was attempting to expose the plight of immigrants in American cities, inadvertently added fuel to the consumer advocacy groups when he published The Jungle in 1906. Some of the characters in The Jungle worked in a Chicago meatpacking plant. In his narrative, Sinclair detailed how rats, rat poison, rat feces, and even human body parts often got mixed in with processed meats and marketed to the public. Sickened, the public, advocacy groups, and Roosevelt himself pressured Congress to once again take up a pure food act. In fact, the Senate had passed a new bill just as Sinclair's book appeared. The public clamor and the weight of the American Medical Association prompted the House to also pass the Pure Food and Drug Act, 1906 (Wells and Sim, 1983).

The act mandated a system of government inspections on meat processed at packing plants. In an age when Americans still had a large measure of faith in the government, a federal stamp on a side of beef meant it had passed inspection. As the name implies, the act also sought to safeguard the purity of drug preparations (Silber, 1983). With no mandated ingredient labeling, "pharmaceutical" companies—often purveyors of quack patent remedies—were free to market preparations for both adults and children containing large quantities of alcohol and opiates. Government inspections after passage of the act largely curtailed such practices.

After a brief detour to supply Allied and American armies in World War I, American industry and agriculture once again sped consumerism in the 1920s. New products—and their concomitant advertising—deluged American buyers. Henry Ford had long since revolutionized automobile manufacturing (all manufacturing, really) with his assembly-line process. Essentially, instead of one team of workers building a car from the ground up, car parts on an assembly line passed by workers who performed one or two specialized tasks. The streamlined process made cars cheaper, but Ford went one better. He made it possible for people to buy cars "on time," or on credit, by making affordable monthly payments (Lowe and Woodroffe, 1980). Ready access to automobiles created a new type of consumerist culture—the car culture. Americans took to the roads, prompting state and local governments to begin paving projects. Motor courts, the forerunners of motels, sprang up to accommodate travellers. Motor courts featured individual bungalows clustered around an office and offered well-appointed bedrooms, bathrooms, and kitchenettes. Automobiles, of course, needed refueling, and oil companies placed filling stations at strategic points along major roadways. Filling station advertising and billboards championed the highest octane in their gasoline; the cleanest restrooms—a must for urgent travellers; and the quickest service (McIlhenny, 1990). Oil companies also issued some of the first credit cards to speed motorists on their way. Roadsides offered new advertising space to merchants. They hawked everything from soft drinks to headache powders on large billboards erected to catch motorists' attention. The most popular of the advertisements, Burma-Shave signs, peddled shave cream with serialized rhyming signs, all ending with the distinctive Burma-Shave logo.

3.2.4.vi. Advertisements

Advertising perhaps preyed on emotion and basic human need as a way to create markets. As the car culture took hold and enabled suburbia to spread, many young housewives and mothers found themselves increasingly isolated from traditional family connections. Advertising stepped up to fill the void, with ad copy that offered thinly veiled familial wisdom: whole grain cereals were the key to health in children; clean bathrooms were the key to social acceptance; mouthwashes and toothpastes the key to sexual appeal. Such advertising barraged women from newspapers, magazines like Good Housekeeping and Ladies' Home Journal, and the newer medium of radio.

Economic historian Don Slater has said that the 1920s marked an ideological milestone in the progression of consumerism. Mass advertising of new products heralded them as the key to modernity, and consumers embraced the idea. Advertising implied that "consumerism itself was the shining path to modernity: it incited the public to modernize themselves, modernize their homes, their means of transport." Indeed, Slater sees in the consumerism of the 1920s a "double face," one which shows mainstream middle America embracing consumerism as a path toward security and contentment and a radical youth/flapper culture embracing it as a license for pleasure. For whatever sector, sociologists would argue that 1920s consumerism pointed both groups away from the carnage of World War I (Onah, 1979).

Late in the decade, however, some consumer advocates voiced concern that advertising was unfairly targeting human fears in order to sell goods, and manifestly lying by saying that new, health-related products had undergone scientific testing and carried the approval of the medical community. In 1927, authors Stuart Chase and F. J. Schlink published Your Money's Worth: A Study in the Waste of the Consumer's Dollar. The authors charged that producers were fleecing consumers and, as in the case of some cosmetics containing harmful chemicals, endangering their health. Consumers' clubs and research groups began to spring up, and state university extension home economists began to champion the rights of consumers. They also attempted to educate consumers on how to make better purchasing decisions.

3.2.4.vii.   The Great Depression and Consumerism

The stock market crash of October 1929 and the advent of the Great Depression shifted the American economy from one of plenty to one of scarcity once again. Across the nation, unemployment averaged more than 30 percent. In some urban areas, where industry fed consumerism, it reached nearly 50 percent. All but the most financially insulated of Americans once again had to save what little money they had. Those lucky enough to remain in a job often found themselves "underemployed," meaning that their wages were significantly less than before the depression began (Silber, 1983). However, depression-era Americans were subtly different than their pre-consumerist forefathers. While the latter had never dreamed of a consumerist culture (and may well have seen it as wretchedly excessive had they done so), the former had tasted it and wanted to remain consumers as best they could. What had been necessity in the 1920s became luxury in the 1930s, but Americans still consumed.

One of the biggest consumer goods in the 1930s was entertainment. It makes sense: faced with financial crisis or unrelenting poverty at home, Americans sought escape when they could. A few extra cents now and then bought a ticket into a theater where people could watch newsreels, cartoons, a serial, teasers, and a feature (McIlhenny, 1990). Indeed, the 1930s were Hollywood's "Golden Age." Movies were cheap to make and relied on writing and acting rather than special effects. Studios could crank out "B" movies in less than a week; "A" movies took a little longer. Such actors as Clark Gable, Humphrey Bogart, John Wayne, Bette Davis, and Katharine Hepburn became stars in the 1930s, and moviegoers saw in their situations a way out of their own troubles. Stan Laurel and Oliver Hardy and the Marx Brothers made classic comedies that poked fun at authorities—symbolic of the same authorities who had steered the country into depression.

If they could not make it to the theater, Americans consumed entertainment in other forms. Pulp novels, long a reading staple, continued to thrive, as did comic books. The 1930s saw the origin of two classic American super-heroes—Superman and Batman—who fought crime and injustice, again metaphors for the trouble in which the United States found itself. And, for cheaper fare, Americans could simply turn on a radio (McGregor and MacDonald, 1997). Radio offered music, concerts ranging from local bluegrass and religious groups to the Metropolitan Opera; dramas in the form of serials and "soap operas," so named because soap manufacturers sponsored them; and comedy with George Burns and Gracie Allen, Bob Hope, and Jack Benny weekly bringing riotous laughter into homes.

In government, President Franklin D. Roosevelt ushered in the New Deal, a program of deficit spending designed to get Americans back on their feet. In 1938, after five years of wrangling, Congress passed new legislation that increased the oversight power of the Food and Drug Administration to protect consumers, and also strengthened the hand of the Federal Trade Commission, which watched over advertising practices (Ramesh, 1989).

3.2.4.viii. World War II Brings Change

The depression gave way to World War II, and while defense spending brought the nation out of the depression and erased unemployment, the war years saw Americans still living in an economy of scarcity. The government rationed perishable goods and food staples, gasoline, and durable goods such as tires and shoes to Americans; the American industrial and agricultural machines had to supply American and Allied soldiers first if they were to defeat global tyranny. In the automobile industry, the 1942 model year was the last for a while; automakers retooled to make army jeeps, tanks, helmets, and a host of other military items.

With millions of men in the armed services, women went to work as they had never done before. In manufacturing plants they built bombers and tanks and aircraft carriers; in business they assumed traditionally male clerk and secretarial roles; at home they managed family finances. With men getting government pay and women at work, some families found themselves, for the first time ever, with two pay checks (Lewis, 2000). They were poised, at war's end, to resume consumerism with a vengeance. After a brief recession in 1946 as the nation reconverted to a peacetime economy, consumerism boomed in 1947. Holding tidy nest eggs, couples began buying homes, often in expanding suburbs. They replaced worn-out automobiles. They began having the children who would become the baby boomers, the most consumer-oriented generation the world had yet seen. The 1950s ushered in an era of consumerism that has rolled on virtually unopposed to the present. Americans purchased homes, cars (sometimes two), television sets, new home furnishings, modern refrigerators, clothes for work and their new found leisure time, barbeque grills, lawn mowers—the list is endless. They continued to consume entertainment as movies continued to boom. Movies also touched off ancillary consumer purchases. When Disney Studios produced a largely fictitious but popular series about Davy Crockett starring Fess Parker, seemingly every boy in America had to have a Disney-marketed coon-skin cap like Parker wore in the films.

The recording industry boomed as kids bought up millions of records to play on compact record players in their bedrooms. The crooning styles of Bing Crosby in the 1930s and Frank Sinatra in the 1940s had now given way to the rock 'n' roll beat of Elvis Presley, Chuck Berry, Jerry Lee Lewis, and Bill Haley and the Comets. But television was beginning to revolutionize entertainment as well (Kerton, 1988). Comedies such as Love Lucy and Love That Bob and westerns like Gun smoke and Maverick ran weekly. All carried corporate sponsors, and series stars frequently hawked merchandise in both televised commercials and coordinated print ads. Situation comedies—the first sitcoms—like Leave It to Beaver, Father Knows Best, and Ozzie and Harriet promoted an idealistic, family-entered American lifestyle. Through set design, product placement, and costuming, they also subtly suggested how American homes should look and how people should dress. Consumerism continued to roll as Americans sought to achieve the televised ideal. Sociologists consider 1950s consumerism as an attempt to achieve contentment and security in a complicated world. The United States had won World War II, defeating the most nefarious enemies the modern world had yet seen—totalitarian Germany and Japan—yet in the 1950s it faced new, ominous threats: an aggressive Soviet Union and nuclear weapons. The United States was a reluctant superpower (Johnston, 1985). Pledged to halt the spread of communism, the country, so recently victorious, looked impotent as China became communist in 1949; as communist aggressors touched off the Korean War in 1950; and as Red-baiter Senator Joseph McCarthy imagined communists at high levels of American government. Faced with such uncertainties and perceived threats, a new washing machine, a roomy sedan, and a clean toilet spelled homogeneity, continuity, and security for many Americans.

3.2.4.ix. A Liberated Consumerism

The 1960s brought a liberated consumerism. Sexually free with the advent of birth control pills in 1960, and encouraged by such books as Betty Friedan's The Feminine Mystique (1963) to drop the June Cleaver wardrobe and attitudes of the 1950s, women sought new and different avenues for their lives. They also became fresh targets for advertisers. Commercials encouraged free lifestyles with portable hair curlers and blow dryers. Women were shown that they need not be tied to motherly chores like cooking with the appearance of such baby boom staples as toaster pastries and instant puddings; they need not dress like their mothers and grandmothers, either, as bell-bottom pants, hip-huggers, and flower-print shirts set a breezy, liberated style for the era (Harland, 1988). Marketing reminded women that to be any less was to be "square"; yet the double face of marketing continued to chide women for having a less-than-spotless kitchen floor or mirrors that did not sparkle.

Advertising also continued to prey on the male psyche as well. Men needed to drink, smoke, and dress like James Bond. Family sedans were passé: instead, muscle cars like the Pontiac GTO and Oldsmobile 442 were the way to go. Better yet, get into sporty pony cars like the Ford Mustang, Chevrolet Camaro, and Pontiac Firebird. If user could afford it, the Chevrolet Corvette was the ultimate expression of male virility on the road, as Martin Milner and George Maharis had proved in the popular television drama

Route 66. Consumer protection took an upswing in 1962 when President John F. Kennedy introduced his Consumer Bill of Rights. Kennedy said that all consumers have a right to safety, the right to be informed about products, the right to choose, and the right to be heard (Hamilton, Jennifer, McIlveen and Strugnell, 2000). His platform set the stage for new investigative hearings into the safety of products ranging from over-the-counter medicines to cosmetics.

Undoubtedly the most influential consumer advocate of the age was Ralph Nader. In 1965 he published Unsafe at Any Speed, an investigation of the automobile industry, charging that car manufacturers gave little concern to motorist safety in the design of their cars. Nader's attack ultimately led to more convenient seat belts in all cars and side turn indicator lights beginning with the 1968 model year. His crusade also spelled the end of the rear-engine Chevrolet Corvair. Deemed patently unsafe, the Corvair's last model year was 1969. Consumer advocacy brought a "truth-in-packaging" bill from Congress in 1966. In the 1960s, Congress also mandated that cigarette packages carry the now-famous surgeon general's warning about tobacco and cancer. And, in 1970, Congress forced an end to televised cigarette commercials.

3.3. The Growth of the Modern Consumer Movement in Comparative Perspective

The modern, comparative-testing form of consumer expertise began in the United States. In 1927, a civil servant for the Labor Bureau, Stuart Chase, and an engineer, F. J. Schlink, published *Your Moneys Worth*, a critique of the exploitation of the consumer in the modern marketplace. Drawing on Veblen-esque attacks on consumption as well as anti-trust traditions within American politics, the book epitomised a desire to empower the consumer that was one of the founding principles of Consumers Research, which began publishing its *Bulletin* in 1929. Consumers' Research sought to overcome the ignorance of the consumer and make him or her adapt at assessing the quality of goods while at the same time maintaining a healthy distance from modern commercial values (Bruun and Schnack 1985). It rode the wave of a developing consumer consciousness in 1930s America which saw the establishment of a consumer infrastructure within the New Deal bodies and the flourishing of several other consumer organizations. However, in 1936, a strike broke out among Consumers' Research staff and in the ensuing split, Arthur Kallet, a former collaborator of Schlink, went on to form the longer lasting, and ultimately more successful, Consumers Union. Schlink would later denounce his former radical colleagues now connected to Consumers Union (CU) as Marxists, especially since the new organization did make efforts to link its model of consumerism with the social and economic concerns of the labour movement (Bloom and Greyser, 1981). But by the end of the 1950s, when it had asserted its non-political role to the House Un-

American Activities Committee, CU had been steered by its President, Colston Warne, and the socially conservative tendencies of the readers of *Consumer Reports*, towards a focus on value-for-money testing. This is not to say that CU has not gone on to support a number of social and economic issues, but its primary focus on testing has proved extremely popular with American shoppers. It has remained a financially successful publishing organization and it has had an uneasy relationship with some of the more aggressive voices in post-war American consumerism, most notably that of Ralph Nader.

Nevertheless, the focus on the testing of goods and services was clearly an inspiration to European shoppers. In the 1950s, a number of consumer testing organizations began to emerge. In France, in 1951, the Union Fédéral des Consommateurs (UFC) was formed and began publishing its testing magazine, *Que Choisir*, in December 1961. The UFC was soon joined by family and rural groups which had formed just previously in the 1940s as well as co-operative organizations and trade unionists through bodies such as the Organization Generale des Consommateurs (ORGECO, 1959), set up specifically to represent consumers who were also union members (Blake and Walters 1987). In response, the state initially created the National Consumer Council (Conseil National de la Consommation) in 1960 to act as a forum for consumers to interact with government, though this has been followed with more comprehensives measures, most notably the National Consumption Institute (Institute National de la Consommation) in 1968, which published *50 millions de consommateurs*from 1970, and the creation in 1976 of a secretariat of State for Consumption, converted into a full ministry by Mitterand in 1981.

Organized consumerism in France has resembled something of a social movement. By 1978, 3% of the adult French population identified themselves as members of a consumer organization, while 27% claimed to be willing to join one. Furthermore, in 1976, 800 clubs de consommateurs around the country were affiliated to the Associations populairesfamiliales, inspired and motivated by such campaigns as the 3-6-9 boycott which urged protesting consumers to stop buying meat for three days, fruit for six, and mineral water for nine (Barker, 1987).

While no other European country witnessed such high levels of grassroots mobilization, it is clear that French consumers were responding in part to a set of general issues facing a rising generation of affluent shoppers. That is, as western economies moved into an increasingly technological and complex age, where the traditional skills attributed to the housewife-shopper were no longer useful in the assessment of products, both male and female consumers sought institutional support to guide and protect them through the marketplace (David, 1975). Thus, it was not only the UFC which mirrored the activities of the American Consumers Union. In the Netherlands,

Consumentenbond was formed in 1953, joining other rural, family and womens bodies, which had increasingly turned their attention to consumer affairs in the period of economic growth. Consumentenbond has, however, remained the pre-eminent consumer organization, its 650,000 members or subscribers to its testing magazine in the late 1990s representing the highest market penetration rate of any consumer publication in the world, reaching one out of every nine Dutch families (Nordic Council of Ministers, 2001).

Similarly, in Belgium, the Association des Consommateurs was formed in 1957 as a private organization of individual shoppers keen to imitate the success of *Consumer Reports*. In 1993, it had 325,000 member subscribers and has played a leading role internationally in promoting consumer organising. At home, while it has always been the most prominent consumer organization, it has also worked alongside a wider network, spearheaded by the women, co-operative and labour movement which came together to form, in 1959, the Union Féminine pour lInformation et la Défense des Consommateurs, although this ended in 1984 when the authorities withdrew their financial support.

In financial terms at least, though, the most successful imitator of the American product-testing model has been the United Kingdoms Consumers Association (CA). Formed in 1956 by a group of professionals broadly, if not entirely, associated with the centre-left traditions of the British Labour Party, CA first began publishing *Which?* in 1957. Its success was immediate and membership peaked in 1987 when subscriptions to *Which?* reached one million (Post, 1986). While its core work has remained servicing its members with better information about the quality of branded products, the income generated from the sale of its magazine has enabled CA to play a leading role internationally and to become a prominent advocate at the national level. Although it is a purely private organization, it has maintained a close relationship with the state and its staff and ideas have heavily influenced such government initiatives as the Consumer Council in the 1960s, the Office of Fair Trading from 1973 and the National Consumer Council from 1975. Furthermore, it also gave rise to something of a social movement. In the 1960s it encouraged the establishment of local consumer groups around the country. For the moderately-minded professionals associated with post-war planning and economic regeneration lawyers, engineers, managers and accountants the groups offered the opportunity for a new type of citizen to play a role in local and national civic life. Although Britain never witnessed the same degree of grassroots consumer mobilization as in France, by March 1963 there were 50 consumer groups in existence with a total of 5,000 members. They had all come together under the National Federation of Consumer Groups (NFCG) and, in 1967; the movement peaked with the existence of 100 groups and a total membership of 18,000 consumers.

While the growth of the western European consumer movement attests to the importance of explaining its rise through variables such as affluence, an increasingly technical marketplace and the growth of advertising and sales techniques which confused individual shoppers, the experience of other countries should not blind the users to the fact that much consumer motivation emerged from adversity and detriment rather than the perplexities of expanding choices. Private testing organizations may have emerged in the 1950s, but they often found themselves working alongside pre-existing consumer groups, most notably co-operatives and women organizations, the former of which had been recognized as the principal consumer experts in periods of necessity, and the latter of which had risen to prominence as consumer experts in the Second World War. In Japan, the main organizations which have become the dominant spokesbodies for consumers in an age of affluence all emerged in the period of shortages, rationing and controls associated with the Allied occupation in the late- 1940s and early 1950s (Pessemier, Bammaor and Hanssens, 1977). Women especially protested against the restrictions of a recovering marketplace, leading to the establishment of organizations such as the Japanese Federation of Housewives Associations (Shufuren) in 1948 which, by the 1990s, consisted of 400 local affiliates from all around the country. Other, more conservative, women organizations have further bolstered the movement and, even as the Japanese began to enjoy unprecedented levels of economic prosperity, local cooperative clubs have flourished, a movement which, if highly diverse, nevertheless boasts 44 million members as housewives in particular have sought to maintain a greater degree of control over an increasingly anonymous and alien marketplace.

What the Japanese situation highlights is the specificity of different national consumption regimes. The factors which gave rise to consumer organising across the industrialized world may have been remarkably similar but how this consumer consciousness manifested itself as a consumer politics varied from one state to the next. Again, in Japan, the collective responsibilities of consumers have been just as relevant as their individual rights and this has meant consumer organizations have recognised the importance of protecting fledgling Japanese industries and agriculture. This has led many commentators on Japan to conclude that its consumer movement has been especially pro-business. Recently, this view has been overturned by Maclachlans in-depth study of consumer politics which stresses the oppositional voice of Japanese consumer groups. Nevertheless, business and commercial interests have clearly eclipsed consumer voices within national public and private institutions and thus a large grass-roots consumer movement has had very little impact on economic and social policy when compared to, for instance, the United States. There, a more plural central bureaucracy has created a diverse number of opportunities and, consequently, strategies for consumer activists to pursue and, prior to an anti-consumer backlash beginning in the late 1970s, a more aggressive form of consumer politics was able to emerge in the US which achieved notable victories both in the courts (through class actions suits) and in the legislature. Different institutional contexts also provide part of the explanation as to why consumer movements have not taken off to the same extent at the grassroots level in other countries. In northern Europe, for instance, stronger state involvement in consumer protection measures has meant consumers have not had to flock to independent, and specifically consumer-based, organizations to realise their interests. In Germany, organizations of consumers emerged as elsewhere in the post-Second World War period, and the Arbeitsgemeinschaft der Verbraucherbände (AgV, Alliance of Consumer Associations) was established as early as 1953 which has subsequently gone on to co-ordinate different groups activities, engage in consumer education and provide information to support its role as an advocacy organization. However, it has not sought to become a mass movement, preferring instead to use its technical expertise to become an equal partner in the development of products and services. It has sought a negotiated role with government and, although business interests have predominated, the German consumer movement has developed a strong representative function. To some extent, this has meant the government has taken the initiative on many consumer activities. Several attempts had been made to start comparative testing magazines, but no lasting publication appeared until *Test* in 1966. German businesses had previously blocked the testing and reporting activities of AgV in the early 1960s, but with the support of the Social Democrats, a government funded testing body, Stiftung Warentest, was established to publish *Test*. By the 1990s, sales had reached one million, and Stifting Warentest was no longer reliant on government subsidies. As the pre-eminent national consumer publication, *Test* differs from other European publications, since the constitution of Stiftung Warentest allows for the input of business at all levels of the product examinations. This, in essence, reflects the German consumer protection regime more generally. German consumers have an impressive representative and negotiating role at the federal level (a situation replicated at the state level thanks to the creation of state-based Verbraucherbände), though this is strongest only in technical areas. What the absence of a strong, independent consumer movement has meant is that German consumer groups have not enjoyed the same freedom of action or ability to set their own agendas as, for instance, in the French case.

In Scandinavia, limited populations have been held to prevent the economies of scale enjoyed by testing magazines with a mass circulation and thus, no such organization as the Consumers Association or Consumers Union has been able to emerge. Beyond this, however, strong co-operative, trade union and social democratic traditions have ensured the state has often initiated a range of consumer interest activities that have elsewhere emerged from below. In Sweden, for instance, involvement in consumer affairs in the 1940s and 1950s by trade unions, cooperatives, voluntary and women organizations was later taken up by the state (i.e., the StatensKonsumentråd). Later still, Sweden established the worlds first consumer ombudsman as well as a Market Court in 1971 and, in 1973, the state-sponsored National Board for Consumer Policies (Konsumentverket, merging with the ombudsman in 1976). With such top-down consumer protection, no national federation of independent consumer groups was thought necessary until the Cooperative Union established a Consumer Policy Council to serve as a forum for the co-operative, labour and consumer movements (becoming the Consumer Council from 1992). In Sweden, then, the role of the state has been particularly strong and it has offered a specifically Scandinavian model of consumer protection which has been an inspiration for consumer movements elsewhere campaigning for greater state intervention. However, it has also ensured a consumer consciousness has been directed away from those organizations usually held to be more typical of a social movement (Scherhorn, 1988).

3.3.1. International Organization of Consumers Unions (IOCU) and the Global Consumer Movement

To varying degrees at the national level, then, the desire for greater guidance in the marketplace gave rise to comparative testing magazines and the emergence of organised consumerism as something of a social movement. However, where the consumer movement has most closely resembled the new social movements of environmentalism or the peace movement, is in the international arena (Lowe and Woodroffe, 1980). In 1960 the First International Conference on Consumer Testing was held to discuss opportunities for future collaborative efforts between the principal national consumer organizations of western Europe and North America. Significantly, this led to the further establishment of the International organization of Consumers Unions (IOCU), consisting of the four comparative testing organizations from France, Belgium, the Netherlands and the UK that had been largely founded on the American model, as well as US Consumers Union. The original aims of the new body were simply to extend and assist comparative testing consumerism, yet it soon extended beyond this model.

The IOCUs growth was impressive. Although in 1970 its Council still consisted of the core of the five founding members, it had also co-opted the state- assisted, publicly-funded consumer organizations of Germany and Scandinavia. Moreover, its membership had grown to include representatives from Asia, Africa and Latin America, if only from the richest nations of these areas (Stanley, 1987). By 1990, however, the IOCU had extended well beyond the affluent West. The Council now consisted of representatives of most

Western European states, but also of consumer organizations in Argentina, Hong Kong, India, Indonesia, Jamaica, Japan, Mauritius, Mexico, Poland and South Korea. An Executive had been formed which showed the domination of the founding members (excluding Belgium) though even here South Korea and Mauritius were represented and the Presidency was held by Erna Witoelar of the Yayasan Lembaga Konsumen, Indonesia (Thorelli, 1981). Today, the IOCU is called Consumers International, and in November of 2003 it held its 17th World Congress in Lisbon, Portugal. Its headquarters are in London, but there are thriving regional offices in Africa, Asia and Latin America. At the turn of the millennium, it had 253 members from 115 different countries which ranged from all the states of the western world to post-communist Eastern Europe and a whole collection of developing states (China, Chad, Guatemala, El Salvador, Gabon, Nigeria, Malawi and Burkina Faso) which, on first instinct, one might suppose had other interests that needed defending than those of consumers (Veblen, 1899). With such a global reach, it clearly extends further and beyond many other, more prominent, international non-government organizations. The significance of the consumer movement as an international phenomenon lies in the political respectability it held within many western states and its ability to reach out to new consumer issues and consumer organizations in the non-affluent global South. Almost from the very beginning of its existence, IOCU decided to structure its activities in a manner in line with the American governments espousal of a rights-based liberalism. In March 1962, President Kennedy made a significant speech in the history of consumer protection. In it, he outlined four basic consumer rights that should act as the guiding principles for legislative and voluntary action: the right to safety; the right to be informed; the right to choose; and the right to be heard. The IOCU immediately incorporated these four rights as its own *raison dêtre*, binding its member organizations to the pursuit of consumer protection ideals articulated and advanced from within a changing US context. Such a rights-based model was also at the heart of liberal politics internationally and IOCU was able to obtain a foothold within the institutions of the United Nations. It quickly had an influence with the UN Economic and Social Council and it went on to have a voice in other bodies such as the World Health Organization and the Food and Agriculture Office. It has been granted Category I status within the General Assembly, enabling it to sit at the table and speak like a national delegation (although it cannot vote on issues). Just as the respectable professionals, who made up the national consumer movements were often able to find a representative role within different states in the 1960s and 1970s, so too were they able to secure a role within the institutions of global governance. Due to IOCU lobbying, in 1982 the UN General Assembly voted to establish a Consolidated List of Banned Products, it has consistently advised on food standards (Codex Alimentarius) and, in 1985, it managed to establish the UN Guidelines on Consumer Protection which have acted as a model law for the implementation of consumer protection regimes around the world. In the mid-1990s, these were subsequently extended by the UN Commission on Sustainable Development and the UN Economic and Social Council to include the promotion of sustainable consumption. Less successfully, but more indicative of the role IOCU was playing in global civil society, was the campaign it spearheaded to obtain a Code of Conduct for Multinational Corporations. This ultimately failed due to US opposition and the weakening of the social and economic role of the UN with the creation of the World Trade Organization and the post-Uruguay Round global trading system. Nevertheless, by the 1980s, IOCU had become a leading NGO as civil society organizations increasingly looked to the UN to implement more socially-minded forms of global justice.

Part of the explanation for IOCUs prominence at this time lies in the absence of other NGOs, compared to the explosion of civil society organizations in the 1990s, and partly because it developed new forms of campaign tactics which gave it a greater legitimacy as the spokes body for civil society. As IOCU expanded into the developing world in the 1970s, it encountered new sets of consumer problems not experienced by affluent westerners. Firstly, it had to deal with the problem of baby food formulas which were marketed to developing world consumers as nutritious substitutes to breast milk. For poor consumers, such an expense was an unnecessary outlay, yet infant formula companies promoted their products as medical advances, even though evidence mounted that poor water supplies meant that babies were being fed disease-ridden foodstuffs (Painter, 1978). Secondly, while the environmental movement and Rachel Carsons pioneering *Silent Spring* had raised the consciousness of American consumers to the dangers of pesticides, the problem seemed all the more acute for developing world consumers who were often exposed to the harmful chemicals in their roles as agricultural labourers as well. Thirdly (although many other examples might also be cited), developing world consumer organizations were increasingly concerned about the high prices of western drugs and the inappropriate marketing of patent medicines which were either ineffective or were dangerous, the international pharmaceutical companies taking advantage of weak consumer protection legislation to dump products which had been banned in western markets.

All three of these issues were subjects which fell within the remit of a variety of developmental NGO concerned with economic and social justice. Not all of these organizations had such a prominent voice as IOCU, however, particularly at the UN, while IOCU, for its part, was too diverse an organization to be able to collect the primary evidence needed to mount campaigns against the alleged market abuses. The solution pioneered by IOCU was to create networks of pre-existing organizations prepared to work together on a specific issue. Although campaigning networks had clearly existed at the national level for some time, and more general networks or Federations existed within the labour and women movements, the creation of single-issue, international campaign networks in the late 1970s was an important precedent which in many ways still has a fundamental influence on the nature of global civil society today. In response to the three issues cited above, IOCU initiated the International Baby Food Action Network in 1979, Health Action International in 1981 and the Pesticide Action Network in 1982. Led and administered by IOCU, the networks brought together a variety of NGOs and enabled many smaller and perhaps in the eyes of those who determined who could obtain a formal voice at the UN less reputable groups to have a say in which issues should be brought to the attention of the UN.

Such campaigns also led to the incremental expansion of the consumer rights at the heart of IOCUs operating philosophy. Over the years, IOCU has added four more rights to those set out by Kennedy in 1962. They now include the right to redress; the right to consumer education; the right to a healthy environment; and the right to basic needs. These latter two rights in particular reflect the influence of the global South on the international consumer movement. The rights to a healthy environment and to basic needs are not so much rights but duties, since they invoke the responsibility of consumers to ensure that all other consumers can enjoy goods and services in an equally inhabitable environment, or else they call upon the duties of affluent western consumers to campaign to ensure that poor consumers around the world can also participate at the most basic level in the consumer society. As developing world consumer activists are keen to point out, if the right to basic needs is not met, then all other consumer rights effectively become meaningless. IOCU expanded in the 1960s and 1970s with a missionary fervour that thought better informed consumers could empower themselves to provide the correctives to imbalances of power within the marketplace. But as the focus of consumer concern in these new countries shifted from cars to rice and refrigeration to water supply, it soon became obvious that the majority of the worlds consumers were facing a very different set of questions (Campbell, 1990). As IOCU set up regional offices, first for the Asia Pacific in 1973 and then for Latin America in the late-1980s and for Africa in the 1990s, it took on board new agendas such that the politics of consumption has more often been concerned with meeting the demands of necessity rather than the desire for luxury.

3.3.2. British reflections on consumer protection and guidance

Unfair trade practices are as old as the trade itself. However, the legal mechanism to curb these practices took it own time to settle. Although, the courts in England from the very beginning were quick to condemn the unfair or misleading conduct in dict, judicially imposed limitations and practical considerations of time and cost confined these remedies to narrow circumstances. The tenderness exhibited towards trade practices of doubtful probity was rooted in the history of market fairs in the medieval England in which trust was neither given nor expected.

In medieval days, transactions of sale and even or barter between strangers were few are rare. When trading cid takes place, it was in the markets and fairs, where goods were openly displayed. So, it was presumed that the buyer relied on his own skill and judgment and the idea of Caveat Emptor well reflected in that practice. At common law, unfair trade practices are subject to legal control through three types of remedies. They are:

(1) Civil Suit by Consumer.
(2) Civil Action by Competitors.
(3) Criminal prosecution.

Only towards the end eighteenth century common law imposed liability for dishonesty. Caveat Emptor (Buyer be beware) has its origin in the middle ages and was dominant feature of the sale of horses in market over. Market overt was an open public place legally constituted market. Since all the sales used to take place in the open market, where seller and buyer were face to face, it was presumed that since buyer is the best judge of his own interest, if he makes a wrong selection by his own choice, he couldn't complain later on against seller. The last quarter of the 19th century saw in England, the enactment of Sale of Goods Act, 1893. This Act represented an important step in the abandonment of the original common law rule of Caveat Emptor (Harland, 1987).

The traditional doctrines of Common Law i.e. caveat emptor. Freedom and sanctity of contract and privatise rule reflected in Market Over were the reflections of the then existing state of values and norms. Even today the spirit of these doctrines holds good. There are no two opinions about the fact that the promise once made must be fulfilled or where person has himself inspected the goods, he should blame none but himself in case of any defect. The Justice demands that only the parties to the contract must be entitled to or liable under the contract. However, the developments of twentieth century has proved that these catch phrases of past have outlived their utility. The market structure of the past has undergone a sea change. Which the profounder of these doctrines might not hate envisaged. The modern paradigms of marketing have proved that these doctrines if implemented in letter and spirit will prove harsh to consumers. The complex nature of the goods hardly provides any scope for an ordinary consumer to detect the defect while inspecting the goods. The aggressive advertising campaign has also added to the confusion of the consumers in making choice (Harland, 1988).

In 1935, a formal 'Consumer Union' came in to existence in Britain. It brought consumer reports thereon and enlightened the public about misleading claims. In Great Britain the consumer movement began to gather momentum during the years following the Second World War mainly through voluntary actions of women's organizations. But in 1955, the Labour Party put out a pamphlet entitled "Battle for the Consumer", It not only argued the case for quality marketing of goods, but also the setting up of Consumers Council. Another major development of the late fifties was the establishment of a Retail Trading Standards Association with the primary objective of helping to resolve disputes between retailers and their consumers.

The British Government appointed the Monopoly Committee in the late fifties to report on, what changes in the law, were desirable for further protection of consuming public and to make recommendations. On the basis of this report, the Government appointed Consumer Council in 1963. A ministry for consumer protection as well as several legislative enactments were passed in the following years. The Consumer Protection Act, 1987 was passed by the British Parliament after extensive debate on. It was a wide-ranging piece of legislation, creating both civil and criminal liability and it would be of major importance throughout industry and commerce (Hendon, 1975).

3.3.3. Russian Reflections on Consumer Protection and Guidance

The Russian movement for Consumer Rights' Protection was given a start in the Soviet Times. The first club for Consumer Rights' Protection was established in 1988 in Leningrad (St. Petersburg). It was followed by the creation of the Russian Consumer Societies' Federation in 1992. The same was converted in to the International Confederation of Consumer Societies, which included Russia and other republics of the former USSR.

In February 1992, the "Consumer rights Protection" law as adopted in Russia. It outlined the consumer rights of the citizens as well as the obligations of organizations engaged in trade and services. Annual Public opinion polls show that in recent years Russian Federation Citizens have grown more resolute to defend their consumer rights in case of the in violation the majority of consumers are ready to stand up for their rights today. The efficiency of consumer's rights protection has increased too. The majority of sellers Goods manufacturers and service providers are ready to satisfy their consumers' lawful demands upon presentation of competently compiled claims, trying to avoid appeals to courts.

3.4. Consumerism in India

"Consumerism" is likely to dominate the Indian market in the next Millennium, thanks to the economic reforms ushered in and the several agreements signed under the World Trade Organization. The transition will be from a predominantly "sellers' market" to a "buyers' market" where the choice exercised by the consumer will be influenced by the level of consumer awareness achieved. By "consumerism" we mean the process of realizing the rights of the consumer as envisaged in the Consumer Protection Act (1986) and ensuring right standards for the goods and services for which one makes a payment. This objective can be achieved in a reasonable time frame only when all concerned act together and play their role. The players are the consumers represented by different voluntary non-government consumer organizations, the government, the regulatory authorities for goods and services in a competitive economy, the consumer courts, organizations representing trade, industry and service providers, the law-makers and those in charge of implementation of the laws and rules.

Consumer protection was part of ancient culture and formed. India has an ancient history of consumer protection the core of its administration. But the introduction of boundless commercialization of activities eclipsed the old rich heritage. As in Europe, in India also the origin of the Consumer Movement was in the form of Consumer Co-operative section.

The people in different parts of the country today celebrate in different ways the dates dedicated to the remembrance of ancient periods during which, it is believed, people's welfare was the first concern of the rulers. 'Onam' in Kerala is one such example. The folk songs relating to Onam celebrate the fact that during the rule of King Mahaballi, people were not at all exploited in any manner. It is believed that there were not shortages or malpractices in weights or measures and nor excessive advertisements. Consumer Protection has its deep roots in the rich soil of Indian civilization, which dates back to 3200 B.C (Rangarajan, 1992).

In ancient India, human values were cherished and ethical practices were considered of great importance. However, the rulers felt that the welfare of their subjects was the primary area of concern. They showed keen interest in regulating not only the social conditions but also the economic life of the people, establishing many trade restrictions to protect the interests of buyers (Prasad, 1998).

3.4.1. Consumer Protection in Ancient India

In ancient India, all sections of society followed Dharma-sastras ("Dharma"), which laid out social rules and norms, and served as the guiding principle governing human relations. The principles of Dharma were derived from Vedas. Vedas were considered the words of God, and law was said to have divine origin, which was transmitted to society through sages. Thus, Vedas were the primary sources of law in India. Many writers and commentators of the ancient period documented the living conditions of the people through their innovative and divine writings, including Smriti (tradition) and Sruti (revelation), and also prescribed codes to guide the kings and rulers about the method of ruling the State and its subjects. Consumer protection was also a major concern in their writings.

Among the Dharmas, the most authoritative texts are a) the Manu Smriti (800 B.C. to 600 B.C.); b) the YajnavalkyaSmriti (300 B.C. to 100 B.C); c) the Narada Smriti (100 A.D to 200 A.D.); d) the Bruhaspati Smriti (200A.D. to 400 A.D.); and e) the Katyayana Smriti (300 A.D. to 600 A.D). Among these, Manu Smriti was the most influential.

Manu Smriti describes the social, political and economic conditions of ancient society. Manu, the ancient law giver, also wrote about ethical trade practices. He prescribed a code of conduct to traders and specified punishments to those who committed certain crimes against buyers. For example, he referred to the problem of adulteration and said "one commodity mixed with another must not be sold (as pure), nor a bad one (as good) not less (than the property quantity or weight) nor anything that is at hand or that is concealed." The punishment "for adulterating unadulterated commodities and for breaking gems or for improperly boring (them)" was the least harsh. Severe punishment was prescribed for fraud in selling seed corn: "he who sells (for seed-corn that which is) not seed-corn, he who takes up seed (already sown) and he who destroys a boundary (mark) shall be punished by mutilation" (Misra, 2007). Interestingly, Manu also specified the rules of competency for parties to enter into a contract. He said "a contract made by a person intoxicated or insane or grievously disordered (by disease and so forth) or wholly dependent, by an infant or very aged man, or by an unauthorized (party) is invalid."

During the ancient period, the king had the power to confiscate the entire property of a trader in two instances: (1) when the king had a monopoly over the exported goods; and (2) when the export of the goods was forbidden (Kane, 1975). There was also a mechanism to control prices and punish wrongdoers. The king fixed the rates for the purchase and sale of all marketable goods. Manu said "man who behaves dishonestly to honest customers or cheats in his prices shall be fined in the first or in the middle most amercement."(Patrick, 2004) There was a process to inspect all weights and measures every six months, and the results of these inspections were duly noted.

All these measures show how effective ancient society was in regulating the many wrongs of the market place. These measures also show how developed the system was in identifying the market strategies of traders. Thus, Manu Smriti effectively dealt with various consumer matters, many of which remain of great concern in modern legal systems (Muller, 2004)

Written subsequent to Manu Smriti, Kautilya's Arthasastra is considered to be a treatise and a prominent source, describing various theories of statecraft and the rights and duties of subjects in ancient society. Though its primary concern is with matters of practical administration, consumer protection occupies a prominent place in Arthasastra (Chaturvedi). It describes the role of the State in regulating trade and its duty to prevent crimes against consumers.

Between 400 and 300 B.C., there was a director of trade whose primary responsibility was to monitor the market situations. Additionally, the director of trade was made responsible for fair trade practices (Chamola, 2007). The director of trade was required to be "conversant with the differences in the prices of commodities of high value and of low value and the popularity or unpopularity of goods of various kinds whether produced on land or in water and whether they arrived along land-routes or water-routes, and also should know about suitable times for resorting to dispersal or concentration, purchase or sale." The director of trade advised to "Avoid even a big profit that would be injurious to the subjects (Rangarajan, 1992). He should not create a restriction as to time or the evil of a glut in the market in the case of commodities constantly in demand."

During this period, several measures were taken to maintain official standards of weights and measures. Kautilya observed, "the superintendent of standardization should cause factories to be established for the manufacture of standard weights and measures." He further said "the superintendent should cause a stamping of the weights and measuresto be made every four months. The penalty for unstamped weights is twenty seven panas and a quarter. Traders shall pay a stamping fee amounting to one kakani every day to the superintendent of standardization."

According to Kautilya, 'the trade guilds were prohibited from taking recourse to black marketing and unfair trade practice." Severe punishments were prescribed for different types of cheating. For example, "for cheating with false cowrie-shells, dice, leather straps, ivory-cubes or by sleight of hand, the punishment shall be cutting-off of one hand or a fine." The rights of the traders were also well protected. Kautilya said, "On the subject of the return of an article purchased or payment of price thereof, there was fixed rule of time, after which an article could not be returned" (Sihag, 2009).

During Chandragupta's period, in which Kautilya lived, good trade practices were prevalent (Spengler, 1971). For example, "Goods could not be sold at the place of their origin, field or factory. They were to be carried to the appointed markets (panyasala) where the dealer had to declare particulars as to the quantity, quality and the prices of his goods which were examined and registered in the books." Every trader was required to take a license to sell. A trader from outside had to obtain permission. The superintendent of commerce fixed the whole-sale prices of goods as they entered the Customs House (Gopal, 1935). He allowed a margin of profit to fix retail prices. Speculation and cornering to influence prices were prohibited. Thus, the State bore a heavy responsibility for protecting the public against unfair prices and fraudulent transactions. There were severe punishments for smuggling and adulteration of goods. For example, public health was guarded by punishing adulteration of food products of all kinds, including grains, oils, alkalies, salts, scents and medicines.

Also during Chandragupta's period, easy access to justice for all, including consumers, was considered of great importance. The king was the central power to render justice. According to Kautilya, "The king should look to the complaints of the people of the town and village in the second part of the day. The mobile and circuit courts worked at night, when necessity arose. They also must have worked on holidays in urgent matters." The king was required to pay full attention to the truth and he was primarily responsible for administering justice. Everyone could approach the king's court for justice. However, standing was strictly followed. The king only entertained cases if the aggrieved presented a valid complaint (Braibanlti and Spengler, 1963). The king was directed not to "foster litigation by starting an action without a complainant, and moreover, the king was told that no complaint should be taken notice of when it proceeded from a person altogether unconnected with the person aggrieved." In addition to this, different set of courts were prevalent in ancient India.

The court system during Kautilya's time was well organized. There were two different benches comprising judges and magistrates to try civil and criminal cases. In civil matters, the judges themselves were empowered to take cognizance of the cases of disadvantaged persons who could not approach the court, for example, the cases concerning ascetics, women, and minors, old, sick and helpless people. Thus, rendering justice was regarded as one of the essential duties of the rulers, and care was taken to ensure that justice was accessible to all. Indeed, this emphasis on justice for all remains a cornerstone of India's legal system.

3.4.2. Consumer Protection in Medieval

Consumer protection was of paramount importance in the medieval period in India ranging from 1000 AD to 1750 AD. Several prominent Muslim rulers had ruled India during this period from their capital in Delhi. The Delhi Sultanate, being the start of such a long period of Islamic rule in India, laid the foundation to the economic, financial and commercial backbone of the Indian medieval period (Nagarajan, 1992).

The most notable achievements in Consumer Protection during the Delhi Sultanate were during the period of Alauddin Khilji (1296 AD to 1316 AD). Alauddin Khilji was the second ruler of the Khilji dynasty. During his reign, there were unprecedented improvements in the weights and measures standardization process bringing about dramatic changes in the transparency practices of traders with consumers. Commodities were weighed and measured through standards established by the Sultan and people who did not follow standards were punished through fines and even capital punishment. The Sultan had judges who were omnipotent in enforcing the rights of the consumers and approaching the courts when injustice occurred was simple and without bureaucracy.

Several generations of rulers following the Khilji did not contribute much to the consumer protection cause until Sher Shah Suri who ruled during the brief period between 1540 and 1545 AD. Sher Shah Suri was a visionary in matters related to commerce. He envisioned that an economy is always dependent on how well its consumers are treated. He emphasized on standardized measures and set forth decimal and centenary systems with respect to measures. He also published quality guidelines especially for produce, grocery, confectionaries and pharmaceuticals. The financial system he introduced along with the currency Rupiyah forms the foundation of the monetary system of modern India. Although his reign was brief, he is thought to be one of the most important medieval ruler who has influenced consumer protection policies of modern India.

During the reign of Akbar (1556-1605), the third Mughal Emperor of India, several significant achievements were made in matters related to consumer protection. The right of the consumer to be informed perhaps found its earliest roots during the period. All traders were required to publish details regarding the quality and quantity of their merchandise including weights, measures, adulteration if any, age, grade, and usability. This law was strictly enforced through prefects and secret service personnel employed by the emperor. Violations and deceitful behavior were dealt with the harshest of punishments including amputation of limbs. Consumers also enjoyed the right to return merchandise which did not meet the standard requirements related to quality and quantity. Akbar's contribution is notable in that his rule improved accountability and transparency in commodity transactions which were perhaps non-existent in the medieval days in India.

Although the Mughal kings that came afterwards did continue the achievements laid by their forefather, they concentrated more on literary, architectural and military pursuits. Eventually by the time the British gained control over the whole Indian peninsula, consumer issues had deteriorated into a stage that needed a rigorous revival. Nevertheless, the awareness, vision and perseverance through which the medieval rulers of India preserved the importance of consumer protection issues have been a source of fascination for international historians and economists.

In the modern period, the British system replaced the age old traditional legal system of India. However, one of the outstanding achievements of

British rule in India was "the formation of a unified nationwide modern legal system." During the British period, the Indian legal system was totally revolutionized and the English legal system was introduced to administer justice. However, it is important to note that the traditions and customs of the Indian legal system were not ignored. "The law itself underwent considerable adaptation. The British institutions and rules were combined with structural features [e.g. a system of separate personal laws] and rules [e.g. Dharma, and local custom] which accorded with indigenous understanding. The borrowed elements underwent more than a century and a half of pruning in which British localisms and anomalies were discarded and rules were elaborated to deal with new kinds of persons, property and transactions." To administer justice, "they were confronted with the problem of the value suitable to attach in practice to the Indian traditions and customs." Despite the challenges of combining the British and Indian legal systems, "the fabric of modern Indian Law is unmistakably Indian in its outlook and operation" and consumer protection is not an exception to this perception.

Some of the laws which were passed during the British regime concerning consumer interests are: the Indian Contract Act of 1872, the Sale of Goods Act of 1930, the Indian Penal Code of 1860, the Drugs and Cosmetics Act of 1940, the Usurious Loans Act of 1918, and the Agriculture Procedure (Grading and Marketing Act) of 1937. These laws provided specific legal protection for consumers.

For fifty-five years, the Sale of Goods Act of 1930 [SGA] was the exclusive source of consumer protection in India. The Sales of Goods Act, drafted with precision, is "an admirable piece of legislation." It is also praised as a "Consumer's Charter." The main protection for the buyer against the seller for defective goods is found in Section 16 of the Act. It provides exceptions to the principle of Caveat emptor ("let the buyer beware") and the interests of the buyer are sufficiently safeguarded. Phrases such as "skill and judgment of the seller", "reliance on sellers' skill", and the test of "merchantable quality" provide effective remedies to buyers. Courts interpreted these rules in the consumer's favor. The Sales of Goods Act was the exclusive consumer legislation until 1986, with the passage of the Consumer Protection Act of 1986, designed to supplement the remedies already provided under the Sales of Goods Act.

Consumer protection was also provided within India's criminal justice system. The Indian Penal Code of 1860 has a number of provisions to deal with crimes against consumers. It deals with offenses related to the use of false weights and measures, the sale of adulterated food or drinks, the sale of noxious food or drink, and the sale of adulterated drugs.

Consumer protection legislation enacted after India's independence from Britain include: the Essential Commodities Act of 1955, the Prevention of Food Adulteration Act of 1954 and the Standard of Weights and Measures

Act of 1976. A benefit of these acts is that they do not require the consumer to prove or show proofs. Rather, "the offenses are of strict liability, and not dependent on any particular intention or knowledge." Criminal law in the field of consumer protection has acquired much significance, as consumers are less inclined to go to civil court for small claims. It has been said that "the functional value of criminal law in the field of consumer protection is a high one and it has a respectable pedigree." Another view is that there has been an attempt to look at consumer protection as "a public interest issue rather than as a private issue" to be left to individuals for settlement in court.

In addition to the remedies under contract and criminal law, consumers have rights under tort law. Based on its numerous legal intricacies, however, tort law is not the ideal remedy for injured consumers in India. For example, the traditional doctrine of negligence imposes heavy responsibility on the plaintiff to prove each of its required elements. These traditional legal requirements naturally encourage injured consumers to pursue legal remedies under different laws. Not surprisingly, it is estimated that for about half a century from 1914 to 1965, only 613 tort cases came before the appellate courts.

The orthodox legal requirements under the law of torts and contracts forced the policy makers to craft specific legislation to protect consumers. As a result, the Consumer Protection Act of 1986 was enacted with the objective of providing "cheap, simple and quick" justice to Indian consumers.

3.4.3. Consumer Movement in the Modern Period

Consumer movement in the present form came into being only in the 1930's in the West and only in the 60's in India. The basic objectives of consumer movement worldwide are as follows:

- To provide opportunity to the consumers to buy intelligently
- Recognition of reasonable consumer requests
- Protection against fraud, misrepresentation, unsanitary and unjust product
- Participation of consumer representatives in management of aspects affecting consumers
- Promoting consumers interests

The basic reason for the development of consumer movement in India, are different from those in the West. In western countries, consumer movement was the result of post-industrialization affluence-for more information about the merits of competing products and to influence producers especially for new and more sophisticated products.86 In India, the basic reasons for the consumers' movement have been:

- Shortage of consumer products; inflation of early 1970's
- Adulteration and the Black Market
- Lack of product choices due to lack of development in technology

- Thrust of consumer movement in India has been on availability, purity and prices

The factors which stimulated the consumer movement in recent years are:

- Increasing consumer awareness
- Declining quality of goods and services
- Increasing consumer ,expectations because of consumer education
- Influence of the pioneers and leaders of the consumer movement
- Organized effort through consumer societies

3.4.4. The Indian Consumer Protection Act of 1986 and the Evolution of a New Legal Culture

The Indian legal system experienced a revolution with the enactment of the Consumer Protection Act of 1986 ["Consumer Protection Act"], which was specifically designed to protect consumer interests. The Consumer Protection Act was passed with avowed objectives. It is intended to provide justice which is "less formal, [and involves] less paper work, less delay and less [expense]". The Consumer Protection Act has received wide recognition in India as poor man's legislation, ensuring easy access to justice. However, the Consumer Protection Act simply gives a new dimension to rights that have been recognized and protected since the ancient period (Thomas, 1978). It is rightly said that "the present-day concern for consumer rights . . . is not new and that consumer's rights like the right to have safe, un-adulterated and defect-free commodities at appropriate prices has been recognized since ancient times."

Two decades of experience with the operation of the Consumer Protection Act shows its popular acceptance and the legal preference of injured consumers to enforce their rights under it. The Consumer Protection Act commands the consumer's support because of its cost-effectiveness and user-friendliness. In fact, the Consumer Protection Act creates a sense of legal awareness among the public and at the same time, brings disinterest to approach traditional courts, especially on consumer matters (Borrie, 1984). It has changed the legal mindset of the public and made them think first of their remedies under the Consumer Protection Act, regardless of the nature of their case. In short, the Consumer Protection Act has instilled confidence among the "teeming millions" of impoverished litigants. The way in which the consumer fora are flooded with cases and the mode in which these cases are being disposed of creates an impression of "judicial populism" in India in the arena of consumer justice.

The greatness of the Consumer Protection Act lies in its flexible legal framework, wider jurisdiction and inexpensive justice. One can find in the Consumer Protection Act a mixture of principles of torts and contracts.

Simply speaking, it is "a shorthand term to indicate all the many different aspects of general law." Basically, the Consumer Protection Act liberalizes the strict traditional rule of standing and empowers consumers to proceed under the Consumer Protection Act. Consumer groups, the central or any state government are all empowered to lodge complaints under the Consumer Protection Act. This liberalization shows the care that has been taken to represent and fight for the cause of weak, indifferent and illiterate consumers. The novelty of the Consumer Protection Act is the inclusion of both goods and services within its ambit (Mahajan, 1980). The consumer can sue for defective products as well as for deficiency of services. In the event of any deficiency, all services, whether provided by the government or private companies, can be questioned under the Consumer Protection Act.

The Consumer Protection Act also liberalized rigid procedural requirements and introduced simple and easy methods of access to justice. To proceed under the Consumer Protection Act, the consumer need only pay a nominal fee and need not send any notices to the opposite party. A simple letter addressed to the consumer forum draws enough attention to initiate legal action (Fetterman and Schiller, 1978). Another major procedural flexibility is the option the consumer has to engage a lawyer. If the consumer prefers, he can represent himself. The simple measures of action drive consumers to avail themselves of the benefits of the Consumer Protection Act.

The Consumer Protection Act initiated a legal revolution by ushering in the era of consumers and developing a new legal culture among the masses to take recourse under the Consumer Protection Act regardless of their grievance. The Consumer Disputes Redressal agencies, the National Commission, the State Commission, and the District Fora are working together in a way that is revolutionizing the present Indian legal system and challenging the traditional system of delivering justice. With easy access to the courts guaranteed by the Consumer Protection Act, consumers now wage legal battles against unscrupulous traders or service providers without any hesitation. The Indian government is also taking an active interest in protecting consumer rights and promoting effective consumer movements. In 2003, the Planning Commission of India identified "Consumer Awareness, Redressal, and Enforcement of the Consumer Protection Act of 1986" as a priority, and as a result, a national action plan was prepared.

The consumer fora created by the Consumer Protection Act have proven to be effective, disposing of thousands of cases with few legal formalities, and leading the way toward well-founded consumer jurisprudence in India. The traditional Indian legal system, in addition to a huge blacklog of cases, is experiencing a litigation explosion in the area of consumer protection. According to one report, the total number of consumer cases pending in different fora was 359,469 cases as of June, 2004. Around 45,798 cases have been filed before the national commission since its inception. At present, 8,884 cases are pending disposal. The huge backlog of consumer cases before consumer fora is forcing the Indian legal systems to think of "alternatives" for speedy disposal of consumer cases. India, home to the majority of the world's consumers, is committed to working for the welfare of consumers through new legal innovations.

3.5. Stages of Development of the Consumer Movement

The Consumer Movement today is undergoing a silent revolution. The movement is bringing qualitative and quantitative changes in the lives of people enabling them to organize themselves as an effective force to reckon with. But the path to reach this stage has not been easy. It has been a struggle against bad business which always put profit before fairness in transactions.

The first stage of movement was more representational in nature, i.e., to make consumers aware of their rights through speeches and articles in newspapers and magazines and holding exhibitions.

The second stage was direct action based on boycotting of goods, picketing and demonstration. However, direct action had its own limitations, which led to **the third stage** of professionally managed consumer organizations. From educational activities and handling complaints, it ventured into areas involving lobbying, litigation and laboratory testing. This gave good results. Thus, for instance business sector has started taking notice and co-operating with the movement. It has played a role in hastening the process of passing the Consumer Protection Act, 1986 which has led to the fourth stage.(Gurg, 2003) The Act enshrines the consumer rights and provides for setting up of quasi-judicial authorities for redressal of consumer disputes. This act takes justice in the socio-economic sphere a step closer to the common man.

3.6. Some Important Consumer Organizations

Consumer movement in India had its beginning in the early part of this century. The first known collective body of consumers in India was set up in 1915 with the 'Passengers and Traffic Relief Association' (PATRA) in Bombay. Women Graduate Union (WGU). Bombay was another organization started in 1915. One of the earliest consumer co-operatives was the 'Triplicane Urban Co-operative Stores' started in late 40's in Madras. It has about 150 branches all over the city. The Indian Association of Consumer (IAC) was set up in Delhi in 1956. This was an All India Association for consumer interests with the government's support. However, even IAC did not make any headway.

The first organization to really make an impact was the Consumer

Guidance Society of India (CGSI), Bombay started by nine housewives in 1966 with Mrs.Leela Jog as its founder secretary. Instead of just holding conferences and meetings and asking questions like earlier consumer associations, it started testing and reporting the quality of items of daily use of foodstuffs and handling' consumer complaints. It has 8 branches at various places carrying on publicity, exhibitions and education. It publishes a magazine called 'Keemat', in English, for consumer information. The second consumer organization which made quite an impact in making the cause of consumers known throughout the country is the Karnataka Consumer Services Society' (KCSS) formed in 1970. The main strength of the KCSS was Mrs. Mandana who spread the word of the movement throughout the country, especially among government circles at a time when the word 'consumer' was not familiar to many. It is based in Bangalore. It organised important seminars on consumers' education in schools and is represented on prevention of Food and Drug Adulteration Committee and Karnataka Food and Civil Supplies Corporation. Visaka Consumers Council (VCC) started in 1973 in Vishakhapatnam, Andhra Pradesh, 'is another pioneering consumer organization which has made a significant contribution to the consumer movement. It represented the plight of the poor ration card holders and LPG gas users, who had to stand in long queues because of the irresponsible attitude of the concerned authorities. Mr. V. K. Parigi with 20 members held meetings, survey of ration card holders and succeeded in achieving necessary changes in the fair price shops and the public distribution system. Besides this about 15 more organizations came up in Andhra Pradesh taking up the task of solving problems of fair price shops and milk distribution in different parts of the state. To wage a war against exploitation by the traders, some organizations came up with the novel idea of buying quality product of everyday use at wholesale and selling these to the consumers at much lower prices than that being sold by the merchants. These are the Akhil Bhartiya Grahak Panchayat (ABGP) started in 1974 in Pune, Mumbai Grahak Panchayat (MGP) in 1979 in Mumbai and Grahak Panchayat in 1979 in Jamshedpur. Another organization which made a significant contribution to the cause of consumers is the Consumer Education and Research Centre (CERC) which started in Ahmedabad in 1978. It added a new dimension to the Consumer movement with Prof. Manubhai Shah, the Managing Trustee of CERC. The organization constantly used legal machinery to bring about changes and protect consumer rights. Its special focus and intervention is against the governments and public corporations. It has a big library, computer centre and a product testing laboratory. Recently, it has also launched a project on comparative testing in Ahmedabad where comparative testing, ranking and evaluation of consumer products are being undertaken with the aim of publication of such findings for consumer education. To begin with, testing of food, pharmaceuticals and domestic appliances had started. Findings will be published and Action may be initiated against unsafe products. CERC also undertakes internship training for any consumer organization, besides routine exhibitions, seminars and publications of the magazine 'Consumer Confrontation.'

The Eighties of the present century saw the dawn of a new era in consumer movement in India. There was mushrooming of consumer organizations, many floated by politicians to earn additional income and capture a gullible vote bank! However some associations were really committed to the cause of the consumers. One of these was 'Jagrut Grahak' in Baroda, Gujarat started in 1980 by ten retired professionals. It imparts consumer education through seminars and publication and runs a network of 45 complaint centres. 'Consumers Forum' is another important organization started in 1980 in a small form in Udupi in South Karnataka. Under the leadership of Dr. P. Narayan Rao, it succeeded in bringing relief to many aggrieved consumers, chiefly from their problems with the state bureaucrats. VOICE, the voluntary organization in the interest of consumer education, was founded by energetic young students and teachers of the Delhi University in 1983 in Delhi to fight against unfair trade practices. It gives consumers information about the benefits of shortcomings of various products and brands and enables them to make informed choices. With Dr.Shri Ram Khanna asthe Managing Trustee, it has launched comparative testing. Its first attempt was directed at comparative testing of well-known brands of colour T.Vs. Consumer Unity and Trust Society (CUTS) started in Jaipur, Rajasthan, in March 1984, made its impact by effectively making use of media and publicity. For example, to tackle problems of garbage, it announced prizes for a photograph depicting the biggest heap rubbish or the biggest pothole, and these galvanized authorities into taking prompt action. Consumer Action Group (CAG) founded in 1985 in Madras concerns itself with the issues of civic amenities, health and environments. For example, shortage in Chennai and Chemical pollution in Adyar river.

To mention now, some individual consumer activities who have been in the forefront of the consumer movement in the country.Mr. R. R. Dollani, an old Gandhian, started a number of associations in Madras. He has been organising meetings and rallies on consumers' issues and other public interest issues in various parts of the city. Mr. H.D. Shourie, Director; Common Cause; Delhi, is a well-known litigant in consumer circles. This organization as 5000 members from all over the country keeping contact with the various consumers outfits and taking up cases on problems of electricity, hospitals, taxation and similar issues. Another consumer activist who works primarily with his pen is Mr. R. Desikan of SMN Consumer Protection Council, Madras.

A new impetus was given to the consumer movement with the

enactment of the Consumer Protection Act, 1986. It applies to the whole of India except J&K. The detailed information on this act is dealt with elsewhere in this course. Here, it is suffice to mention that this act is unique since it provides for setting up of quasi-judicial bodies vested with jurisdiction concurrently with the established courts for redressal of consumer disputes at the district, state and national levels. The basic objective is to provide inexpensive justice to consumers. For the enactment of this legislation, the late Prime Minister, Mr. Rajiv Gandhi deserves special mention from several ministries and public sector monopolies and after vested interests, he went ahead and got the act passed. The Nineties saw the fulfillment of efforts towards a unified approach. It had been always felt that there were benefits in collective and united approach. In March, 1990 the Federation of Consumer Organizations (FEDCOT) was established in Tamil Nadu to bring together as many consumer groups as possible in the state under one umbrella. In 1992, consumer groups of Guiaratioins hands to form a federation, Guiarat State, Federation of Consumer Organizations (GUSFECO). Now nine states in the country have federations. Besides Tamil Nadu and Gujarat, they are Kerala, Karnataka, Andhra Pradesh, Maharashtra, Rajasthan. Orissa, and Uttar Pradesh. Besides, at the apex level, there are Confederation of Indian Consumer Organization (CICO), New Delhi, formed in February 1991 and Consumer Coordination Council (CCC), New Delhi, formed in April 1992. The primary reason for firming these apex bodies is networking of consumer groups coming together for a common cause.

Consumer organizations improve awareness of regarding consumer rights and advice on the legal recourse a user can take when his consumer rights are violated. Following are the major consumer organizations functional in India.

3.6.1. Consumer Coordination Council (CCC)

Consumer Coordination Council (CCC) was established in March 1993 as a Society registered under the Societies Registration Act of 1860. Before taking the present shape, a group of consumer activists representing various Consumer Organizations gathered (in April 1992) to work as one body, to raise one voice on issues related to consumer interests and various Government policies and programmes affecting the interest of the Consumers. CCC has been actively involved in various consumer-related projects and programmes funded by UNICEF, UNDP, Ford Foundation, Consumer Welfare Fund and other funding agencies as also grants from various Ministries of Govt. of India such as MNES, MOH&FW, MOFPI, Department of AR & PG etc. for specific projects. Earlier CCC had a long-term partnership with a German Foundation called Friedrich-Naumann-Stiftung (FNST), which helped in establishing the organization and provided full support for its programmes including infra-structural expenditure till 31st March 2002. From 1st April 2002 onward CCC is being managed entirely by such project-related funds. By now CCC has completed a decade of service to the consumers of the country in general and its Member Consumer Organizations in particular.

CCC presently has a membership reach of over 72 leading Consumer Organizations, spread over different parts of the country, which are, or have been members of the Central Consumer Protection Council (CCPC), set up under the Consumer Protection Act. It may also be added that many more Consumer Organizations including some new Members of CCPC have applied for Membership of CCC. These are under process. Its Governing Council of 12 Members consists of well-known consumer activists belonging to established Consumer Organizations of long standing.

Aims & Objectives of CCC:

- Influencing policies, legislation and administrative framework towards promoting consumer interests.
- Empowering consumer protection groups to work towards strengthening the civil society in the democratic system of the country.

One of the major concerns of CCC has been Good Governance. CCC had accordingly launched a National Campaign on Citizens' Charter in July 1996 for implementing the principles of Transparency, Accountability, Standards of Service, Availability of Information and an Effective Grievance Redressal System in Public Service and has been continuing its pioneering work in this direction. In the process, CCC has been involved both in the drawing up of appropriate Citizens' Charters for various organizations, as also in the evaluation of their implementation in the Health, Telecom, Railways, Insurance & Banking Sectors (www.cccindia.co).

3.6.2. Consumer Guidance Society of India

Since independence, India has been striving to develop and strengthen its industrial base. In this pursuit of "self-sufficiency", however, the consumer has been made to endure sub-standard products and services: adulterated foods, short weights and measure, spurious and hazardous drugs, exorbitant prices, endemic shortages leading to black marketing and profiteering, unfulfilled manufacture guarantees, and a host of other ills. In one infamous case, forty persons were struck with dropsy and glaucoma after consuming groundnut oil adulterated with toxic argimon oil. The culprits were never brought to justice. This outrage energized nine ladies to organize a movement to fight for consumer rights. They formed the Consumer Guidance Society of India (CGSI) to resist consumer exploitation of all forms.

Following are some of the landmarks achieved by CGSI:

1. CGSI is the earliest consumer organization in India, founded in 1966.
2. CGSI was the first to demand a Consumer Protection Act with Consumer Courts to implement it. This became a reality in 1986.
3. To date, 70% of the thousands of complaints referred to CGSI have been redressed.
4. CGSI established formal Product Testing in India.
5. CGSI was the first to publish a monthly magazine "Keemat" carrying information of importance to consumer.
6. CGSI promotes consumer education; initiates training projects in rural areas; Promotes publicity drives; represents consumer interests with Government and other bodies.
7. CGSI received the National Award for consumer Protection in 1991.
8. CGSI is the only Indian consumer organization to be a council member of Consumer International for 25 years.
9. CGSI is a member of the Maharashtra State Consumer Protection Council.
10. CGSI participates in a large number of technical committees and government decision-making bodies.

CGSI was the first consumer organization to demand special Consumer Court for redressal of consumers' complaints. In 1975, CGSI led a delegation of five consumer organizations from different parts of India to the then Minister for food and Civil Supplies, Mr.T.A. Pai, to press for a comprehensive Consumer Protection Act, Special Consumer Court and a Directorate for implementation of the Act. The first two have now become a reality.

CGSI handles consumer complaints and offers legal guidance to those wishing to file suits in the Consumer Court. In case where there are a number of complaint against a particular party, both sides are brought together to resolve the issue. The CGSI'S Complaints Committee meets twice a week. Many thousands of grievances have been handled over the years, with 70% success in favour of the complaints cover medical/surgical malpractice and negligence; insurance non-payment; sub-standard drugs and medicines; home remedies; defective household appliances; poor quality foods and drinks; misleading advertising claims; and grievances concerning investments, real estate, insurance, telephones, electricity supply, etc.

As early as 1977, CGSI established the facility of product testing. It first assessed the safety and performance of domestic pressure stoves and found that two-third of the samples tested failed in safety Parameters. CGSI sent the results to the government and Indian Standards Institution (ISI) with a demand for mandatory certification. In 1986, the Pressure Stoves Quality Control Order was passed. Later, ISI Certification for pressure stoves became mandatory. Subsequently tests were carried out on electrical appliances and fittings - irons, immersion heaters, this culminated in the enactment of the Household Electrical Appliances (Quality Control) Order. A food adulteration testing kit has been developed for use by the lay consumer. Many other products were tested and reports published in the Society's monthly Journal, "Keemat": edible oils, powdered spices, 'surma', geysers, clinical thermometers, plastic water bottles, rubber teats, milk, mineral water, bread, soft drinks, bath soaps and toothpaste.

CGSI's Education Committee members had been working with other likeminded educationists to formally introduce Consumer Education in the school curriculum. After nearly two years of meetings and discussions, our efforts were fruitful. In 1994, the Maharashtra Education Board introduced Consumer Education at the 9th Standard Level, progressively covering students from the 4th Standard upwards. The subject taught are the Consumer Moment, Rights & Responsibilities of Consumers, the Consumer in the Market Place, Food Adulteration, Weights and Measures, the Environment, etc. This topics included under existing subjects like Civics, Economics and Home science, are project-based and more practical in nature then theoretical or examination-oriented.

CGSI started a rural project in the villages of Thane and Raigad districts (Maharashtra) in 1997, with a staff of six and funding from Action aid. Consumer training was given to people in 112 villages by 1999. Over 32,300 people have received Consumer Education through 750 talks and demonstrations in the 2 years of the project, 107 training programmes were organized and 5,767 potential activists have been given special training in Consumer Activision. Three local Consumer groups have been setup in different areas by the Consumers themselves, and these are now actively organizing exhibitions, holding talks and redressing complaints. More are expected to come up soon.

"Keemat" is now in its 32th year of publications, the first Consumer magazine in India to be published regularly every month. CGSI has also produced Consumer Guides on subject like Electrical Appliances, Edible Oils, Pesticides, Food, Adulteration, Safety At Home, Safe Blood, etc.

In 1991, CGSI received the National Award for Consumer Protection in its 25th year for service to Consumers. CGSI hopes to reach out to more and more consumers in the new millennium and to developed newer and more effective methods of serving consumers interest.

3.6.3. Citizen Consumer and Civic Action Group (CAG)

CAG came into existence on 7 October 1985 as a non-profit, non-political, non-religious, voluntary and professional citizens group based in Chennai, India. S. Govind Swaminadhan, legal practitioner and former Advocate General of the State of Tamil Nadu, was the founding trustee of CAG. The initial trustees included S. Guhan (former Finance Secretary,

Government of Tamil Nadu), S.L. Rao (former Chairman, Central Electricity Regulatory Commissioner), Shyamala Nataraj (development journalist with the South India Aids Action Program) and Sriram Panchu (Senior Advocate).

The Group was originally christened Consumer Action Group. After nearly a decade of our existence, we decided to change it to CAG (Citizen, consumer and civic Action Group), keeping in mind the larger role that groups such as ours have to play. Specifically, issues affecting the common citizen such as extreme pollution, lack of access to information, poor quality health care and civic amenities have emerged as priorities in the work undertaken by CAG.

Over the last five years, our main activities have ranged from campaigning for greater access to information, monitoring the functioning of public utilities and advocating for greater transparency and accountability in governmental and private sector functioning to decentralized and localized urban planning, and the protection of open spaces and our natural environment. A Board of Trustees consisting of persons from different walks of life, but with a common objective of improving the quality of life for citizens oversee the Groups' activities.

CAG's activities are carried out by a team of young professionals with different academic and work backgrounds. In the implementation of our programmes we draw upon the resources of a wide range of experts skilled professionals, government officials academia, journalists and fellow civil society and NGO activists. This informal consultation with the 'Friends of CAG' results in an inclusive, comprehensive and informed kaleidoscope of ideas that we analyze and apply appropriately.

Every activity of ours is characterized by the identification of the one critical intervention, which will directly impact the citizen-consumer in a significant way. We arrive at this core conclusion by the following steps:

Collect Data – Through a variety of sources like original research, government and other publications, expert reports etc. we build our case.

Diagnose the problem – Very often what is observed from data collection are just symptoms of a deeper problem, we identify the core issue from the data collected. Subsequently we carry out any or all of the following steps depending on the need of the intervention.

Halt the problem – Through a variety of tools including advocacy, signature campaigns, formal complaints, public interest litigation and igniting public participation.

Evolve a Solution – In order to bring about an equitable solution, which would address the core issue, we collaborate with academia/ academicians, civil society activists and government agencies.

Help present the solution – Through our network of contacts we help present the solution in the appropriate fora.

Disseminate Information: We carry out capacity-building exercises for the citizenry through outreach programmes, publications and other communication tools, which would make them aware of the issue and its solution.

Implement /Monitor the Solution: We provide the expertise and resources to ensure solutions are appropriately implemented and monitored (www.cag.org.in).

3.6.4. Association for Consumers Action on Safety and Health (ACASH)

ACASH is an independent, non-profit, voluntary organization addressing health- related consumer issues and advocating for the rights of the consumers and the general public. ACASH was founded by a group of doctors, lawyers and other concerned individuals in 1986. ACASH serves as an information center to educate, guide and disseminate information in the field of health and safety issues.

ACASH is a member of Consumers International, Globalink, International Network of Women Against Tobacco (INWAT), International Baby Food Action Network (IBFAN), International Lactation Consultant Association (ILCA), World Alliance for Breastfeeding Action (WABA), Health Action International (HAI), Breastfeeding Promotion Network of India (BPNI), All India Drug Action Network (AIDAN), Bureau of Indian Standards (BIS) and Voluntary Health Association of India (VHAI).

ACASH has representation on various government committees like the Central Pollution Control Board (CPCB) (Ecomark technical subcommittee), Bureau of Indian Standards (BIS) Subcommittee on soaps and detergents and Maharashtra Breastfeeding Promotion Initiative(MBPI). ACASH has been appointed by the Government of India, Ministry of Human Resources Development (Department of Women and Child Development) as per gazette notification GSR 540(E) to monitor and report violations of the "Infant Milk Substitutes, Feeding Bottles and Infant Foods (Regulation of Production, Supply and Distribution) Act,1992" (www.acash.org).

The Objectives of the Association are:

a) To inform, educate, and organize consumers so as to enable them to secure, protect and preserve their interests and assert their rights as consumers of goods and services pertaining to health and safety, including but not restricted to pharmaceutical drugs, medical services, health care, nutrition including infant and child nutrition, tobacco and other harmful substances, potable water and cosmetics, toiletries and the like;

b) To disseminate information aimed at improving the status of health and nutrition of all human beings, and at protecting all classes of people from unsafe products and services, health and safety violations, unsafe testing of drugs, cosmetics and toiletries, unscrupulous marketing practices of products used for health, nutrition, cosmetics, toiletries, human consumption, and the like;

c) To protect and promote the interests of the consumers of goods and services referred to in Clause (a) by all lawful means;

d) To collaborate with, and to work in co-operation with other organizations engaged in consumer activism, education, research and mobilization in the fields of health, safety and nutrition;

e) To provide a forum for redressal of consumer grievances related to safety and health issues;

f) To provide for, undertake, aid and promote the study, research, testing, investigation and evaluation of consumer products and services in the fields of health care, nutrition, safety, cosmetics, toiletries, tobacco and other products of human consumption;

g) To promote, aid and popularize the use of cost-effective, economical and affordable solutions for health care, nutritional and safety issues, and to mobilize public opinion against uneconomical, wasteful, irrational, or otherwise damaging solutions or nostrums or goods and services referred to in Clause (a) above;

h) To do all such other lawful things which are closely akin to and identical with or conducive to the attainment of any or all the above objects of the Association which the Trustees may, in consultation with the Founder Members, believe to be necessary for the fulfillment of the Association's aims and goals;

i) To take all lawful steps necessary for the achievement of the above objects including but not limited to printing, publication and dissemination of information, lobbying with Government agencies, international organizations, private bodies and other persons, initiating, filing or appearing in support of Court proceedings, holding meetings, seminars, demonstrations, organizing boycotts, and adopting other peaceful and constitutional means of raising public consciousness and mobilizing public opinion;

j) To protect the rights of all the consumers including those who are deprived and disfranchised (www.acash.org).

3.6.5. Consumer Education and Research Centre

Consumer Education and Research Centre is the leading consumer rights organization in India. CERC is a nonprofit, non-government body, dedicated to the protection and promotion of consumer interests through active use of research, media, law, and advocacy and information dissemination. CERC does not belong to any political party, nor does it subscribe to any political ideology. CERC is recognized as a research institute by the Government of India and as a consumer organization by the Government of Gujarat. The

United Nations has recognized CERC as one of the approved non-government organizations.

Since April 2013 the INSIGHT has merged with the consumer magazine, Right Choice, published in India by BGG Information Pvt. Ltd., Mumbai, and set up by the Which?, the UK's largest consumer magazine. Both the Which? and Right Choice are magazines with the same ethos as the INSIGHT and accept no advertising or any benefits from manufacturers or retailers; their sole income is derived from subscriptions to their magazines.

The merger has benefited the former INSIGHT subscribers. The Right Choice is an 84 - page monthly magazine; the INSIGHT was a 52 - page bi-monthly. The Right Choice, with its larger coverage of comparative product tests, provides many more product test assessments and hence offers consumers a lot more advice on what to buy. The INSIGHT's consumer protection advice, counselling and news are now available within the Right Choice, with exclusive CERS content in each issue, covering consumer protection, advocacy and consumer news. Besides, access to the CERC's legal advice service and consumer redress advice will continue as previously.

3.6.6. Consumers Association of India

The past decade has witnessed a dramatic growth in consumerism in India. With the economic liberation implemented by the Government of India, as well as the emergence of India on the global trade stage, followed by a change in not only disposable incomes but also the attitude of the Indian consumer, the floodgates have opened for a deluge of products and services in every possible sector. As a consumer, it is an overwhelming situation to be in. To make the right choices, you must be adequately armed with enough information to handle this deluge.

The average consumer in India has access to absolutely no information on the safety of the products he uses. Shockingly, this is particularly true of household electrical appliances, health products, food products, cosmetics and toiletries. Hence he is totally reliant on the manufacturer's claims. He has no guidelines to decide whether the product matches his needs. Manufacturers and distributors do not necessarily disseminate enough information to the user to enable him to make an informed choice. As a result, the user may find the product unsatisfactory or he may pay for unnecessary features.

The products may not be safe to use even if they are certified and approved.. This may be because the standards themselves may be defective or because the manufacturers compromise on standards during manufacture. With two decades of experience in the consumer movement, the founders of CAI felt keenly the need to build an effective and meaningful lobby to represent the consumer. This led to the registration of the Consumers Association of India (CAI) as a voluntary charitable trust on 15th March

2001, World Consumer Rights Day.

The objectives of the Consumers Association of India are:

- To spread awareness amongst citizen consumers
- Educate consumers about their responsibilities and rights
- Make CAI a strong all India body to represent consumers and to ensure that their voices are heard

CAI has the necessary expertise and experience in brand marketing, publishing, editing and legal counseling. CAI achieved a membership base of 6000 within its first two years of operation, reflecting the timeliness and appropriateness of its mission. Over the past six years, CAI has filed several petitions before the District Consumer Disputes Redressal Forum and State Consumer Disputes Redressal Commission. Over the same period, CAI has handled more than 7500 complaints (based on an average of enquiries and complaints received per day); of these 95% have been settled by arbitration. Two percent decided to take legal action after receiving advice from CAI and were represented by lawyers in the Consumer Forum. By educating you, the consumer, about the various products and services available to help you make the right choice for YOU Consumer's Digest, the CAI's bi-monthly publication, offers a wealth of useful information on the safety and other standards that products in different sectors must comply with and how products must be used CAI takes up complaints received from consumers about the deficiencies in products and services with the concerned organizations for redress of their grievances CAI conducts seminars that provide opportunities for consumers to air their grievances and an opportunity for government and regulatory agencies to become aware of the consumer's problems (www.caiindia.org).

3.6.7. Mumbai Grahak Panchayat

Mumbai Grahak Panchayat (MGP), or Bombay Consumer Forum, started as an agitation against the increase of consumer prices near festival season for fair and free distribution of consumer goods. The distribution system that flourished was registered under the Indian Societies Registration Act 1960 and Indian Public Trust Act 1950 in the name of MGP. MGP promotes consumerism by bringing the consumer to the forefront of the logistics and supply chain of consumer goods as decision makers, executors and monitors. MGP's primary objectives include organizing the consumers for common causes, educating them and protecting consumer interest through legal and other means (www.mumbaigrahak).

3.6.8. Adhikaar - The Rights Path

Adhikaar – the rights path is an NGO registered with the Govt. of Haryana in 2006-07 and is actively working in the NCR (National Capital Region) for Civil, Consumer and Human Rights for all sections of society. It is supported by an active team of volunteers comprising of eminent people from various walks of life. We have our dedicated team of lawyers, scholars, retired judges, retired senior officers from civil and military working on purely voluntary basis with an aim to raise awareness and also to take up cases with appropriate authorities when brought to our notice. We also offer following services to public at large:-

- Free consultations
- Advice on above matters
- Organise campaigns, seminars and lectures to spread awareness about citizen rights!

The mission of Adhikaar is to empower people to realize their rights, to assist in capacity building for upholding such rights and to act as a dependable source of intellectual capital to the people for doing so. Adhikaar - the rights path is an attempt to create awareness provide help and take up issues on various rights of the citizens guaranteed by the law. With the primary aim of addressing the area of NCR, Adhikaar has been in the field for more than three years now and has led many campaigns on various issues (www.adhikaar.in).

3.6.9. Bharat Jyoti

Bharat Jyoti was established in 1986 with a vision and a mission to create awareness of consumers' Rights and duties among the masses. It was a first N.G.O. to established a Consumer Protection Cell in UP in 1989. Bharat Jyoti has come to the succor of a large number of aggrieved consumers by guiding and consulting them in the District Consumer Forum.

Aims and Objects

1. To uphold protect and develop and the cultural heritage of India.
2. To promote creativity of ideas and bring together scientists, technologies, sociologists economists and intellectuals on a single platform for the development of a modern prosperous, democratic India.
3. To create conditions for greater vocational awareness, employment and self-employment among youth.
4. To promote and encourage the participation of citizens in social, political, economical main stream with a national and secular outlook.
5. To assist and cooperate with Government as well as voluntary bodies engaged in the Human Development Programmer and schemes of social welfare.
6. To establish education institutions, hospitals, adult literacy centers, vocational guidance centers for the welfare of people.
7. To motivate poors for gainful activities and help them for better living standard for occupying dignified place in the society.

8. To assist in implementation of various rural development programmes of State and Central Government.

Credits and Awards

Having noticeably observed the meritorious services rendered in the field of Consumer Protection, Department of Food and civil Supplies, Government of U.P has awarded SECOND PRIZE in 1996. Not satisfied with the services rendered to the consumers, it ventured into more areas of involvement and attracted more people into its services, The Department of Food and civil Supplies awarded FIRST Prize. Besides the state government, the government of India too recognized its selfless assistance given to various categories of people, it was compelled to award THIRD Prize in 1997. A helpline came into existence to receive, register and counsel to all queries/references from consumers specially those under the preview of Consumer protection Act 1986. It gives online interim reply to the consumers and allot to them registration number for further reference. The helpline sends forth the queries to the concerned authorities/departments for providing requested reply/information. Bharat Jyoti got deeply involved in motivational educational programmes, upliftment of poor and downtrodden, particularly women and children, distribution of clothes to the needy, medicines, food, etc. Contributions by generous and humanitarian personalities of the organization brought resource for weddings of destitute girls. With a motive of educating the uneducated children of the society, Bharat Jyoti distributed scholarships to the helpless children, physically and mentally challenged siblings which have motivated them to pursue the studies and not to drop out of school (www.bharatjyoti.org).

3.6.10. Akhil Bharatiya Grahak Panchayat

Akhil Bharatiya Grahak Panchayat was started in 1974. It started not merely as an institution but as a consumer movement to create a society free from exploitation. It was registered under Co-operative Societies Act in 1986. In 1974, there was an acute shortage of goods of daily use and essential commodities. To ease and lessen the suffering of the consumers in getting essential commodities at reasonable prices, a group of young people started this movement. Initially, they formed a group of 25 families staying in proximity. About 500 such groups were formed. As a combined effort, material was purchased in wholesale as well as from manufacturers, which resulted in economy of prices. This material was handed over to the leader of the above-mentioned family group for subsequent distribution to its members. Later on, it was felt that the ordinary consumer in his individual capacity could not get justice in his day-to-day life. Hence, the organization now known as Grahak Panchayat was formed.

The main objective of this organization is to educate the people about their rights as consumers. It provides free counseling and legal-aid to people who are not satisfied with the quality of goods or services purchased by them or have suffered exploitation form the seller. The volunteers include retired people from various fields with knowledge and expertise. They teach, those aggrieved about their rights and ways in which they can get redressal. They help parties in reaching a compromise to avoid filing complaint in the consumer court. Every day of the week (except Wednesday) is fixed for a particular issue. For e.g. issues related to banking and financial institutions are handled every Thursday. Likewise, days are fixed for problems related with agriculture, builders, PMC, MSEB etc. The Grahak Panchayat also holds seminars to generate awareness about consumer rights.

Within a span of 30 years, 'Grahak Panchayat' has opened branches all over the country including Andaman. At present, they are running counseling centers where free advice is given to consumers (www.citizencentre.virtualpune.com).

3.6.11. Akhil Bhartiya Upbhokta Uthan Sangathan (AICPO)

Akhil Bhartiya Upbhokta Uthan Sangathan (AICPO), name gives the objective of organization. Organization wants to be famous by giving the people's their rights. Organization came in existence for making people to know their rights. Organization was made by Mr. H. S. Shukla (President) in 1990 as Madhya Pradesh Cooking Gas Upbhokta Sangathan, but in1996 to make movement of sangathan countrywide, name of sangathan was changed and the new name was Akhil Bartiya Upbhokta Uthan Sangathan (All India Consumer Protection Organization).

In Present sangathan is working in 7 states in India. These states are: Madhya Pradesh, Chattishgarh, Delhi, Maharastra, Punjab, Uttar Pradesh, and Tamil Nandu. Akhil Bhartiya Upbhokta Uthan Sangathan have many level working committee. Which are working for making organization strong enough to fight against the exploitation of consumer. Such as:

1. National Committee
2. State Committee
3. Divisonal Committee
4. District Committee

The aim of organization is stop black marketing and worthless business in every area of country.

Aim of Organization

- Unitize own members and develop feeling of mutuall brotherhood and help on them.
- Seeing, protecting and expanding the collective benefit of own members.
- Doing every thing to stop black marketing in each area.

- Advertise and extent the consumer education ,to make strong consumer revolution
- Play an effective role to execution of consumer protection act.
- Doing anything for stop monopoly, obstructing and improper business.
- Solving general problems of own member.
- Working under the rule of organization, to support the other organization of same motive for their benefit.
- For completion of own aim, to use valid behavior define under the citizen rights.
- To give importance benefit of country in each of our activity.
- Increase the collective benefit of consumer working under the consumer protection act.
- To run health awareness program, for this purpose advertise and extent the schemes of government with help of organization.
- In backward areas, by the beneficial schemes of government educating the peoples of sc\st, and work for their social and moral progress.
- To work against the makers and sellers of duplicate and inferior goods (www.aicpo.org.in).

3.6.12. The Consumer Rights Education and Awareness Trust (CREAT)

The Consumer Rights Education and Awareness Trust (CREAT) is a not for profit consumer advocacy group. CREAT was established in December 1993 and was registered as a public charitable trust in July 1994 at Bangalore. CREAT is administered by a Board of Trustees assisted by a Committee consisting of eminent persons (www.creatindia.org).

Areas of work

1. **Consumer Protection:** Consumer protection has been one of the core areas of work involved in by CREAT. Since its inception in 1993 CREAT has taken special interest in protecting the interests of the consumers. This is done through handling consumer complaints, representing consumers in various policy making bodies, filing complaints in consumer forum, mediation etc. CREAT has filed some complaints in the forum and has been successful.

2. **Governance and Right to Information:** As part of its program on empowering civil society in Governance, CREAT has been focusing on issues relating to citizens' Right to Information, Citizens' Charters and strengthening grievance redressal machinery in government departments. CREAT has launched a campaign on

Right to Information in Karnataka from June 2004. This is being supported by Commonwealth Human Rights Initiative, New Delhi.

3. **Consumer Participation in Power Sector Regulation and Reform:** The process of economic reforms and liberalization has ushered in an era of regulation. Public services like telecom, banking and power sector have come under the umbrella of independent regulation. However the benefits of regulation will accrue to the public only through an active involvement and participation of civil society organizations. Realising the importance of consumer involvement in power sector reforms, CREAT launched a project entitled 'Public Understanding and Participation'(PUP) in October 2003 with the assistance of USAID. The project was successfully completed in June 2004. At present CREAT is continuing the project independently. The activities include training programs, seminars, workshops, publications and participating in public hearings organized by the electricity regulatory Commission.

4. **Consumer Education:** Since its establishment in 1993 CREAT has been actively involved in consumer educating consumers both formal and informal. CREAT has established consumer clubs in schools and colleges. Activities include debates, essay and quiz competitions, exhibitions, drawing competitions etc. A Consumer Educators Network (CENET) has been constituted to assist schools, colleges and educational institutions to set up consumer clubs. In addition a Students Consumer Action Network (SCAN) has been established to coordinate the activities of various consumer clubs.

5. **Consumer Information Centre:** CREAT has established a Consumer Information Centre with financial assistance from Ministry of Food, Consumer Affairs and Public Distribution, Government of India. The CIC acts as a Consumer guidance and counseling hub. The CIC consists of a library with over 3000 books, 25 magazines, 7000 paper clippings and a large number of workshop reports, papers, presentations, monographs etc. CIC is a repository of judgments delivered by consumer forum/commission. Judgments from 1987 is available for reference and study.

6. **Clipping Service:** CREAT has a clipping service. Documents, judgments, reports, paper clippings etc. are made available to consumers, students, researchers, media persons on payment of actual cost of Xerox, postage/courier.

7. **Trade, economics and Globalization:** CREAT believes that globalization and its effect is a major concern for consumer safety and security. Trade and globalization is another area of focus of CREAT. At present CREAT is involved in a campaign called

GRANITE on trade and globalization supported by Consumer Unity and Trust Society (CUTS) Jaipur. The project involves conducting meetings (www.creatindia.org).

3.6.13. EMPOWER

EMPOWER was established in the year 1991 by Mr. A. Sankar with a voluntary participation of a team of dedicated Development activists, Health Care Professionals , Academicians and Researchers who are committed to Social Justice.

EMPOWER is registered under Tamil Nadu Societies Act in the year 1991 and engaged in developmental work for the past 15 years in Southern Districts of Tamil Nadu.

Legal Status

- EMPOWER is registered under Tamilnadu Societies Act in the year 1991.
- Donations to EMPOWER are exempted under section 80G of the Income Tax Act.
- EMPOWER is registered with the Ministry of Home Affairs to receive Foreign Contributions under the Foreign Contributions Regulation Act (FCRA).
- Mr.A.Sankar is the Chief Functionary and Executive Director.

Vision

Empowered gender just communities leading sustainable and quality livelihood.

Objectives

- To empower the marginalized communities such as Women, Children and Youth of socially and economically disadvantaged communities.
- To promote women's rights and campaign against violence against women
- To promote child rights and campaign against exploitation of children
- To impart consumer awareness education, offer consumer guidance, campaign against unfair trade practices, to work on civic and environmental issues affecting the people through research and social action
- To prevent the spread of STD/HIV/AIDS among high-risk behaviour groups and care to those affected by HIV/AIDS.
- To enhance reproductive rights and to carry out research in the area of reproductive health
- To prevent alcoholism and drug abuse and to offer de-addiction and Rehabilitation.

- To promote art and craft to enhance the quality of life of the community.
- To promote Science and Technology to improve the quality of life
- To impart skill development training for promoting micro enterprise among women and youth.
- To create awareness to protect, preserve and promote environmental equilibrium for harmonious living with nature (www.empowerindia.org).

3.6.14. Grahak Raja Jagaho

Grahak Raja JagaHo is an organization working in the field of consumer awareness. Grahak Raja JagaHo is registered as a charity organization with Government of India under Societies Registration Act 1860. The registration number of Grahak Raja JagaHo is Maharashtra/2210/2006/Pune. Grahak Raja JagaHo is providing free guidance for all queries related consumer problems. Grahak Raja JagaHo is providing free legal help to fight the cases in consumer courts. Grahak Raja JagaHo is also providing the guidance for effective usage of Right to Information Act 2005. Grahak Raja JagaHo is committed to spread consumer awareness among general public. Grahak Raja JagaHo conducts seminars to spread consumer awareness & Right to Information Act 2005. Grahak Raja JagaHo is founded by Mr. Manoj Ovhal, a consumer activist from Pune, Maharashtra (www.grahakraja.org)

The mission of Grahak Raja JagaHo is to build India as a Greater Nation. To achieve this mission Grahak Raja JagaHo has started following initiatives.

- Consumer Awareness.
- Grahak Raja Jaga Ho.
- Wake up customer, You are the King.
- Awareness about the rights of common citizens.
- Matadar Raja Jaga Ho
- Don't waste your vote, Its your Right as well as Duty.
- Your single vote has the power to change Indian Politics.
- Awareness about Right to Information Act 2005.
- Don't accept bribe, Don't give bribe
- Build a Great India.

3.6.15. MAHADHIKAR

'MAHADHIKAR' is citizens' initiative dedicated to promotion and effective but responsible use of the Right to Information Act (RTI) & Consumer Protection. RTI, a fundamental right of every citizen of India, has not been widely used by citizens in the past due to lack of awareness. More recently however, now awareness is being created all over the country by activists/NGOs. As a result, the use of RTI is rapidly increasing in all parts of India. Some of us involved in RTI, felt the need for a citizen-oriented platform that would interact with the government in getting hurdles and problems removed, propagate RTI amongst citizens desirous of its responsible use and pursue at least some of the matters dug-up thru use of RTI to their logical conclusion, by holding 'Jansunwai' (Peoples' Court), filing Public Interest Litigations (PIL), etc. Hence, *'MAHADHIKAR'* was established in 2003 as an informal group, without any rigid structure. It is a movement - independent of any existing group and in fact, inviting in its fold, activists from all groups.

'MAHADHIKAR'is active on RTI & Consumer Protection (Consumer Protection Act-1986). MAHADHIKAR'is envisaged to be a group of responsible citizens, firmly believing in the rule of law and mature and constructive interaction with the administration; yet it would like to be generally a friend of the administration and not an adjunct. *'MAHADHIKAR'* has conducted several Workshops on RTI for urban & rural citizens/adivasis and Trainers' Training Workshops for Activists/Government Staff, in Marathi, Hindi, Gujarati & English.

In order to promote the use of the RTI Act amongst common citizens, *'MAHADHIKAR'*, in association with Tarun Mitra Mandal (TMM), launched 'Jan Adhikar Abhiyan' and have extensively trained over 75 Activists (Engineers, Advocates, Solicitors, Architect, Doctors, CAs, MBAs plus businessmen, self-employed & students), so as to extend help to citizens in the effective and responsible use of RTI. Already 12 RTI Clinics are functioning, one each in Dombivali & Thane & 10 in Gr. Mumbai, who provide one-to-one help to citizens, atleast once a week. (list enclosed on RTI Clinic page).

'MAHADHIKAR' had organized First State Level Moot Court Competition on Right to Information Act - 2005 (Central), in association with Jitendra Chauhan College of Law, JVPD, Mumbai 400056, on 10 & 11 September 2005, for students of all the law colleges in Maharashtra (65). For the benefit of interested citizens, NGOs, social organizations, educational institutions, government & public sector staff, 'MAHADHIKAR' will be happy to facilitate training programs and workshops.

MAHADHIKAR has launched the 'Road Cell' in association with Satark Nagarik Sanghatan (SNS). Citizens can send their complaints on bad Roads/Footpaths and these will be forwarded to the concerned authorities and then followed-up for action. This entire process would be participatory and would involve citizen action in ensuring better roads and pavements.

3.6.16. The Society for Consumers and Investors Protection (SCIP)

The Society for Consumers and Investors Protection (SCIP) was formed by a group of eminent professionals comprising of people drawn from areas as diverse as academics, law, administration, media, industry and others. The Society is registered with the Registrar of Societies, New Delhi since June 1989 and has been duly recognized by Ministry of Corporate Affairs (MCA) Securities and Exchange Board of India (SEBI).

Government of India and the Society regularly receives complaints from a large number of aggrieved investors & consumers. It helps to resolve these grievances by taking them up at various legal platforms including district state and national consumer redressal forums, district courts and High Courts and other legal avenues available in the country. The society's success rate in its legal battles has been almost hundred percent.

The society has done commendable research work with the most significant being constituting an Investor Sentiment Index a first of its kind for India. The project was sponsored by Ministry of Corporate Affairs. The society has also made investor education programs for various business channels including Doordarshan. It won the case against DLF to get justice to about 1400 shareholders who overnight turned millionaires and also won the case at Delhi High Court for registrants of DDAs Rohini Scheme. It regularly organizes seminars in NCR of Delhi to promote investor education & awareness.

The aims and objectives of the Society are to:

- Educate Consumers and Investors about their rights and create awareness enabling them to protect themselves from being exploited.
- Provide a forum for redressal of Consumers' and Investors' grievances and to discuss the contemporary issues facing them so that concrete steps can be suggested for providing better and improved services to them.
- Undertake effective contact programme and liaison with agencies, governmental and non-governmental, involved in the task of Consumers' and Investors' protection.
- Guide Consumers' about malpractices such as misinformation, cheating and overcharging, non-adherence to various legislation etc leading to their exploitation.
- Suggest the Government and various other agencies about the steps, including the enactment of various legislation that could be taken to protect the interest of consumers and investors. Also assist the Government/ non- government agencies Consumers/Investors by bringing in light the various latent malpractice's followed by different agencies against the interests of Consumers/Investors.
- Guide and counsel the consumers and investors about products and services, and other such innovations in the broader areas of marketing to maximize the utility and return to them.

- Guide, counsel and create awareness amongst agencies serving Consumers' and investors of the investment and marketing ethics for creating an atmosphere of trust and confidence amongst consumers and investors.
- Carry survey and research in the areas of consumer behavior and marketing of different products/services in India and abroad to facilitate the diffusion of useful products and services effectively, introduced by various Government/non-Government agencies providing an effective marketing system aimed at effective, and efficient utilization of scarce national resources and maximizing the Consumers Welfare as also to improve their living standards.
- To offer recognition and awards to agencies, corporations and individuals involved in the task of Consumers/Investors protection and known to be working effectively for providing better services to consumers/investors.
- To cooperated with other similar organizations within the country and abroad.

The Society for the attainment of the above objectives does the following:

- Organize conferences, seminars, symposia, workshops, lectures.
- Summer Schools, short-term courses, debates, discussions, competitions, contests and other such programmes.
- Publish and facilitate the publication of journals and magazines, research studies, books, bulletins, newsletters, pamphlets and other survey and research materials.
- Under-take and promote research and impart education about relevant legislation enacted to protect consumers and other related fields.
- Provide a forum for interaction to various agencies concerned or involved in the broader areas of consumers and investors protection, corporate and financial market studies as also the various aspects of marketing discipline etc.
- Conduct various courses in the areas of marketing and finance as are related to the consumer and investor protection after getting due approval from the concerned authorities.
- Represent itself at conferences etc. both, national and international.
- Undertake projects sponsored by Government and various other agencies within the broad framework of the objectives of the Society.
- Affiliate regional and other Associations/Societies with similar objectives and establish its own local chapters.

Sum Up

The consumer movement stands for the organized efforts of consumers seeking to redress, restitute and remedy for the dissatisfaction of the standard of living. It is a social movement seeking to challenge the rights and powers of the buyers in relation to those of sellers. Consumerism, like democracy, is a movement by the people and for the people where the role of common man is uncommon. Consumerism has weak links with the Western world, but is in fact an international phenomenon. People purchasing goods and consuming materials in excess of their basic needs is as old as the first civilizations (e.g. Ancient Egypt, Babylon and Ancient Rome). A great turn in consumerism arrived just before the Industrial Revolution. The industrial revolution and the development in the international trade and commerce has led to the vast expansion of the business and trade. Due to the international character of trade and industry having well organized and highly professionalized producers and traders on one side and illiterate and unorganized consumers with little time on the other, the exploitation of the consumers is common. Various international organizations like ILO, WHO, UNESCO, UNCTAD and UNICEF, have contributed a lot for the protection of the rights of the consumers in the international sphere. In addition, the world Industrial Property Organization, International Organization of Consumer Union and the Inter-Scandinavian Committee on Consumer Matters are also busy in protecting the interests of the consumers at the international level. Many factors and elements are responsible for the development of consumerism. These include technological development, uniformity and speed in manufacturing, development and expansion of transportation, emergence of new society, etc. in India, also, many organization and non-government organizations are working to improve awareness regarding consumer rights and advice on the legal recourse a user can take when his consumer rights are violated.

References

Evers, Myrlie (1983), "Consumerism in the Eighties," *Public Relations Journal* (August): p. 25.

Barker, A. Tansu (1987), "Consumerism in New Zealand," *International Marketing Review*, 4 (Autumn): pp. 63-74.

Ryans, John K. Jr., Saeed Samiee, and James Wills (1985), "Consumerist Movement and Advertising Regulation in the International Environment: Today and the Future," *European Journal of Marketing*, 19(1): pp. 5-11.

Scherhorn, Gerald (1988), "Self-fulfillment, Consumer Policy, and Consumer Research," in *The Frontier of Research in the Consumer Interest*, E. Scott

Maynes (ed.), Columbia, MO: American Council on Consumer Interests: pp. 589-594.

Julius O. Onah(1979), "Consumerism in Nigerin", in Marketing in Nigeria: Experience in a Developing Economy, Jilius O. Onah (ed.), London: Cassell Ltd, p-139.

Scherhorn, Gerald (1988), *op.cit.*, p. 596.

McGregor, Sue & Susan MacDonald (1997): Canadian university consumer studies courses: a content analysis. *Journal of Consumer Studies & Home Economics*;21: pp. 291-309.

Maynes, E. Scott (1990), "*The Future of Consumerism,*" *At Home with Consumers*, 11(April): pp. 6-7.

Susan MacDonald (1998): Critical thinking in consumer studies: part 2 of a content analysis of Canadian university consumer studies courses. *Journal of Consumer Studies & Home Economics*; 22,1: pp. 3-14.

McIlhenny, James H. (1990), "The New Consumerism: How Will Business Respond," *At Home with Consumers*, 11(April): 5, pp. 9-10.

N. I. Silber, (1983), Test and protest; The influence of Consumers Union, Holmes & Meier Publishers, London, p. 172.

Nicouland, Brigitte M. M. (1987), "Consumerism and Marketing Management's Responsibility," *European Journal of Marketing*, 21(3): pp. 7-16.

Harland, David (1987), "The United Nations Guidelines for Consumer Protection," *Journal of Consumer Policy*, 10(September): pp. 245-246.

Harland, David (1988), "The United Nations Guidelines for Consumer Protection, Reply to the Comment by Weidenbaum," in JCP (1987), 10: 4, *Journal of Consumer Policy*, 11(March): pp. 111-115.

Harland, David (1987), *op.cit.*, pp. 249-250.

Hendon, Donald W. (1975), "Toward a Theory of Consumerism," *Business Horizons*, 18(August): pp. 16-24.

Herrmann, Robert O. (1970), "Consumerism: Its Goals, Organizations and Future," *Journal of Marketing*, 34(October): pp. 45-46.

Herrmann, Robert O. (1980), "Consumer Protection: Yesterday, Today and Tomorrow," *Current History*, 78(May): pp. 126-127.

I. Cooper, (1986), *Consumer Education*, Oxford University Press, Oxford, p. 39.

IOCU Japan (1980), *Law and the Consumer; Background readings*, IOCU, Hong Kong, p. 97.

Harland, David (1988), *op.cit.*, pp. 121-122.

John R. Nelson (1979), "Alexander Hamilton and American Manufacturing: A Reexamination". The Journal of American History ,Vol. 65, p. 975.

Harland, David (1988), *op.cit.*, p. 135.

Douglas, Susan P. and C. Samuel Craig (1983), *International Marketing Research*, Englewood Cliffs, NJ: Prentice Hall, Inc.

Bloom, Paul N. and Stephen A. Greyser (1981), "The Maturing of Consumerism," *Harvard Business Review*, 59 (November-December): pp. 130-139.

Johnston, William L. (1985), "*Consumerism Alive and Well*," News Notes, Center for Consumer Services, 8(1, April): 3.

Blake, David H. and Robert S. Walters (1987), *The Politics of Global Economic Relations*, Third Edition, Englewood Cliffs, NJ: Prentice Hall, Inc.

Douglas, Susan P. and C. Samuel Craig (1983), International Marketing Research, Englewood Cliffs, NJ: Prentice Hall, Inc.

Consumer Education in The Nordic Countries. Proposal of objectives and content of consumer education in the compulsory school and at upper secondary school level in the Nordic Countries. Revised (draft) version. The Nordic Council of Ministers, September 1999.

Cattell, Raymond B. (1978), *The Scientific Use of Factor Analysis in the Behavioral and Life Sciences*, New York: Plenum Press.

Kaynak, Erdener and Solveig Wikstrom (1985), "Methodological Framework for a Cross-National Comparison of Consumerism Issues in Multiple Environments," *European Journal of Marketing*, 19(1): pp. 31-46.

McGregor, Sue & Susan MacDonald (1997): Canadian university consumer studies courses: a content analysis. *Journal of Consumer Studies & Home Economics*; 21: pp. 291-306.

Julius O. Onah(1979), "Consumerism in Nigerin", in Marketing in Nigeria: Experience in a Developing Economy, Jilius O. Onah (ed.), London: Cassell Ltd, pp 126-127.

Lee, Martyn J., (2000), ed. *The consumer society reader.* Malden, Mass.: Blackwell Publishers, p. 156.

Thorelli, Hans B. (1990), "Performance Audits: The MNC through the Glasses of the LDC," in Hans B. Thorelli and S. Tamer Cavusgil (eds.), *International Marketing Strategy*, Third Edition, Oxford, England: Pergamon Press, pp. 605-617.

Kerton, Robert R. (1988), "Time for a 'Wingspread': The Contributions of Professors Olander and Thorelli," in *Frontier of Research in the Consumer Interest*, E. Scott Maynes (ed.), Columbia, MO: American Council on Consumer Interests: pp. 585-588.

M. K. Ramesh, Consumer Interest in Legal Profession-Problems and Perspectives, Cochin University Law Review, Vol. No. 13 December 4, 1989, p. 405-425.

Thorelli, Hans B. (1990), "Performance Audits: The MNC Through the Glasses of the LDC," in Hans B. Thorelli and S. Tamer Cavusgil (eds.), International Marketing Strategy, Third Edition, Oxford, England: Pergamon Press, 605-617.

T. Wells and E. G. Sim, Till they have Faces; Women as Consumers, International Organization of Consumers Union, Penang, 1987, p. 142.

N. I. Silber, Test and protest; The influence of Consumers Union, Holmes & Meier Publishers, London, 1983, p. 172.

R. Lowe and G. Woodroffe, Consumer – Law and Practice, Sweet & Maxwell ltd, London, 1980, p. 368.

McIlhenny, James H. (1990), "The New Consumerism: How Will Business Respond," At Home with Consumers, 11(April): 5, pp. 9-10.

Onah, Julius O. (1979), "Consumerism in Nigeria," in Marketing in Nigeria: Experience in a Developing Economy, Julius O. Onah (ed.), London: Cassell Ltd.: pp.126-134.

N. I. Silber, Test and protest; The influence of Consumers Union, Holmes & Meier Publishers, London, 1983, p. 179.

McIlhenny, James H. (1990), " The New Consumerism: How Will Business Respond," At Home with Consumers, 11(April): 5, pp. 9-10.

McGregor, Sue & Susan MacDonald (1997): Canadian university consumer studies courses: a content analysis. In:J Consumer Studies & Home Economics;21 : pp. 291-306

M. K. Ramesh, Consumer Interest in Legal Profession-Problems and Perspectives, Cochin University Law Review, Vol. No. 13 December 4, 1989, pp. 405-425.

Lewis, David: The soul of the new consumer / David Lewis, Darren Bridger. - Nicholas Brealey Publishing, 2000 (ordered by JB).

Kerton, Robert R. (1988), "Time for a 'Wingspread': The Contributions of Professors Olander and Thorelli," in The Frontier of Research in the Consumer Interest, E. Scott Maynes (ed.), Columbia, MO: American Council on Consumer Interests: pp. 585-588.

Johnston, William L. (1985), "Consumerism Alive and Well," News Notes, Center for Consumer Services, 8(1, April): p. 3.

Harland, David (1988), "The United Nations Guidelines for Consumer Protection, Reply to the Comment by Weidenbaum," in JCP (1987), 10: 4, Journal of Consumer Policy, 11(March): 111-115.

Hamilton, Jennifer, McIlveen, Heather & Christopher Strugnell (2000): Educating young consumer – a food choice model. In:J Consumer Studies & Home Economics;24,2: pp. 113-123.

Bruun Jensen, B. & Schnack, K., eds.: *Action and Action Competence as Key Concepts in Critical Pedagogy*. Studies in Educational Theory and Curriculum. Vol. 12. Royal Danish School of Educational Studies, 1985.

Bloom, Paul N. and Stephen A. Greyser (1981), "The Maturing of Consumerism," Harvard Business Review, 59(November-December): pp. 130-139.

Blake, David H. and Robert S. Walters (1987), The Politics of Global Economic Relations, Third Edition, Englewood Cliffs, NJ: Prentice Hall, Inc.

Barker, A. Tansu (1987), "Consumerism in New Zealand," International Marketing Review, 4(Autumn): pp. 63-74.

N. David, Reference Guide to Consumers, R. R. Broker Co, New York, 1975, p.327.

Nordic-Baltic conference on Consumer Education in school. September 11-13, 2000, Riga, Latvia. Nordic Council of Ministers, Consumer. TemaNord 2001: pp. 531.

Post, James E. (1986), "International Consumerism in the Aftermath of the Infant Formula Controversy," in The Future of Consumerism, Paul N. Bloom and Ruth Belk Smith (eds.), Lexington, MA: Lexington Books: pp. 165-178.

Pessemier, Edgar A., Albert C. Bammaor, and Dominique M. Hanssens (1977), "Willingness to Supply Human Body Parts: Some Empirical Results," Journal of Consumer Research, 4(December): pp. 131-139.

Scherhorn, Gerald (1988), "Self-fulfillment, Consumer Policy, and Consumer Research," in The Frontier of Research in the Consumer Interest, E. Scott Maynes (ed.), Columbia, MO: American Council on Consumer Interests: 589-594.

R. Lowe and G. Woodroffe, Consumer – Law and Practice, Sweet & Maxwell ltd, London, 1980, p. 368.

Stanley, Guy (1987), "The Third World Tackles Consumer Protection," Business and Society Review, 62 (Summer): pp. 31-33.

Thorelli, Hans B. (1981), "Consumer Policy for the Third World," Journal of Consumer Policy, 3: pp. 197-211.

Veblen, Thorstein (1899): The Theory of the Leisure Class: an economic study of institutions, Dover Publications, Mineola, N.Y., 1994, p.236.

A. A. Painter (1978), *Guide to Consumer Protection Law*, Barry Rose (Publishers) Ltd., London, p. 173.

Campbell, Colin: (1990), Character and consumption: an historical action theory approach to the understanding of consumer behaviour. In: *Culture & history*;7: pp. 37-48

Harland, David (1987), "The United Nations Guidelines for Consumer Protection," *Journal of Consumer Policy*, 10(September): pp. 240-243.

Harland, David (1988), "The United Nations Guidelines for Consumer Protection, Reply to the Comment by Weidenbaum," in JCP (1987), 10: 4, *Journal of Consumer Policy*, 11(March): pp. 165-166.

Hendon, Donald W. (1975), "Toward a Theory of Consumerism," *Business Horizons*, 18(August): pp. 16-24.

Kautilya-The Arthashastra (1992), L.N. Rangarajan ed., Penguin books India, p. 385.

A. Rajendra Prasad, (1998), "Historical Evolution of Consumer Protection and Law in India", *Journal of Texas Consumer Law*, p. 133.

Misra, V.S. (2007). Ancient Indian Dynasties, Mumbai: Bharatiya Vidya Bhavan, p.48.

Kane, P. V., (1975), *History of Dharmaśāstra*, Bhandarkar Oriental Research Institute, Pune, Volume I, Part I, p. 566.

Patrick, Olivelle (2004), *Manu's Code of Law: A Critical Edition and Translation of the Manava-Dharmasastra*, Oxford University Press, p. 546.

Muller, F. Max. (2004), *The Laws of Manu: The Sacred Books of The East*, Oxford University Press, p. 705.

Chaturvedi, B. K. (2006), *Kautilya's Arthshastra*, Diamond Pocket Books, New Delhi, p. 23.

Chamola, S.D.Chamola. (2007), *Kautilya Arthshastra and the science of management: relevance for the contemporary society*, Hope India Publications, Gurgaon, p.53.

Kauṭalya, L. N. Rangarajan, (1992), *The Arthashastra*, Penguin Books India, New Delhi, p. 458.

Balbir S. Sihag, (2009) "Kautilya on principles of taxation", *Humanomics*, Vol. 25 Iss: 1, pp.59.

Spengler, Joseph J (1971) Indian Economic Thought, Durham, NC: Duke University Press, p.752.

Gopal, M. H. (1935), *Mauryan Public Finance*. London, England: George Allen & Unwin Ltd. p. 353.

Braibanlti, Rarlpn end Joeeph J. Spengler, (1963) eds. *Administration and Economic Development in India*, Durham, NC: Duke University Press. p.24.

Nagarajan, V., (1992), *Evolution of Social Polity of Ancient India*. Delhi, India: Dattsons.p. 43.

Bill Thomas, (1978), *The Legal Framework of Consumer Protection, in Marketing and the Consumer Movement*, (Jeremy Mitchell ed., p. 49.

Gordon Borrie, (1984), *The Development of Consumer Lawand Policy: Bold Spirits and Timorous Souls* p. 3.

B. M. Mahajan, (1980), *Consumer Behavior in India; An Economic Study*, NaurangRai, New Delhi, 1980, p. 382.

E. Fetterman and M. K. Schiller, (1978), *Let the Buyer Be Aware; consumer Rights and Responsibilities*, Fairchild Publications, New York, 1978, p. 217.

M. J. Gurg, (2003), *Consumer Rights*, Clarion Books, New Delhi, p. 139.

"Consumer Coordination Council", available at http://www.cccindia.co/aboutus.asp accessed on 08-10-2013.

"Citizen Consumer and Civic Action Group (CAG)", available at http://www.cag.org.in/overview accessed on 08-10-2013.

"Association for Consumers Action on Safety and Health", available at http://www.acash.org/index.htm accessed on 09-10-2013.

____ , "Association for Consumers Action on Safety and Health", available at http://www.acash.org/objectives.htm accessed on 09-10-2013.

"Consumer Education and Research Centre", available at accessed on Tuesday, 24 September 2013 12:13.

"Consumers Association of India", available at http://www.caiindia.org/about.aspx accessed on 09-10-2013.

"Mumbai Grahak Panchayat", available at http://www.mumbaigrahak panchayat.org/index.asp?msgid=introduction accessed on 01-10-2013.

"Adhikaar - The Rights Path", available at http://adhikaar.in/ accessed on 18-09-2013.

"Bharat Jyoti, Consumer Protection and Social Welfare Organization", available at http://bharatjyoti.org/aboutus.php accessed on 09-10-2013.

"Akhil Bharatiya Grahak Panchayat", available at http://citizencentre.virtualpune.com/html/grahak_panchayat.shtml accessed on 09-10-2013.

"Akhil Bhartiya Upbhokta Uthan Sangathan (AICPO)", available at http://aicpo.org.in/about.htm accessed on 24-09-2013.

"The Consumer Rights Education and Awareness Trust (CREAT)", available at http://www.creatindia.org/ accessed on 09-10-2013.

"The Consumer Rights Education and Awareness Trust (CREAT)", available at http://www.creatindia.org/areas-of-work.html accessed on 09-10-2013.

"EMPOWER", available at http://www.empowerindia.org/about.html , accessed on 09-10-2013.

"Grahak Raja JagaHo", available at http://www.grahakraja.org/ accessed on 09-10-2013.

"Grahak Raja JagaHo", available at http://www.grahakraja.org/mission.html accessed on 09-10-2013.

CHAPTER – 4
VARIOUS LEGISLATIONS RELATED TO CONSUMER PROTECTION

When the world was younger and communities smaller, consumer resistance was virtually unnecessary to ensure fair trade practices. Unfair trade was almost impossible in the life-style of those items. One could not comfortably cheat someone in the market-place in the morning and break bread with him the same evening. The industrial revolution and a shift in population from rural areas to towns and the anonymity of urban living gave plenty of scope for malpractices. Consumer came to mean more than just eating, drinking and wearing clothes. It extended to cover the whole business of life and living.

Consumer education began with the realization that hardly any goods or service in the world exists that some man cannot make a little worse and sell a little chapter. Consumer resistance, initially, took the form of comparative or selective shopping - taking one's custom elsewhere, or returning the shoddy product for exchange if the shopkeeper could be prevailed upon to agree to it. In America, formal consumer education started in 1930's - a result of the depression. With falling money income the customers looked for ways and means to get the best value for his money. It was in the 60s. However, that consumerism became a vital social movement. It began to encompass the evolving set of activities of government, business, independent organizations and concerned citizens, designed to protect the rights of the consumers in the market place.

In order to control the market, the government has introduced a number of laws giving customers rights about the quality of the goods they buy. It has created criminal offences if sellers mis-describe, charge the wrong price or sell unsafe products. Hence, present chapter is an attempt to examine various legislations for consumer protection at the international level as well at the national level in India.

4.1 Legislation for Consumer Protection at Global Level: A Brief Description

In view of a number of undesirable and unfair trade practices being followed by producer distributors, government have resorted to certain legislations designed to protect the interest of the consumers, almost in every part of the world. In U.K., for instance, the Trade Description Act, 1968 prohibits the use of misleading description of goods or services or misleading representation of price reductions. Similarly, such practices have been checked Sweden through 'The False or Deceptive Marketing Practices of Goods Act, 1971'. Also, in 1972 was passed the 'Food Products Law', which was concerned with the handling and packaging of foodstuffs, both domestic and imported. In a number of countries, the producer – consumer legislations provide for compensation for loss or damage suffered by a consumer because of certain prohibited practices. This is true of the Sherman Act and the Clayton Act of the U.S.A., the Trade practices Act of Australia, the Combines Investigation Act of Canada, Act against Restraint of Competition of Spain, etc.

In some countries statutory bodies are empowered to require the advertiser to substantiate the claims made in the advertisements. For instance, the Federal Trade Commission (FTC) of the United States can seek affirmative disclosures. That is, if information in an advertisement is considered insufficient by the FTC, the Commission may require a company to disclose in advertisements some of the deficiencies or limitations of its product or service so that the consumer can judge the product's negative, as well as positive attributes. The FTC can also require the advertisers to submit, on demand by the Commission, data to back up advertising claims for a product's safety, performance, and quality or price comparability.

The intent of this substantiation is to help consumers make more reasoned choices by having information available to them. Members of many industry groups including automobiles, appliances, so; and detergents, television sets, hearing aids, and all over-the-counter drugs have been order to provide the Commission with documentation in support of their designated advertising claims. Corrective advertising requirements have increasingly been a part of many FTC consent orders. Corrective advertising doctrines are based upon the notion that inaccurate information has already been communicated by advertisers, and that corrective advertising is needed to eliminate the lingering effects of such information.

The Warner-Lambert v. Trade Commission is an interesting illustration. In that case, the FTC had issued an order requiring the Warner-Lambert to cease and desist from advertising its product, 'Listerine' - mouth-wash, as a preventive, cure or palliative, for the common cold. The FTC also directed that in all future advertising, both print and electronic, Warner-Lamb must include the following corrective statement: "contrary to prior advertising, Listerine will not help prevent colds or sore throats or lesson their severity." In addition, the FTC required that the statement be included in all Listerine advertising until the company has spent $10 million on advertising, a sum equivalent to that spent on publicizing Listerine from April 1962 to March, 1972. The Court of Appeals upheld all the Commission's orders except the required use of the phrase "Contrary to prior advertising" (Kapoor, 20063).

4.2 Legislations for Consumer Protection in India

A large number of legislations have been enacted over all these years to safeguard the interest of the consumers. These legislations are designed to control product, supply, distribution, price and quality of a large number of goods and services. Government has also been empowered regulate the terms and conditions of sale, nature of trade and commerce etc.

Important legislations designed to protect consumers' interests have been discussed as below.

4.2.1. Indian Contract Act, 1872

Indian Contract Act 1872 (www.vakilno1.com) is the main source of law regulating contracts in Indian law, as subsequently amended. It determines the circumstances in which promise made by the parties to a contract shall be legally binding on them. All of us enter into a number of contracts everyday knowingly or unknowingly. Each contract creates some right and duties upon the contracting parties. Indian contract deals with the enforcement of these rights and duties upon the parties. The Indian Contract Act 1872 sections 1-75 came into force on 1 September 1872. It applies to the whole of India except the state of Jammu and Kashmir. It is not a complete and exhaustive law on all types of contracts.

Definition

Section 2(h) of the Act defines the term contract as "any agreement enforceable by law". There are two essentials of this act, agreement and enforceability.

Section 2(e) defines agreement as "every promise and every set of promises, forming the consideration for each other."

Again Section 2(b) defines promise in these words: "when the person to whom the proposal is made signifies his assent thereto, the proposal is said to be accepted. Proposal when accepted, becomes a promise."

Essential Elements of a Valid Contract

According to Section 10, "All agreements are contracts, if they are made by the free consent of the parties, competent to contract, for a lawful consideration with a lawful object, and not hereby expressly to be void."

Essential Elements of a Valid Contract are proper offer and proper acceptance, Lawful consideration, Competent to contract or capacity, Free Consent, Lawful Object and Agreement, Agreement not declared void or illegal, Intention to Create Legal Relationships, Certainty, Possibility of Performance, and Legal Formalities.

Offer

Proposal is defined under section 2(a) of the Indian contract Act, 1872 as "when one person signifies to another his willingness to do or to abstain from doing anything with a view to obtain the assent of that other to such act or abstinence, he is said to make a proposal/offer". Thus, for a valid offer, the party making it must express his willingness to do or not to do something. But mere expression of willingness does not constitute an offer. An offer should be made to obtain the assent of the other. The offer should be communicated to the offeree and it should not contain a term the non compliance of which would amount to acceptance.

Acceptance

According to Section 2(b), "When the person to whom the proposal is made signifies his assent thereto, the proposal is said to be accepted." Acceptance must be absolute and unqualified, Communicated to offeror, Acceptance must be in the mode prescribed, Acceptance must be given within a reasonable time before the offer lapses, Acceptance by the way of conduct, and Mere silence is no acceptance.

Lawful Consideration

According to Section 2(d), Consideration is defined as: "When at the desire of the promisor, the promisee has done or abstained from doing, or does or abstains from doing, or promises to do or abstain something, such an act or abstinence or promise is called consideration for the promise."

In short, Consideration means quid pro quo i.e. something in return. An agreement must be supported by a lawful consideration on both sides.

The consideration or object of an agreement is lawful, unless and until it is- 1. forbidden by law, or 2. is of such nature that, if permitted, it would defeat the provisions of any law, or 3. is fraudulent, or involves or implies injury to the person or property of another, or 4. the court regards it as immoral, or opposed to public policy. 5. consideration may take in any form- money, goods, services, a promise to marry, a promise to forbear etc.

Competent to Contract

Section 11 of The Indian Contract Act specifies that every person is competent to contract provided he should not be a minor i.e. an individual who has not attained the age of majority i.e. 18 years; he should be of sound mind while making a contract. A person with unsound mind cannot make a contract; he is not a person who has been personally disqualified by law.

Free Consent

According to Section 13, "two or more persons are said to be consented when they agree upon the same thing in the same sense (Consensus-ad-idem). A consent is said to be free when it not caused by coercion or undue influence or fraud or misrepresentation or mistake.

Elements Vitiating free Consent

1. Coercion (Section 15): "Coercion" is the committing, or threatening to commit, any act forbidden by the Indian Penal Code under(45, 1860), or the unlawful detaining, or threatening to detain, any property, to the prejudice of any person whatever, with the intention of causing any person to enter into an agreement.

2. Undue influence (Section 16): "Where a person who is in a position to dominate the will of another enters into a contract with him and the transaction appears on the face of it, or on the evidence, to be unconscionable, the burden of proving that such contract was not induced by undue influence shall lie upon the person in the position to dominate the will of the other."

3. Fraud (Section 17): "Fraud" means and includes any of the following acts committed by a party to a contract, or with his connivance, or by his agent, with intent to deceive another party thereto of his agent, or to induce him to enter into the contract.

4. Misrepresentation (Section 18): "causing, however innocently, a party to an agreement to make a mistake as to the substance of the thing which is the subject of the agreement".

5. Mistake of fact (Section 20): "Where both the parties to an agreement are under a mistake as to a matter of fact essential to the agreement, the agreement is void".

Revocation of Offer

A proposal may be revoked at any time before the communication of its acceptance is complete as against the proposer, but not afterwards. An acceptance may be revoked at any time before the communication of the acceptance is complete as against the acceptor, but not afterwards.

A proposal is revoked by the communication of notice of revocation by the proposer to the other party; by the lapse of the time prescribed in such proposal for its acceptance, or, if no time is so prescribed, by the lapse of a reasonable time, without communication of the acceptance; by the failure of the acceptor to fulfill a condition precedent to acceptance; or by the death or insanity of the proposer, if the fact of the death or insanity comes to the knowledge of the acceptor before acceptance.

Agency

In law, the relationship that exists when one person or party (the principal) engages another (the agent) to act for him, e.g. to do his work, to sell his goods, to manage his business. The law of agency thus governs the legal relationship in which the agent deals with a third party on behalf of the principal. The competent agent is legally capable of acting for this principal vis-à-vis the third party. Hence, the process of concluding a contract through an agent involves a two-fold relationship. On the one hand, the law of agency is concerned with the external business relations of an economic unit and with the powers of the various representatives to affect the legal position of the principal. On the other hand, it rules the internal relationship between principal and agent as well, thereby imposing certain duties on the representative (diligence, accounting, good faith, etc.). The principal also cannot revoke the agent's authority after it has been partly exercised, so as to bind the principal (Section 204), though he can always do so, before such authority has been so exercised (Sec 203).

Further, as per section 205, if the agency is for a fixed period, the principal cannot terminate the agency before the time expired, except for sufficient cause. If he does, he is liable to compensate the agent for the loss caused to him thereby. The same rules apply where the agent, renounces an agency for a fixed period. Notice in this connection that want of skill continuous disobedience of lawful orders, and rude or insulting behavior has been held to be sufficient cause for dismissal of an agent. Further, reasonable notice has to be given by one party to the other; otherwise, damage resulting from want of such notice, will have to be paid (Section 206). As per section 207, the revocation or renunciation of an agency may be made expressly or impliedly by conduct. The termination does not take effect as regards the agent, till it becomes known to him and as regards third party, till the termination is known to them (Section 208). When an agent's authority is terminated, it operates as a termination of subagent also. (Section 210)

4.2.2. Sale of Goods Act, 1930

Sale of Goods Act (www.vakilno1.com) is one of very old mercantile law. Sale of Goods is one of the special types of Contract. Initially, this was part of Indian Contract Act itself in chapter VII (sections 76 to 123). Later these sections in Contract Act were deleted, and separate Sale of Goods Act was passed in 1930. The Sale of Goods Act is complimentary to Contract Act. Basic provisions of Contract Act apply to contract of Sale of Goods also. Basic requirements of contract i.e. offer and acceptance, legally enforceable agreement, mutual consent, parties competent to contract; free consent, lawful object, consideration etc. apply to contract of Sale of Goods also.

Contract of Sale - A contract of sale of goods is a contract whereby the seller transfers or agrees to transfer the property in goods to the buyer for a price. There may be a contract of sale between one part-owner and another. [Section 4(1)]. A contract of sale may be absolute or conditional. [section 4(2)].

Thus, following are essentials of contract of sale - * It is contract, i.e. all requirements of 'contract' must be fulfilled * It is of 'goods' * Transfer of property is required * Contract is between buyer and seller * Sale should be for 'price' * A part owner can sale his part to another part-owner * Contract may be absolute or conditional.

How Contract of sale is made - A contract of sale is made by an offer to buy or sell goods for a price and the acceptance of such offer. The contract may provide for the immediate delivery of the goods or immediate payment of the price or both, or for the delivery or payment by installments, or that the delivery or payment or both shall be postponed. [section 5(1)]. Subject to the provisions of any law for the time being in force, a contract of sale may be made in writing or by word of mouth, or partly in writing and partly by word of mouth or may be implied from the conduct of the parties. [section 5(2)]. Thus, credit sale is also a 'sale'. - - A verbal contract or contract by conduct of parties is valid. e.g. putting goods in basket in super market or taking food in a hotel.

Two parties to contract - Two parties are required for contract. - - "Buyer" means a person who buys or agrees to buy goods. [section 2(1)]. "Seller" means a person who sells or agrees to sell goods. [section 2(13)]. A part owner can sale his part to another part-owner. However, if joint owners distribute property among themselves as per mutual agreement, it is not 'sale' as there are no two parties.

Contract of Sale includes agreement to sale - Where under a contract of sale the property in the goods is transferred from the seller to the buyer, the contract is called a sale, but where the transfer of the property in the goods is to take place at a future time or subject to some condition thereafter to be fulfilled, the contract is called an agreement to sell. [section 4(3)]. An agreement to sell becomes a sale when the time elapses or the conditions are fulfilled subject to which the property in the goods is to be transferred. [section 4(4)]. The provision that contract of sale includes agreement to sale is only for the purposes of rights and liabilities under Sale of Goods Act and not to determine liability of sales tax, which arises only when actual sale takes place.

Transfer of property - "Property" means the general property in goods, and not merely a special property. [Section 2(11)]. In layman's terms 'property' means 'ownership'. 'General Property' means 'full ownership'. Thus, transfer of 'general property' is required to constitute a sale. If goods are given for hire, lease, hire purchase or pledge, 'general property' is not transferred and hence it is not a 'sale'.

Possession And Property- Note that 'property' and 'possession' are not synonymous. Transfer of possession does not mean transfer of property. e.g. - if goods are handed over to transporter or godown keeper, possession is transferred but 'property' remains with owner. Similarly, if goods remain in possession of seller after sale transaction is over, the 'possession' is with seller, but 'property' is with buyer.

Goods - "Goods" means every kind of movable property other than actionable claims and money; and includes stock and shares, growing crops, grass, and things attached to or forming part of the land which are agreed to be severed before sale or under the contract of sale. [Section 2(7)].

Price - "Price" means the money consideration for a sale of goods. [Section 2(10)]. Consideration is required for any contract. However, in case of contract of sale of goods, the consideration should be 'price' i.e. money consideration.

Conditions and Warranties - Opening para of section 16 makes it clear that there is no implied warranty or condition as to quality of fitness of goods for any particular purpose, except those specified in Sale of Goods Act or any other law. - - This is the basic principle of caveat emptor' i.e. buyer be aware. However, there are certain stipulations which are essential for main purpose of the contract of sale of goods. These go the root of contract and non-fulfilment will mean loss of foundation of contract. These are termed as 'conditions'. Other stipulations, which are not essential are termed as 'warranty'. These are collateral to contract of sale of goods. Contract cannot be avoided for breach of warranty, but aggrieved party can claim damages. - - A breach of condition can be treated as breach of warranty, but vice versa is not permissible.

A stipulation in a contract of sale with reference to goods which are the subject thereof may be a condition or a warranty. [section 12(1)]. A condition is a stipulation essential to the main purpose of the contract, the breach of which gives rise to a right to treat the contract as repudiated. [section 12(2)]. A warranty is a stipulation collateral to the main purpose of the contract, the breach of which gives rise to a claim for damages but not to a right to reject the goods and treat the contract as repudiated. [section 12(3)]. Whether a stipulation in a contract of sale is a condition or a warranty depends in each case on the construction of the contract. A stipulation may be a condition, though called a warranty in the contract. [section 12(4)].

Where a particular stipulation in contract is a condition or warranty depends on the interpretation of terms of contract. Mere stating 'Conditions of Contract' in agreement does not mean all stipulations mentioned are 'conditions' within meaning of section 12(2).

When condition to be treated as warranty - Where a contract of sale is subject to any condition to be fulfilled by the seller, the buyer may waive the condition or elect to treat the breach of the condition as a breach of warranty and not as a ground for treating the contract as repudiated. [section 13(1)]. Where a contract of sale is not severable and the buyer has accepted the goods or part thereof, the breach of any condition to be fulfilled by the seller can only be treated as a breach of warranty and not as a ground for rejecting the goods and treating the contract as repudiated, unless there is a term of the contract, express or implied, to that effect. [section 13(2)].

Nothing in this section shall affect the case of any condition or warranty fulfillment of which is excused by law by reason of impossibility or otherwise. [section 13(3)].

Time of payment is not essence of contract but time of delivery of goods is, unless specified otherwise - Unless a different intention appears from the terms of the contract, stipulations as to time of payment are not deemed to be of the essence of a contract of sale. Whether any other stipulation as to time is of the essence of the contract or not depends on the terms of the contract. [section 11]. As a general rule, time of payment is not essence of contract, unless there is specific different provision in Contract. In other words, time of payment specified is 'warranty'. If payment is not made in time, the seller can claim damages but cannot repudiate the contract.

Caveat Emptor - The principle termed as *'caveat emptor'* means 'buyer be aware'. Generally, buyer is expected to be careful while purchasing the goods and seller is not liable for any defects in goods sold by him. This principle in basic form is embodied in section 16 that subject to provisions of Sale of Goods Act and any other law, there is no implied condition or warranty as to quality or fitness of goods for any particular purpose. As per section 2(12), "Quality of goods" includes their state or condition.

Transfer of property as between seller and buyer - Transfer of general property is required in a sale. 'Property' means legal ownership. It is necessary to decide whether property in goods has transferred to buyer to determine rights and liabilities of buyer and seller. Generally, risk accompanies property in goods i.e. when property in goods passes, risk also passes. If property in goods has already passed on to buyer, seller cannot stop delivery of goods even if in the meanwhile buyer has become insolvent. - - - Where there is a contract for the sale of unascertained goods, no property in the goods is transferred to the buyer unless and until the goods are ascertained. [section 18].

Property passes when intended to pass - Where there is a contract for the sale of specific or ascertained goods the property in them is transferred to the buyer at such time as the parties to the contract intend it to be transferred. [section 19(1)]. For the purpose of ascertaining the intention of the parties regard shall be had to the terms of the contract, the conduct of the parties and the circumstances of the case. [section 19(2)]. Unless a different intention appears, the rules contained in sections 20 to 24 are rules for ascertaining the intention of the parties as to the time at which the property in the goods is to pass to the buyer. [section 19(3)].

Specific goods in a deliverable state - Where there is an unconditional contract for the sale of specific goods in a deliverable state, the property in the goods passes to the buyer when the contract is made, and it is immaterial whether the time of payment of the price or the time of delivery of the goods, or both, is postponed. [section 20].

Auction sale - Auction sale is special mode of sale. The sale is made in open after making public announcement. Buyers assemble and make offers on the spot. Person offering to pay highest price gets the goods. Usually, auctioneer is appointed to conduct auction. Higher and higher bids are offered and sale is complete when auctioneer accepts a bid.- - - In the case of a sale by auction— (1) where goods are put up for sale in lots, each lot is *prima facie* deemed to be the subject of a separate contract of sale; (2) the sale is complete when the auctioneer announces its completion by the fall of the hammer or in other customary manner; and, until such announcement is made, any bidder may retract his bid; (3) a right to bid may be reserved expressly by or on behalf of the seller and, where such right is expressly so reserved, but not otherwise, the seller or any one person on his behalf may, subject to the provisions hereinafter contained, bid at the auction; (4) where the sale is not notified to be subject to a right to bid on behalf of the seller, it shall not be lawful for the seller to bid himself or to employ any person to bid at such sale, or for the auctioneer knowingly to take any bid from the seller or any such person; and any sale contravening this rule may be treated as fraudulent by the buyer; (5) the sale may be notified to be subject to a reserved or upset price; (6) if the seller makes use of pretended bidding to raise the price, the sale is voidable at the option of the buyer. [section 64].

Delivery of goods to buyer - The Act makes elaborate provisions regarding delivery of goods to buyer. It is the duty of the seller to deliver the goods and of the buyer to accept and pay for them, in accordance with the terms of the contract of sale. [section 31]. Unless otherwise agreed, delivery of the goods and payment of the price are concurrent conditions, that is to say, the seller shall be ready and willing to give possession of the goods to the buyer in exchange for the price, and the buyer shall be ready and willing to pay the price in exchange for possession of the goods. [section 32]. - - Note that this is *'unless otherwise agreed'*, i.e. buyer and seller can agree to different provisions in respect of payment and delivery.

Acceptance of goods by buyer - Contract of Sale is completed not by mere delivery of goods but by acceptance of goods by buyer. 'Acceptance' does not mean mere receipt of goods. It means checking the goods to ascertain whether they are as per contract. - - - Where goods are delivered to the buyer which he has not previously examined, he is not deemed to have accepted them unless and until he has had a reasonable opportunity of examining them for the purpose of ascertaining whether they are in conformity with the contract. [section 41(1)]. - - Unless otherwise agreed, when the seller tenders delivery of goods to the buyer, he is bound, on request, to afford the buyer a reasonable opportunity of examining the goods for the purpose of ascertaining whether they are in conformity with the contract. [section 41(2)].

Buyer's and Seller's duties - The Act casts various duties and grants certain rights on both buyer and seller.

Rights of unpaid seller against the goods - After goods are sold and property is transferred to buyer, the only remedy with seller is to approach Court, if the buyer does not pay. Seller has no right to take forceful possession of goods from buyer, once property in goods is transferred to him. However, the Act gives some rights to seller if his dues are not paid.

Suits for breach of the contract - Unpaid seller can exercise his rights to the extent explained above. In addition, seller can exercise following rights in case of breach of contract. Buyer has also rights in case of breach of contract.

Measure for compensation and damages – The Sale of Goods Act does not specify how to measure damages. However, since the Act is complimentary to Contract Act, measure of compensation and damages will be as provided in sections 73 and 74 of Contract Act.

4.2.3. The Agricultural Produce (Grading And Marking) Act, 1937

An Act to provide for the grading and marking of *agricultural* and other produce. Whereas it is expedient to provide for the grading and marking of agricultural and other produce; it is here by enacted as follows (www.vakilno1.com):-

1. **Short title and extent**
   (1) This Act may be called the Agricultural Produce (Grading and Marking) Act, 1937.
   (2) It extends to the whole of India.
2. **Explanations**
   In this Act, unless the contrary appears from the subject or context-
   1. "agricultural produce" includes all produce of agriculture or horticulture and all articles of food or drink wholly or partly manufactured from any such produce, and fleeces and the skins of animals;
   2. "counterfeit" has the meaning assigned to that word by Section 28 of the Indian Penal Code (XLV of 1860);
   3. "covering" includes any vessel, box, crate, wrapper, tray or other container;
   4. "grade designation" means a designation prescribed as indicative of the quality of any scheduled article;
   5. "grade designation mark" means a mark prescribed as representing a particular grade designation;
   6. "quality" in relation to any article includes the state and condition of the article;
   7. "prescribed" means prescribed by rules made under this Act;
   8. "Scheduled article" means an article included in the Schedule;

9. An article is said to be marked with a grade designation mark, if the article itself is marked with a grade designation mark or any covering containing or label attached to such article is so marked.

10. an article is said to be misgraded if :-

a. the article is not of the quality prescribed for the grade designation with which it is marked;

b. the composition of the article offered for grading is altered in any way after a sample has been drawn for analysis and determination of the grade designation of the article in accordance with the rules made under this Act;

c. the article is tampered with in any manner, and

d. any false claim is made for the quality prescribed for its grade designation, upon thelabel or throughadvertisement or in any other manner.

3. Prescription of grade designations

1. The Central Government may, after previous publication by notification in the Official Gazette, make rules to carry out the provisions of this Act.

2. In particular, and without prejudice to the generality of the foregoing power, such rules may provide for all or any of the following matters; namely:-

a) fixing grade designation to indicate the quality of any scheduled article,

b) defining the quality indicated by every grade designation,

c) specifying grade designation marks to represent particular grade designations,

d) authorising a person or a body of persons, subject to any prescribed conditions, to mark with a grade designation mark any article in respect of which such mark has been prescribed or any covering containing or label attached to any such article,

e) specifying the conditions referred to in clause (d) including in respect of any article conditions as to the manner of marketing, the manner in which the article shall be packed, the type of covering to be used and the quantity by weight, number or otherwise to be included in each covering.

f) providing for the payment of any expenses incurred in connection with the manufacture or use of any implement necessary for the reproduction of a grade designation mark or with the manufacture or use of any covering or label marked with a grade designation mark or with measures for the control of the quality of articles marked with grade designation marks including testing of samples and inspection of such articles or with any publicity work carried out to promote the sale of any class of such articles.

g) providing for the confiscation and disposal of produce marked otherwise than in accordance with the prescribed conditions with a grade designation mark,

h) any other matter which required to be, or may be, prescribed.

3. Every rule made by the Central Government under this Act shall be laid, as soon as may be after it is made, before each House of Parliament, while it is in session for a total period of thirty days which may be comprised in one session or in two or more successive sessions and if, before the expiry of the session immediately following the session or the successive sessions aforesaid, both Houses agree in making any modification in the rule or both houses agree that the rule should not be made, the rule shall thereafter have effect only in such modified from or be of no effect as the case may be, so, however, that any such modification or annulment shall be without prejudice to the validity of anything previously done under that rule.

3A. Powers of entry inspection and search

1. Any officer of the Central Government or a State Government, or any authority, being an officer of a Gazetted rank or of equivalent rank, authorised by the Central Government, may, if he has reason to believe that any provision of this Act or the rules made thereunder has been, or is being, contravened, enter any premises at any reasonable time and make necessary inspection of, and search for, the agricultural produce in relation which such contravention has been, or is being made.

2. Every authorisation made under sub-section (1) shall be deemed to be a warrant referred to in section 93 of the code of Criminal Procedure, 1973.

3B. Powers of authorised officer to seize agricultural produce

1. An officer authorised under sub-section (1) of Section 3-A may seize and detain any agricultural produce in relation to which an offence under this Act or the rules made thereunder is being, or appears to have been committed, or which is intended or likely to be used in the commission of such offence;

2. Provided that where any agricultural produce seized under this sub-section is subject to speedy or natural decay, the officer so authorised may dispose of such produce in such manner as may be prescribed.

3. The provisions of Section 102 of the code of Criminal Procedure, 1973, shall apply to every seizure made under this section.

4. Penalty for an authorised marking with grade designation mark Whoever marks any scheduled article with a grade designation mark, not being authorised to do so by rule made under Section 3, shall be

punishable with imprisonment for a term not exceeding six months and fine not exceeding five thousand rupees.

5. Penalty for counterfeiting grade designation mark.

Whoever counterfeits any grade designation mark or has in his possession any die, plate or other instrument for the purpose of counterfeiting a grade designation mark, shall be punishable with imprisonment for a term not exceeding three years and fine not exceeding five thousand rupees.

4.A. Penalty for selling misgraded articles

Whoever sells any scheduled article which is misgraded shall be punishable with imprisonment for a term not exceeding six months and fine not exceeding five thousand rupees.

4.B. Power to prescribe compulsory grade designations in respect of certain articles

1. Where the Central Government is of the opinion that it is necessary in the public interest or for the protection of consumers that any scheduled article or class of articles shall not be sold or distributed except after such article or class of articles is marked with the grade designation mark, it may, by notification in the Official Gazette, make declaration to that effect.

2. Any notification issued under sub-section (1) shall specify the area or areas in relation to which the notification shall have effect.

3. Where a notification under sub-section (1) is issued in respect of any area or areas, no person shall sell or offer to sell or distribute or offer to distribute any scheduled article or class thereof in the area or areas except in accordance with the provisions of this Act or the rules made thereunder.

4. Whoever contravenes the provisions of this section shall be publishable with imprisonment for a term not exceeding six months and fine not exceeding five thousand rupees

4.2.4. The Essential Commodities Act, 1955

The Essential Commodities Act, 1955 (www.vakilno1.com) is a Central Act. It gives powers to control production, supply, distribution etc. of commodities for maintaining or increasing supplies and for securing their equitable distribution and availability at fair prices. Under this Act, a number of Control Orders have been issued by the Govt. of India and State Governments for regulating production, distribution, quality aspects, movement etc. pertaining to the commodities such as food grains, edible oils, pulses, kerosene, sugar etc. which are essential and administered by them. The Central Government monitors the action taken by the State Governments to implement the Act.

Delegation of powers:

Under Section 5, the Central Government may, by notified order delegate powers to Officers and authorities of the Central Government or subordinate to the State Government. Section 6A provides for confiscation of the essential commodity or any property like package, animal, vehicle, vessel or other conveyance by the Collector/Joint Collector.

Before passing an order of confiscation of the stocks, packages, vehicles, vessels, animals etc. by the Collector/Joint Collector a notice under Section 6B should be issued to the party from whom stocks have been seized and he should be given an opportunity for making his representation in writing. He should also be afforded an opportunity of being heard in person or through his counsel. No order of confiscation of the vehicle or animal vessel etc., shall be passed if the owner or his agent proves to the satisfaction of the Collector/Joint Collector that the vehicle, vessel, animal etc. had been used without their knowledge or connivance. In respect of animal, vehicle or other conveyance shall be given the to pay in view of its confiscation, a fine not exceeding the market price at the date of seizure of the essential commodity sought to be carried by such animal, vehicle, vessel etc.

Appeal against orders of confiscation by the party aggrieved by the Order lies to the judicial authority viz. the District & Sessions Courts authorized by the State Government within 30 days from the date of communication to him. Order of confiscation shall not prevent infliction of punishment to which the person affected is liable under the Act.

Penalties:

If any person contravenes any order made under Section 3, he shall be punishable

1. With imprisonment upto one year and fine for contraventions pertaining to violations in respect of information or statistics maintenance and production of books and accounts and records of their business for inspection

2. With imprisonment not less than three months but extend upto seven years and fine. However, for a punishment less than three months the court may mention adequate and special reasons in the judgment.

3. Any property in respect of which order have been contravened shall be forfeited. Any packing covering or receptacle in which the property was found or the animal, vehicle, vessel or other conveyance used for carrying the commodity shall be forfeited. If any person contravening the direction given by the authorized controller for complying the undertaking or any part of such undertaking regarding the production and supply of the

164

commodity shall be liable for imprisonment with not less than three months but which may extend up to seven years and fine.

If a person is convicted for an offence again under the same provision, he shall be punishable with imprisonment for the second and for every subsequent offence for a term of not less than six months and extend up to 7 years and fine. However, for a punishment less than six months, the court may mention adequate and special reasons in the judgment.

If a person is liable to pay any amount in pursuance of an order issued under Section 3 of the Essential Commodities Act, it shall be recoverable as arrears of land revenue or as a public demand.

Any person who attempts to contravene the order made under Section 3 of the EC Act is deemed to have contravened that Order.

Offences to be cognizable and bailable:

All the offences are cognizable and bailable.

The list of commodities under the Essential Commodities Act, 1955.

Declared under Clause (a) of Section 2 of the Act

Cattle fodder, including oilcakes and other concentrates, Coal, including coke and other derivatives, Component parts and accessories of automobiles, Cotton and woolen textiles, Drugs, Foodstuffs, including edible oilseeds and Oils, Iron and Steel, including manufactured products of Iron & Steel, Paper, including newsprint, paperboard and strawboard, Petroleum and Petroleum products, Raw Cotton, either ginned or unginned and cotton seeds, and Raw Jute.

Declared under sub-clause (xi) of clause (a) of Section 2 of the Act

Jute textiles, Fertilizers, whether inorganic, organic or mixed, Yarn made wholly from cotton, seeds of food crops and seeds of fruits and vegetables, seeds of cattle fodder and jute seeds.

The control Orders issued under this Act provide for action - (1) to confiscate the stock seized; 2) to suspend/cancel licences, if any and 3) impose punishments like imprisonment.

4.2.5. The Prevention Of Food Adulteration Act, 1955

This law was enacted to eradicate the anti-social evil of food adulteration and ensuring purity in the articles of food. It provides for constitution of a Central Committee for Food Standards to advise the Central and State Governments on matters arising out of the administration of the Act and to carry out other functions assigned to it (www.vakilno1.com).

The Act has some general provisions as to Food and incorporates certain provisions as regards analysis of food. For this purpose the office of a Public Analyst has been created. The duty of the Public Analyst is to analyse the sample of food sent to him. Further, the Act provides that purchaser of any article of food, or a recognized consumer association, (whether the purchase is a member of that association or not) can get such article analyzed by the public Analyst. The Public Analyst shall send the report of the result of analysis of any article of food to the Local (Health) Authority. If the food article as per report is found to be adulterated, prosecution proceedings against the person from whom the sample was taken shall be instituted.

4.2.6. The Trade And Merchandise Marks Act, 1958

This Act provides a comprehensive law in tune with consumer protection relating to registration and better protection of trade marks in the country. Also, it provides for the prevention of the use of fraudulent marks on merchandise in the interest of the consumer in particular and the public in general (www.vakilno1.com).

4.2.7. MRTP ACT, 1969

The objectives of the Act are ((www.vakilno1.com):

a) *To prevent concentration of economic power to the common detriment*

With the initiation of market economy and the consequent liberalisation of economic policy since July 1991, this objective has been substantially diluted. The MRTP (Amendment) Act, 1991 has omitted provisions regarding Central Government's permission for substantial expansion, establishment of a new undertaking, mergers, takeovers, etc. Establishments, howsoever big are now tree to expand, or establish new undertakings, or effect mergers. Consequently, strategic alliance between Godrej Soaps and Procter and Gamble could not be questioned.

Likewise merger of Hindustan Lever with TOMCO, though objected by certain quarters was allowed by the Supreme Court. However, checking concentration of economic power still remains as one of the objectives of the MRTP Act but only in so far as a large undertaking is likely to result in the practice of monopolistic, restrictive or unfair trade practices. Sections 27 and 27A of the Act, in such cases empower the Central Government to order division of an undertaking or severance of inter-connection between undertakings. The order for severance or interconnect bans shall be made by the Central Government on a recommendation by the MRTP Commission after due inquiry in this regard.

b) *To prohibit monopolistic trade practices*

The Act provides to control such practices through initiation of an enquiry at the instance of the central government or the Director General or even on its own motion. Besides, Section 32 mentions certain practices which are deemed to be prejudicial to the public interest.

c) *To prohibit restrictive trade practices and unfair trade practices*

The MRTP Commission has been vested with full powers to regulate restrictive trade practices (such as tie-up sales, exclusive dealings, area restrictions, formation f carters, etc.) through investigation and final orders. The Act has also made provisions for a scheme of registration of certain agreements pertaining to restrictive trade practices, enquiry into such practices at the instance of the Central Government, State Government, Director General, a trade association, a registered consumers' association or even from an individual consumer. Unfair trade practices (like false claims about quality, quantity, collaboration, price, warranty, organizing promotional contests, etc.) are also sought to be checked under the Act.

The executive arm for implementation of the MRTP Act is primarily MRTP Commission. MRTP Commission, particular 1984 (when a chapter on unfair trade practices was added) has been looked upon as a consumer protection body. It aims to offer protection to the consumers by curbing undesirable trade practices, viz. restrictive, monopolistic and unfair trade practices. Restrictive and unfair trade practices are entirely within the Commission's own initiative and the Commission can pass 'cease and desist' order regarding these trade practices (i.e., the trade practices shall not be repeated) or declare that these shall be void or the agreement relating thereto shall stand modified in the manner suggested. The Commission is empowered even to award compensation for any loss that may be caused to a person because of any restrictive or unfair trade practice. The role of the Commission in relation to monopolistic trade practice is of an advisory nature. It can only recommend an action to the Central Government.

4.2.8.   The Standards Of Weights And Measures Act, 1976

This Act was enacted to establish standards of weights and measures, to regulate inter-State trade or commerce in weights, measures and other goods which are sold or distributed by weight, measure or number, to provide for matters connected therewith or incidental thereto. Under the Act, weight and measures also include 'weighing or measuring instrument' which means "any object, instrument, apparatus or device, or any combination thereof, which is, or is intended to be, used, exclusively or additionally, for the purpose of making any weighment or measurement, and includes any appliance, accessory or part associated with any such object, instrument, apparatus or device"(www.vakilno1.com).

The main features of this Act are:

1. Every unit of weights or measures shall be based on the units of the metric system, which is the international system of units as recommended by the General Conference on Weights and Measures, and such additional units as may be recommended by the International Organisation of Legal Metrology. For example, the base unit of length to be the metre; mass - kilogram; time - second; electric current - ampere; thermodynamic temperature - kelvin;

luminous intensity - candela; amount of substance - mole; and of numeration - unit of the international form of Indian numerals.

2. The Act prohibits the use of any non-standard weight or measure or numeral. Thus, use of stones, bricks, copies, or weights made of non-standard material is strictly prohibited.

3. The Central Government shall, in relation to any weight or measure, prescribe the physical characteristics, configuration, constructional details, materials, equipment, performance, tolerances, methods or procedures of tests in accordance with the recommendations made by the International Organisation of Legal Metrology.

4. When commodities are sold or distributed in packaged form in the course of Inter-State trade or commerce, it is essential that every package bears a definite, plain and conspicuous declaration thereon showing the identity of the commodity in the package; the net quantity, in terms of the standard unit of weight or measure, or the commodity in the package; where the commodity is packaged or sold by number, the accurate number of the commodity contained in the package; the Unit sale price of the commodity as well as the sale price of that particular package of that commodity. The name and address of the manufacturer as well as of the packer or distributor should also be mentioned on the package.

5. The Act states that no person shall sell, distribute or deliver for sale a package containing a commodity which filled less than the prescribed capacity of such package, except where it is proved by such person that the package was so filled with a view of (i) giving protection to the contents of such package; or (ii) meeting the requirements of machines used for enclosing the contents of such package.

6. Where any weight or measure, sent from a transferor State (the State from which any weight or measure made or manufactured therein, or kept therein for sale or use, is sent to, or delivered in any other State) for delivery, sale or use in a transferee State (the State in which any weight or measure is delivered or received for sale or use therein from any other State), is such that (i) it is not required to be dismantled before its dispatch to the transferee State and is not likely to lose its accuracy by reason of such dispatch, it shall be known as a weight or measure of the first category;(ii) it is required to be dismantled before its dispatch to the transferee State and re-assembled and installed for use in the transferee State, it shall be known as a weight or measure of the second category.

7. Weight or measure of the first category shall, before it is dispatched to any transferee State, be produced before the local Inspector in the

transferor State and if such Inspector is, after verification of such weight or measure, satisfied that such weight or measure conforms to the standards established by or under this Act, stamp the same with such special seal as may be specified by rules made under this Act. While, weight or measure of the second category shall not be verified and stamped in the transferor State but shall be verified and stamped, after its reassembly and installation for use, by the local Inspector in the transferee State.

8. The fees for the verification and stamping of every weight or measure of (i) the first category shall be levied and collected by the transferor State; and (ii) the second category shall be levied and collected by the transferee State.

9. A weight or measure, whether of the first or second category, shall not require periodical re-verification if it is exclusively intended for domestic use and is not used by any member of the medical profession in the course of such profession.

10. No dealer or manufacturer shall export or import any weight or measure unless he is registered as exporter or importer, as the case may be. Every person who intends to commence or continue business as an exporter or importer of any weight or measure shall make, within prescribed time, an application for the inclusion of his name in the register to be maintained for the purpose. The application shall be made to the Director and every such application shall be made in prescribed form and on payment of prescribed fees. On receipt of an application, the Director shall, if he is satisfied after such inquiry as he may think fit, that it is expedient in the public interest so to do, include the name of the applicant in the register and issue to the applicant a certificate to the effect that his name has been so included and send a copy of the said certificate to the Controller of Legal Metrology in the State in which such exporter or importer is carrying on his business.

4.2.9. The Prevention Of Black-Marketing And Maintenance Of Essential Commodities Act, 1980

This Act is a supplement to the essential Commodities Act, 1955 (www.vakilno1.com). The object of this Act is to deal with certain malpractices indulged in by unscrupulous elements like black-marketers, hoarders, profiteers. Its penal provisions are very stringent. Under this Act, the Central Government, State Government and specified officials of the Government have been empowered to order detention of a person who is found to be acting in any manner prejudicial to the maintenance of supplies of commodities essential to the community.

The maximum period for which any person may, be detained in

pursuance of any detention order cannot exceed 6 months from the date of detention. However, the person detained has a right to know the grounds of his detention, vide Section 8, unless disclosure of the grounds is considered against the public interest in general. Further, Section 16 grants protection to the authorities for having taken action in good faith. It provides that no suit or other legal proceeding shall lie against the Central Government or a State Government, and no suit, prosecution or other legal proceeding shall lie against any person for anything in good faith done or intended to be done in pursuance of this Act.

4.2.10. Consumer Protection Act, 1986

Inspite of various Acts the consumers did not have any effective mechanism or institutional arrangement for the speedy redressal of their grievances and also the lack of effective popular movement isolated the consumer and his plight only increased. Seeing the pressure mounting from various consumer protection groups and the consumer themselves the Parliament enacted the Consumer Protection Act in 1986.

The Consumer Protection Act, 1986 (www.vakilno1.com) was enacted for better protection of the interests of consumers. The provisions of the Act came into force with effect from 15-4-87. Consumer Protection Act imposes strict liability on a manufacturer, in case of supply of defective goods by him, and a service provider, in case of deficiency in rendering of its services. The term "defect" and "deficiency", as held in a catena of cases, are to be couched in the widest horizon of there being any kind of fault, imperfection or shortcoming. Furthermore, the standard, which is required to be maintained, in services or goods is not to be restricted to the statutory mandate but shall extend to that claimed by the trader, expressly or impliedly, in any manner whatsoever.

A latest addition to the list of legislations is the Competition Act, 2002. A high level Committee was constituted in October 1999 under the Chairmanship of Shri SVS Raghavan, which submitted its report on May 2000. The committee framed the new Competition Policy which proposed repeal of Monopolies and Restrictive trade Practices Act, 1969 and enactment of a new Competition Law and establishment of a regulatory authority Competition Commission for implementation of Competition Act. On recommendation of the Committee the Competition Act was passed and the Monopolies and Restrictive Trade Practices Act, 1969 has been repealed. The Competition Act is a comprehensive legislation, which deals with matters of competition and monopolies.

Objectives of the Act

The purpose of the Act is to provide for the establishment of the Commission :

1.   To prevent practices having adverse effect on competition;

2.   To promote and sustain competition in markets;

3.   To protect the interests of consumers and

4.   To ensure freedom of trade carried on by other participants in the markets, in India

The major focus of the Act is on the following areas:

1.   Prohibition of anti competitive agreements;

2.   Prohibition against abuse of dominant position;

3.   Regulation of combinations;

4.   Advocacy of competition policy.

The legislative intention behind this Act is to clear all hurdles in promoting competition among business units whether of domestic or foreign origin. The Consumer Protection Act of 1986 was enacted with an objective to provide better protection of the interests of the Consumers, to make provision for the establishment of Consumer Councils and other authorities for the settlement of consumer disputes. This is indeed a very unique and highly progressive piece of Social Welfare Legislation. The provisions of this Act are intended to provide effective and efficient safeguards to the consumers against various types of exploitations and unfair dealings. Unlike other laws, which are basically punitive or preventive in nature, the provisions of the Act are compensatory. It is a matter of great satisfaction that we can legitimately boast that we now have in our country a statute, which provides more effective protection to the consumers than any corresponding legislation in force in countries, which are considered to be much more advanced and industrialized. Consumer Protection Act has been in operation for about 18 years. A number of deficiencies and shortcoming in respect of its operation have come to light thereby requiring amendments thrice, still leaving scope for further improvements. Despite all this it is a handy weapon for consumers to ensure accountability of producers of goods and providers of services. In the International Conference on Consumer Protection held in Malaysia in 1997, the Indian Consumer Protection Act was described as one "which has set in motion a revolution in the field of consumer rights, the parallel of which has not been seen anywhere else in the world".

Important Features of the Consumer Protection Act

1.   It covers all the sectors whether private, public, and cooperative or any person. The provisions of the Act are compensatory as well as preventive and punitive in nature and the Act applies to all goods covered by sale of goods Act and services unless specifically exempted by the Central Government;

2.   It enshrines the following rights of consumers:

(a)   right to be protected against the marketing of goods and services which are hazardous to life and property;

(b) right to be informed about the quality, quantity, potency, purity, standard and price of goods or services so as to protect the consumers against unfair trade practices;

(c) right to be assured, wherever possible, access to a variety of goods and services at competitive prices;

(d) right to be heard and to be assured that consumers' interests will receive due consideration at the appropriate fora;

(e) right to seek redressal against unfair trade practices or unscrupulous exploitation of consumers; and

(f) right to consumer education;

3. The Act also envisages establishment of Consumer Protection Councils at the central, state and district levels, whose main objectives are to promote and protect the rights of consumers;

4. To provide a simple, speedy and inexpensive redressal of consumer grievances, the Act envisages three-tier quasi-judicial machinery at the national, state and district levels. These are: National Consumer Disputes Redressal Commission known as National Commission, State Consumer Disputes Redressal Commissions known as State Commissions and District Consumer Disputes Redressal Forum known as District Forum; and

5. The provisions of this Act are in addition to and not in derogation of the provisions of any other law for the time being in force.

Consumer Rights under the Act

The Act enshrines the following rights:

1. The right to be protected against the marketing of goods which are hazardous to life and property;

2. The right to be informed about the quality, quantity, potency, purity, standard and price of goods so as to protect the consumer against unfair trade practices;

3. The right to be assured, wherever possible access to variety of goods at competitive prices;

4. The right to be heard;

5. The right to seek redressal against unfair trade practices or unscrupulous exploitation of consumer; and

6. The right to consumer education.

The Act provides for the establishment of the Consumer Protection Councils at the National, State and District levels. The objectives of these councils are to help the respective governments in adopting and reviewing policies for promoting and protecting the rights of the consumers. The composition of these consumer councils are broad based. The citizens and organizations representing different interest groups having implications for consumer's rights protection are members of these councils. One may like to add, that the Consumer Councils are required to be constituted on public-private partnership basis for better feedback and thereby review of the policy in the area of consumer's rights protection. The main objective of these councils is to promote and protect rights and interests of consumers in the society.

It also provides for Consumer Disputes Redressal Adjudicatory bodies established at three levels i.e. District, State and National. They are known as District Forums, State Commissions and National Commission. District Forum is composed of President and two members (one member is woman). Every member of the District Forum shall hold office for a term of five years or up to the age of 65 years, whichever is earlier and shall be eligible for reappointment. Now graduation is the minimum educational qualification for a member. The State Commission is presided over by Retired High Court Judge. The National Commission is presided over by the retired Supreme Court Judge.

The District Forum can adjudicate on the matter up to Rs. 20 lakhs, State Commission up to one crore and National Commission above Rs. one crore. The proceedings before these adjudicatory bodies are regulated in accordance with the principles of natural justice. At present 571 District Fora and 35 State Commissions are functioning all over the country besides the National Commission. Now State Commissions and National Commission have started sitting in Circuit Benches. It may, however, be highlighted that there are 253 Vacancies of the Presidents and Members of the Forums in the entire Country. It may also be mentioned that at present there are 73 District Forums, which are non-functional.

Now complaints filed are required to be accompanied with such amount of fee and payable in such manner as may be prescribed. Fee structure for the cases filed in the District Forums has been prescribed by the Ministry of Consumer Affairs, Food and Public Distribution by Rule 9A of the Consumer Protection (Amendment) Rules, 2004, which is as follows:

Value of goods or services and compensation claimed	Amount of fee payable
Upto one lakh rupee	Rs. 100
One lakh and above but less than five lakh rupees	Rs. 200
Five lakh rupees and above but less than Rs.10 lakh	Rs. 400
Ten lakh rupees and above but not exceeding Rs.20 lakh	Rs. 500

As on 30.9.2004 the total number of cases field and disposed of in the National Commission, State Commissions and as on 30.06.2004, District Forums are as below:

The National Commission, State Commissions and District Forums are required to decide complaint, as far as possible, within a period of three months from the date of notice received by the opposite party where complaint does not requires analysis or testing of commodities and within five months if it requires analysis or testing of commodities. The Appeals are allowed within 30 days against the order of the District Forum to the State Commission and against the order of the State Commission, to the National Commission. Appeal can also be preferred to the Supreme Court against the order of the National Commission within a period of 30 days. No appeal by a person who is required to pay any amount in terms of an order of the National Commission shall be entertained by the Supreme Court unless that person has deposited in the prescribed manner fifty percent of that amount or rupees fifty thousand, whichever is less. Similarly there is a requirement for depositing Rs. 35000/- and Rs. 25000/- in case of appeals to National Commission and State Commission.

From the various reports and feedback received by the Central Government, it is evident that many of the consumer forums have not been provided with adequate accommodation, infrastructure facilities and staff. In many State Commissions and District Forums, vacancies of Presidents/Members have not been filled up which adversely affects the disposal of cases. It should be remembered that the confidence of the consumer ultimately depends upon the successful functioning of the Consumer Commissions/Forums. It is, therefore, a matter of utmost importance that these agencies must function effectively, efficiently and without any interruption. For this to happen state governments are having definite role to perform.

Other Important Aspects of Consumer Protection Act
Definition of 'Defect' and 'Consumer'

Under the Consumer Protection Act, Consumer Forums at the District, State and National level have been specifically constituted to adjudicate claims of consumers for any "defect" in goods. A "defect" has been defined in Section 2(1) (f) of the Act as "any fault, imperfection or shortcoming in the quality, quantity, potency, purity or standard which is required to maintained by or under any law for the time being in force or under any contract, express or implied, or as is claimed by the trader (which includes the manufacturer) in any manner whatsoever in relation to any goods."

It is important to mention herein that by virtue of Section 2 (1)(d) persons/entities who had purchased goods for 'commercial purpose' (other than those persons who have purchased goods for using them to earn their livelihood by means of self-employment) are excluded from the scope of Consumer Protection Act; they cannot institute proceedings under the Consumer Protection Act even if there is any 'defect' in the goods purchased by them for using the goods for commercial purposes.

Who is a Complainant?

Complainant means

1   A Consumer;

2   Any Voluntary Consumer Association;

3   The Central Government;

4   The State Governments or Union Territory Administration;

5   One or more consumers, where there are numerous consumers having the same interest and

6   In case of death of a consumer, his legal heir or representative.

What Constitute a Complaint?

- An allegation in writing made by the complainant that
- Any unfair trade practice or restrictive trade practice has been adopted by any trader.
- The goods bought or agreed to be bought suffer from one or more defects.
- Services hired /availed or agreed to be hired /availed suffer from deficiencies in any respect.
- That a trader has charged for the goods or services mentioned in the complaint, a price in excess of the stipulated price

(i)   fixed by or under any law for the time being in force; or

(ii)   displayed on goods; or

(iii) displayed on any package containing such goods that goods or services which are hazardous to life and safety of the public are being offered to the public

Who can file a Complaint?

A complaint can be filed by

1   A consumer to whom goods are sold or delivered or agreed to be sold or delivered or such services provided or agreed to be provided.

2   Voluntary Consumer Organization

3   The Central Government;

4   The State Governments or Union Territory Administration;

5   One or more consumers, where there are numerous consumers having the same interest

The definition of consumer is wide but only a consumer to whom goods are sold or delivered or agreed to be sold or delivered or such services provided or agreed to be provided can file complaint. The definition as provided under Sec. 2(1) (b) is different from list of persons who can file complaint. The legal heirs or representatives of the deceased have been included in definition of 'complainant' by 2002 amendment but have not been specified in Sec. 12(1) as person who can file complaint, which, creates a doubt that he cannot file and can only continue as a complainant after the death of the complainant.

A Complaint should contain the following information

(a) The name, description and address of the complainant;

(b) The name, description and address of the opposite party or parties;

(c) The facts relating the complaint and when and where it arose;

(d) Documents 'if any' in support of allegations and

(e) The relief which the complainant is seeking.

The complaint should be signed by the Complainant or his/ her authorized agent.

Reliefs Available to Consumers

Following reliefs are available to the Consumers under the Act:

1 Removal of defects from the goods;

2 Replacement of the goods;

3 Refund of the price paid;

4 Award of compensation for the loss or injury suffered;

5 Discontinue and not to repeat unfair trade practice or restrictive trade practice;

6 Not to offer hazardous goods for sale;

7 To withdraw hazardous goods from sale;

8 To cease manufacture of hazardous goods and desist from offering services which are hazardous in nature;

9 If the loss or injury has been suffered by a large number of consumers who are not identifiable conveniently, to pay such sum (not less than 5% of the value of such defective goods or services provided) which shall be determined by Forum; to issue corrective advertisement to neutralize the effect of misleading advertisement;

10 To provide adequate costs to parties.

Validity of Limitation of liability clauses

Contractual liability has a role to play in product liability claims under the Consumer Protection Act. Courts in India have upheld limitation of liability clauses, which parties have specifically agreed to in the contract as recognized by the Supreme Court in Bharathi Knitting Company v DHL Worldwide Express Courier (1996) 4 SCC 704. However, such clauses may be struck down if found to be unconscionable in nature. In MarutiUdyog v. Susheel Kumar Gabgotra, [(2006) 4 SCC 644], the manufacturer of the vehicle had stipulated a warranty clause limiting its liability to merely repair the defects found if any. In view of this clause, the Supreme Court reversed the findings of the National Commission to replace the defective goods and held that the liability of the manufacture was confined to repairing the defect. Compensation was, however, awarded for travel charges to the complainant, which was incurred due to the fault of the car manufacturer.

Applicability of other laws

Section 3 of the Consumer Protection Act provides that the Act is in addition to and not in derogation of any other law. The Supreme Court in Secretary, Thirumurugan Co-operative Agricultural Credit Society v. M. Lalitha, [(2004) 1 SCC 305] has interpreted the above provision to mean that the remedies provided under the Consumer Protection Act are in addition to the remedies provided under other statutes. Hence, the fact that a remedy is specifically provided for under another statute would not necessarily oust the jurisdiction of the appropriate authority under the Consumer Protection Act. It has been further held that if forums under one statute and the Consumer Protection Act are approached, then it is for the appropriate authority to permit the parties to opt between the consumer forum and the other forum, depending on the facts and circumstances of the case.

Establishment of Consumer forums

At present, there are 34 State Commissions, one in each State/UT and 571 district fora besides the National Commission. The state governments are responsible to set up the district fora and the State Commissions. States have been empowered to establish additional District Forum and also additional members in the State Commission to facilitate constituting benches and also for holding circuit benches. The Central Government is empowered to establish the National Commission. It has been empowered to appoint additional members to facilitate creation of more benches and holding of circuit benches. The second bench of the National Commission started functioning from 24 September 2003. The government is monitoring the disposal of cases by the consumer courts through National Commission. As per the current statistics, since its inception and up to 5.9.2008 , 2559451 cases were filed out of which 2327035 cases were disposed of by the District forums in various states of India .

Jurisdiction under Consumer Protection Act 1986

The District Forum has the jurisdiction to entertain complaints where the value of the goods or services and the compensation, if any, claimed, is less than INR 50,000. A State Commission has the jurisdiction to entertain complaints where the value of the goods or services and the compensation, if any, claimed exceeds 500,000 rupees but does not exceed 2 million rupees. It is also appellate forum for orders of the District forum. The National Commission has the jurisdiction to entertain complaints where the value of goods and services and the compensation exceeds two million rupees and also hears the appeals against the orders of the State Commission.

Period of limitation

A complaint is only admitted by any of the competent forums under Consumer Protection Act if it is filed within two years from the date on which the cause of action has arisen but it may be entertained after the said period after recording its reasons for condoning such delay , if the complainant satisfies that he had a sufficient cause for not filing the complaint within period of two years .

Class actions

Under Consumer Protection Act Section 2 (1) (b) permits filing of a complaint by a consumer, any voluntary consumer association registered under companies Act 1956 or under any other law, the State government or Central Government, one or more consumers where number of consumers have same interest, incase of death of a consumer , his legal representative may ,make a complaint.

Penalty under Section 27 Consumer Protection Act

According to Consumer Protection Act ,where a trader or the complainant fails to comply with an order made by the relevant consumer forum , such person is liable to a punishment with imprisonment for a term which is not less than one month but which may extend to three years or with fine of not less than two thousand rupees but which may extend to ten thousand rupees or with both.

Major Amendments in Consumer Protection Act, 1986

Time and again, some amendments have been made into consumer protection act, 1986 with the idea of covering more products and services, and making the act more efficient. Following is the discussion related to major amendments which have been brought out in the consumer protection act, 1986.

1. In case of death of a consumer, his legal heir or representative a new sub-clause (1) under Section 2 of the Principal Act. Exclusion of a person who avails of such service for any commercial purpose from the category of the consumer.However, the "Commercial purpose" does not include use by a person of goods bought and used by him and services availed by him exclusively for the purpose of earning his livelihood by means of self-employment.

2. "Spurious goods and services" in the form of new clause (oo) after clause (o) under Section 2 of the Principal Act.

3. With a view to promote and protect within the district the rights of the consumer laid down under the Principal Act "establishment of the District Consumer Protection Council" under the Chairmanship of the District Collector, insertion of new Sections 8A and 8B; is proposed.

4. Qualifications including academic and also disqualifications for members.

5. Re-appointment of a member for another term of five years or up to the age of sixty-five years, whichever is earlier.

6. Substitution of new Section for Section 12 dealing with the manner in which complaint shall be made.

7. Provisions dealing with adjournment - "no adjournment shall be ordinarily granted". Proviso to the new sub-clause (3A) under Section 13 of the Principal Act.

8. Power to make "interim order" new sub-clause (3B) of Section 13.

9. Power to grant "punitive damages" new proviso to clause (d) of Sub-Section (1) of Section 14.

10. Power to issue "corrective advertisement" to neutralize the effect of misleading advertisement at the cost of the opposite party, new clause (nc) under Sub-Section (1) of Section 14. Benches of the State Commission may be constituted by the President of the State Commission with one or more members.

11. Insertion of new Section 17A authorising the State Commission, on the application of the complainant or of its own motion, to transfer any complaint pending before the District Forum to another District Forum within the State in the interest of justice.

12. Creation of benches of the National Commission.

13. Power of the National Commission to review its own order, when there is an error apparent on the face of record.

14. Provision in regard to the execution of orders of the District Forum, the State Commission or the National Commission.

15. All offences under the Consumer Protection Act may be tried summarily, notwithstanding anything contained in the code of Criminal Procedure, 1973. The District Forum, the State Commission or the National Commission shall have the power of a judicial magistrate of the first class for the trial of offences.

16. New Section 28 A dealing with the procedure for service of notice.

Sum Up

The anonymity of urban living has been responsible for a number of malpractices on the part of the producers, sellers, suppliers, distributors, etc. These malpractices, in turn, resulted in a number of consumer protection legislations. Each of these legislations is designed to protect the interests of the consumers in one way or the other. Consumer Protection Act has been the major umbrella legislation or act which deals directly with consumer rights and problems. Apart from it, The Essential Commodities Act, empowers the Central Government to regulate production, supply, distribution, storage, transport, price, etc. of essential commodities. Likewise, the Prevention of Food Adulteration Act is designed to eradicate the evil of food adulteration and to ensure purity in the articles of food. Standards of Weights and Measures Act aims at introducing standards in relation to weights and measures used in trade, and commerce. The Trade and Merchandise Marks Act offers protection to the consumers by preventing the use of fraudulent marks.

'AGMARK' under Agricultural Produce (Grading and Marking) Act is an assurance of quality with respect to agricultural products. Then, the Indian Contract Act offers protection to consumers by declaring those contracts which are the result of fraud, misrepresentations, coercion, and undue influence as terminable at the option of the party aggrieved. Besides, damages can also be claimed. Against Sale of Goods Act, protects consumers by subjecting every contract of sale and purchase of goods to certain conditions and warranties. Sale by a person not having a clear title entitles the buyer at full refund of price. Buyer is also protected by latent defects in the goods rendering the un-merchantable.

The efficient and effective program of Consumer Protection is of special significance to all of us because we all are consumers. Even a manufacturer or provider of a service is a consumer of some other goods or services. If both the producers/providers and consumers realize the need for co-existence, adulterated products, spurious goods and other deficiencies in services would become a thing of the past. The active involvement and participation from all quarters i.e. the central and state governments, the educational Institutions, the NGO's, the print and electronic media and the adoption and observance of a voluntary code of conduct by the trade and industry and the citizen's charter by the service providers is necessary to see that the consumers get their due. The need of the hour is for total commitment to the consumer cause and social responsiveness to consumer needs. This should, however, proceed in a harmonious manner so that our society becomes a better place for all of us to live in.

References

G. K. Kapoor, (2006), *Defective Goods And Deficiency Of Service Vis-À-Vis Consumer*, Indian Institute of Public Administration, New Delhi, pp. 345-364.

INDIAN CONTRACT ACT, 1872, Retrieved from http://www.vakilno1. com /bareacts/indiancontractact/indiancontractact.html, 16 October 2013.

SALE OF GOODS ACT, 1930, Retrieved from http://www.vakilno1.com/ bareacts/saleofgoods/saleofgoods.html, 18 March 2013.

THE AGRICULTURAL PRODUCE (GRADING AND MARKING) ACT, 1937, Retrieved from http://www.vakilno1.com/bareacts/laws/ agricultural-produce-grading-and-marking-act-1937.html , 16 October 2013.

THE ESSENTIAL COMMODITIES ACT, 1955, Retrieved from http://www.vakilno1.com/bareacts/essencom/essencom.html,16 October 2013.

THE PREVENTION OF FOOD ADULTERATION ACT, 1954, Retrieved from http://www.vakilno1.com/bareacts/prevfood1954/prevfood.html, 16 October 2013.

TRADE AND MERCHANDISE MARKS ACT, 1958, Retrieved from http://www.vakilno1.com/bareacts/trademerchand1958/trademercha ndisemrks.html, 16 October 2013.

MRTP ACT, 1969, Retrieved from http://www.vakilno1.com /bareacts/mrtpact/mrtpact.html

THE STANDARDS OF WEIGHTS AND MEASURES ACT, 1976, Retrieved from http://www.vakilno1.com/bareacts/stdsweights1976/ standardswcights.html , 18 March 2013.

THE PREVENTION OF BLACK-MARKETING AND MAINTENANCE OF ESSENTIAL COMMODITIES ACT, 1980, Retrieved from http://www.vakilno1.com/bareacts/preblakm1980/preblakm.html , 18 March 2013.

CONSUMER PROTECTION ACT, 1986, Retrieved from http://www.vakilno1.com/bareacts/consumerprotectionact/consumer protectionact.html. 18 March 2013.

CHAPTER – 5
CONSUMER DISPUTES AND CONSUMER REDRESSAL FORUMS IN INDIA

Consumer protection is a group of laws and organizations designed to ensure the rights of consumers as well as fair trade competition and the free flow of truthful information in the marketplace. The laws are designed to prevent businesses that engage in fraud or specified unfair practices from gaining an advantage over competitors; they may also provide additional protection for the weak and those unable to take care of themselves. Consumer protection laws are a form of government regulation, which aim to protect the rights of consumer (www.answers.com).

In India, Consumer Protection Act of 1986 is the law governing consumer protection. Under this law, Separate Consumer tribunals have been set up throughout India in each and every district in which a consumer [complaint can be filed by both the consumer of a goods as well as of the services] can file his complaint on a simple paper without paying any court fees and his complaint will be decided by the Presiding Officer of the District Level. Appeal could be filed to the State Consumer Disputes Redressal Commissions and after that to the National Consumer Disputes Redressal Commission (NCDRC). The procedures in these tribunals are relatively less formal and more people friendly and they also take less time to decide upon a consumer dispute when compared to the years long time taken by the traditional Indian Judiciary. In recent years, many effective judgement have been passed by some state and National Consumer Forums (Eradi, 2013).

The Grievance redressal mechanism of an organization is the gauge to measure its efficiency and effectiveness as it provides important feedback on the working of the Organization. The main purpose of a Grievance Policy is to place an appropriate mechanism whereby the Customer who believe(s) that he/ she has been wronged by any act of the Company is afforded a fair opportunity to redress his/ her Grievance. Putting the importance and necessity of consumer protection and redressal of grievances in mind, this chapter reviews the frameworks for consumer dispute resolution and redress in India.

5.1. Consumer Disputes In India

Consumer dispute means dispute where the person against whom a complaint has been made, denies or disputes the allegation contained in the complaint (www.nishasharmadavpushpanjali.blogspot.in). Before reviewing the consumer redressal forums, it is important to know the different types of consumer disputes. A consumer can approach consumer forum for redressal of following types of disputes.

1   Electricity consumption and Bills
2   Insurance
3   Medical facilities
4   Hospitals
5   Phone manufacturers (Nokia, Samsung, LG etc.)
6   Telecommunication companies (Airtel, Idea, Tata Indicom, Reliance etc.)
7   Builder and Developers
8   Hotel and Restaurants (Maurya Sherton, Hayaat etc.)
9   Airlines (Air India, Jet Airways, Go, Indigo, Lufthansa etc.)
10 Travel Agencies (makemytrip.com, yatra.com, clertrip.com etc.)
11 Auto Companies (TATA, Maruti, Honda, Hyundai etc.)
12 Banking Services
13 Sale and purchase of consumables and any other goods
14 Manufacturer of any goods
15 Any other service provider
16 Deficiency in service
17 Defect in goods
18 Main Service Providers in our country are:
19 Telecommunication companies
20 Electricity Distribution Companies
21 Builders
22 Shopkeepers
23 Manufacturer of Goods
24 Auto Companies
25 Banks
26 Transport Companies or Government including Railways
27 Service Stations
28 Repair Centers

The above mentioned list is not exhaustive. The categorization of disputes will depend upon the facts. It is essential that public authorities have a place and play an active role in consumer policy and justice. The simple fact that one or several authorities are responsible for consumer policy has an influence on consumer protection and the role of consumer organizations. Some Member States have a single public authority that deals with consumer law; some have several public authorities that are competent. Yet, in other Member States, consumer organizations are the only body responsible for enforcement of consumer protection law.

5.2. Consumer Courts In India

Protecting the interests of consumers has been one of the major concerns of the Indian Government. Several policies and legislations have been in place in order to promote the concerns of the consumers and grant them the rights of choice, safety, information and redressal. Accordingly, there is a well-placed departmental set up both at the Central and State level in the form of a separate department.

Fostering the development of effective, low cost ways for consumers to resolve their disputes and obtain monetary compensation for losses sustained is a key consumer policy objective. The particular features of consumer disputes require tailored mechanisms that can provide consumers with access to remedies that do not impose a cost, delay and burden disproportionate to the economic value at stake (www.oecd.org). Hence, in India, under the Consumer Protection Act, 1986, consumer courts have been established for the redressal of consumer grievances.

Consumer Court is the name given to special purpose courts, mainly in India, that deal with cases regarding consumer disputes and grievances. These are judiciary set ups by the government to protect the consumer rights. If any consumer is cheated by the seller he/she can approach the redressal forum to seek justice. Their main function is to maintain the fair practices by the sellers towards consumers.

Consumer Protection Act provides for the creation of consumer courts. The central government is given the responsibility to create and maintain the National Consumer Disputes Redressal Commission in New Delhi. The state government is given the responsibility to create a State Consumer Disputes Redressal Commission at the state level and a District Consumer Disputes Redressal Forum at the district level.

5.2.1. National Consumer Disputes Redressal Commission

The National Commission was constituted in the year 1988. The National Consumer Court must ordinarily be functioning in New Delhi and is presided over by a person who is currently or has been in the past a judge of the Supreme Court. The President of the National Consumer Disputes Redressal Commission (NCDRC) is appointed by the Central Government after consultation with the Chief Justice of India. The National Consumer Commission has a minimum of four other members and is appointed by a committee chaired by a Supreme Court judge as recommended by the Chief Justice of India. Members of the NCDRC can have a term of up to five years or up to 70 years, whichever is earlier (en.wikipedia.org).

If your complaint seeks more than one crore rupees of compensation from a company, then the National Consumer Commission has the pecuniary jurisdiction over your complaint. In order to attain the objects of the Consumer Protection Act, the National Commission has also been conferred with the powers of administrative control over all the State Commissions by calling for periodical returns regarding the institution, disposal and pendency of cases. It is empowered to issue instructions regarding: (1) adoption of uniform procedure in the hearing of the matters; (2) prior service of copies of documents produced by one party to the opposite parties; (3) speedy grant of copies of documents; and (4) generally over-seeing the functioning of the State Commissions or the District Forums to ensure that the objects and purposes of the Act are best served without in any way interfering with their quasi-judicial freedom (www.ifmr.co.in).

The National Consumer Court handles five types of complaints:

- Appeals from State Consumer Disputes Redressal Commissions
- Consumer complaints that occurred in India, except in the State of Jammu and Kashmir
- Cases from State Consumer Commissions where there has been accusations or proof of material irregularity or illegal activities
- Cases where ex-parte (where verdicts have been passed in the absence of either parties) orders have to be set aside.
- Complaints that has been sought or need to be transferred from one State Consumer Commission to another in the interest of justice.

If you are not satisfied by the verdict from the National Consumer Court, you can appeal in the Supreme Court, within a period of 30 days. If a verdict has been given against the company, it can appeal only after depositing 50% of the compensation to be paid to you or Rs.50000/-, whichever is lesser.

Commission-wise detail of complained filed, disposed off and pending has been given in Table 5.1.

Table 5.1 depicts that since the inception of consumer protection Act, out of total filed cases, 87.29 per cent of cases have been disposed off by the National commission, 80.49 per cent of cases has been disposed off by state commission and 91.46 per cent of cases has been disposed off by district forums.

Table 5.1

Detail of Consumer complaints filed, disposed off and Pending at the National, State and District Forums (Updated on 28.01.2011)

Sr. No.	Name of Agency	Cases since inception			
		Filed	Disposed off	Pending	% of total Disposal
1	National Commission	67764	59151	8613	87.29%
2	State Commissions	528747	425569	103178	80.49%
3	District Forums	2932228	2681798	250430	91.46%
	TOTAL	3528739	3166518	362221	89.74

Source: ncdrc.nic.in/National Consumer Dispute Redressal Commission, Delhi.

5.2.2. State Consumer Disputes Redressal Commission

Under the Consumer Protection Act, 1986 a State Consumer Disputes Redressal Commission shall be set up by the State Government for the respective State. At present there are 35 State Commissions functioning in differ States. The law provides that the State Consumer Commission function in the state capital, but the government has the powers to move it as needed. The President of the State Consumer Commission shall be or should have been a High Court judge and should be appointed only after consultation with the Chief Justice of the High Court with the states jurisdiction. The remaining members of the commission are appointed by a committee with the President of the State Consumer Court as its chairman, and they can have a term of up to five years or up to 67 years, whichever is earlier (Srinivasan, 2013).

The State Consumer Disputes Redressal Commission deals with a pecuniary jurisdiction of only those complaints where the compensation sought is higher than twenty lakhs but lesser than one crore.

The State Consumer Forum usually hears cases of three types:

1 Appeals from District Consumer Forums

2 Cases against companies that operates an office or a branch in the state.

3 Cases where the actual reason why you are filing the complaint (such as signing of an agreement or payment of a bill) partially or fully occurred within the state.

The State Consumer Court also has the powers to transfer a case from one District Consumer Forum to another Forum provided there is such a request or it is in the interest of the law. If you are not satisfied by the verdict from the State Consumer Court, you can appeal in the National Consumer

Disputes Redressal Commission, within a period of 30 days. If a verdict has been given against the company, it can appeal only after depositing 50% of the compensation to be paid to you or Rs.35000/-, whichever is lesser.

The state-wise details of cases filed, disposed off and pending in the state commission has been shown in Table 5.2.

Table 5.2

State-wise details of cases filed, disposed off and pending in the state Commission

Sr. No.	Name of State	As on	Cases since inception			
			Filed	Disposed off	Pending	% of Disposal
1	Andhra Pradesh	30.11.2010	26172	23399	2773	89.40
2	A & N Islands	31.01.2008	42	38	4	90.48
3	Arunachal Pradesh	30.11.2010	56	52	4	92.86
4	Assam	31.12.2010	2361	1484	877	62.85
5	Bihar	30.11.2010	14063	10101	3962	71.83
6	Chandigarh	31.12.2010	11091	10700	391	96.47
7	Chattisgarh	31.12.2010	6804	6470	334	95.09
8	Daman & Diu and DNH	30.06.2010	23	16	7	69.57
9	Delhi	31.12.2010	31529	30262	1267	95.98
10	Goa	31.12.2010	2180	2074	106	95.14
11	Gujarat	31.12.2010	35355	30731	4624	86.92
12	Haryana	30.11.2010	39219	28853	10366	73.57
13	Himachal Pradesh	30.11.2010	6995	6384	611	91.27
14	Jammu & Kashmir	31.03.2010	5884	5175	709	87.95
15	Jharkhand	30.09.2010	4547	3657	890	80.43
16	Karnataka	31.12.2010	37516	34269	3247	91.35
17	Kerala	31.12.2010	23374	22061	1313	94.38
18	Lakshadweep	31.12.2010	16	15	1	93.75
19	Madhya Pradesh	31.07.2010	36159	31953	4206	88.37
20	Maharashtra	30.09.2010	51852	34137	17715	65.84
21	Manipur	30.09.2008	139	96	43	60.06
22	Meghalaya	30.06.2009	238	152	86	63.87
23	Mizoram	31.10.2010	177	169	8	95.48
24	Nagaland	31.12.2006	94	64	30	68.09
25	Orissa	30.11.2010	19910	13564	6346	68.13
26	Puducherry	31.12.2010	899	852	47	94.77
27	Punjab	30.11.2010	25449	19449	6000	76.42
28	Rajasthan	30.11.2010	45309	41829	3480	92.32
29	Sikkim	31.12.2010	37	36	1	97.30
30	Tamil Nadu	30.11.2010	21867	19150	2717	87.57
31	Tripura	31.12.2010	1239	1223	16	98.71
32	Uttar Pradesh	30.11.2010	59687	30256	29431	50.69
33	Uttarakhand	30.11.2010	4088	3285	803	80.36
34	West Bengal	31.10.2010	14376	13613	763	94.69
	TOTAL		**528747**	**425569**	**103178**	**80.49**

Source: scdrc.nic.in/State Consumer Dispute Redressal Commission, Delhi.

Table 5.2 reveals that consumers in all the States and Union Territories have filed cases/complaints against the wrong done by the service/goods providers. The percentage of disposal of cases is highest in Tripura (that is, 98.71 per cent) and lowest in Uttar Pradesh (that is 50.69 per cent).

The State Commission shall ordinarily function in the State Capital but may perform its functions at such other place as the State Government may, in consultation with the State Commission, notify in the Official Gazette, from time to time (www. ncdrc.nic.in).

5.2.3. District Consumer Disputes Redressal Forum

Under the Act, the State Government shall establish a District Forum in each district of the State, though, more than one District Forum may be established in a district if it is deemed fit. Presently, there are 629 District Forums functioning in different States. The President and members are directly/indirectly appointed by the state government and he shall be eligible to be a district judge. All members of the court can have a term of up to five years or up to 65 years, whichever is earlier. The District Consumer Forum cannot conduct a hearing without the President and at least one other member.

This consumer court deals with complaints where the compensation sought is less than twenty lakhs. This limit is commonly known as the 'pecuniary jurisdiction' of the District Consumer Disputes Redressal Forum.

A District Consumer Forum can hear cases for any company that operates an office or a branch in the district. It can also hear cases provided the actual reason why you are filing the complaint (such as sale or maintenance service that led to the defect) partially or fully occurred within the district. For this same reason, it is very important that you do not do business with any company that does not have local representation or one that makes you sign an agreement regarding the jurisdiction of the dispute (www. ncdrc.nic.in).

The law provides that the District Consumer Disputes Redressal Forum has the same powers as a civil court under Code of Civil Procedure 1908, but you may be surprised as to how much of this power in law books actually manifests when put to practice. The District Consumer Forum can order the company to take the following actions once it hears the complaint and decides that the company is at fault:

1 Correct deficiencies in the product to what they claim
2 Repair defect free of charges
3 Replace product with similar or superior product
4 Issue a full refund of the price
5 Pay compensation for damages/ costs/ inconveniences
6 Withdraw the sale of the product altogether
7 Discontinue or not repeat any unfair trade practice or the restrictive trade practice
8 Issue corrective advertisement for any earlier misrepresentation

If one is not satisfied with the verdict from the District Consumer Court, you can appeal in the State Consumer Disputes Redressal Commission within a period of 30 days. If a verdict has been given against the company, it can appeal only after depositing 50% of the compensation to be paid to you or Rs.25000/-, whichever is lesser.

Table 5.3

State-wise details of Cases filled, disposed off and pending in District Forums (updated on 28.01.2011)

Sr. No.	Name of State	As on	Cases filed since inception	Cases disposed of since inception	Cases Pending	% of Disposal
1	Andhra Pradesh	30.11.2010	182369	177591	4778	97.38
2	A & N Islands	31.03.2006	330	301	29	91.21
3	Arunachal Pradesh	30.11.2010	310	270	40	87.10
4	Assam	31.08.2010	13704	11976	1728	87.39
5	Bihar	30.11.2010	79000	68294	10706	86.45
6	Chandigarh	31.12.2010	42245	40853	1392	96.70
7	Chattisgarh	31.12.2010	32052	29486	2566	91.99
8	Daman & Diu and DNH	30.06.2010	153	129	24	84.31
9	Delhi	30.09.2010	214314	202712	11602	94.59
10	Goa	31.12.2010	6046	5462	584	90.34
11	Gujarat	30.11.2010	158904	140162	18742	88.21
12	Haryana	30.11.2010	198958	180898	18060	90.92
13	Himachal Pradesh	31.12.2010	52560	49476	3084	94.13
14	Jammu & Kashmir	31.12.2007	20792	18855	1937	90.68
15	Jharkhand	30.09.2010	31986	29571	2415	92.45
16	Karnataka	31.12.2010	138692	132997	5695	95.89
17	Kerala	31.12.2010	168679	161298	7381	95.62
18	Lakshadweep	31.12.2010	68	59	9	86.76
19	Madhya Pradesh	31.07.2010	155236	142553	12683	91.83
20	Maharashtra	30.09.2010	235578	217522	18056	92.34
21	Manipur	30.09.2008	1037	1012	25	97.59
22	Meghalaya	31.03.2007	322	308	14	95.65
23	Mizoram	31.12.2006	2065	2011	54	97.38
24	Nagaland	30.6.2006	246	205	41	83.33
25	Orissa	30.11.2010	84120	78511	5609	93.33
26	Puducherry	31.12.2010	2771	2536	235	91.52
27	Punjab	30.11.2010	135519	130913	4606	96.60
28	Rajasthan	30.11.2010	253945	230657	23288	90.83
29	Sikkim	31.12.2010	260	245	15	94.23
30	Tamil Nadu	30.11.2010	95859	89960	5899	93.85
31	Tripura	30.09.2008	2015	1807	208	89.68
32	Uttar Pradesh	30.11.2010	512222	429627	82595	83.88
33	Uttarakhand	30.11.2010	32241	30599	1642	94.91
34	West Bengal	30.09.2010	77630	72942	4688	93.96
	TOTAL		2932228	2681798	250430	91.46

Source: ncdrc.nic.in/ National Consumer Dispute Redressal Commission, Delhi.

There are important differences regarding the (legal) position of consumer organizations in relation to different authorities. The rights and possibilities which consumer organizations have at their disposal may vary significantly from country to country, but also within the national context. Consumer organizations may be explicitly designated and granted the status of an "interested party" in the procedures initiated by a certain authority, e.g. a "consumer protection" authority. They may be entitled to request certain measures to be taken, to receive responses to complaints they filed with the authority within a certain time period and they may even have the right to challenge decisions taken by the authority before courts. This special status may be granted in relation to a consumer authority, but not in relation to a competition authority for example. Consumer organizations can use such a "qualified" position to put more pressure on public authorities and to render the enforcement system more efficient.

State-wise details of cases filed, disposed off and pending in district forums has been given in Table 5.3.

Table 5.3 reveals that District Forums in Mizoram has disposed off 97.59 per cent of cases, which highest among the states/UTs. The lowest percentage is recorded in Nagaland (that is, 83.33 per cent).

A person cannot file a complaint in a consumer court if two years have elapsed after the cause of action (such as payment of a bill or the incident that started the dispute with the company).

If a consumer is not satisfied by the decision of the District Forum, he/she can challenge the same before the State Commission and against the order of the State Commission a consumer can come to the National Commission.

To provide speedy and simple redressal to consumer disputes, a quasi-judicial machinery is sought to be set up at the District, State and Central levels. These quasi-judicial bodies will observe the principles of natural justice and have been empowered to give reliefs of a specific nature and to award, wherever appropriate, compensation to consumers. Penalties for non-compliance of the orders given by the quasi-judicial bodies have also been provided (www.delhistatecommission.nic.in).

5.3. Some Of The Cases Pertaining To Consumer Grievances Redressal

Following examples show the efforts of consumer forums for redressal of the consumers' grievances:

5.3.1. Case against Indian Air Lines

Common cause filed a petition before the National Consumer Commission against the Indian Air Lines, Airport Authority of India and the Director General of Civil Aviation. The Complaint was filed against the alleged lack of attention to the safety of the aircrafts and the passenger travelling by the airlines; lack of facilities, against inconvenience caused to the passengers due to the delay in operation in flights, failure to give information regarding the delayed or cancelled flights, delay in baggage clearance and unsatisfactory catering. In response to the complaint the respondents gave the assurance that detailed course of action would be taken up in immediate future for the redressal of the consumers grievances as pointed out by the common cause. In another case involving the Indian Airlines, the CERC on the basis of a newspaper, filed a petition before the National Commission. The petitioner alleged that the passengers travelling by an Indian Airlines No IC-401 from Calcutta to Delhi on May 13, 1989 were made to stay at the Airport for long time. It was due to the delay in flight by 90 minutes because the Chief Minister of Tripura who was to board the flight could not reach the airport in time.

The complainant argued that the passengers travelled by air mainly to shorten the travelling time. Due to the delay, they not only wasted time but faced inconvenience also; such delay had become frequent in India, the complainant argued. The National Commission dismissed the petition on the ground that the complainant has not been authorised to represent the passengers of the flight. The complaint was based on the newspaper which might not be correct. The commission argued that the Act of 1986 was enacted to give redressal to the consumers if there was any defect in the goods purchased or there was any deficiency in the service hired or breach of the promise to be made.

It is necessary to note that social action litigation was initially used in the late 1970s, and even report published in the newspapers were treated as *soumotto* writ petition by the judges of Supreme Court and high courts. For example, in Rain Pyari vs. Union of India AIR 1988 Rajasthan 124, on 10th September, 1985, a local newspaper of Rajasthan reported that an 80 years old widow of a soldier ran from pillar to post for forty years to get the pension of her husband. in vain. It was only after the direction of the court to the government of Rajasthan that the woman was paid her husband's pension (www. indiankanoon.org).

5.3.2. Case of Inconvenience Caused in the Availability of Service

CUTS (Consumer Unity and Trust Society) a Calcutta based NGO tiled a petition before the, National Consumer Commission alleging the inconvenience caused to the consumer due to the strike of the employees of Bank of Baroda who went on strike. The national commission declared the strike of the employees as "anti-consumer Acts". It passed the structure against the striking employees that "they have been totally indifferent to the interests of the consumers, the depositors, the account holders, and the borrowers, whom the bank including its workmen are expected to serve." It directed the bank to see to it that the innocent consumers did not suffer. The commission hoped that the department of Banking, finance ministry, Government of India and RBI would urgently give attention to the matter of evolving some worltable arrangements for rendering skeleton service.

In another case the society for civic rights filed a complaint against the Government of India before National Consumer Commission. The complainant was regarding the inconvenience caused to the consumers by the strike of the engineers of the telecommunication. The complaint argued that the striking employees had damaged the telecommunication system. As the telephone service is ail essential service, it is the duty of the telecommunication department to provide the service to public. The NGO demanded that the consumers should be provided relief in turns of reduction in the rent for the period when service was disrupted by the strike; the payment of punitive compensation to the customers, and fixing the responsibility on agitating engineers for tampering with communication system and causing hardship and injury to the customers. The consumer commission, however, rejected the plea that the complaint was filed regarding the unspecified users of the telephone services, and that the law provided the provisions for the strike. Therefore, the complaints were dismissed (www.lawsenate.com).

5.3.3. Case of Adulterated Goods

Two ration shops in West Bengal supplied contaminated rapeseeds oil. The consumer suffered from service disability due the consumption of this oil seed. The CUTS filed a petition against union of India and others. It demanded ex-gratia payment to the sufferers,their prompt medical treatment, disablement pension to the affected persons, and rehabilitation of the victims of oil seed tragedy. The National Commission appreciated the efforts of the CUTS. Common cause of Delhi had also filed a petition in before the national commission regarding the failure of the state and central governments in providing the iodinated edible oil supplied to the general public in goitre-prone areas of the country. It demanded that the governments should take necessary action in this regard. The government responded to the commission and explained the government was introducing appropriate policy measure in this regard. It said that by 1992 the idionised salt will be sold throughout the country (www.lawsenate.com).

5.3.4. Deficiency and Negligence of Service

In 1991 Madras Provincial Consumer Association took up the grievances of a dental surgeon involving the case of deficiency and negligence of Southern Railway. The Consumer association filed a petition on behalf of the consumer against the General Manager, Southern Railway. The petition complained that the customer, the dental surgeon got railway reservation journey from Trichy to Madras. But after the confirmation of ticket it was found that the train did not start from Madras. This caused mental agony to the customer, apart from wastage of his time, money and energy. The consumer form demanded that the railways should pay compensation to the customer for the agony and the loss suffered by him. The consumer commission held that this was a case of "patent error and palpable negligence" on the part of railway staff. On the order of the commission, the complainant was paid by the railway Rs.7,500/- as compensation (www. en.wikipedia.org).

5.3.5. Case against the Electricity Board

In a case of the fault of the Himachal Pradesh Electricity Supply Board, the Himachal State Consumer Protection Council filed a petition before the consumer Forum against the secretary, Himachal Pradesh Electricity Board. It was alleged that supply of low voltage of electricity during the peak hour was virtually of no use. It affected the studies of the students as well as the activities in business and agriculture. It demanded compensation to the consumers. The commission refused to give the compensation and the complaint was disposed of. However, the HPSEB gave the undertaking for regulating the supply of electricity by installing an additional transfer on or before June 1992.In a case the Maharashtra State Consumer Commission ordered the LIC to pay compensation of Rs. 20,0001- to the LIC policy holders who had grievances against LIC.

An NGO Akhil Bharatiya Grahak Panchayat had filed a petition before the Maharashtra State Consumer Commission. It alleged that the consumer had suffered mental and physical loss due to the hostile and indifferent attitude of the LIC. The NGO alleged that the LIC had denied the customer to know about the surrender value, special surrender value and bonus in respect of insurance policy. The commission held the LIC responsible for the deficiency in service and ordered the LIC to make the payment of compensation to the consumer.

Similarly in another case also filed by the consumer Education and Research Society against the LIC, the commission ordered the LIC to pay the compensation of Rs. 2 lakhs along with running interest at the rate of 18% p.a. which was to be paid within three months. In this case wife of a complainant had taken LIC policy with-the accident benefit and paid the premium up-to-date. The ensured died during the existence of the policy and after completion of all formalities the claim was filed with the insurance company. The LIC repudiated the claim under the clause 4B of the policy on the ground that death has occurred as a result of an accident in a public place before the expiry of three years from the date of the policy. The commission repudiated the claim of the LIC and ordered payment of the compensation (www. indiankanoon.org).

5.3.6. Case against Misleading Advertisement

In the 1980s, a manufacturer of automobiles (two-wheelers) launched an ambitious plan to increase the number its customer through manipulative and misleading advertisements. It exhorted its prospective customers to get their names registered by way of payment of Rs.5001-, and promised them that the delivery of the automobile will be made to them after a year or so. The registration amount was to carry an interest rate ranging between 7% to 9% per annum. The fixation of the interest rate depended on the discretion of the company. In certain cases it was said that "reasonable interest will be paid". Advance deposit paid by the customer was to paid the customer was to paid at the time of the deliver of the vehicle. Stringent conditions were laid down in the whole scheme. If a customer cancelled his booking within one year of the deposit, the amount was not to carry any interest. In such cases the amount was to be refunded by a demand draft to be posted to the customer within 60 days from the receipt of the cancellation advice.

A lot of people got registration done. Even after three years of registration, they were not informed about the delivery. And those who got their booking cancelled were not refunded their money. In some cases letter of request, applications, reminders and even legal noticed did not have any effect on the business corporation. These companies had collected huge sum of money. People lost all hope for redressal of their grievances. Following the passage of Consumer Protection Act, 1986, a large number of SAL petitions were filed against the automobile manufacturers in various states of the country.

The manufacturers on their part argued that the relief could be given only to the persons named in the petition. The consumer associations had asked for relief even for those who 'were not named in the petition. The association argued that there were thousands of consumers, who could not file petition and urged that their petitions should be treated as Public Interest Litigations. As a result the National Commission in Mumbai Grahak Panchayat vs. Lohia Machines Ltd. took liberal view of the case and directed the business corporations to furnish list containing names and particulars of persons to whom refund deposits remained outstanding as unpaid.

The commission also directed the respondent company to pay Rs. 5,0001- cause to the petitioner association as "the enormous expenditure incurred in collecting the data concerning the 934 persons." In March, 1992, the Mumbai Gralialc Panchayat and M/s. Lohia machines ultimately reached a compromise. Both the consumer association and Lohia Machines Ltd. submitted an agreed joint scheme before the National Commission for repayment of the outstanding amount of scooter deposits to all remaining customers who had also cancelled their booked scooters. The company ultimately agreed to release, every month a sum of Rs. 50 lakh and was ordered by the National Commission to complete the process of repayment to all unpaid customer not later than 30September, 1995 (www.lawsenate.com).

Sum Up

Consumer Court is the special purpose court, mainly in India that deals with cases regarding consumer disputes and grievances. These are judiciary set ups by the government to protect the consumer rights. Its main function is to maintain the fair practices by the sellers towards consumers. Consumers can file a case against a seller if they are harassed or exploited by sellers. The court will only give a verdict in favour of the consumers/customers if they have proof of exploitation, i.e., bills or other documents. If a consumer does not have the proper documents required for filing a case then it would be very difficult for the consumer to win or even file a case. A nation level court works for the whole country and deals with amount more than Rs 1 crore. A state level court works at the state level with cases valuing less than 20 lakhs and : A district level court works at the district level with cases valuing upto 20 lakhs. The District Consumer Forum is established in all the District of India, The State Consumer Commission is established in all the State Capitals of India, The "National Consumer Disputes Redressal Commission" situated in New Delhi and the governing law is "Consumer Protection Act, in India". It is important to note that the goods purchased or services availed for commercial purposes cannot be challenged under the Consumer Protection Act of India.

References

"West Encyclopedia of American Law. Consumer. Answers.com. Retrieved on January 31, 2010

V. Balakrishna Eradi, "Consumer Protection and National Consumer Disputes Redressal Commission". New Delhi: National Consumer Disputes Redressal Commission. Accessed 25 June 2013.

http://nishasharmadavpushpanjali.blogspot.in/2008/02/meaning-of-consumer-dispute-under.html. Accessed 17 October 2013-10-17

http://www.oecd.org/internet/consumerpolicy/36456184.pdf. Accessed on 12 March 2013.

http://en.wikipedia.org/wiki/Consumer_Court#cite_note-NCDRC_Website - 2 .Accessed on 17 October 2013

http://www.ifmr.co.in/blog/2012/03/23/evolution-of-consumer-protection-laws-in-india-part-1/. Accessed on 23 March 2013.

Jayanth Srinivasan, *Evolution of Consumer Protection Laws in India*. Retrieved from 17 October 2013-10-17

http://ncdrc.nic.in/. Retrieved from 23 April 2012.

http://ncdrc.nic.in/. Retrieved from 13 September 2012.

http://delhistatecommission.nic.in/. Retrieved from 23 April 2012

http://indiankanoon.org/search/?formInput=consumer+cases+against+air+lines. Accessed on 9 January 2009

http://www.lawsenate.com/case-studies/ Inconvenience- Caused- Availability- of- Service.html. Retrieved from 15 January 2009

http://www.lawsenate.com/case-studies/ Adulterated- Goods-html. Retrieved from 15 January 2009

http://en.wikipedia.org/wiki/Consumer_Court#cite_note- NCDRC_Website-2 **Deficiency_ and_ Negligence_ of_ Service.** Retrieved 6 October 2010

http://indiankanoon.org/search/?formInput=consumer+cases+against+ **Electricity Board.** Accessed on 26 January 2010

http://www.lawsenate.com/case-studies/Misleading-Advertisement-html. Retrieved from 15 January 2009

CHAPTER – 6
EVALUATION OF WORKING OF CONSUMER PROTECTION SETUP IN HIMACHAL PRADESH

Organization occupies an important place in the administration. Without proper organization, whole system of administration would have collapsed. In ordinary sense of the term organization is an arrangement in which different parts have their functions to perform and all these are interlinked and interconnected as well as interdependent to each other (Jayapalan, 2010). An organization is a collectivity with relatively identifiable boundary, a normative order, authority ranks, communications system, and membership coordinating systems; this collectivity exists on a relatively continuous basis in an environment and engages in activities that are usually related to a goal or a set of goals (Hall, 1972).

Organization is the process of combining the work which individuals or group have to perform with the facilities necessary for this execution, that the duties so performed provide the best channels for the efficient, systematic, positive and coordinated application of the available efforts. Thus organization concerns itself with combining as well as grouping activities in an enterprise. In this sense organization structure can be thought of as the machine through which management works to accomplish its tasks (Trivedi, 1999). An organization may be described as a system with a purpose or a goal, accomplish through the efforts of individuals operating in its several departments, contributing to the main goal in one way of another. In effect we can define an organization as a purposeful system with several sub-systems in which individuals are organized to achieve certain predetermined goals through the division of labour and coordination of activities (Sekaran, 2004).

Organizational success is on its structure. It is the structure in which human beings can perform most effectively. Organizational structure is a group of people working together to attain the desired objectives. People in an organization do not start working together automatically unless they are provided with some mechanism of coordination and control. One of the mechanisms is the organization structure. It provides an invisible framework to integrate all the people working together towards a common goal. Organization structure is essential for exercising leadership. It provides an indispensable sort of co-ordination in an organization (Malik, **2006**). Organizational structure is the configuration of the hierarchical levels and specialized units and positions within an organization, and the formal rules governing these arrangements (Malhotra, **2006**). Organization structure defines how job tasks are formally divided, grouped, and coordinated (Robbins, Judge & Sanghi, 2008). Organization structure helps in the achievement of goals with the help of well-defined hierarchical position which carry with them authority and responsibilities. Thus, a well-established organizational structure is an essential pre-requirement for the proper implementation of laws, rules and regulations, policies and programmes.

The organization of government is not an end in itself, but a means for achieving national objectives. The purpose is to allocate the tasks of government so that they are performed in a manner that is both efficient and economical, with a minimum of duplication and overlapping. It is important to define the areas of authority and responsibility of administrative units, so that they may be properly subject to constitutional and political controls (Malhotra, **2006**).

Consumer protection consists of laws and organizations designed to ensure the rights of consumers as well as fair trade competition and the free flow of truthful information in the marketplace. The laws are designed to prevent businesses that engage in fraud or specified unfair practices from gaining an advantage over competitors and may provide additional protection for the weak and those unable to take care of themselves. Consumer protection laws are a form of government regulations, which aim to protect the rights of consumers. On the other hand, organizations are set up to enforce the laws in their original form and to hear complaints and finally to pass verdicts. Earlier chapters have covered Consumer Protection Laws.

This chapter aims at explaining the organizational setup for the consumer protection along with its evaluation in Himachal Pradesh. Before discussing the organizational setup, it is important to discuss the socio-economic profile of Himachal Pradesh. Thus, present chapter has been divided into two sections, namely, Section A and Section B. section A presents a picture of socio-economic profile of Himachal Pradesh and in Section B an examination of organizational structure for the consumer protection along with evaluation in Himachal Pradesh has been made.

Section – A

This section presents a picture of socio-economic profile of Himachal Pradesh.

6.A.1. Profile of Himachal Pradesh

The word HIMACHAL derives its origin from two Hindi words, 'Him' and 'Anchal' meaning 'Snow' and 'Lap' respectively. Thus etymologically, Himachal Pradesh (Hill State) stands for the region which lies in the slopes of foot-hills of snow, that is, Himalaya (Ahluwalia, 1993). Himachal Pradesh, the *Dev Bhumi* as it is known to the ancients, lies in the heart of the Western Himalaya (Singh, 1999). Himachal literally means 'Land of Snowy-Mountains' (Balokhra, 2010). Himachal situated in the heart of the western Himalaya, identified as "Dev Bhumi" and is believed to be the abode of Gods and Goddesses. The entire State is punctuated with stone as well as wood temples. The rich culture and traditions have made Himachal unique in itself. The shadowy valleys, rugged crags, glaciers and gigantic pines and roaring rivers and exquisite flora and fauna compose the symphony that is forever Himachal (www.india.gov.in). Now, it is known as 'the Country's Orchard', 'Nature's Paradise' and an 'Abode of Peace'.

6.A.1.i   Administrative History

Himachal Pradesh came into being on 15th April 1948, as a Centrally Administered Territory by the integration of 30 erstwhile princely states. At that time, the state had four districts viz., Chamba, Mahasu, Mandi and Sirmaur and its area was 25,839 square kilometers. Later, in 1951, it became a Part 'C' state under a Governor with a 36 Member Legislative Assembly and a three member's cabinet. In 1954, Bilaspur, another Part 'C' state was merged with Himachal Pradesh thereby adding one more district with an area of 1,168 square kilometers. And the strength of its assembly was raised to 41. In 1956, despite the majority recommendation of the State Reorganization Commission for its merger with Punjab, Himachal Pradesh retained its separate entity. On 1st November, 1956, it again became a Union Territory under an Administrator designated as Lieutenant Governor and its assembly was abolished. In 1960, a new border district of Kinnaur was carved out of Mahasu district. Then in 1963, Assembly was revived and a regular ministry was formed. Till October, 1966 the Old Himachal Pradesh comprised the six hill districts of Bilaspur, Chamba, Kinnaur, Mahasu, Mandi and Sirmaur with an area of 27,007 square Kilometers. Having a population of 13,51,144 persons (1951 Census). On 1st November 1966 it was enlarged by merging the district of Kangra, Shimla, Kullu, Lahaul-Spiti, Nalagarh, tehsil of Ambala district, some parts of Una Tehsil of Hoshiarpur district and Dalhousie of Gurdaspur District of the then Punjab state. With this merger the total area of Himachal Pradesh increased to 55,673 square kilometers and its population to 28,12,463 persons (1961 Census) (Department of Economics and Statistics, 2010). Upon the formation of the state of Himachal Pradesh in 1971 (25th of January 1971, Himachal got full statehood), Shimla was named as its capital.

On 1st September, 1972, two more districts viz., Hamirpur and Una were created by trifurcation of Kangra district and the Mahasu and Solan districts were reorganized as Shimla and Solan districts (Department of Economics and Statistics, 2004). Presently, the strength of Legislative Assembly of Himachal Pradesh is 68. To the Union Legislature, Himachal Pradesh is represented by 4 members to Lok Sabha and 3 members to Rajya Sabha. The Pradesh has got a High Court and a Public Service Commission located at Shimla (Department of Economics and Statistics, 2010). Presently, Himachal Pradesh is comprised of 3 Administrative Divisions, 12 districts, 51 sub-divisions, 77 developmental blocks, 117 Tehsils/Sub-tehsils, 59 urban areas and 20690 villages. There are 12 Zila Parishads, 77 Panchayat Samities and 3243 Gram Panchayats (Himachal in Figures 2010-11)

6.A.1.ii   Location and Climate

Himachal Pradesh is the third largest hill state of India, which is situated in the western Himalayan region (Tiwari, 2007). Its location is between 30°22′ 40″ to 33°12′40″ North latitude and 75°45′55″ to 79°04′20″ East longitudes (Planning Department, 2010). To the East, it forms India's border with Tibet, to the North lies state of Jammu and Kashmir, Uttrakhand in South-East, Haryana in the South and Punjab in the West. The entire territory of Himachal Pradesh is mountainous with altitude varying from 350 to 7000 meters above the mean sea level (Balokhara, 2010).

Physiographical, the state can be divided into five zones, namely, (i) wet sub-temperate zone, (ii) humid sub- temperate zone, (iii) dry temperate (alpine high lands), (iv) humid sub-tropical zone, and (v) sub-humid sub-tropical zone ((Balokhara, 2010). These vary from wet humid sub-temperate situation to dry temperate alpine high lands. Himachal Pradesh can be divided into three regions – (i) The Shivalik ranges (the height from plain upto 915 meters); (ii) Colder Zone (the height is about 4500 meters); and (iii) the Axis and Crystalline core of the whole system (the height above 4500 meters). The climatic conditions, therefore, vary from the semi-tropical to semi-artic. Besides the seasonal variations, the climate of Himachal Pradesh varies at different altitudes. The average rainfall is 152 cms. (60 inches). The highest rainfall occurs in Kangra district followed by Shimla district (Planning Department, 2010). Himachal Pradesh can be called an *'India-in-miniature'* as almost all climatic conditions prevailing in our country are found in the state (Balokhra, 2010).

6.A.1.iii   Area and Population

The area of Himachal Pradesh is 55,673.00 square kilometers. The provisional population of the state is 68,56,509 as on 1st March, 2011. Out of this, 34,73,892 are males and 33,82,617 females.

Table 6.1
District-Wise Area, Total Population, Rural Population and Sex Ratio in Himachal Pradesh

District	Area (in Sq. Kms.)	Total population (in Number) 2001 Census	Total population (in Number) 2011 (P) Census	Decennial growth (2001 – 2011 (P)	2011 (P) Census Density of population (in per sq. Kms.)	2011 (P) Census Rural population (in number)	2011 (P) Census Sex ratio (women per 'ooo males)
Bilaspur	1167	340885	382056	12.08	327	356930 (93.42)	981
Chamba	6528	460887	518844	12.58	80	482653 (93.02)	989
Hamirpur	1118	412700	454293	10.08	406	422880 (93.09)	1096
Kangra	5739	1339030	1507223	12.56	263	1420864 (94.27)	1013
Kinnaur	6401	78334	84298	7.61	13	84298 (100.00)	818
Kullu	5503	381571	437474	14.65	79	396216 (90.57)	950
Lahaul Spiti	13835	33224	31528	-5.10	2	31528 (100.00)	916
Mandi	3950	901344	999518	10.89	253	936894 (93.73)	1012
Shimla	5131	722502	813384	12.58	159	611884 (75.23)	916
Sirmaur	2825	458593	530164	15.61	188	472926 (89.20)	915
Solan	1936	500557	576670	15.21	298	474592 (82.30)	884
Una	1540	448273	521057	16.24	338	476140 (91.38)	977
Total	55673	6077900	6856509	12.81	123	6167805 (89.96)	974

Source: State Statistical Abstract of Himachal Pradesh 2010-11, Table 1.02 and 1.03, Department of Economics and Statistics, Government of Himachal Pradesh, Shimla.
Note: 'P' represents 'Provisional'.

The proportion of male population is 50.67 per cent and the female 49.33 per cent. During the decade of 2001-11, the population of Himachal Pradesh has increased by 7,78,609 persons, thus yielding a growth rate of 12.81 per cent as against 17.54 per cent in the preceding decade. The population of the state constitutes 0.57 per cent of India's population and ranks 21st amongst all states and union territories of the country (Directorate of Census, 2011).

Kangra district ranks first among the districts with population of 15,07,223 persons accounting for 21.98 per cent of the total population of the state in 2011 census about half of population is concentrated in district Kangra, Mandi and Shimla. The rank of districts according to size of population has undergone few changes during 2001-11. Sirmaur and Una district which has improved its position to 5th and 6th place as against 6th and 7th place in 2001 census. Chamba district has moved down to 7th position in 2011 census against the 5th place in 2001 census (Directorate of Census, 2011).

6.A.1.iv   State Economy

The economy of Himachal Pradesh is predominantly dependent upon agriculture and in the absence of strong industrial base, any fluctuation in the agricultural or horticultural production causes significant change in economic growth also. During 2010-11 about 15.81 per cent of state income has been contributed by agriculture sector alone (Department of Economics and Statistics, 2012).

Gross State Domestic Product or State income is the most important indicator for measuring the economic growth of a state. According to quick estimates, the total State Domestic Product for the year 2010-11 is Rs. 39,066 crore against Rs. 35,907 crore in 2009-10 thereby registering a growth of 8.8 per cent at constant prices (2004-05). The total Gross State Domestic Product of the Pradesh at current prices is estimated at Rs. 54,695 crore in 2010-11, as against Rs. 46,969 crore in 2009-10, thereby registering an increase of 16.4 per cent (Department of Economics and Statistics, 2012). Another indicator of the economy is per capita income. According to quick estimates based on new series, that is, 2004-05 series, the per capita income of Himachal Pradesh at current prices in 2010-11 stood at Rs. 65,535. This shows an increase of 15.6 per cent over 2009-10 (Rs. 56,706). At constant prices (2004-05) the per capita income during 2010-11 is estimated at Rs. 47,106 against Rs. 43,305 in 2009-10 witnessing an increase of 8.8 per cent (Department of Economics and Statistics, 2012).

6.A.1.v   Agriculture and Allied Activities

Agriculture is the largest and most important sector in the economic life of Himachal Pradesh. Agriculture being the largest single industry and main occupation of the people of the Pradesh has special place in the prosperity and development of the state. Agriculture feeds the process of development. It meets the needs for foodgrains on account of rise in incomes, as also of increase in population. It also supplies raw materials for many consumer items like edible oils, sugar cloth, etc (Balokhra, 2010).

Agriculture is the main occupation of the people of Himachal Pradesh and has an important place in the economy of the state. The state of Himachal Pradesh is only state in the country whose 89.96 per cent as per 2011 Census of Population lives in rural areas. Therefore, dependency on agriculture/horticulture is eminent as it provides direct employment to the workers of the state. Agriculture happens to be the premier source of State Income (GSDP). About 16 per cent of the total Gross State Domestic Product comes from agriculture and its allied sectors. Out of the total geographical area of 55.67 lakh hectares, the area of operational holdings is about 9.68 lakh hectares and is operated by 9.33 lakh farmers. The average holding size comes to 1.04 hectare. Distribution of land holdings according to 2005-06 Agricultural Census shows that 87.03 per cent of the total holdings are of small and marginal farmers, 12.54 per cent of holdings are owned by semi-medium/medium farmers and only 0.43 percent by large farmers (Department of Economics and Statistics, 2012).

The rich diversity of agro-climatic conditions, topographical variations and altitudinal differences coupled with fertile, deep and well drained soils favour the cultivation of temperate to sub- tropical fruits in Himachal Pradesh. The region is also suitable for cultivation of ancillary horticultural produce like flowers, mushroom, honey and hops. This particular suitability of Himachal has resulted in shifting of land use pattern from agriculture to fruit crops in the past few decades ((Department of Economics and Statistics, 2012). Apple is so far the most important fruit crop of Himachal Pradesh, which constitutes about 48 per cent of total area under fruit crops and about 87 per cent of the total fruit production (Department of Economics and Statistics, 2012).

6.A.1.vi   Industries

Industrialization in Himachal Pradesh is comparatively a recent phenomenon. The severe climatic conditions, topographical and geographical severities are the main hurdles in this process. In such a scenario, the monetary and fiscal benefits in the form of incentives and subsidies as well as the development of appropriate infrastructure are the main instruments to woo industrial investment in the state. Though the industrialization in the state has not been able to gather momentum as compared to the neighboring states like Punjab, Haryana, U.P. and Uttrakhand, yet with investment in infrastructural facilities, formulation of well-defined policies, scientific management marshaling and optimization of scarce resources, Himachal Pradesh have been able to offset the locational and geographical disadvantages to a considerable extent (Planning Department, 2010).

Himachal Pradesh has made significant achievements in the field of industrialization in the past few years. With ushering in the liberalized economy and consequent de-licensing and notification of special package of incentives for the state, the flow of investment in the Pradesh has increased manifold resulting in very good response for setting up new industrial ventures in the state. As on December 2011, there were 474 medium and large-scale industries and about 38,409 small-scale industries with a total investment of about Rs. 14,146.58 crore working in the state. These industries have provided employment to about 2.61 lakh persons (Department of Economics and Statistics, 2011).

6.A.1.vii   Power

Power is a critical infrastructure for the socio-economic development of the country. This century would be dependent on the availability of adequate, reliable and quality power at competitive rate. Therefore, the basic responsibility of Electricity Industry is to provide adequate power at economical cost, while ensuring reliability and quality of supply. Development of hydro-power is essential for the sustainable development of the country and efforts for accelerating the pace of hydro power development shall give an impetus for the economic growth in the new globalized economy (Planning Department, 2010).

Himachal Pradesh is blessed with abundant water resources in its five major rivers, that is, Chenab, Ravi, Beas, Satluj and Yamuna, which emanate from the western Himalayas and flow through the state (Planning Department, 2010). There are various sources, from which energy can be obtained namely, burning coal, oil, gas, wood waste and nuclear materials. However, the most vital source of energy, which man found, is the power of water when it falls from a height. Himachal Pradesh has a vast hydel power potential (Balokhra, 1995). The state has a potential to generate 23,560 MW hydel power through various major, medium, small, mini and micro projects on the five river basins. In view of the technological advancement and environment-friendly techniques, total potential of the state of Himachal for power generation can go up to 25,000 MW (Chaudhry, 2006).

6.A.1.viii   Water Resources and Drainage System

Himachal has a distinction of supplying water to Indus river system and Ganga river system, that is, part of the state's river drain into the Arabian Sea and part into Bay of Bengal. The state is drained by a number of rivers and streams (Jreat, 2004). Five perennial rivers (Satluj, Beas, Ravi, Chenab and Yamuna) flow through its territory. The utility of these rivers for irrigation is very much limited due to the rugged and undulating terrain of the state. Nevertheless, these rivers possess immense potential for generation of Hydroelectricity. Thus, what these rivers lack is their potential contribution to agricultural productivity is amply compensated for in the form of hydro-electric potential, the modern engines of overall socio economic development (Sharma, 1987). There are few lakes in Himachal, necessarily small in sizes, but well known for their scenic beauty. Himachal Pradesh has one of the largest artificial lakes in India, Govind Sagar. The other lakes are those of Riwalsar, Khajjiar, Manimahesh, Prashar, Renuka, Chander Tal and Suraj Tal, etc (Thakur, 1996).

6.A.1.ix   Tourism

Tourism in Himachal Pradesh has been recognized as one of the most important sectors of the economy as it is being realized as a major engine of growth for future. State is endowed with all the basic resources necessary for thriving tourism activity like geographical and cultural diversity, clean, peaceful, and beautiful streams, scared shrines, historic monuments and friendly and hospitable people. Tourism industry in Himachal Pradesh has been given very high priority and the government has developed appropriate infrastructure for its development which includes provision of public utility services, roads, communication network, airports, transport facilities, etc. for the year 2011-12 there is an allotment of Rs. 2,094.44 lakh for development of Tourism and Rs. 167.97 lakh for Civil Aviation (Department of Economics and Statistics, 2012).

6.A.1.x   Education

From the lowest literacy level at the time of independence, Himachal today ranks 11th among the states and UTs in India. Its literacy rate was recorded at 77.1 per cent as against the national average of 65.4 per cent in the 2001 Census (Planning Commission, 2005). As per the 2011 (P) Census, literacy rate of Himachal Pradesh is 83.8 per cent and male and female literacy rate is 90.8 per cent and 76.6 per cent respectively (Himachal in Figures 2010-11). Education receives priority in the state and allocation of resources is much higher in Himachal Pradesh than in Punjab, Haryana, Kerala and at the all-India level. The age-specific enrolment rate is also much higher. The state has also reduced its dropout rates considerably up to the elementary level (Planning Commission, 2005).

Section – B

This section evaluates the organizational structure for the consumer protection in Himachal Pradesh. Firstly, it reviews the organizational setup and secondly, it evaluates the performance of state commission and district forums in Himachal Pradesh.

6.B.1. The Department Of Food, Civil Supplies And Consumer Affairs

The Department of Food, Civil Supplies and Consumer Affairs came into existence as a separate unit in the State during the year 1966. It was a part of co-operative department prior to this arrangement. This department is the backbone of the State Government. The organization of Weights and Measures was also merged with the department during the year, 1981. The department mainly deals with the demand and supply of various essential commodities in the open market as well as Public Distribution System. The basic responsibility of the department is the enforcement of various control orders against the Essential Commodities Act, 1955 for Price Stabilization and matter relating to Weights & Measures.

The main motives of the department are:

1 To strengthen the Targeted Public Distribution System.
2 To ensure easy availability of Essential Commodities on reasonable rates.
3 To create awareness amongst the consumers about their rights.

6.B.1.i. Structure Of The Department

The Department of Food, Civil Supplies and Consumer Affairs is headed by a Minister, who is the political head of the department. He is assisted by the Additional Chief Secretary (Food, Civil Supplies and Consumer Affairs) to the Government of Himachal Pradesh. They have the overall responsibility of the department. The Additional Chief Secretary is responsible for the smooth functioning of the department.

6.B.1.i.a) Directorate

The department has two separate organizations at the directorate level, namely, Food, Civil Supplies & Consumer Affairs and Weights & Measures. He is assisted at the Directorate Level by one Additional/ Joint/ Deputy Director (Admin) of H.A.S. cadre, one Joint Director, two Deputy Directors, one Law Officer and one Deputy Controller (Finance & Accounts) besides other supporting staff. Hierarchical structure of the Department of Food, Civil Supplies and Consumer Affairs at the secretariat and directorate level has been shown in Figure 6.1.

6.B.1.i.b) Zonal Office

There is a Zonal Office at Dharamsala in Kangra District headed by a Joint Director. He is assisted by one Food & Supplies Officer and the other supporting staff. He carries out the duties and responsibilities as assigned by the Government from time to time besides supervision of the working of 8

Districts under his control. These Districts are Kangra, Hamirpur, Una, Chamba, Kullu, Bilaspur, Mandi and Lahaul & Spiti (Department of Food, Civil Supplies and Consumer Affairs, 2013). Zonal level hierarchical structure has been shown in Figure 6.2.

Figure 6.1
Organizational Structure at the Secretariat and Directorate level in Himachal Pradesh

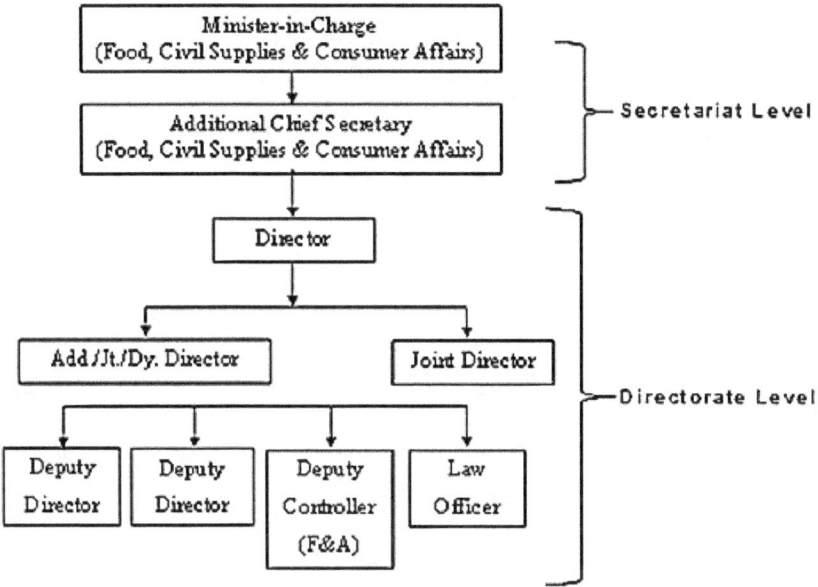

Note: Add. = Additional; Jt. = Joint; Dy. = Deputy; F&A = Finance and Account.

Figure 6.2
Organizational Hierarchy at Zonal Level

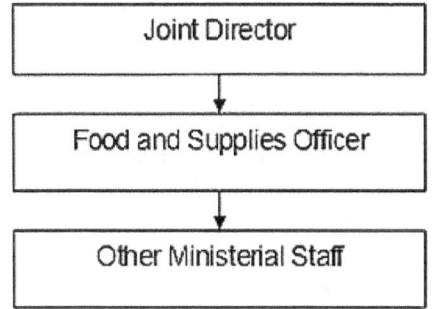

6.B.1.i.c) District Level Set Up

There are 12 District Officers of the department in the State. Each District Office is headed by a District Controller, Food, Civil Supplies and

Consumer Affairs. These District Heads are assisted by a Food & Supplies Officer, Inspector and other supporting staff (Department of Food, Civil Supplies and Consumer Affairs, 2013). District level organizational setup for the protection of consumer in Himachal Pradesh has been shown in Figure 6.3.

Figure 6.3
Organizational Hierarchy at the District Level

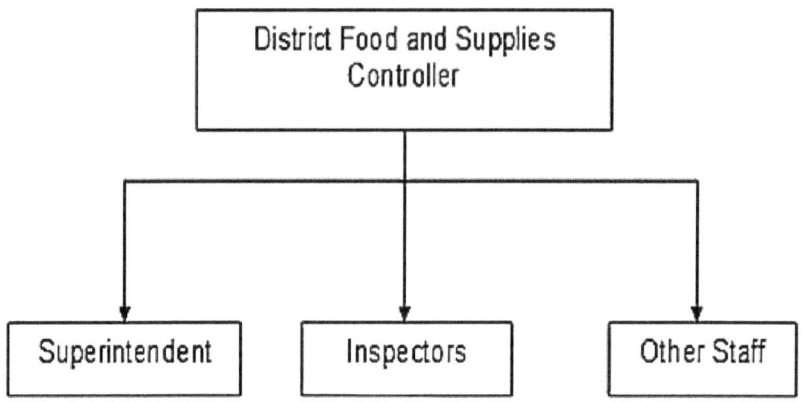

6.B.1.ii. Functions Of The Department

The department functions differently at various levels of the administration in District, State and Centre respectively. Again, at each level there are following jobs related to monitoring of (Department of Food, Civil Supplies and Consumer Affairs, 2013):

- Market Rates
- Allocation and Lifting
- Ration Cards
- Fair Price Shops
- Inspections/Raids
- Issuances of Licenses

The information relating day to day activities are being reported on Daily, Weekly basis to the Ministry of Food & Civil Supplies, Govt. of India. The information generated at Fair Price Shops and Inspectorate level is compiled at District Level and sent to the State H. Q. where it is again compiled and consolidated and then conveyed to the Centre.

The department performs many functions related to supply of food-grains, managing public distribution system and other related activities. A detailed discussion on various schemes of the department has been presented as below.

6.B.1.ii.a)   Targeted Public Distribution System

Public Distribution System is the main area of thrust, which has been renamed as 'Targeted Public Distribution System' with   effect from 1.6.1997. The entire population of the State has been covered under the Targeted Public Distribution System. It is being implemented through a network of Fair Price Shops.

Table 6.2
Breakup of Fair Price Shops in Himachal Pradesh

Cooperative	Panchayats	HPSC SC	Individuals	Mahila Mandals	Total
2927	40	129	1302	5	4403

Source: Department of Food, Civil Supplies and Consumer Affairs, District Una (Himachal Pradesh).

The sector-wise breakup of fair price shops in Himachal Pradesh in Table 6.2. reveals that there are 4403 Fair Price Shops as on 31/03/2009.

Table 6.3
District-wise Details of APL, BPL and AAY Families in the State

Sr. No.	District Name	Number of Families			
		A.P.L.	B.P.L.	A.A.Y	Total
1.	Bilaspur	58132	18225	12272	88629
2.	Chamba	47419	35043	31607	114069
3.	Hamirpur	86055	21373	13601	121029
4.	Kangra	254513	68900	43579	366992
5.	Kinnaur	11771	4744	1870	18385
6.	Kullu	67181	18323	7811	93315
7.	Mandi	171784	47929	28932	248645
8.	Shimla	118251	35105	21691	175047
9.	Sirmaur	68429	21130	10219	99778
10.	Solan	72589	22381	12420	107390
11.	Una	83802	21079	11508	116389
12	Lahaul & Spiti	4167	2668	1590	8425
	Total	1044093	316900	197100	1558093

Source: Department of Food,Civil Supplies and Consumer Affairs, Delhi
Note: APL = Above Poverty Line; BPL = Below Poverty Line and AAY= Antodya Anna Yojana

Under the Targeted Public Distribution System, the consumers have been categorized as (Above Poverty Line (APL) and Below Poverty Line (BPL) families. District-wise details of APL, BPL and AAY families in Himachal Pradesh has been shown in Table 6.3.

The families living below the poverty line have been categorized as

Below Poverty Line (BPL) families. There are 15,58,093 ration cardholders in the State out of which the no. of (Above Poverty Line (APL) families in the State are 10,44,093 whereas the no. of Below Poverty Line (BPL) families in the State are 3,16,900 and under antodaya yojna 1,97,100 families.

The scale of allotment of food grains and other essential commodities from the Govt. of India at present has been presented in Table 6.4.

Table 6.4
Scale of Allotment of Good Grains and other Essential Commodities

Sr. No.	Commodity	Allocation Per month			Total	Central Issue Price (in Qtl./kl.)		
		AAY	BPL	APL		AAY	BPL (w.e.f. 12/7/2001)	APL (w.e.f. 12/7/2001)
1	Wheat	3942	6338	14490	24770	Rs. 200	Rs. 415	Rs. 610
2	Rice Grade - A	2953	4757	7118	14828	Rs. 300	Rs. 565	Rs. 830
3	Levy Sugar	-	-		4722	Rs. 1350		
4	Kerosene Oil	-	-		5411 Kl	Rs. 8066.61 to Rs. 8533.56 per Kl		

Source: Department of Food, Civil Supplies and Consumer Affairs, Delhi
Note: APL = Above Poverty Line; BPL = Below Poverty Line and AAY= Antodya Anna Yojana

Two major schemes have been implemented under Public Distribution System in Himachal Pradesh. These schemes are as under.

a) Annapurna Scheme

'ANNAPURNA' a centrally sponsored scheme has been introduced by the State Govt. in the Pradesh w.e.f. 1.4.2000. The numerical ceiling of the beneficiaries to be covered under this scheme fixed by the Govt. of India at 3426 persons for this State for providing food security to the old destitute/indigent citizens of 65 years of age or above who are eligible for Old Age Pension under the 'National Old Age Pension Scheme' (NOAPS), but are not receiving the same under the scheme. This ceiling has further been fixed by the Govt. of India to 6373 persons. Out of this target 3646 persons have been identified. Under this scheme the beneficiaries are being provided 10 Kgs of Wheat/ Rice free of cost per month.

b) Antodaya Anna Yojna

The Govt. of India has launched another scheme titled as 'ANTODAYA ANNA YOJNA' throughout the country for the poorest of the poor families which has been introduced in this State w.e.f. 01/03/2001. Ceiling of 156000 poorest of the poor families to be covered under this scheme has been fixed for this State by the Govt. of India. The same number of families against the ceiling fixed have been identified under the scheme out of 142181 families already identified under B.P.L. At present, these families are being provided 35 Kgs. of food grains i.e. 15 Kgs of Wheat at the rates of Rs. 2.00 per Kg and 20 Kg of Rice at the rates of Rs. 3.00 per Kg per family per month.

6.B.1.ii.b) Availability of Food Grains

The population of the State as based on the ration cards is 72,32,983 as on 31/03/2009 and taking 15 Kgs. of food-grains as an average consumption per unit, the requirement of food grains comes to 108495 MTs. per month and 13.10 Lac MTs. per annum. Due to easy availability of food grains, there is no restriction on interstate movement at present. The requirement of food-grains under the Public Distribution System (PDS) is being made by the Govt. of India to the State on historic basis, through the Food Corporation of India (FCI) for which this deptt. is required to make advance financial arrangements with the FCI through the HIMACHAL PRADESH State Civil Supplies Corporation. Ltd. to procure the allotted and required quantity from the declared principal distribution centers of the FCI. The sub-allocation of food grains and the financial arrangements thereof is made as per the requirement placed by the District Officers. At present 35 Principal Distribution Centres of F.C.I. are functioning in the State i.e. 12 at each district headquarter and the remaining 23 at Bharmour, Tisa, Baijnath, Dehra, Rampur Bushar, Hatkoti, Karsog, Naura-Dhar, Sarkaghat, Jaisinghpur, Killar(Pangi), Kaza, Janjehli, Banjar, Udaipur, Dodrakawar, Chopal, Narkanda, Anni, Pooh, Arki, Bara-bangal & Shillai.

Under the T.P.D.S. network the State Govt. is required to arrange lifting of food grains through the HIMACHAL PRADESH State Civil Supplies Corporation Ltd. from the declared P.D.Cs of F.C.I. and arrange its transportation to its wholesale godowns for further distribution to fair price shops as per their requirements.

6.B.1.ii.c) Control over the Prices

The State of Himachal Pradesh depends upon all the Essential Commodities from Neighboring States of Punjab, Haryana and Delhi for its requirement. The price fluctuation in the wholesale market of the neighboring States directly influences the wholesale and retail prices in the Pradesh. The State Government has practically no control over the prevailing prices at the source. However, the Government has been exercising control over the availability and prices of Essential Commodities in the open market by enforcing various statutory provisions under the following Acts and Control Orders:-

1 The Essential Commodities Act, 1955.
2 The Prevention of Black Marketing and Maintenance of Supplies of Essential Commodities Act, 1980.

3   Himachal Pradesh Commodity Price Marking and Display Order, 1977.

4   Himachal Pradesh Hoarding and Profiteering Prevention Order, 1977.

5   Himachal Pradesh Specified Articles (Regulation of Distribution) Order, 2003.

6   Himachal Pradesh Trade Articles (Licensing and Control) Order, 1981.

7   Liquefied Petroleum Gas (Regulation of Supply and Distribution) Order, 2000.

8   Himachal Pradesh Bricks (Control) Act, 1969.

9   Himachal Pradesh Bricks (Control) Order, 1970.

10 Himachal Pradesh Coal (Licensing and Price Control) Order, 1989.

11 Motor Spirit and High Speed Diesel (Prevention of Mal-Practices in Supply and Distribution)Order,2005.

12 Kerosene (restriction on Use and Fixation of Ceiling Price) Order, 1993.

13 The Consumer Protection Act, 1986.

14 Himachal Pradesh Consumer Protection Rules, 1998.

15 Edible Oil (Packaging and Regulation) Order, 1998.

16 Public Distribution System (Control) Order, 2001.

17 Himachal Pradesh Rice Procurement (Levy) Order,2001.

18 The Solvent Reffinate and Slop(Acquisition, Sale, Storage and Prevention of use in Automobiles) Order, 2000

19 Naptha (Acquisition, Sale, Storage and Prevention of use in Automobiles) Order, 2000

20 Liquefied Petroleum Gas (Regulation of Use in Motor Vehicles) Orders, 2001.

21 Household Electrical Appliances (Quality Control) Orders, 1981.

The brief introduction of the above mentioned Acts and Orders are as under:

i)   The Essential Commodities Act, 1955:

It is a Central Act to provide, in the interests of the general public, for the control of the production, supply, and distribution of, and trade and commerce in, certain commodities.

ii)   The Prevention Of Black Marketing And Maintenance Of Supplies Of Essential Commodities Act, 1980:

Vide this order the Officer/Official of the Food and Supplies and Consumer Affairs Deptt. are empowered for detention in certain cases for the purpose of prevention of black-marketing and maintenance of supplies of commodities essential to the community/consumers and for the matter connected therewith.

iii) Himachal Pradesh Commodities Price Marking And Display Order, 1977:

Vide this letter, every shopkeeper is under obligation to display the ultimate retail prices including taxes etc. payable by a consumer at the business premises for information of the consumers. These prices are to be marked/displayed on the packets, containers of such articles per unit and on every meter of cloth.

iv) Himachal Pradesh Hoarding And Profiteering (Prevention) Order, 1977:

Vide this order, Director of Food and Supplies or District Magistrates of the concerned Districts are empowered to fix through notifications maximum margin of profit which a dealer in a specified commodity can charge over his landed cost besides the maximum retail prices to be charged by the dealer among other provisions for possession and sale of any commodity by a dealer and consumer at a given time in the event of scarcity of any commodity listed in the schedule appended thereto.

v) Himachal Pradesh Specified Articles (Regulation Of Distribution) Order, 2003:

This order lays down the provisions and procedures for distribution of specified commodities to the consumer through the Distribution Card (Ration Card) in the fair price shops, which are regulated under the network of Targeted Public Distribution system.

vi) Himachal Pradesh Trade Articles (Licensing And Control) Order, 1981:

Vide this composite statutory Order, the trade is being regulated through licenses issued to a dealer dealing in specified commodities over and above a specified quantity at a given time. This order enables the Department to exercise check over the stocks of commodities of daily use by the dealers in the State for regulating their equitable distribution on fixed prices.

vii) The Liquefied Petroleum Gas (Regulation And Distribution) Order, 2000:

Vide this order, the detailed provisions and procedure for distribution of Liquefied Petroleum Gas through the network of Public Distribution System is being regulated through licenses/authorization issued to a dealer/oil companies dealing in L.P.G. over and above at a given time. This order enables the Department to exercise check over the stocks of L.P.G. in the State for regulating their equitable distribution on fixed price.

viii)   The Himachal Pradesh Bricks (Control) Act, 1969:

Vide this Act, the Govt. has empowered the Officer/Official of the Food and Supplies Deptt. for maintaining or increasing the supply of Bricks for their equitable distribution and availability at fair price and it may by order notified in the Official Gazetteer, provide for regulating by licenses, permits or otherwise the manufacture, storage distribution, transport, acquisition of disposal of Bricks, for collecting any information or statistics with a view to the regulation of the aforesaid matters, for grant or issue of licenses, permits or other documents and the charging of fee therefore, for controlling the price at which bricks may be bought or sold, for requiring dealers or kin owners to maintain and produce for inspection such accounts and records regarding bricks and to furnish such information relating thereto, as may be specified to in the order.

ix)   The Himachal Pradesh Bricks (Control) Order, 1970:

This order lays down detailed provisions and procedure for obtaining licenses for brick-kilns as also for fixation of sale rate for bricks manufactured by such brick-kilns.

x)   The Himachal Pradesh Coal Licensing And Price Control Order, 1989:

The provisions of this order enable the Department to regulate through licenses the procurement, distribution and price control of the coal/coke against the sponsored quota as also through other sources.

xi)   The Motor Spirit And High Speed Diesel (Prevention Of Malpractices In Supply And Distribution) Order, 2005:

Under this order, the supply of Motor spirit and High Speed Diesel through the network of Public Distribution System is being regularized.

xii)   Kerosene (Restriction On Use And Fixation Of Ceiling Price Order, 1993:

This order lays down the procedure for obtaining the licenses for Kerosene dealers dealing in Kerosene through the network of Public Distribution System.

xiii) Consumer Protection Act, 1986:

This Act lays down detailed provisions and procedures for redressel of grievances and to provide for better protection of the interests of the consumers and for that purpose to make provisions for the establishment of consumer councils and other authorities for the settlement of consumers, disputes and for matter connected therewith.

xiv) Himachal Pradesh Consumer Protection Rules, 1998:

These rules are made under sub clause 2 of clause 30 of the Consumer Protection Act, 1986. Vide these rules, the three-tier system of the consumer forums are defined. Vide this system, the functions, sittings, staff and salary etc. of the Distt. Forum, State Commission and National Commission are clarified.

xv) The Edible Oil (Packaging And Regulation) Order, 1998:

This order is strictly enforced by the State Goa, which would minimize contamination, maintain hygienic conditions, check deterioration in quality, ensure correct weight and provide information in respect of its contents, price and date of manufacture. The State of HIMACHAL PRADESH has empowered the Officers/Officials of the Food and Supplies Deptt. for implementation of the order.

xvi) Public Distribution System (Control) Order, 2001:

This order is mainly meant for the smoothly functioning of the Targeted Public Distribution System in various States. Under clause 5 of the annexure attached with this order, the Govt. of India shall authorise all the State Govt. to issue a separate control order is their States for proper functioning of the Targeted Public Distribution System. The State of HIMACHAL PRADESH has already issued HIMACHAL PRADESH Specified Articles(Regulation of Distribution) Order 2003. This order lays down the provisions and proceedings for distribution if specified commodities to the consumers through the Distribution Card(ration card) in the fair price shops, which are regulated under the network of Targeted Public Distribution System.

xvii) H. P. Rice Procurement (Levy) Order, 2001:

This order has been issued by the State Govt. for the purpose of procurement of Rice by the Govt. procurement agencies for maintaining the Stocks of Rice for being distributed to the public through the Targeted Public Distribution System as also ensuring remunerative price of Rice to the farmers.

xviii) The Solvent Reffinate and Slop (Acquisition, Sale, Storage And Prevention Of Use In Automobiles) Order, 2000:

This order has been issued by the Govt. of India for the purpose of restriction on sale and use of solvents, reffinates, slops and other products. This order lays down detailed provisions and procedure for obtaining license, for acquire, store or sell solvent, raffinate, slops or their equivalent and other products issued by the State Govt. or the District Magistrate or any other officer authorized by the Central/State Govt. According to this order no person shall either use or help in any manner the user of solvents, raffinated, slops or their equivalent or other products except Motor Spirit and High Speed Diesel in any automobile.

xix) Naptha (Acquisition, Sale, Storage And Prevention Of Use In Automobiles) Order, 2000:

This order has been issued by the Govt. of India for the purpose of restriction on sale and use of Naptha. This order lays down detailed provisions and procedure for obtaining license, for acquire, store or sell Naptha issued by the State Govt. or the District Magistrate or any other officer authorised by the State Govt. According to this order no person shall either use or help in any manner the user of Naptha except Motor Spirit and High Speed Diesel and/or any other fuel permitted by the Central Govt. in any automobile.

xx) Liquefied Petroleum Gas(Regulation Of Use In Motor Vehicles)) Order, 2001:

This order has been issued by the Govt. of India for the purpose of acquire, store for sale, supply, fill or distributed auto LPG to a consumer except according to the provisions contained in this order. According to this order no person shall store, supply, sell or dispense aoto LPG unless he is aoto LPG dispensing dealer. This order enables the Department to check over the acquire, store for sale, supply, fill or distributed auto LPG to a consumers according to the provisions.

6.B.2. Consumer Courts for the Redressal of Consumer Grievances in Himachal Pradesh

Consumer Protection has a wide agenda. It not only includes educating consumers about their rights and responsibilities, but also helps in getting their grievances redressed. It not only requires judicial machinery for protecting the interests of consumers but also requires the consumers to get together and form themselves into consumer associations for protection and promotion of their interests. For the redressal of consumer grievances a well-organized structure of consumer courts has been established in Himachal Pradesh. The system of judicial setup has been established as per the provision Consumer Protection Act, 1986.

6.B.2.i. Himachal Pradesh State Consumer Disputes Redressal Commission

The Government of India enacted a Statue through Parliament named as Consumer Protection Act, 1986. Its implementation was left to the State Governments. The State Government implemented it on different dates. Under the Act, there is a provision for the formation of State Consumer

Protection Councils and National Consumer Protection Council. There is a provision for the establishment of three tire redressal machinery known as National Consumer Disputes Redressal Commission i.e. National Commission, the State Consumer Disputes Redressal Commission known as State Commission and the District Consumer Disputes Redressal Forum known as District Forum.

In Himachal Pradesh, the State Government has established the State Commission in the first instance with its headquarters at State Capital Shimla which started functioning w.e.f. *01.11.1989* and also the Himachal Pradesh State Consumer Protection Council was formed. The posts were created in the Department of Food and Supplies, Himachal Pradesh and Director Food and Supplies, being the Head of Department filled up all these posts. In the lone District Forum, at Shimla, staff was provided by the Director Food and Supplies, Himachal Pradesh

The First President of State Commission was Mr. Justice V. P. Gupta a retired Judge of Himachal Pradesh High court. There were two whole time Members. The male Member was Mr. Hem Chand , a retired I.A.S. Officer and the other was the Female Member Mrs. Devendera Kumari from Chamba. At that time the peculiar jurisdiction of the District Forum was up to 1 lac and that of the State Commission was from 1 lac to 5 lacs. Mr. Justice V. P. Gupta assumed the charge on *01.11.1989* and retired after attaining the age of 65 years on *24.01.1991*.

The State Government then appointed Mr. Justice D. P. Sood, a sitting Judge of High Court of Himachal Pradesh as its President in addition to his own duties as a Judge of the High Court. The Member Mrs. Devendera Kumari resigned After the resignation of Mrs. Devendera Kumari, Mrs. Subh Mahajan was appointed as Member of the State Commission. After the 2 years tenure of Mr. Hem Chand as its Member, Mr. V. Verma, a retired Secretary, Vidhan Sabha was appointed as its Member. During the year 1992, Mr. Justice R. B. Mishra, a retired Judge of Supreme Court of India was appointed as President of the State Commission. Thereafter in 1993, the State Government appointed Mr. Justice S. K. Seth, a retired Chief Justice of the High Court of Himachal Pradesh as President, State Commission. [1]

Hierarchy of State Consumer Disputes Redressal Commission in Himachal Pradesh has been given in Figure 6.4.

The Commission is headed by a President (of the rank of High court Judge). He is assisted by a registrar and two members, that is, one male and one female. Then there is Assistant Registrar, Private Secretary, Personal Assistant and Superintendent and other supporting staff.

---

[1] History of consumer protection at Himachal Pradesh, retrieved on 14-09-2012 from website http://hpconsumercommission.nic.in/hist.htm.

6.B.2.i.a) Jurisdiction of State Commission

The jurisdiction of Himachal Pradesh State Redressal Commission has been defined by the act. The act provides the following.

Subject to the provisions of the Consumer Protection Act, the State Commission shall have jurisdiction:-

i) To entertain complaints where the value of the goods or services and compensation, if any, claimed exceeds rupees five lacs but does not exceed rupees twenty lakhs ; and appeals against the orders of any District Forum within the State; and

ii) To call for the records and pass appropriate orders in any consumer dispute which is pending before or has been decided by any District Forum within the State, where it appears to the State Commission that such District Forum has exercised a jurisdiction not vested in it by law, or has failed to exercise a jurisdiction so vested or has acted in exercise of its jurisdiction illegally or with material irregularity.

Figure 6.4
Hierarchy at Himachal Pradesh State Consumer Disputes Redressal Commission

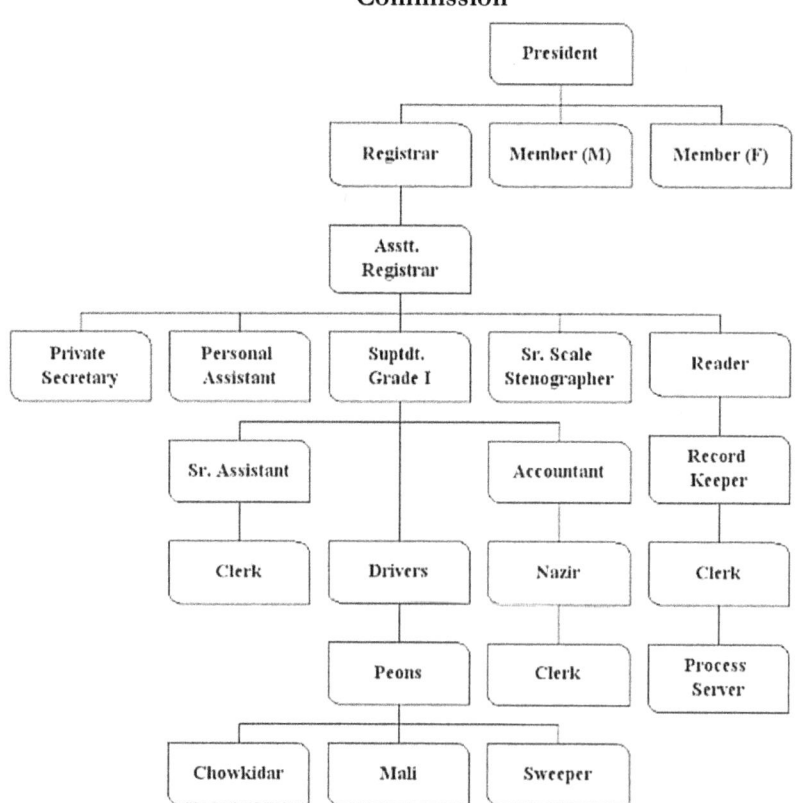

6.B.2.ii. Himachal Pradesh District Consumer Redressal Forums

President Session judge Rank. In Himachal Pradesh, the State Government has established the State Commission in the first instance with its headquarters at State Capital Shimla which started functioning w.e.f. 01.11.1989. During March,1995, the State Government established two whole time District Forums one at Mandi and the other at Kangra at Dharamshala in addition to one at Shimla which was already functioning as whole time District Forum.

The State Government during the year 1997 set up another whole time District Forum, at Una with its jurisdiction for the Districts of Una, Hamirpur and Bilaspur. With the opening of this District Forum, the jurisdiction of all the whole time District Forums, is as under:-

Shimla District Forum: Shimla, Solan, Sirmour and Kinnaur Districts.

Mandi District Forum: Mandi, Kullu, and Lahaul Spiti Districts.

Kangra District Forum: Kangra , Chamba and Una Districts.

Una District Forum: Una , Hamirpur and Bilaspur Districts.

Figure 6.5

Hierarchy at Himachal Pradesh District Consumer Disputes Redressal Commission

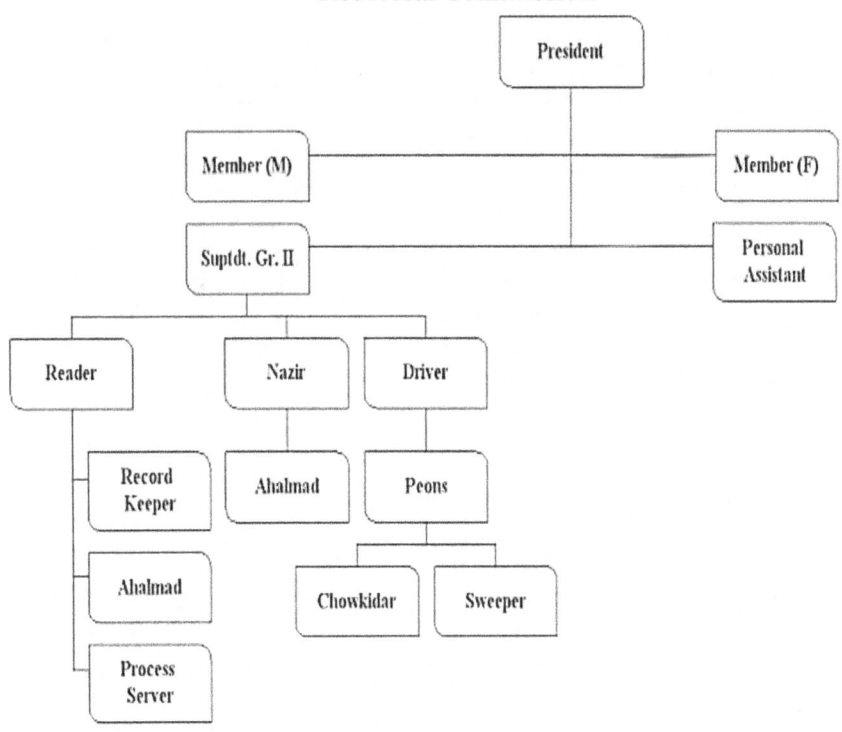

In all other remaining eight Districts only one male and one female Member on part-time basis have been appointed by the State Government. On circuit court to these Districts within their jurisdiction the President, Staff is required to visit the concerned District for sittings where the Members of that District participate in the sittings.

The act states following as the jurisdiction of Himachal Pradesh district forums.

Subject to the provisions of the Consumer Protection Act, the District Forum shall have jurisdiction to entertain complaints where the value of the goods or services and the compensation, if any, claimed does not exceed rupee five lacs.

A complaint shall be instituted in a District Forum within the local limits of whose jurisdiction,-

a) the opposite party or each of the opposite parties, where there are more than one, at the time of the institution of the complaint, actually and voluntarily resides or carries on business or has a branch office or personally works for gain, or

b) any of the opposite parties , where there are more than one, at the time of the institution of the complaint, actually and voluntarily resides, or caries on business or has a branch office, or personally works for gain, provided that in such case either the permission of the District Forum is given, or the opposite parties who do not reside, or carry on business or have a branch office, or personally work for gain, as the case may be, acquiesce in such institution ; or

c) the cause of action, whole or in part, arises.

6.B.3. Performance Of Himachal Pradesh State Commission And District Consumer Forums

In this section, an effort has been made to make a comparative analysis of working performance of both state commission and district forums. Information related to various district forums has been clubbed and consolidated to make an overall review. Performance of these agencies has been examined from various angles like number of cases resolved and pending out of total number of cases filed, time taken to resolve case if within or beyond prescribed time limits, year-wise changes in the proportionate number of cases disposed off and pending, and finally sectoral classification of complaints filed and disposed off.

6.B.3.i. Performance of Himachal Pradesh State Commission

The performance of Himachal Pradesh State Commission has been evaluated under various headings as under.

6.B.3.i.a) Year-wise Performance of Cases Resolved and Pending

In this case, to examine if the proportion of pending cases has been increasing year by year, an analysis of year wise performance separately for state commission and district forums has been made. The information below has been firstly presented for state commission and then for district forums. In some years, the number of cases disposed off is more than the number of cases filed. It has happened because in those years, a number of cases related to previous years have been resolved. Year-wise number of cases filed, disposed off and pending at the state commission has been shown in Table 6.5 and graphically in Chart 6.1.

Table 6.5
Year-wise Number of Cases Filed, Disposed off & Pending at State Commission

Years	STATE COMMISSION		
	Cases Filed in the year	Cases Disposed off in the year	Cases pending at the end
2001	6067	4324	1743
2002	984	2147	580
2003	1384	1361	603
2004	1369	1273	699
2005	1195	851	1043
2006	1664	2040	667
2007	1077	981	763

Source: Collection from State Consumer Dispute Redressal Commission, Shimla.

Table 6.5 shows that in case of state commission, the maximum number of cases was filed in the year 2001. In the subsequent years, the number has reduced significantly. Again, in the year 2002, the number of cases disposed off has been maximum. However, the speed of case resolving has been found to be quiet low in 2005 as the number of cases pending increased.

In Chart 6.1, red portion of bars shows the percentage of cases pending with the state commission. The chart shows that in the period ranging from year 2002 to year 2005, there is an increasing trend in the number of pending cases with the state commission. After this period, there has been a marginal decline in pending cases proportion. Thus it may be said that, after the year 2005, there has been an increase in the pace of resolving cases at the state commission.

221

Graph 6.1
Year-wise Performance of State Commission

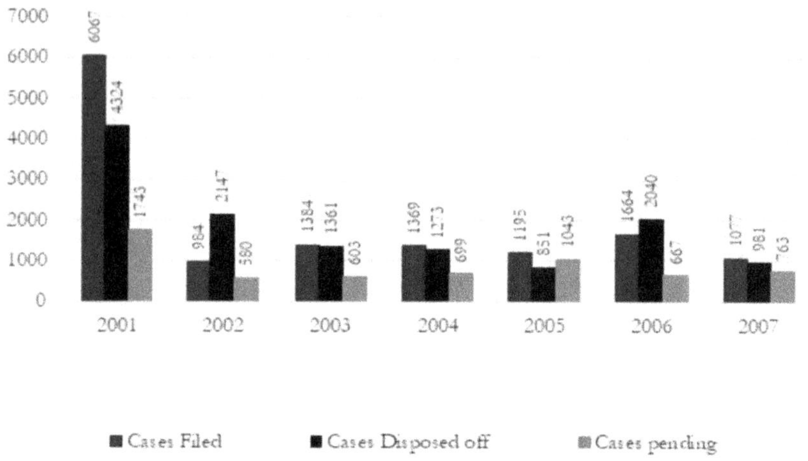

Cases Filed ■ Cases Disposed off ■ Cases pending

6.B.3.i.b) Category –wise Break Up of Cases

This part deals with the category wise break up of consumer cases. Categories include, banking services, medical services, telecom services, insurance services, housing services, electricity services, airlines, railways and other services. The purpose of this exercise has been to find which type of service has been reported for the maximum number of consumer disputes. And also to find the services where the dispute redressal has been speedy or services where the redressal has been extremely low. The category-wise break-up of cases at State Commission has been shown in Table 6.6 and Chart 6.2.

Table 6.6, in reference to state commission, shows that in case of insurance services, maximum number of consumer disputes has arisen. Hence, this industry has been reported for maximum number of consumer cases also. At the next are telephone or telecommunication services. After that is the category others. In the remaining of the cases, the number of complaints filed has been relatively low. It is worthwhile to note that case resolving has been extremely quick in case of airlines and railways. Thus, it can be said that telecom and insurance are the services where the consumer problems or consumer exploitations are the maximum.

The Chart 6.2 shows the proportional resolved and pending cases at state commission with regards to different industries or services. It is rather surprising that the proportion of pending cases has been at maximum in case of medical services followed by insurance and housing services.

Table 6.6
Category wise Break up of Cases at State Commission

Sr. No.	Category	Total No. of Cases Filed since inception	Total No. of Cases Disposed off since inception	Total No. of Cases pending since inception
1.	Banking	180	170	10
2	Medical	44	26	18
3.	Telephone	1430	1294	136
4	Insurance	1971	1692	279
5.	Housing	241	210	31
6.	Electricity	146	136	10
7.	Airlines	6	6	NIL
8.	Railways	20	20	NIL
9.	Others	1192	1102	90

Source: Collection from State Consumer Disputes and Redressal Commission, Shimla.

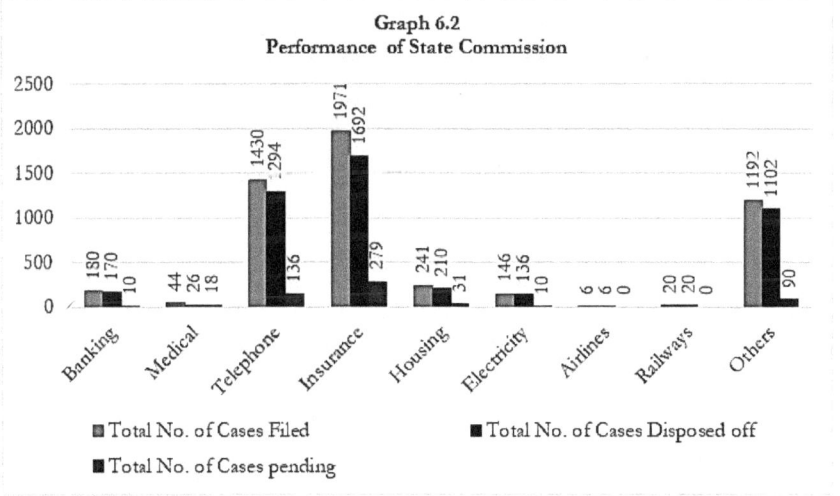

Graph 6.2
Performance of State Commission

Hence, it may be interpreted that it takes long time for state commission to dispose of cases of deficiency in medical and insurance services.

6.B.3.ii. Performance of District Forums in Himachal Pradesh

The performance of Himachal Pradesh State Commission has been evaluated under various headings as under.

6.B.3.ii.a) Year-wise Performance of Cases Resolved and Pending

Year-wise performance of cases filed, resolved and pending has been presented in Table 6.7 and graphically shown in Chart 6.3.

In case of district forums, as shown by table, there is a clear declining trend in all the years for number of cases filed, disposed off and pending. It is encouraging to see that the number of pending cases which were at 5197 in 2001, reduced to almost 2800 by the end of 2007. The reducing number of cases filed may be an indicator of reduced malpractices of business concerns and sellers due to increased level of awareness of consumers.

Table 6.7
Year-wise No. of Cases Filed, Disposed off & Pending at District Forums

Years	DISTRICT FORUMS		
	Cases Filed in the year	Cases Disposed off in the Year	Cases pending at the end
2001	29320	24123	5197
2002	4502	5306	4393
2003	3497	4633	3257
2004	2435	2781	2911
2005	1868	1913	2866
2006	2096	1880	3082
2007	973	1256	2799

Source: Collection from State Consumer Disputes and Redressal Commission, Shimla.

Graph 6.3
Year-wise Performance of District Forum

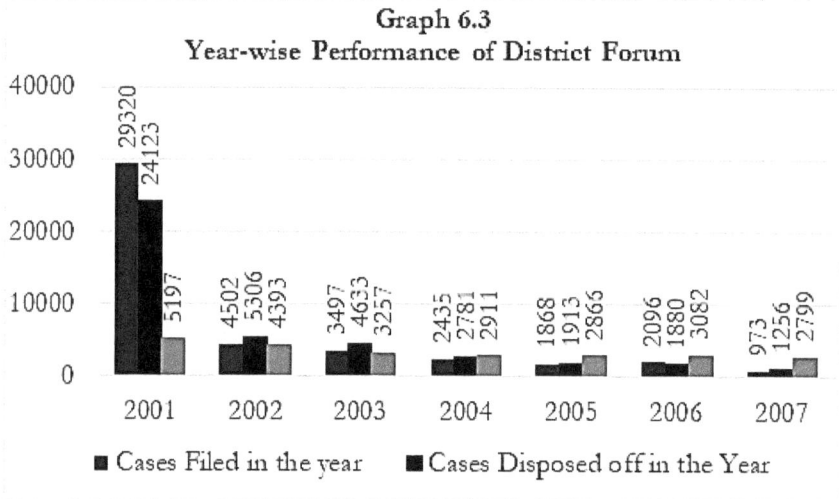

■ Cases Filed in the year   ■ Cases Disposed off in the Year

224

A contrasting result is available however, if percentage bar diagram is used. Chart shows that though the number of cases pending has been reducing constantly, yet the number of cases resolved has also come down. Due to this fact, the proportion of pending cases in total number of cases of district forums has also increased. Thus, it may be said that the number of cases filed has decreased significantly which accounted for decreased number of pending cases also. But, the speed of resolving cases at district forums has not been really impressive.

6.B.3.ii.b)   Category –wise Break Up of Cases

Category-wise break up of cases at District forums in Himachal Pradesh has been presented in Table 6.8 and shown in Chart 6.4.

Table 6.8

Category wise Break up of Cases at District Forums (Consolidated)

Sr. No	Category	Total No. of Cases Filed since inception	Total No. of Cases Disposed off since inception	Total No. of Cases pending since inception
1.	Banking	956	823	133
2.	Medical	63	52	11
3.	Telephone	9409	8596	813
4.	Insurance	8735	8354	381
5.	Housing	2687	2545	142
6.	Electricity	2020	1945	75
7.	Airlines	6	6	NIL
8.	Railways	20	20	NIL
9.	Others	20804	19560	1244

Source: Collection from State Consumer Disputes and Redressal Commission, Shimla.

Table shows that maximum number of consumer cases in district forums has been filed in others like groceries, travel or anything else. Out of the remaining services, telephone service has been reported for many consumer cases followed by insurance services. So it is clear that both the state commission and district forums face or handle quite a lot of consumer cases with regards to deficiency in insurance and telecommunication services. Chart shows that cases on medical services have been taking maximum time to get resolved followed by banking services at district forums.

Other services are taking comparatively less time. The reason may be that in case of particularly medical services, it is never an easy task to hold doctors or hospitals responsible for negligence or deficiency in services. Establishing deficiency in both the medical and banking services is a tough task.

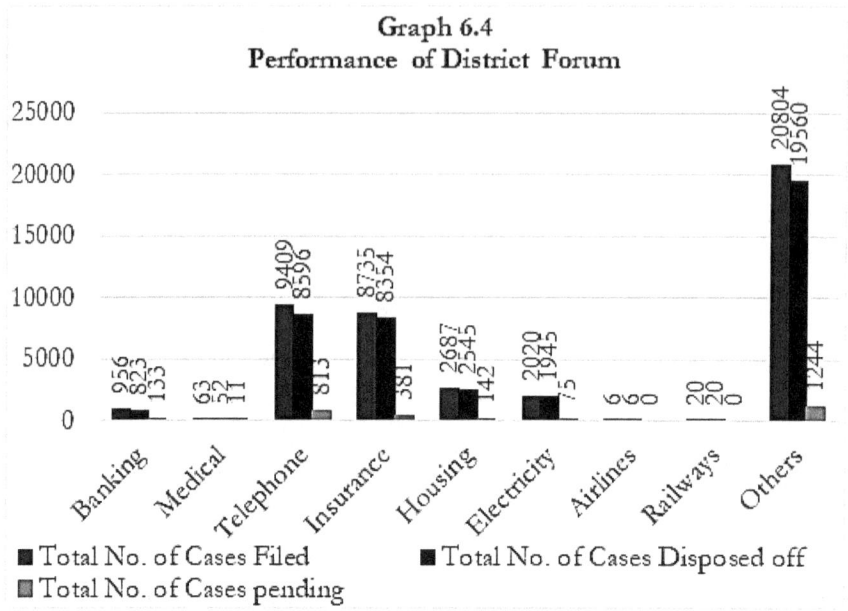

Graph 6.4
Performance of District Forum

■ Total No. of Cases Filed   ■ Total No. of Cases Disposed off
■ Total No. of Cases pending

6.B.3.iii. Performance of Various District Forums in Himachal Pradesh

This section covers district wise performance of eight out of twelve district forums of Himachal Pradesh. The performance evaluation of district forums has been carried out based on number of cases filed, number of cases resolved, and finally number of cases pending. It has been assumed that efficient district forums should resolve cases fast. Thus, there must be a higher proportion of cases disposed off as compared to the proportion of pending cases. The performance evaluation of these eight district forums for the last ten years is as below.

6.B.3.iii.a) Performance of District Forum Kullu

In case of Kullu district forum, the number of cases filed had been quite high in the beginning of the period of study. However, lately many of the cases have been disposed off. Due to this, the number of cases pending has come down drastically. Thus, this district forum is performing well. Year-wise detail of cases filed, disposed off and pending at the District Forum of Kullu has been enumerated in Table 6.9 and graphically shown in Chart 6.5.

Table 6.9 shows that number of cases disposed off were quite good in the first two years and towards the mid of the study. However, towards ending, the number of cases disposed off has come down. It seems that due to the speedy disposal of problems, the number of pending cases is also declining. However, this district forum should try to speedily dispose off cases now.

Table 6.9
Year-wise detail of Cases Filed, Disposed off and Pending in District Forum Kullu

Year	Cases filed in the years	Cases disposed of in the years	Cases pending at the end
2001-02	309	160	149
2002-03	275	194	81
2003-04	181	21	160
2004-05	244	122	122
2005-06	228	149	79
2006-07	230	101	129
2007-08	302	223	79
2008-09	100	64	36
2009-10	132	61	71
2010-11	150	71	79

Source: Collection from District Consumer Forum, Mandi.

Graph 6.5
Performance of District Forum Kullu

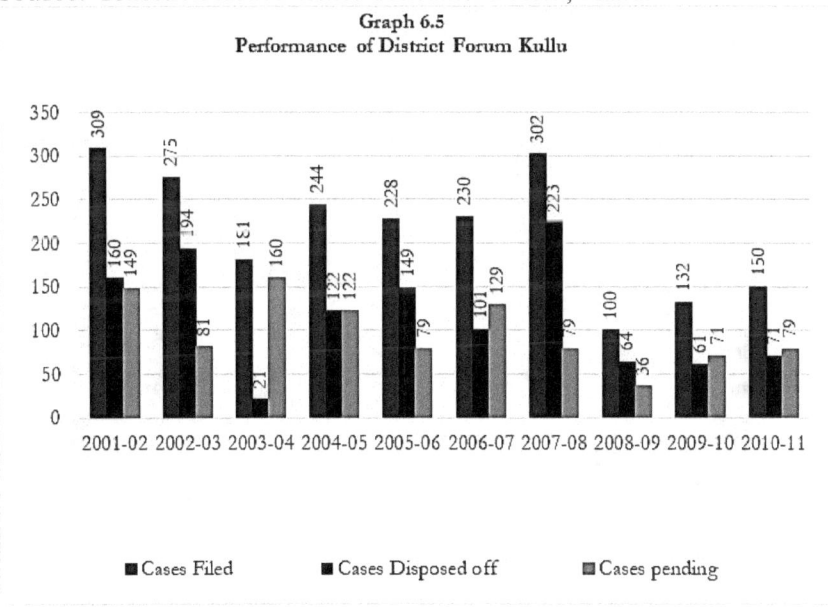

6.B.3.iii.b) Performance of District Forum Lahaul-Spiti

Lahaul Spiti district forum has been small in case of number of complaints filed. The number of complaints has never gone in two digits in this district forum. Besides, for two years 2005-06 and 2006-07, there has been no complaint filed in this district forum. Year-wise detail of cases filed, disposed off and pending at the District Forum Lahaul-Spiti has been enumerated in Table 6.10 and graphically shown in Chart 6.6.

Table 6.10

Case Disposal Performance of Lahaul-Spiti District Forum

Years	Cases filed in the years	Cases disposed off in the years	Cases pending at the end
2001-02	6	4	2
2002-03	2	1	1
2003-04	3	3	0
2004-05	2	2	0
2005-06	0	0	0
2006-07	0	0	0
2007-08	1	1	0
2008-09	2	0	2
2009-10	6	0	6
2010-11	7	0	7

Source: Collection from District Consumer Forum, Mandi.

Graph 6.6
Performance of District Forum Lahaul Spiti

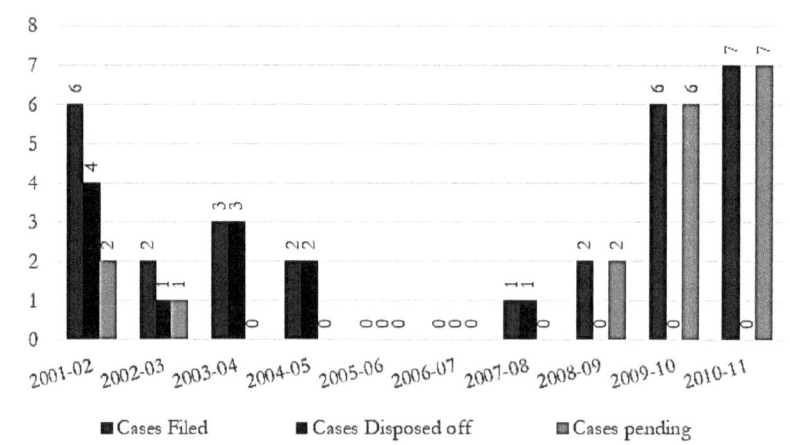

Table 6.10 shows that Lahaul Spiti district forum has been doing well, though the number of cases filed has been too low to comment strongly. However, for this particular district forum, for the last three years of study, not even a single consumer case has been disposed off. Thus, this district

forum almost seems to be non-functional. Hence, it should be considered as alarming situation.

6.B.3.iii.c) Performance of District Forum Mandi

Mandi district forum has been quite big in terms of number of cases filed. Hence, evidently this district forum has been a busy one. Here, the good thing is that of late, there has been a steep decline in the number of cases filed. Because of this, the number of cases disposed off and the number of cases pending with this district forums have been declining. Year-wise detail of cases filed, disposed off and pending at the District Forum Mandi has been enumerated in Table 6.11 and graphically shown in Chart 6.7.

Table 6.11 shows that in the first three years of the study, the number of cases filed had been more than two thousand in number. However, due to fast disposal of cases in the same period, there has been a decline in all numbers. Towards the end of the study, this district forum has maintained a good proportion disposed off cases. It can be said that, though there had been a large number of consumer cases filed, yet this forum has managed to dispose off nearly fifty percent of the total cases every year.

Table 6.11

Year-wise detail of Cases Filed, Disposed off and pending in District Forum Mandi

Year	Cases filed in the years	Cases disposed of in the years	Cases pending at the end
2001-02	2391	1053	1338
2002-03	2734	1491	1243
2003 04	2304	1415	889
2004-05	1266	774	492
2005-06	783	405	378
2006-07	726	375	351
2007-08	668	365	303
2008-09	396	234	162
2009-10	516	322	194
2010-11	553	311	242

Source: Collection from District Consumer Forum, Mandi.

Table 6.11 shows that in the first three years of the study, the number of cases filed had been more than two thousand in number. However, due to fast disposal of cases in the same period, there has been a decline in all numbers. Towards the end of the study, this district forum has maintained a good proportion disposed off cases. It can be said that, though there had been a large number of consumer cases filed, yet this forum has managed to dispose off nearly fifty percent of the total cases every year.

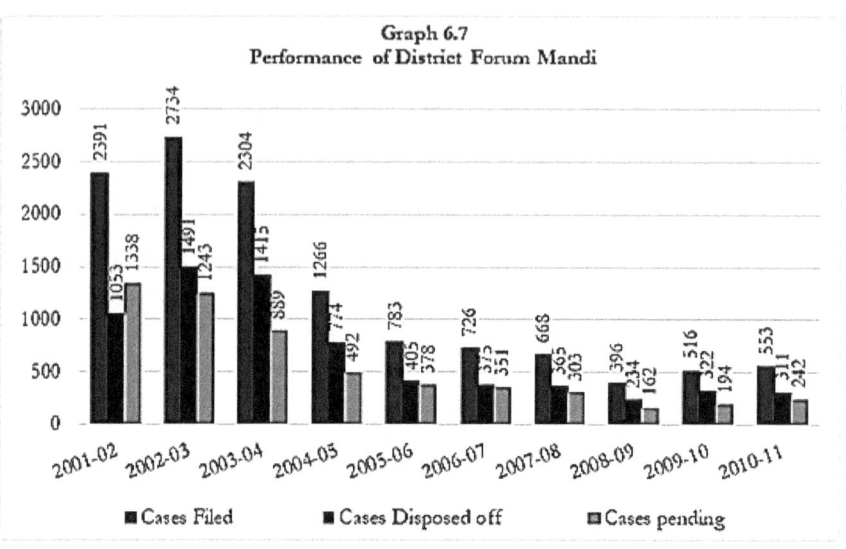

Graph 6.7
Performance of District Forum Mandi

■ Cases Filed   ■ Cases Disposed off   ▣ Cases pending

6.B.3.iii.d) Performance of District Forum Una

Una district forum has evidenced a lot many pending cases in the very first year of the study. Up to that time, the number of cases filed was 436. However, of late, there has been a steep decline due to which the number of pending cases has come down. Also, later, the number of cases filed is gradually coming down. It may be observed that sellers and manufacturers might have learnt a lesson. Year-wise detail of cases filed, disposed off and pending at the District Forum Una has been enumerated in Table 6.12 and graphically shown in Chart 6.8.

Table 6.12
Year-wise detail of Cases Filed, Disposed off and pending in District Forum Una

Year	Cases filed in the years	Cases disposed of in the years	Cases pending at the end
2001-02	436	92	344
2002-03	177	44	133
2003-04	184	47	137
2004-05	171	41	130
2005-06	82	9	73
2006-07	118	103	15
2007-08	166	107	59
2008-09	180	52	128
2009-10	119	4	115
2010-11	155	73	82

Source: Collection from District Consumer Forum, Una.

Graph 6.8
Performance of District Forum Una

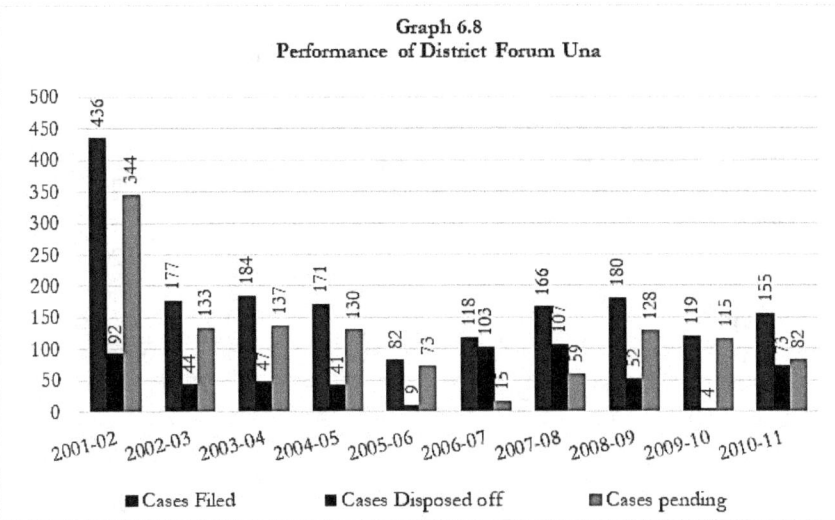

■ Cases Filed   ■ Cases Disposed off   ▣ Cases pending

Table 6.12 shows that the number of cases disposed has been more than hundred in 2006-07 and 2007-08. However, in the remaining of the period, there has been a low number of cases disposed off as compared with the number of pending cases

Thus, it may be observed that though there has been a decrease in the number of pending cases over the last ten years, yes this has mainly been due to a similar decline in the number of cases filed and not due to number of cases disposed off.

6.B.3.iii.e) Performance of District Forum Bilaspur

In case of Bilaspur district forum, the number of cases filed has decreased significantly over the last ten years. But the performance of this district forum in terms of number of cases disposed off is not very impressive. Hence, in almost all the years of study, there has been a big pile up of pending cases waiting to be resolved. Year-wise detail of cases filed, disposed off and pending at the District Forum Bilaspur has been enumerated in Table 6.13 and graphically shown in Chart 6.9.

Table 6.13 shows that in the beginning of 2001-02, there has been a high number of filed cases. Even in the next year, though the number was not that big, yet many cases were filed. However, in the subsequent years, the number of cases filed has been steeply decreasing. A dismal performance, however, is visible in case of case disposal. Particularly, in 2005-06 and 2008-09 the number of cases disposed has been only two and four. In other years also, there has been times when case disposal has been extremely low. Hence, Bilaspur district forum should look into the matter.

Table 6.13
Year-wise detail of Cases Filed, Disposed off and pending in District Forum Bilaspur

Year	Cases filed in the years	Cases disposed of in the years	Cases pending at the end
2001-02	1145	166	979
2002-03	671	215	456
2003-04	146	26	120
2004-05	93	34	59
2005-06	45	2	43
2006-07	171	79	92
2007-08	96	19	77
2008-09	114	4	110
2009-10	250	20	230
2010-11	242	105	137

Source: Collection from District Consumer Forum, Una.

Graph 6.9
Performance of District Forum Bilaspur

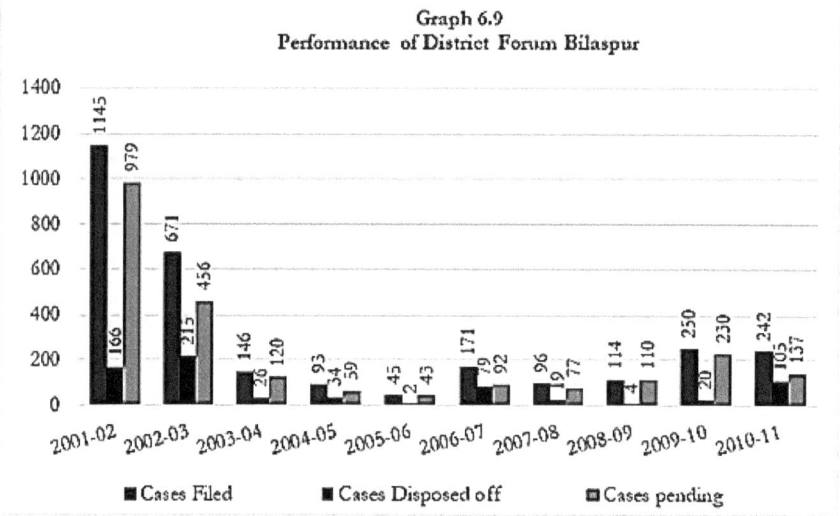

6.B.3.iii.f) Performance of District Forum Hamirpur

Hamirpur district forum has relatively lower number of cases filed with it. Though, in the initial years, there has been a rising trend in the number of cases filed, yet, later there has been a decline. The case disposal performance has been average. This has resulted into a significant backlog of pending cases at this district forum. Year-wise detail of cases filed, disposed off and pending at the District Forum Bilaspur has been enumerated in Table 6.14 and graphically shown in Chart 6.10.

Table 6.14

Year-wise detail of Cases Filed, Disposed off and pending in District Forum Hamirpur

Year	Cases filed in the years	Cases disposed of in the years	Cases pending at the end
2001-02	282	51	231
2002-03	319	44	275
2003-04	302	163	139
2004-05	107	27	80
2005-06	102	28	74
2006-07	184	60	124
2007-08	118	49	69
2008-09	117	15	102
2009-10	124	18	106
2010-11	124	62	62

Source: Collection from District Consumer Forum, Una.

Table 6.14 shows that there has been a decline in both the cases filed and pending cases with Hamirpur district forum throughout the period of study. However, as fas as performance of this district forum is concerned, it is neither very good nor poor. Except few years towards the end where the number of cases disposed was under twenty, the performance is average. Thus, Hamirpur district forum can still do better.

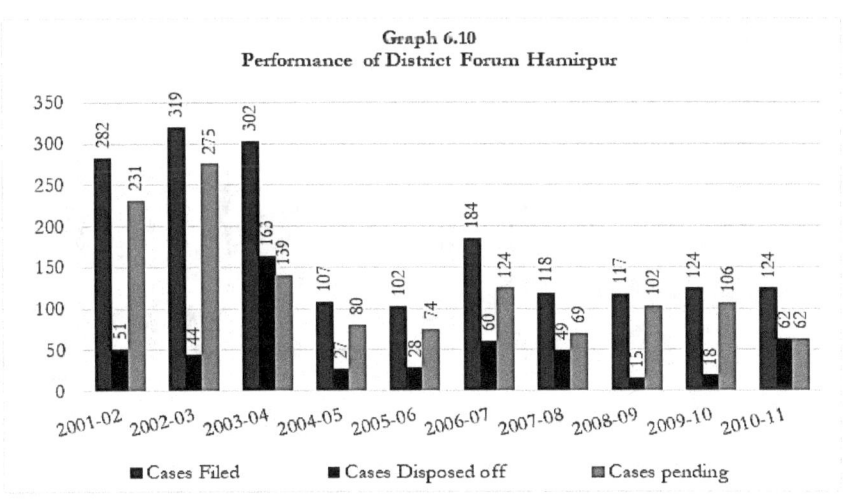

Graph 6.10
Performance of District Forum Hamirpur

6.B.3.iii.g) Performance of District Forum Kangra

In case of Kangra district forum, the number of cases filed had been quite high in the beginning of the period of study. However, lately many of the cases have been disposed of. Due to this, the number of cases pending has come down drastically. Thus, this district forum is performing well. As compared to many other district forums, the number of cases disposed in Kangra district forum is better.Year-wise detail of cases filed, disposed off and pending at the District Forum Bilaspur has been enumerated in Table 6.15 and graphically shown in Chart 6.11.

Table 6.15

Year-wise detail of Cases Filed, Disposed off and pending in District Forum Kangra

Year	Cases filed in the years	Cases disposed of in the years	Cases pending at the end
2001-02	1359	1108	251
2002-03	838	404	434
2003-04	1018	671	347
2004-05	891	445	446
2005-06	827	370	457
2006-07	871	384	487
2007-08	905	905	591
2008-09	992	484	508
2009-10	884	443	441
2010-11	831	366	465

Source: Collection from District Consumer Forum, Kangra.

Graph 6.11
Performance of District Forum Kangra

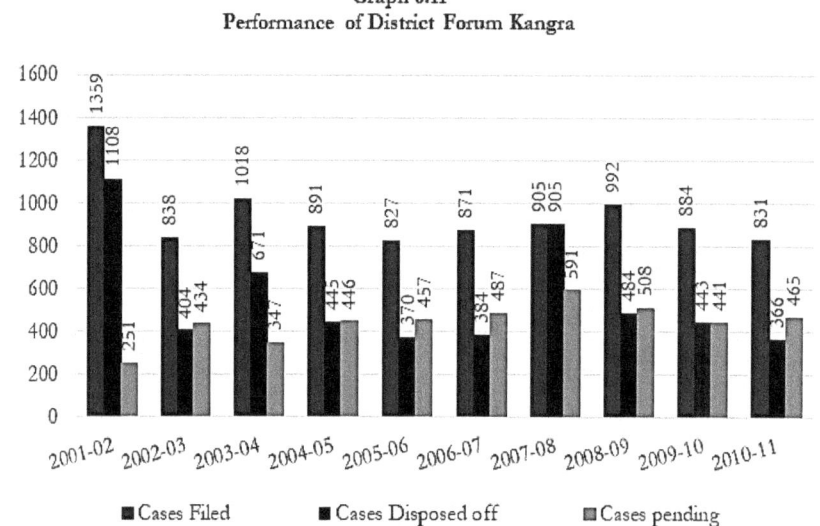

Table 6.15 shows that number of cases disposed off was quite good in the first year and towards the mid of the study. However, towards ending, the number of cases disposed off has come down. It seems that due to the speedy disposal of problems, the number of pending cases is also declining.

234

However, this district forum should try to speedily dispose off cases now. However, relatively the performance of Hamirpur district forum is apprecialble.

6.B.3.iii.h) Performance of District Forum Chamba

At Chamba district forum, given the lower number of cases filed and moreover consistency in the number of cases filed, the number of cases disposed off is at reasonably good level. Unlike other district forums, here the numbers of cases filed, disposed off and pending are consistently at similar levels. Thus, a reasonably speedy disposal of pending cases is there at Chamba district forum.Year-wise detail of cases filed, disposed off and pending at the District Forum Bilaspur has been enumerated in Table 6.16 and graphically shown in Chart 6.12.

Table 6.16 shows that in the beginning of 2002-03, there has been a high number of filed cases. Even in the next year, though the number was not that big, yet many cases were filed. However, in the subsequent years, the number of cases filed has been gradually decreasing. A reasonably good performance, however, is visible in case of case disposal. Particularly, in 2002-03 and 2003-04 the number of cases disposed has been high. In other years also, there has been times when case disposal has been somewhat low. Hence, Chamba district forum among others is doing well.

Table 6.16
Year-wise detail of Cases Filed, Disposed off and pending in District Forum Chamba

Year	Cases filed in the years	Cases disposed of in the years	Cases pending at the end
2001-02	133	49	84
2002-03	262	178	84
2003-04	161	119	42
2004-05	143	81	62
2005-06	120	74	46
2006-07	88	27	61
2007-08	119	30	89
2008-09	141	63	78
2009-10	146	79	67
2010-11	114	75	39

Source: Collection from District Consumer Forum, Kangra.

Briefly, it can be observed that over the period of last ten years, the number of cases filed is declining significantly. Major reason seems to be the increasing awareness of consumers in almost all the districts. This move has actually forced manufacturers and sellers to stay away from various malpractices. However, the number of cases disposed off in comparison to number of cases filed is still very low.

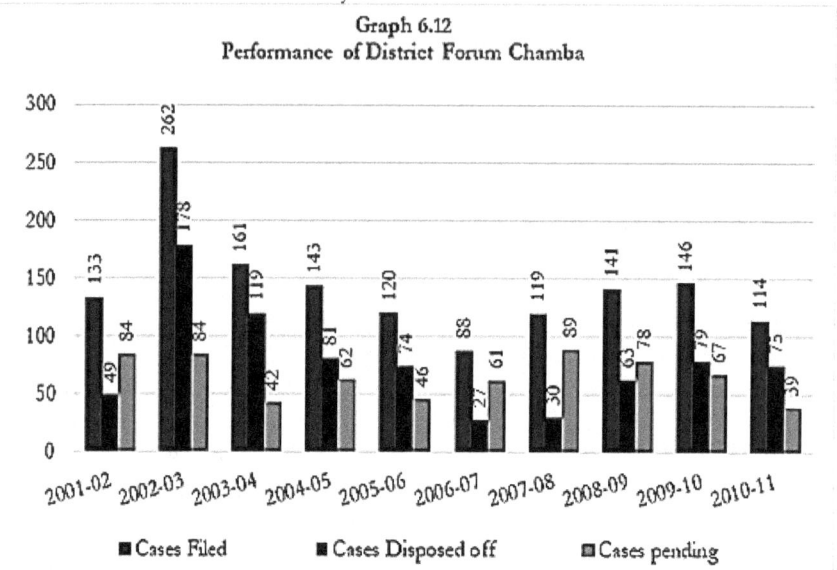

Graph 6.12
Performance of District Forum Chamba

This has caused a huge backlog of pending cases. May it be due to vacancy at district forums or less awareness of legal procedures among consumers, the process needs to be simplified and vacancies to be filled fast.

6.B.4. Comparative analysis of Performance of State Commission and District Forums

In this part, information related to total number of complaints or cases received, number of cases resolved or pending and their respective percentages have been presented. Both the percentage of cases disposed off and cases pending have been calculated on total number of cases filed in respective consumer protection agencies.

6.B.4.i. Cases Filed, Disposed off and Pending

Comparative analyses of cases filed, Disposed off and Pending in State Commission and District Forum in Himachal Pradesh has been illustrated in Table 6.17 and graphically shown in Chart 6.13.

Table 6.17 displays the information related to overall performance of state commission and district forums. It is clear that the overall performance of both these agencies is quite satisfactory and similar to each other. Thus, it deserves to be appreciated as more than ninety percent of cases filed with Himachal Pradesh state commission and district forums have been successfully resolved.

Table 6.17

Detail of Cases Filed, Disposed off and Pending Since the Inception of Consumer Protection Act 1986

Commission/ Forum	Cases filed since inception	Cases disposed off since inception		Cases pending since inception	
		Number	%	Number	%
State Commission	3740	12977	94.44	763	5.56
District Forums	44700	41901	93.73	2799	6.27

Source: Collection from State Consumer Dispute Redressal Commission, Shimla.

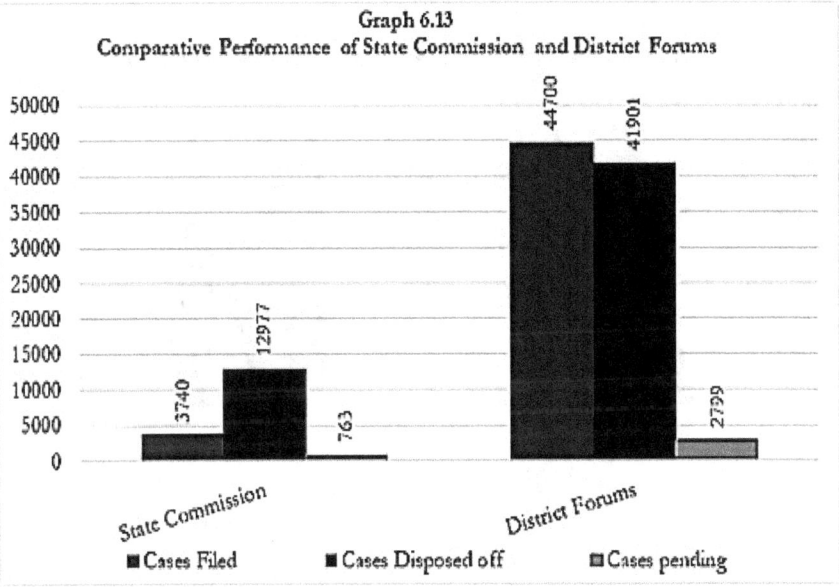

Graph 6.13
Comparative Performance of State Commission and District Forums

6.B.4.ii. Comparative Analysis of Cases Resolved within the Prescribed Time Limit

After the number of cases disposed off or pending, the next issue to be addressed is the resolution within the prescribed time limits. Consumer protection act has prescribed time limits to resolve cases. Also, it is said that delayed justice is no justice at all. Thus, time plays a crucial role in Indian judicial systems. Here, it has been examined if the cases have been resolved in time or not. Comparative analysis of cases resolved within the prescribed time limit in State Commission and District Forums in Himachal Pradesh have been given in Table 6.18 and shown in Chart 6.14.

Table 6.18
Comparative detail of Cases Resolved within the Prescribed Time Limit in Himachal Pradesh

Commission/ Forum	Total no. of Cases disposed off since inception	No. of cases disposed off in Prescribed time limits		No. of cases disposed off with delay of time	
		Number	%	Number	%
State Commission	12977	9244	71.23	3733	28.73
District Forums	41901	28400	67.78	13501	32.28

Source: Collection from State Consumer Dispute Redressal Commission, Shimla.

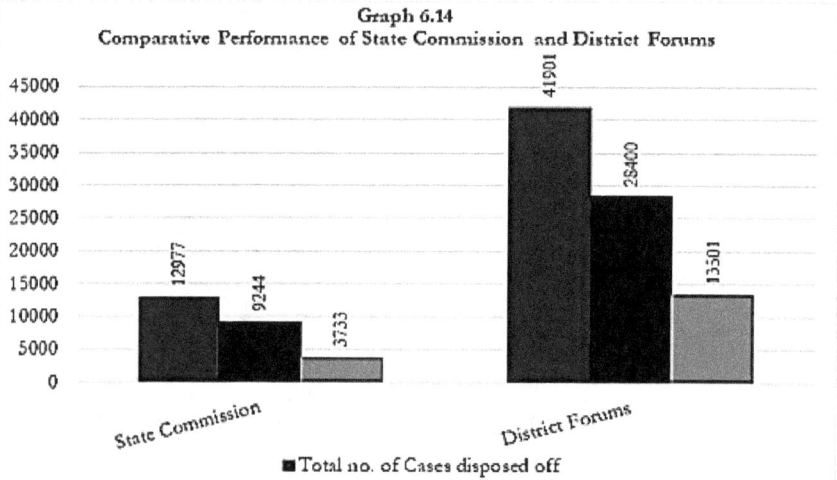

Graph 6.14
Comparative Performance of State Commission and District Forums

It is clear from the Table 6.18 that more than two-third of the total cases filed with **both** the state commission and district forums have been resolved within the prescribed time limits. However, this should not be the end as still many cases are pending with both the consumer courts. Timely justice assures and maintains the faith of people in judiciary. Hence, efforts should be made to even more increase the pace of resolving cases.

Sum up

In brief, it may be said that the number of cases filed with both state commission and district forums have been increasing. However, more than ninety percent of the cases have already been resolved. Though the crucial element of prescribed time limit has sometimes not been followed. After the year 2005, the speed of resolving consumer cases has increased. Finally, insurance and telecom services have been sued most of the times for deficiency in services. So these service providers should look for the major causes of such cases. And due to critical and technical assessment problems, it takes longer time to resolve cases in medical and banking services.

References

Jayapalan, N. (2000). *Public Administration*. New Delhi: Atlantic Publishers and Distributors, p. 46.

Hall, Richard H. (1972). *Organization: Structure and Process*, Englewood Cliffs, New Jersey: Prentice Hall, Inc., p. 9.

Trivedi. K.D. quated Oliver Sheldon in (1999). *Organization and Administrative Theories*, Jaipur: Research Publication, p. 10

Sekaran. Uma (2004). *Organizational Behaviour: Text and Cases (2ⁿᵈ ed.)*. New Delhi. Tata McGraw Hill Publishing Company Ltd., pp. 1-2.

Malik, A.S. (2006). Rural Development Administration in india, in Surat Singh and Mohinder Singh, ed., *Rural Development in the 21ˢᵗ Century: A Multi-Dimensional Study*, New Delhi: Deep and Deep Publications Pvt. Ltd., p. 833.

Malhotra, Girish (2006). *Public Administration*. New Delhi: Murari Lal and Sons, p. 61.

Robbins, Stephen P. Timothy A. Judge & Seema Sanghi. (2008). *Organizational Behavior*, New Delhi: Pearson Prentice Hall, Dorling Kindersley (India) Pvt. Ltd., p. 590, 65 - 66..

Ahluwalia, M.S. (1993). *History of Himachal Pradesh (2ⁿᵈ ed.)*. New Delhi: Intellectual Publishing House, p. 2.

Singh, Mian Goverdhan (1999). *Wooden Temples of Himachal Prades*. New Delhi: Indus Publishing Company, p. 13.

Balokhra, Jag Mohan (2010). *The Wonderland Himachal Pradesh: An Encyclopedia on the State of Western Himalayas*. New Delhi: H.G. Publications, p. 5, 927-928, 921, 976.

http://www.india.gov.in/knowindia/state_uts.php?id=10, retrieved on 21ˢᵗ March 2012.

Department of Economics and Statistics. (2010). *Brief Facts: Himachal Pradesh 2009-10*, Shimla: Government of Himachal Pradesh, pp. ii-iii, iii.

Government of Himachal Pradesh. (2004). *Brief Facts: Himachal Pradesh 2004* Shimla: Department of Economics and Statistics, p. i.

See *Himachal in Figures 2010-11*, Department of Economics and Statistics. Shimla: Government of Himachal Pradesh,

Tiwari, A.K. (2007). *Spatial Dimension of Socio-Economic Development: A Case Study of Himachal Pradesh*. New Delhi: Kanishka Publishers and Distributors, p. 21.

Planning Department. (2010). *Draft Annual Plan 2010-11*. Shimla: Government of Himachal Pradesh, p. 2.

Directorate of Census Operations, *Census of India 2011: Provisional Population Totals, Paper 1 of 2011 Himachal Pradesh Series-3*. Shimla: Government of Himachal Pradesh, p. 29, 30.

Department of Economics and Statistics. (2012). *Economic Survey 2011-12*. Shimla: Government of Himachal Pradesh, p. 13, 13-14, 40, 52, 123.

Planning Department (2010). *Draft Annual Plan 2010-11*, Shimla: Government of Himachal Pradesh, p. 290, 54.

Department of Economics and Statistics (2011). *Economic Survey 2010-11*, Shimla: Government of Himachal Pradesh, p. 78.

Chaudhry, Minakshi (2006). *Himachal: A complete Guide to the Land of Gods*. New Delhi: Rupa and Company, p. 149.

Jreat, Manoj (2004). *Tourism in Himachal Pradesh*. New Delhi: Indus Publishing Company, p. 19.

Sharma, L.R. (1987)., *The Economy of Himachal Pradesh: Growth and Structure: A Study in Development Performance*. New Delhi: Mittal Publications, p. 20.

Thakur, Laxam S. (1996). *The Architectural Heritage of Himachal Pradesh: Origin and Development of Temple Styles*, New Delhi: Munshiram Manoharlal Publishers, p. 3.

Planning Commission (2005*), Development Report*, Government of India, New Delhi. p. 29, 29.

See *Himachal in Figures 2010-11*, Department of Economics and Statistics, Shimla: Government of Himachal Pradesh.

Department of Food, Civil Supplies and Consumer Affairs. *About the Department*. 12 August 2013, from http://admis.hp.nic. in/ehimapurti/aboutus.htm

History of consumer protection at Himachal Pradesh, retrieved on 14-09-2012 from website http://hpconsumercommission.nic.in/hist.htm.

CHAPTER – 7
ANALYSIS OF CONSUMER ALERTNESS AND AWARENESS ABOUT CONSUMER PROTECTION IN HIMACHAL PRADESH

This chapter deals with a detailed data analysis on the alertness, awareness, and sources of information of respondents in relation to consumer protection. This chapter starts with a brief introduction of sample respondents on their demographic features. Besides, it covers a detailed analysis of their alertness while buying something and awareness. Awareness has been examined from three different perspectives viz. awareness of consumer protection laws, awareness of consumer rights, and general consumer protection.

Later, analysis has been carried out to find those products and services in relation to which maximum consumer disputes have been filed by the respondents. Also, various types of malpractices witnessed by respondents have been covered. Finally, use of various sources of information has been highlighted. To measure the difference, if any, regarding alertness and awareness of respondents belonging to different demographic attributes, analysis of variance (ANOVA) has been carried out.

7.1. Sample Description

For the purpose of the study, a sample of 1250 respondents was selected. This sample has been analyzed from four different demographic attributes of the respondents. These demographic attributes include gender of the respondents, occupation of the respondents, age of the respondents, and educational qualification of the respondents. A detailed description of the sample covering various demographic attributes is as below.

7.1.1. Gender of the Respondents

In this segment, gender based classification of the respondents has been made. Information related to gender of the respondents has been collected with the objective of testing gender related hypotheses in the research. Later in the thesis, differences between awareness and alertness of male and female respondents have been analyzed with this information. Gender-wise classification of sample respondents has been presented in Table 7.1 and graphically shown in Graph 7.1.

Table 7.1
Gender-wise classification of Respondents

Gender	Frequency	Percentage
Male	875	70.0
Female	375	30.0
Total	**1250**	**100.0**

Source: *Primary Probe.*

Graph 7.1
Gender-wise classification of Sample Respondents

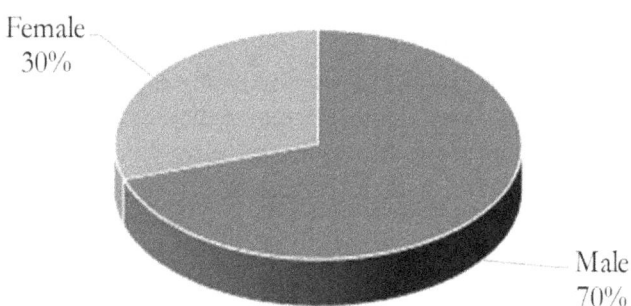

Table 7.1 shows that out of a total of 1250 respondents, 875 respondents have been male and 375 respondents female. Thus, the sample has consisted of 70 per cent of males and 30 per cent of female respondents.

7.1.2. Occupation status of Sample Respondents

Second demographic attribute covered in the sample is the occupation of respondents. Four occupational classes have been covered in the sample viz. Business, Service (Including Public and Private Service), Students, and Housewives. This information has been collected to find differences in relation to awareness among various occupational categories.

Table 7.2
Occupation of the Respondents

Occupation	Frequency	Percentage
Business	325	26.0
Service	635	50.8
Student	160	12.8
Housewife	130	10.4
Total	**1250**	**100.0**

Source: Primary Probe.

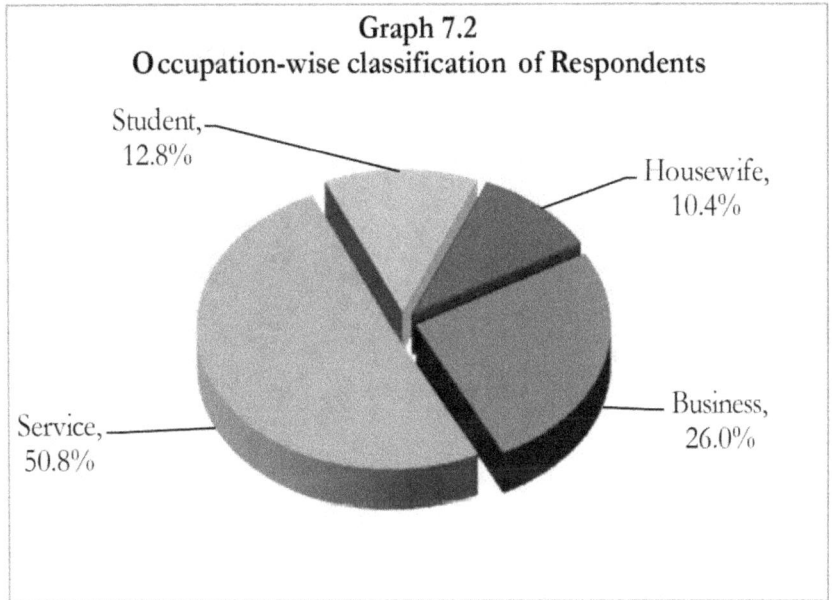

Graph 7.2
Occupation-wise classification of Respondents

Table 7.2 shows that the sample has a majority of respondents from service class. Almost half of the sample consists of such respondents only.

Thereafter, the second highest number of respondents is from business class. 26 per cent respondents in the sample belong to business class. Number of students in the sample are 160 and housewives are 130. Hence, the sample covers a representation from four different occupations.

7.1.3. Age-wise distribution of Sample Respondents

Third demographic attribute covered in the sample is the age of respondents. Again, the idea behind considering such information has been to find out the difference in alertness, if any, in the various age groups. This information serves the purpose of testing if any specific age group has a high or low degree of awareness as compared to other groups.

Table 7.3
Age Group-wise distribution of sample Respondents

Age group	Frequency	Percentage
15 – 18 years	300	24.0
18 - 25 years	365	29.2
25 - 35 years	445	35.6
35 years or above	140	11.2
Total	**1250**	**100.0**

Source: Primary Probe.

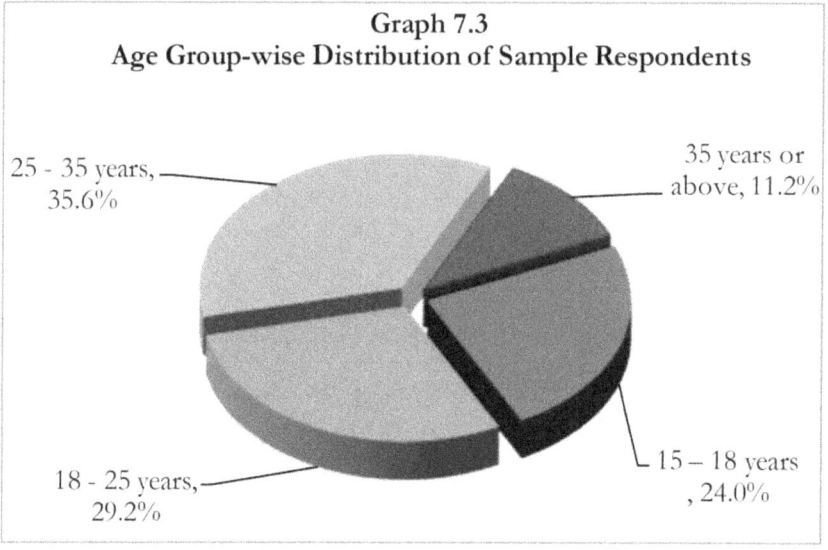

Graph 7.3
Age Group-wise Distribution of Sample Respondents

Table 7.3 shows that majority of the respondents belong to age group of 25 yrs to 35 yrs. 445 respondents consisting of 35.6 per cent of the sample are from this age group. This has been followed by age group 18 yrs to 25 yrs. As many as 365 respondents are from this age group. 24 per cent of the respondents have been in the age group 15 yrs to 18 yrs. Finally, 140 respondents consisting of 11.2 per cent of the sample belong to age group of 35 years or above. Thus the representation of various age groups in the sample has been covered.

7.1.4. Educational Status of Sample Respondents

Last demographic attribute of the sample is qualification of the respondents. As indicated earlier in the review of literature that less qualified customers can be easily cheated and exploited by business concerns, information related to awareness among different levels of qualification can help to test the empirical hypothesis. The sample for this purpose has been divided in four educational qualifications viz. matriculate or below, higher secondary, graduates, and post graduates or above.

Table 7.4
Educational Status of Sample Respondents

Educational Status	Frequency	Percent
Matriculate or below	280	22.4
Higher Secondary	375	30.0
Graduate	280	22.4
Post Graduate or above	315	25.2
Total	**1250**	**100.0**

Source: *Primary Probe.*

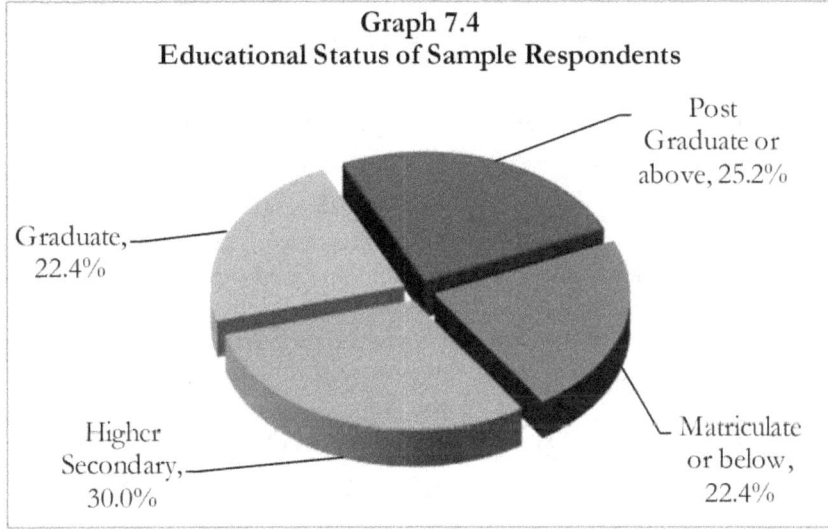

Graph 7.4
Educational Status of Sample Respondents

Post Graduate or above, 25.2%

Graduate, 22.4%

Higher Secondary, 30.0%

Matriculate or below, 22.4%

Table 7.4 shows that out of 1250 respondents, 30.0 were higher secondary pass, 25.2 per cent were post graduate or above, 22.4 per cent were graduate and same were matriculate. Hence, it can be said that majority of sample consists of respondents with higher secondary educational level, followed by post graduate or above and graduates.

Therefore, it can be concluded that the sample consists of representations from all the qualification categories except illiterate.

7.2. Alertness Among Consumers

Alertness among customers while making any purchases protects them from being cheated by the sellers. There may be comprehensive sets of acts, rules, and regulations. However, nothing can substitute alertness while buying. An alert customer will automatically check the price, quality and quantity before finalizing buy deals. Hence, this section deals with the assessment of alertness generally exercised by the customers while making purchases.

Alertness in this context has been defined as a set of various activities or parameters. Primarily, such activities can be to examine the expiry date the food items and medicines, to ask for a bill whenever purchase something, to look for the company's name on the product, to check the Maximum Retail Price (M.R.P.) before buying the products, to look for ingredients details of the product, to verify the rate printed on the product cover/bottle/carton, to check for the ISI/AGMARK or other Mark on the product, to inquire whether any discounts or any other offers available, to cross checked the weights of the products, to check the prices, of goods one buys, from alternative sources, and to look for the trade mark on the product. Results of such activities of alertness among customers have been tabulated and interpreted as below.

7.2.1. Examination of the expiry date the food items and medicines

There are many goods or products which come with expiry date. Most of the food products and medicines fall in this category. After the expiry date is over, these products may lose their utility. In case of medicines, it can be a health hazard to consume expired medicines. Hence, customers are supposed to be alert if they check the expiry date of food products and medicines while making a purchase of such items.

Table 7.5
Examination of the Expiry Date of the Food Items and Medicines

Response	Frequency	Percent
Never	120	9.6
Few Times	365	29.2
Sometimes	120	9.6
Frequently	380	30.4
Always	265	21.2
Total	**1250**	**100.0**

Source: Primary Probe.

Analyses of the degree of alertness of respondents regarding examination of expiry date while purchasing food products or medicines in Table 7.5 reveals that 30.4 per cent of respondents frequently examined the expiry date of the food items and medicines, 29.2 per cent of were few times examined and 21.2 per cent were always examined the expiry date of the food items and medicines.

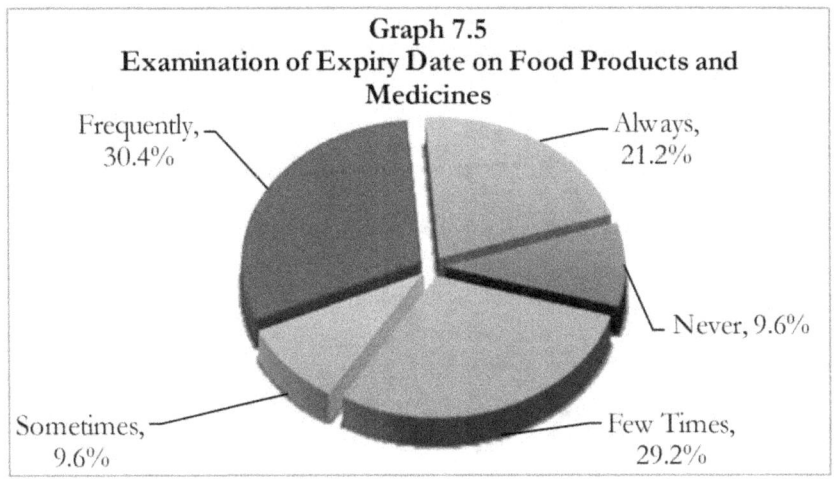

Graph 7.5
Examination of Expiry Date on Food Products and Medicines

Frequently, 30.4%
Always, 21.2%
Never, 9.6%
Sometimes, 9.6%
Few Times, 29.2%

Further, Table depicts that almost 50 per cent of the respondents have stated that they either never or few times or sometimes checked the expiry date of food products and medicines. Around 50 per cent of the respondents frequently or always check the same. Remaining consumers sometimes check the expiry date.

Hence, it indicated towards an alarming situation as about 50 per cent consumers do not remain alert while buying medicines or food products in relation to the expiry date.

7.2.2. Asking for a Bill While Purchase

Asking for a bill while making any purchase can help in a long way. A seller who issues bills automatically binds himself with that transaction and cannot deny the same. Also, a bill can be used to file a case in the consumer court. However, many a times, consumers either ignorantly or for tax avoidance and saving few rupees, ignore bills. An alert consumer should ask for a bill every time he purchases any goods or services.

Table 7.6
Ask for a bill on purchases

Response	Frequency	Percent
Never	215	17.2
Few Times	465	37.2
Sometimes	55	4.4
Frequently	405	32.4
Always	110	8.8
Total	1250	100.0

Source: *Primary Probe.*

Table 7.6 shows that 37.2 per cent of respondents few times ask for a bill, 32.4 per cent frequently ask and 17.2 per cent were never demand the bill for their purchasing. Thus, it can be inferred that about 60 per cent of respondents were not found alert regarding taking bill of their purchase, as they ask for bill either few times or never or sometimes.

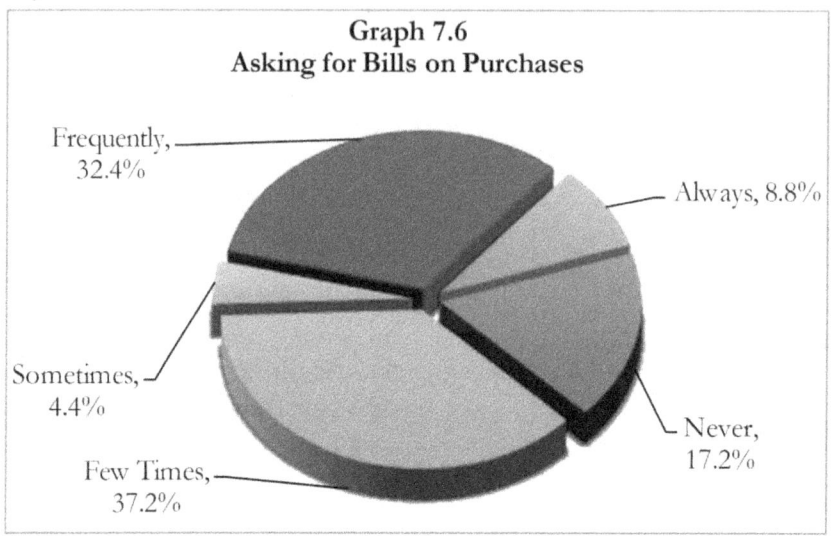

This can really be a threatening situation. If all the consumers start asking for bills on purchases, it would be beneficial from two points. Firstly, sellers would be more conscious while selling low quality or defective goods. And secondly, tax evasion would not be easy.

7.2.3. Looking for the Company's Name on the Product

In India, there are many inferior products, which resemble to some known brands in their size, shapes, and even in color combination. However, the quality is no way near to those popular products. Consumers should be very alert and they should read the name of company and brand very carefully on the product they are buying. It would assure that no duplicate or low quality product is being sold to the customers.

Results in Table 7.7 show that out of 1250 respondents, 36.8 per cent of respondents few times check the name of the company on the product and19.2 per cent of respondents sometimes check the name of the company on the product. These customers can be prone to be sold duplicate products. 24.4 per cent of respondents check the name of the company as a routine which indeed is a good sign while, 19.6 per cent respondents frequently check the brand name.

Table 7.7
Look for the company's name on the product

Response	Frequency	Percent
Never	0	0.0
Few Times	460	36.8
Sometimes	240	19.2
Frequently	245	19.6
Always	305	24.4
Total	**1250**	**100.0**

Source: Primary Probe.

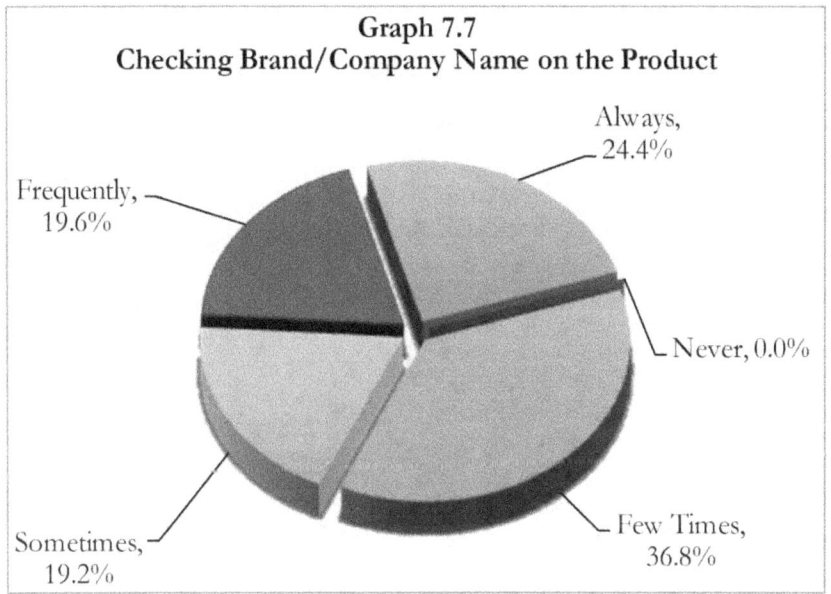

Graph 7.7
Checking Brand/Company Name on the Product

Thus, it may be noted that roughly 37 per cent respondents may be easy targets for the sellers to sell duplicate products.

7.2.4. Checking M.R.P. (Maximum Retail Prices) Before Buying the Products

MRP more popularly known as the maximum retail price is the maximum price that can be charged by any shopkeeper for different products. No customer can be charged any more than the MRP of the product. As an alert consumer, people should frequently check the MRP of products and make sure that they have not been charged beyond MRP.

However, the Table 7.8 narrates a different story. Almost one fourth of the total sample has never checked the MRP of the products. 37.2 per cent of respondents were of the opinion that they few times check MRP on the product. Surprisingly, only twenty five out of 1250 respondents always check MRP of the products they buy. Hence, it shows that customers need to be more alert.

Table 7.8
Checking Maximum Retail Prices (M.R.P.) before buying the Products

Response	Frequency	Percent
Never	290	23.2
Few Times	465	37.2
Sometimes	40	3.2
Frequently	430	34.4
Always	25	2.0
Total	**1250**	**100.0**

Source: *Primary Probe.*

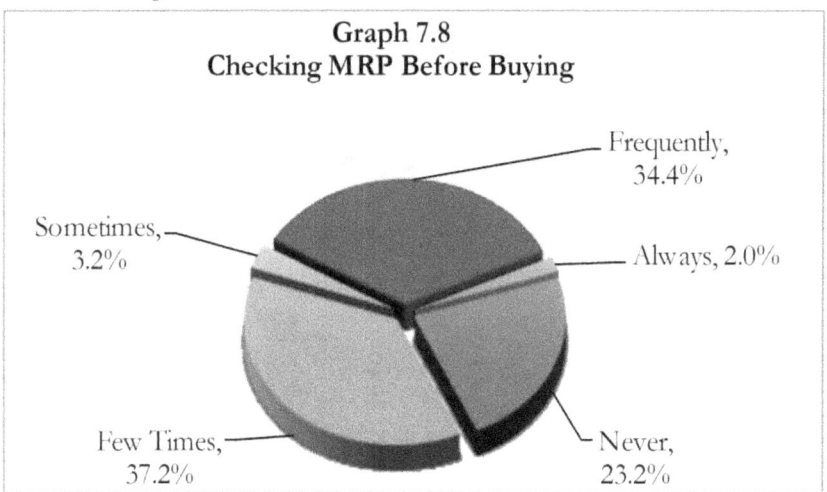

Graph 7.8
Checking MRP Before Buying

Frequently, 34.4%

Sometimes, 3.2%

Always, 2.0%

Few Times, 37.2%

Never, 23.2%

7.2.5. Looking for Ingredient Details of the Product

Ingredient details of products refer to the various inputs used in the manufacturing of products. Especially food products and medicines carry ingredient details mentioned on their packing or labels. These details can be extremely important in many cases where a particular mixture is desired to be purchased. In such cases, an alert customer would definitely check the ingredient details.

Here again in Table 7.9, only few customers seem to be alert in context of ingredients. 24.4 per cent and 4.0 per cent of respondents look ingredients details of the product frequently and always respectively. More than half of the sample respondents were either never checked or even if they checked, it was few times only.

Table 7.9
Look for ingredients details of the product

Response	Frequency	Percent
Never	425	34.0
Few Times	210	16.8
Sometimes	260	20.8
Frequently	305	24.4
Always	50	4.0
Total	**1250**	**100.0**

Source: Primary Probe.

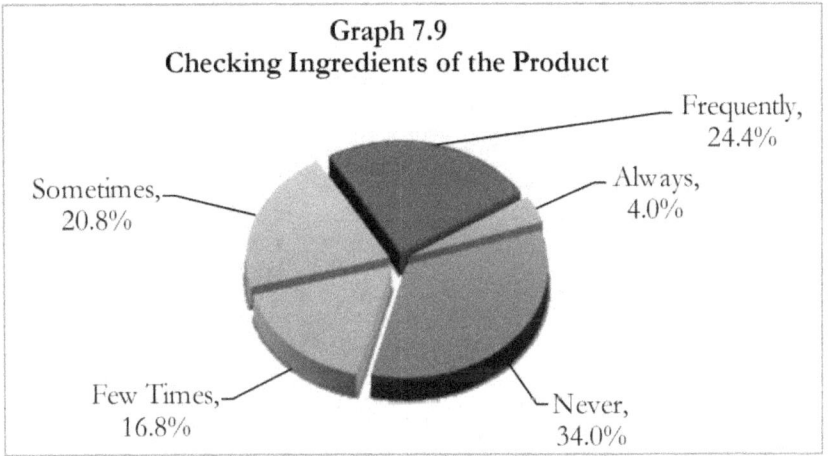

Graph 7.9
Checking Ingredients of the Product

Frequently, 24.4%

Always, 4.0%

Sometimes, 20.8%

Few Times, 16.8%

Never, 34.0%

There are only fifty customers in the entire sample which have always checked the ingredients mentioned on the labels. Thus, there can be chances of sales of products with undesired ingredients.

7.2.6. Check for the ISI/AGMARK or Other Mark on the Product

Many of the products we use in routine are certified and standardized products. There are many popular standards or marks which assure the good quality of the product. These mainly include ISI mark for electric and electronic appliances, AGMARK for food products, Hallmark for testing the purity of gold, and BEE for the energy efficiency of electronic appliances. Alert customers would never take chances and buy only products with such standard marks.

Table 7.10
Check for the ISI/AGMARK or other Mark on the product

Response	Frequency	Percent
Never	225	18.0
Few Times	405	32.4
Sometimes	180	14.4
Frequently	345	27.6
Always	95	7.6
Total	**1250**	**100.0**

Source: Primary Probe.

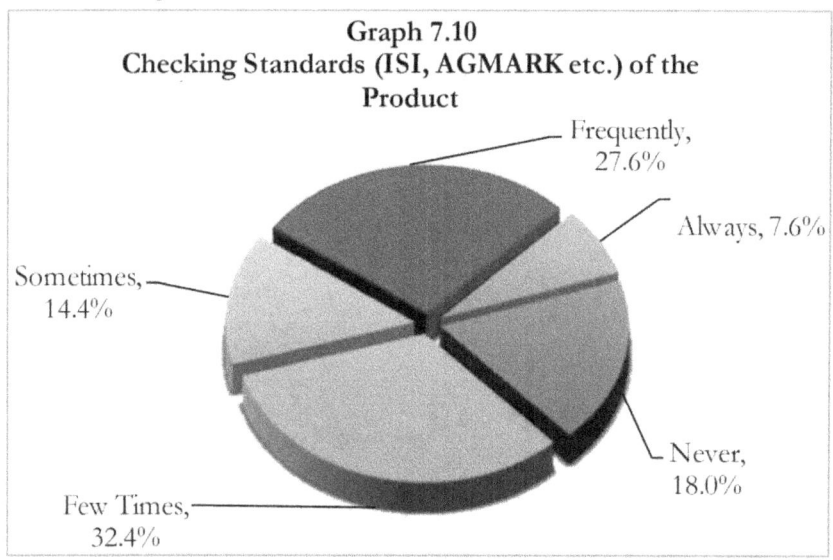

Graph 7.10
Checking Standards (ISI, AGMARK etc.) of the Product

Table 7.10 shows that there are only 95 (7.6 per cent) customers in the sample which always check for such standard marks on the products. Again, more than half of the respondents either never (18.0 per cent) look for standards or only few times (32.4 per cent) do it. Thus again, it is alarming situation as the use of non-standard or sub-standard products can be a safety hazard when put into use.

7.2.7. Inquire Whether any Discounts or any other Offers Available

Companies, nowadays, introduce many discount offers and promotional offers to enhance their sale. However, many a times, these discounts are enjoyed by the retailers only and not passed to the final consumers. This can adversely affect many companies. An alert customer should always look for products which are attached as free with the main product. Also any discount mentioned on the product should be availed to its full.

Table 7.11
Inquire about discounts or any other offers available

Response	Frequency	Percent
Never	295	23.6
Few Times	215	17.2
Sometimes	200	16.0
Frequently	260	20.8
Always	280	22.4
Total	**1250**	**100.0**

Source: *Primary Probe.*

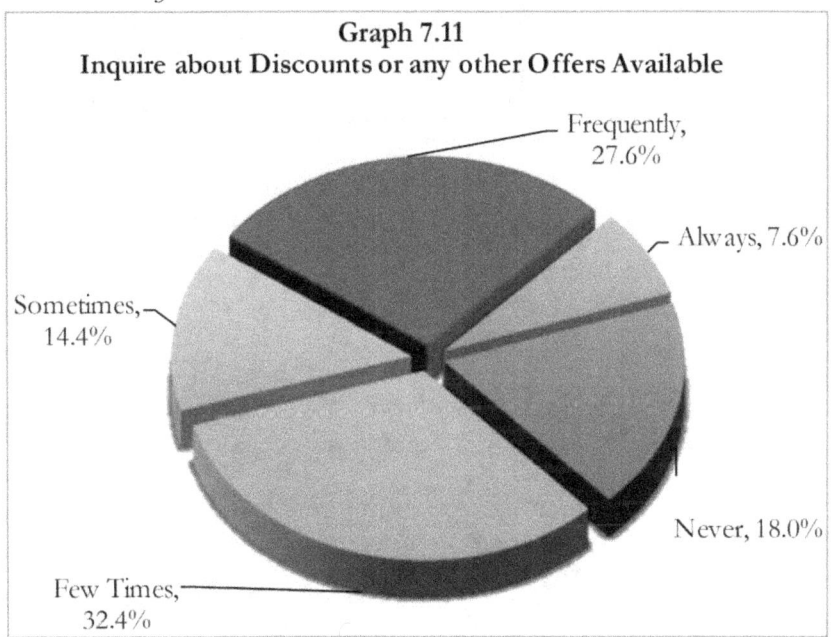

Graph 7.11
Inquire about Discounts or any other Offers Available

Frequently, 27.6%
Always, 7.6%
Never, 18.0%
Few Times, 32.4%
Sometimes, 14.4%

Table 7.11 depicts that out of total respondents, 23.6 per cent of respondents were never inquired discounts or other promotional offers. On the other hand, 22.4 per cent of respondents always inquired it. 20.8 per cent frequently, 17.2 per cent few times and 16.0 per cent sometimes inquired discounts and other offers.

Thus, analyses reveals that around 43 per cent of the respondents always or frequently check and make enquiry with the shopkeepers about discounts or free gifts available with the main products. However, around 41 per cent respondents are also such which never or few times make such enquiries.

These customers can easily fall prey to shopkeepers' malpractices.

7.2.8. Cross Checking the Weights of the Products

Many shopkeepers or trading firms though do not play with the prices of products, yet are involved in malpractices related to weights of the products. As per regulations, products need to mention the gross and net weight on packing. Similarly, alert customers should check the weight mentioned on the products and cross check the accuracy by actually weighing the product.

Table 7.12
Cross Checking the Weights of the Products

Response	Frequency	Percent
Never	460	36.8
Few Times	540	43.2
Sometimes	250	20.0
Total	**1250**	**100.0**

Source: *Primary Probe.*

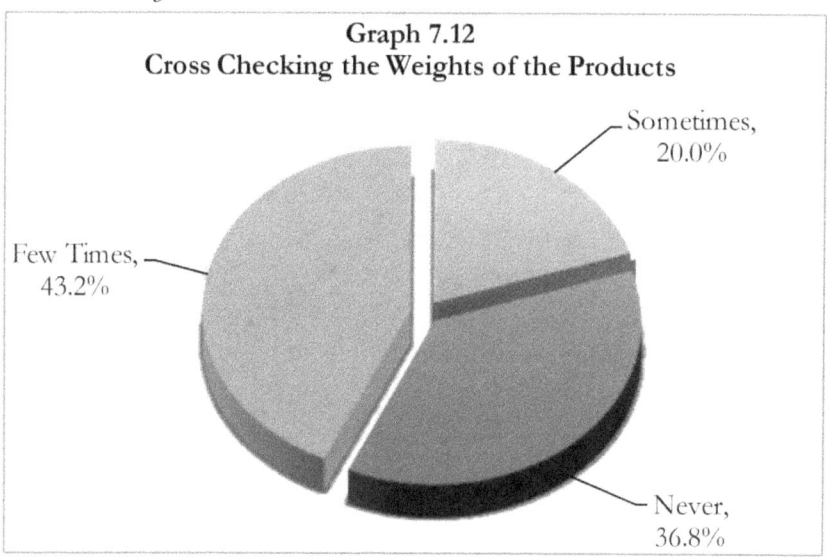

Graph 7.12
Cross Checking the Weights of the Products

Table 7.12 shows that 36.8 per cent of the respondents have never cross checked the weights of products they have purchased. 43.2 per cent of the respondents have done it but few times. 20.0 per cent of the respondents have cross checked weights sometimes. Here, it is clear that no respondents always or frequently cross check the weights. But, customers should remain alert also. This will assure that no underweight product is being sold to the consumers.

7.2.9. Checking Prices of Goods from Alternative Sources

Even though the prices charged by one shopkeeper are less than MRP, the customers can check the prices with alternative sources like other sellers. The other sellers may be offering higher rate of discounts than the present seller. Thus, the customers should always keep themselves updated with the prices of various products.

Table 7.13
Check the prices of goods from alternative sources

Response	Frequency	Percent
Never	225	18.0
Few Times	225	18.0
Sometimes	300	24.0
Frequently	300	24.0
Always	200	16.0
Total	**1250**	**100.0**

Source: Primary Probe.

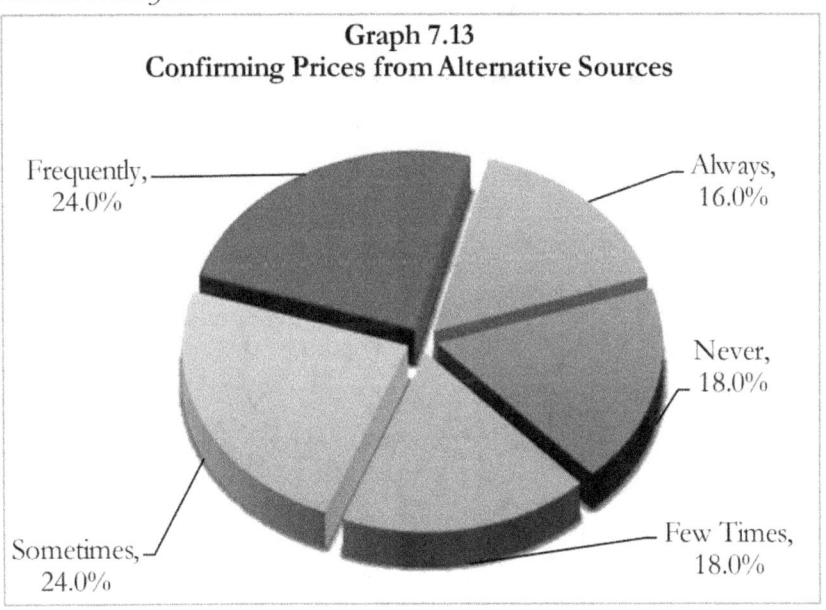

Graph 7.13
Confirming Prices from Alternative Sources

Table 7.13 shows that out of total 1250 respondents, 18.0 per cent of respondents never check the prices of goods from alternative source, while 18.0 per cent few times check it. On the other hand, table reveals that in 24.0 per cent of cases people sometimes check the price of goods from alternative sources and in same percentage of cases people frequently check the price of goods.

Thus, it can be concluded that about 60 per cent of consumers were either sometimes or never or few times check the prices of goods from alternative sources.

7.2.10. Look for the Trade Mark on the Product

In India, many duplicate products with same color combinations and same shapes can be found selling on roads. However, trademarks, copyrights or patents are not copied generally. Copying patents and trademarks is considered to be a serious legal offence. Hence, an alert customer should know trademarks of various popular products and further check these trademarks as printed on the products.

Table 7.14
Look for the Trade Mark on the Product

Response	Frequency	Percent
Never	295	23.6
Few Times	245	19.6
Sometimes	220	17.6
Frequently	260	20.8
Always	230	18.4
Total	**1250**	**100.0**

Source: *Primary Probe.*

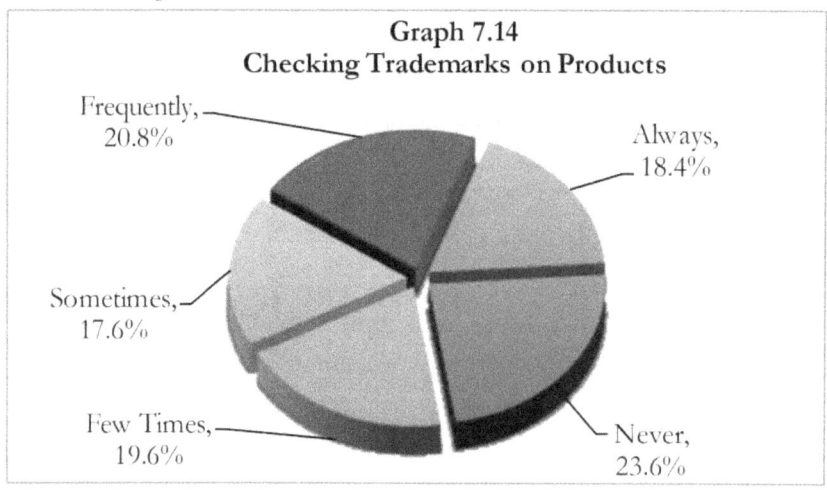

Graph 7.14
Checking Trademarks on Products

Frequently, 20.8%
Always, 18.4%
Sometimes, 17.6%
Few Times, 19.6%
Never, 23.6%

Table 7.14 shows that an average response is prevalent in all the categories. Majority of respondents, that is, 32.6 per cent, were never checked the trademark on the products. 20.8 per cent of respondents frequently checked trademark, 19.6 per cent were sometime checked it. Approximately 40 per cent of the respondents frequently or always look for the trademarks mentioned on the product labels. However, around 43 per cent are also such respondents who never or few times look for the company trademarks on the products.

7.2.11. Descriptive Related to Alertness

This segment presents a brief snapshot of the entire consumer related activities and the degree of alertness displayed by the sample respondents.

Table 7.15

Relative Alertness among Consumer for Various Activities

	Alertness	Mean	Std. Deviation
A1	Verify the rate printed on the product cover/bottle/carton	3.58	0.808
A2	Look for the company's name on the product	3.32	1.202
A3	Examine the expiry date the food items and medicines	3.24	1.333
A4	Check the prices, of goods you buy, from alternative sources	3.02	1.337
A5	Inquire whether any discounts or any other offers available	3.01	1.493
B1	Look for the trade mark on the product	2.91	1.444
B2	Ask for a bill whenever you purchase something	2.78	1.302
B3	Check for the ISI/AGMARK or other Mark on the product	2.74	1.251
B4	Check the M.R.P.(Maximum Retail Prices) before buying the products	2.55	1.235
B5	Look for ingredients details of the product	2.48	1.290
C1	Cross checked the weights of the products	1.83	0.736

Note: Mean and Standard deviation has been calculated from the frequencies of Table 7.5 to 7.14.

Table 7.15 includes calculation of arithmetic mean and standard deviation values. Maximum value can be five as per the scale which would indicate that activity is done always by all the customers. Going by that, mean values in 3+ categories are the activities which are performed frequently or sometimes by the consumers. Hence, it may be said that on average consumers frequently or sometimes verify the rate printed on the product cover/bottle/carton, look for the company's name on the product, examine the expiry date the food items and medicines, check the prices from alternative sources, and enquire whether any discounts or any other offers available.

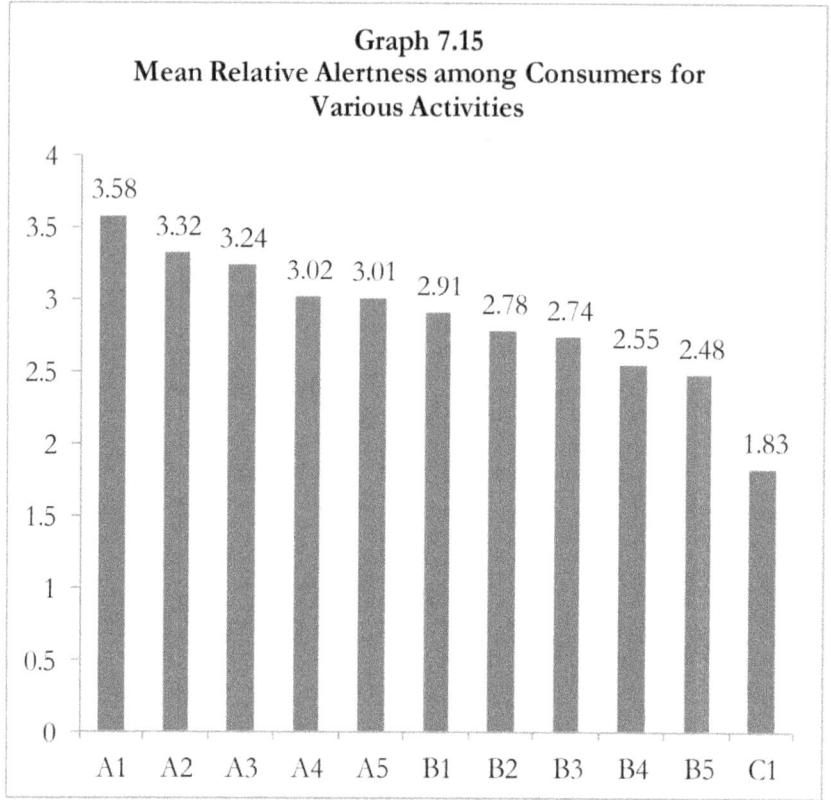

Graph 7.15
Mean Relative Alertness among Consumers for Various Activities

Thereafter, second category deals with the activities, which are carried out by consumers but only few times. Customers generally ignore these activities but sometimes do take interest in such activities. These activities include to look for the trade mark on the product, ask for a bill while purchasing, check for the ISI/AGMARK or other Mark on the product, check the M.R.P. (Maximum Retail Prices) before buying the products, and look for ingredients details of the product.

Finally cross checking the weight of products by actually weighing is the least performed activity. Not many customers like to cross check the weights of the products they buy. But, as an alert customer, one should not ignore any activity mentioned in the list.

7.3. Consumer Alertness and Demographic Attributes

Here, an effort has been made to see if any demographic attribute of the customer has any say in doing or not doing any particular activity. For this purpose, four demographic attributes viz., gender of the respondents, age of the respondents, occupation of the respondents, and qualification of the respondents have been covered and analyzed. This exercise has been done for grand score of alertness taking into account all the nine questions related to alertness discussed earlier. Thereafter, mean alertness scores have been calculated for all the groups based on demographic features.

7.3.1. Gender Based ANOVA

This part deals with the exploration of difference, if any, in males and females with regards to doing or not doing any such activity showing consumer alertness.

Table 7.16
Descriptive-Gender vs. Level of Alertness

Gender-wise Level of Alertness	N	Mean	Std. Deviation
Male	875	31.3371	4.32788
Female	375	31.7733	4.13153
Total	1250	31.4680	4.26635

Table 7.16 shows that the average alertness scores which represents the sum of all alertness related activities is marginally high in case of females than males.

To find the significance of difference, ANOVA has been used. Null hypothesis for ANOVA states no difference between male and female respondents with regards to level of alertness. However, ANOVA value 2.757 is quite low. Due to it, p-value of significance is 0.097. It indicates that no significant difference exists in male and female respondents in relation to level of alertness.

Table 7.16 (a)
ANOVA - Gender vs. Level of Alertness

Gender-wise Level of Alertness	Sum of Squares	d.f.	Mean Square	F	Sig.
Between Groups	49.944	1	49.944	2.757	.097
Within Groups	22611.276	1248	18.118		
Total	22661.220	1249			

Thus, the null hypothesis stating no difference in males and females in relation to their level of alertness while buying stands accepted.

7.3.2. Occupation Based ANOVA

This ANOVA deals with the examination of differences, if any, in different occupational categories. Null hypothesis in this case states that respondents belonging to different occupational backgrounds have no difference in their level of alertness. Descriptive and ANOVA of Occupation vs. level of alertness has been presented in Table 7.17 and Table 7.17 (a) respectively.

Table 7.17
Descriptive - Occupation vs. Level of Alertness

Occupation-wise Level of Alertness	N	Mean	Std. Deviation
Business	325	31.0154	4.56718
Service	635	31.7008	4.30267
Student	160	31.9375	3.04734
Housewife	130	30.8846	4.65039
Total	**1250**	**31.4680**	**4.26635**

Descriptive in Table 7.17 show that students have the lowest mean level of alertness whereas all the remaining three types of respondents have a better degree of alertness. So it may be said that students are generally of casual attitude when it comes to consumer alertness.

Table 7.17 (a)
ANOVA - Occupation vs. Level of Alertness

Occupation-wise Level of Alertness	Sum of Squares	df	Mean Square	F	Sig.
Between Groups	180.503	3	60.168	3.335	.019
Within Groups	22480.717	1246	18.042		
Total	**22661.220**	**1249**			

ANOVA value in this case is 3.335, which is quite low. Also the p-value is 0.019 which indicates significant variation. Hence, it may be concluded that difference exists in respondents with regard to alertness. Service and student class have higher levels of alertness as compared to other two categories. Hence, null hypothesis assuming no difference of alertness among respondents belonging to different occupations stands rejected.

7.3.3. Age Based ANOVA

Age based ANOVA has been calculated in this part to examine any possible difference of level of alertness among respondents belonging to different age groups. Here null hypothesis statement is that respondents belonging to different age groups do not significantly differ on their level of alertness while making purchases. Descriptive and ANOVA of Age vs. level of alertness has been presented in Table 7.18 and Table 7.18 (a) respectively.

Table 7.18 shows that level of alertness has been minimum in case of age group 35 years or above, followed by age group of '25 years to 35 years' and '18 years to 25 years'. The maximum alertness has been found in the respondents in age group '15 years to 18 years'. Besides, standard deviation is not too high. So it seems that alertness decreases as one grows older.

Table 7.18
Descriptive- Age vs. Level of Alertness

Age vs. Level of Alertness	N	Mean	Std. Deviation
15 - 18	300	32.2500	4.26505
18 - 25	365	31.5342	4.67583
25 - 35	445	31.3146	4.07764
35 or above	140	30.1071	3.49962
Total	**1250**	**31.4680**	**4.26635**

Table 7.18 (a)
ANOVA - Age vs. Level of Alertness

Age vs. Level of Alertness	Sum of Squares	d.f.	Mean Square	F	Sig.
Between Groups	454.800	3	151.600	8.506	.000
Within Groups	22206.420	1246	17.822		
Total	**22661.220**	**1249**			

F-value in this case is 8.506 which is high. That's why p-value is 0.000. It indicates that there is significant difference among various age groups with regards to their level of alertness. Thus, it can be stated that in the young people with age group of '15 yrs. To 18 yrs.' tend to be alert. However, this alertness decreases with the increase in age. Hence, null hypothesis assuming no difference of alertness among consumers belonging to different age groups stands rejected.

7.3.4. Education Based ANOVA

In this case, ANOVA has been used to examine the possibility of significant difference of degree of alertness of various respondents having different levels of education. It has been assumed that education makes a person more alert and educated people cannot be cheated easily. Here the null hypothesis is that respondents having been from various levels of education do not differ significantly with respect to degree of alertness. Descriptive and ANOVA of Education vs. level of alertness has been presented in Table 7.19 and Table 7.19 (a) respectively.

Table 7.19
Descriptive – Education vs. Level of Alertness

Education vs. Level of Alertness	N	Mean	Std. Deviation
Matriculate or below	280	31.5357	4.30207
Higher Secondary	375	31.2533	4.14629
Graduate	280	31.8929	4.05274
Post Graduate or above	315	31.2857	4.61913
Total	**1250**	**31.4680**	**4.26635**

Table 7.19 shows that the degree of alertness was maximum in case of graduates followed by matriculate or below and post graduates. Higher secondary education people have been on the lower side.

Table 7.19 (a)
ANOVA – Education vs. Level of Alertness

Education vs. Level of Alertness	Sum of Squares	df	Mean Square	F	Sig.
Between Groups	79.572	3	26.524	1.464	.223
Within Groups	22581.648	1246	18.123		
Total	**22661.220**	**1249**			

As far as level of education is concerned, F-value has been quite low at 1.464 with p-value of significance at 0.223. This clearly indicates that level of alertness has been almost similar in all categories of education. Hence, the null hypothesis stating no difference of alertness among various education levels stands accepted.

7.4. Awareness Of Consumer Protection Laws

A number of laws have been passed by the Government of India over the years to protect the interest of consumers. It can be said that if all these laws are implemented properly, not even a single instance of exploitation of consumer can take place. However, awareness of legal machinery is very important to protect consumers. Thus, an effort has been made to examine the level of awareness of consumers with regards to consumer protection laws. The results are as below.

7.4.1. Awareness of Consumer Court

Consumer Court is the name given to special purpose courts, mainly in India, that deal with cases regarding consumer disputes and grievances. These are judiciary set ups by the government to protect the consumer rights. If any consumer is cheated by the seller he/she can approach the redressal forum to seek justice. Their main function is to maintain the fair practices by the sellers towards consumers. Awareness among about the consumer courts has been depicted in Table 7.20 and graphically shown in 7.16.

Table 7.20

Awareness of consumer courts

Awareness	Frequency	Percent
Not at all Aware	220	17.6
Not Very Aware	460	36.8
Somewhat Aware	225	18.0
Adequately Aware	75	6.0
Fully Aware	270	21.6
Total	**1250**	**100.0**

Source: *Primary Probe.*

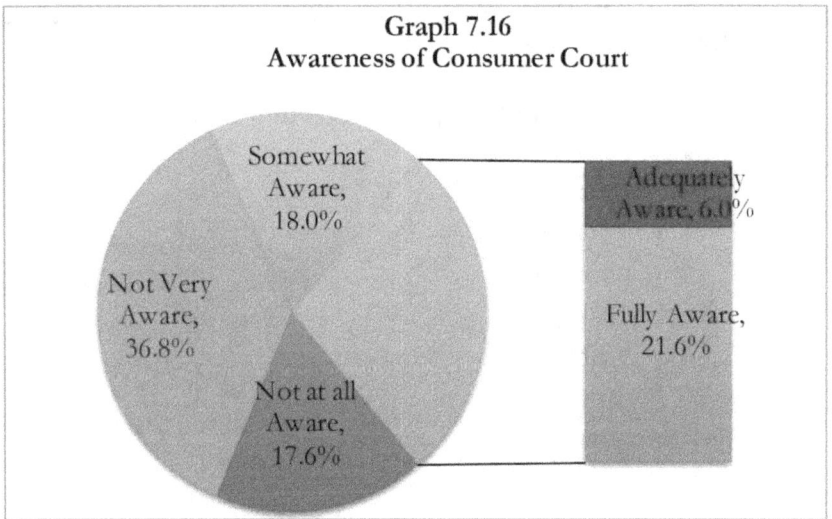

Graph 7.16
Awareness of Consumer Court

Table 7.20 shows that majority of respondents (that is, 36.8 per cent 'not very aware' and 17.6 per cent 'not at all aware') of consumer courts. While on the other hand, 21.6 per cent were fully aware of consumer courts and 18.0 per cent were somewhat aware.

Thus, it can be inferred that majority of respondents were not aware of consumer courts. Around 28 per cent of respondents were found either fully aware or adequately aware of consumer courts in Himachal Pradesh. It seems to be a threatening situation to consumer protection efforts as consumers are not aware of courts of justice.

7.4.2. Awareness of Consumer Protection Act

The Consumer Protection Act 1986 is a social welfare legislation, which was enacted as a result of widespread consumer protection movement. The main object of the legislature in the enactment of this act is to provide for the better protection of the interests of the consumer and to make provisions for establishment of consumer councils and other authorities for settlement of consumer disputes and matter therewith connected. The awareness among the respondents about the Consumer Protection Act has been enumerated in Table 7.21 and shown in Graph 7.17.

Table 7.21
Awareness of Consumer Protection Act

Awareness	Frequency	Percent
Not at all Aware	495	39.6
Not Very Aware	285	22.8
Somewhat Aware	285	22.8
Adequately Aware	185	14.8
Total	**1250**	**100.0**

Source: *Primary Probe.*

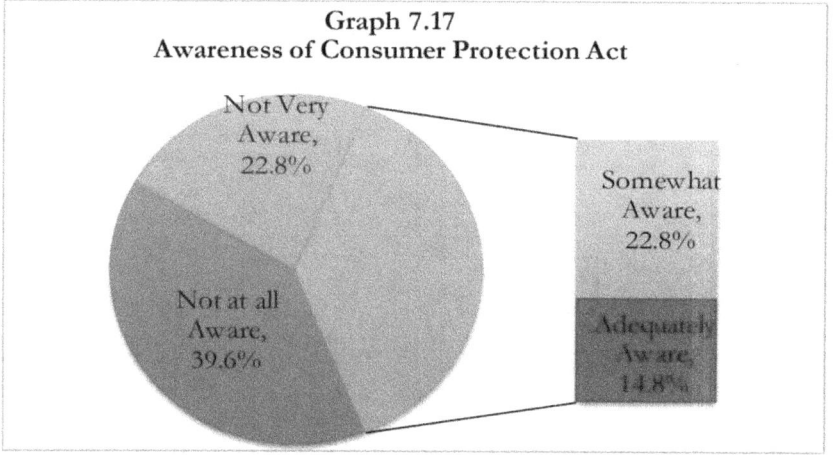

Graph 7.17
Awareness of Consumer Protection Act

Table 7.21 shows that more than 62 per cent of the respondents are either not at all aware or not very aware of consumer protection act, 1986. As this act contains many provisions related to consumer protection, appealing, and seeking remedies,

It seems to be important for consumers to be aware of it. Hence, the situation is not so good in Himachal Pradesh. Only around 15 per cent of the respondents are adequately aware of this act.

7.4.3. Awareness of Standards of Weights & Measures Act

This act aims at introducing standards in relation to weights and measures used in trade and commerce. The ultimate objective is to sub serve the interests of the consumers. The Act, therefore, is essentially a consumer protection measure as every article of manufacture, subject to the standards of weights and measures under the Act, ultimately finds its application or use by or for the benefit of consumer. The data regarding the awareness among the respondents about the standards of Weights and Measures Act has been presented in Table 7.22 and shown in Graph 7.18.

Table 7.22
Awareness of Standards of Weights & Measures Act

Awareness	Frequency	Percent
Not at all Aware	675	54.0
Not Very Aware	490	39.2
Somewhat Aware	85	6.8
Total	**1250**	**100.0**

Source: Primary Probe.

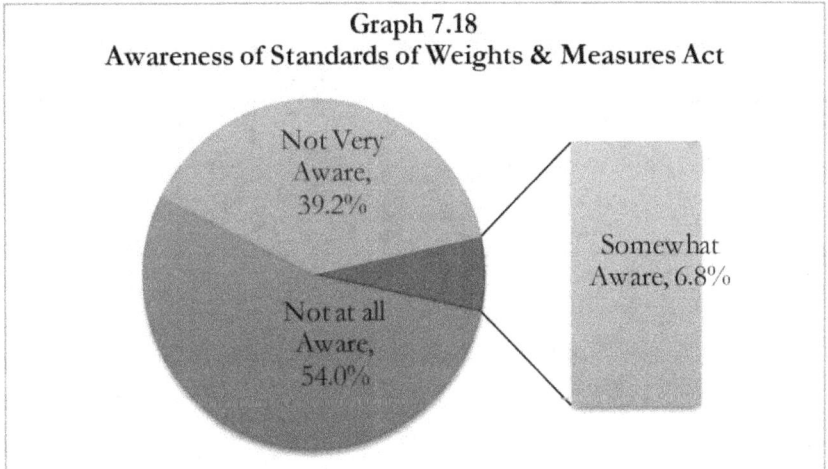

Graph 7.18
Awareness of Standards of Weights & Measures Act

Table 7.22 reveals that awareness of Standards of Weights and Measures Act among the people was not found good. Out of total respondents, 54.0 per cent of respondents were not at all aware of this Act, 39.2 per cent of respondents were not very aware and 6.8 per cent of respondents were somewhat aware of the Act. In this regard it was observed that respondents have never even heard of this act.

Thus, it can be inferred that majority of people are not aware of Standards of Weights and Measures Act in Himachal Pradesh.

7.4.4. Awareness of Consumer Protection Laws - Definition of Consumer

Consumer means any person who, buys any goods for a consideration which has been paid or promised or partly paid and partly promised, or under any system of deferred payment and includes any user of such goods other than the person who buys such goods for consideration paid or promised or partly paid or partly promised or under any system of deferred payment when such use is made with the approval of such person but does not include a person who obtains such goods for resale or for any commercial purpose; or hires or avails of any services for a consideration which has been paid or promised or partly paid and partly promised, or under any system of deferred payment and includes any beneficiary of such services other than the person who hires or avails of the services for consideration paid or promised, or partly paid and partly promised, or under any system of deferred payment, when such services are availed of with the approval of the first mentioned person but does not include a person who avails of such services for any commercial purpose. The data regarding the awareness among the respondents about the consumer or definition of consumer has been shown in Table 7.23 and shown in Graph 7.19.

Table 7.23
Awareness of Consumer Protection Laws - Definition of consumer

Awareness	Frequency	Percent
Somewhat Aware	805	64.4
Adequately Aware	210	16.8
Fully Aware	235	18.8
Total	**1250**	**100.0**

Source: Primary Probe.

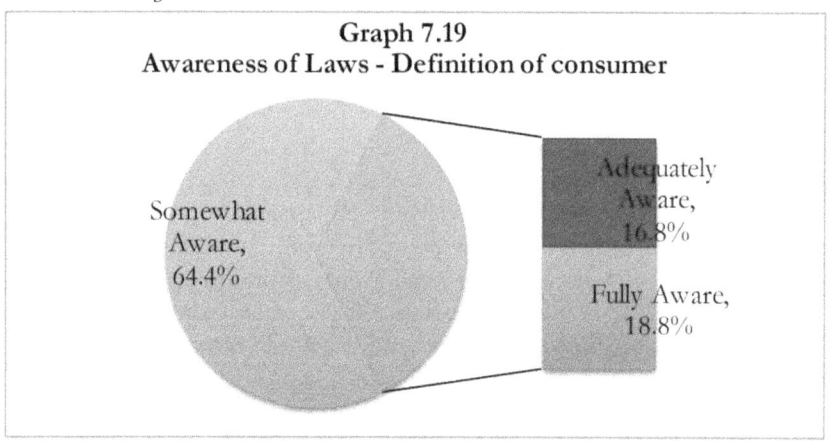

Graph 7.19
Awareness of Laws - Definition of consumer

Somewhat Aware, 64.4%

Adequately Aware, 16.8%

Fully Aware, 18.8%

Table 7.23 shows that level of awareness among consumers regarding the concept of consumer or definition of consumer is quite good. More than 35 per cent of the respondents are adequately or fully aware of the concept of consumer under legal terminology. Even remaining of the respondents is somewhat aware of the definition of consumer which is really encouraging.

7.4.5. Awareness of Consumer Protection Laws - Who Can Make Complaint

A complaint can be filed by a consumer to whom goods are sold or delivered or agreed to be sold or delivered or such services provided or agreed to be provided, by any voluntary consumer organization, by the central government, by the state governments or union territory administration; and/or by one or more consumers, where there are numerous consumers having the same interest. To know the awareness among the sample respondents about who can make complaint has been illustrated in Table 7.24 and in Graph 7.20.

Table 7.24

Awareness of Consumer Protection Laws - Who can make complaint

Awareness	Frequency	Percent
Not at all Aware	215	17.2
Not Very Aware	580	46.4
Somewhat Aware	455	36.4
Total	**1250**	**100.0**

Source: Primary Probe.

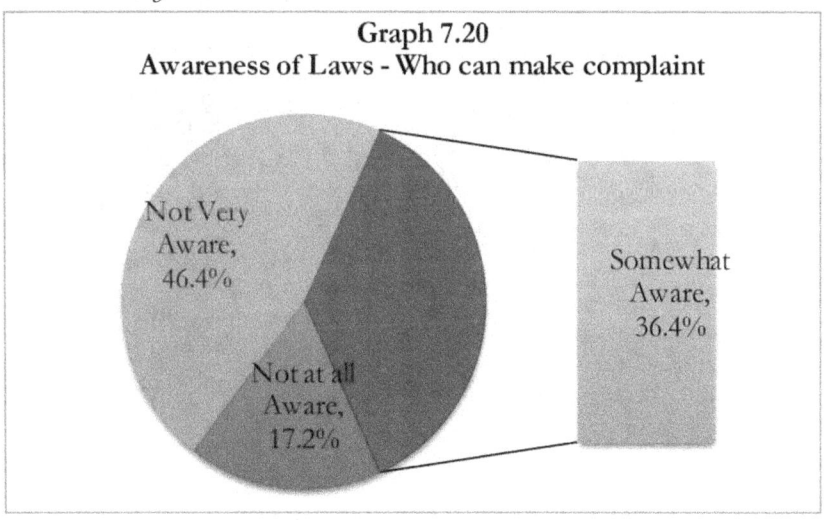

Graph 7.20
Awareness of Laws - Who can make complaint

Not Very Aware, 46.4%

Somewhat Aware, 36.4%

Not at all Aware, 17.2%

Table 7.24 shows that people in Himachal Pradesh are not very much aware of who can make a complaint in case of any deficiency in a product or service takes place. Out of total, 46.4 per cent of respondents were not very aware, 36.4 per cent of respondents were somewhat aware and 17.2 per cent of respondents were not at all aware about who can make complaint. Thus, it can be inferred that people in Himachal Pradesh were not aware about who can make complaint.

7.4.6. Awareness of District Consumer Protection Councils

The Consumer Protection Act provisions the central and state governments to create councils at the central, state and district level to promote consumerism. These consumer protection councils have very little statutory powers and as such any direct benefit one can get as a consumer from these councils is low to none. Yet, it is good if the consumers are aware of such consumer protection councils. In this regard data has been present in Table 7.25 and shown in Graph 7.21.

Table 7.25
Awareness of District Consumer Protection Councils

Awareness	Frequency	Percent
Somewhat Aware	830	66.4
Adequately Aware	200	16.0
Fully Aware	220	17.6
Total	**1250**	**100.0**

Source: *Primary Probe.*

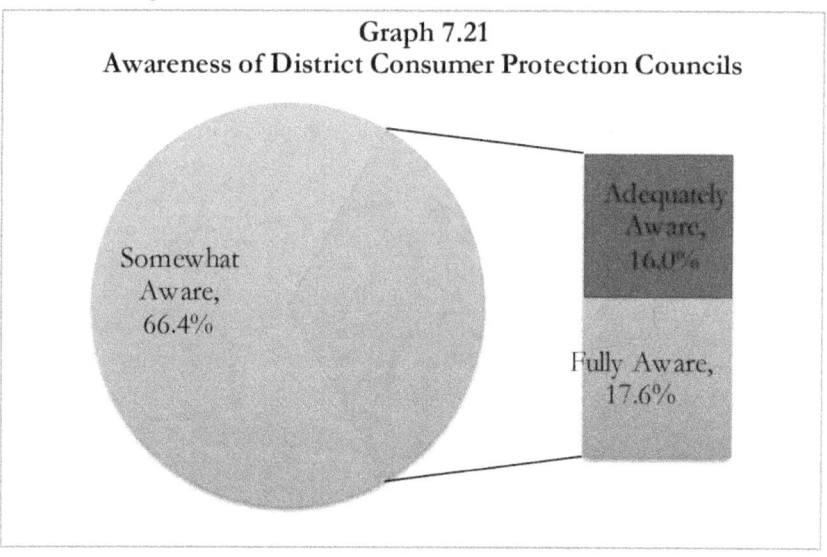

Graph 7.21
Awareness of District Consumer Protection Councils

Table 7.25 depicts that out of total respondents, 66.4 per cent of respondents were somewhat aware of district consumer protection councils. On the other hand, 17.6 per cent of respondents were fully aware and 16.0 per cent were adequately aware of these councils. The analyses gives an impression that through majority of respondents were somewhat aware, yet the awareness level of about 34 per cent of respondents was found reasonably good enough. It indicates good sign.

7.4.7. Awareness of District Consumer Forums

This consumer court deals with complaints where the compensation sought is less than twenty lakh. This limit is commonly known as the 'pecuniary jurisdiction' of the District Consumer Disputes Redressal Forum. For more details on how to file a complaint with a District Consumer Court, please refer to our article about filing complaints in consumer courts. A District Consumer Forum can hear cases for any company that operates an office or a branch in the district. It can also hear cases provided the actual reason why you are filing the complaint (such as sale or maintenance service that led to the defect) partially or fully occurred within the district. Data with regard to the awareness about district consumer forums has been depicted in Table 7.26 and shown in Graph 7.22.

Table 7.26
Awareness of District Consumer Forums

Awareness	Frequency	Percent
Not at all Aware	270	21.6
Not Very Aware	420	33.6
Somewhat Aware	500	40.0
Adequately Aware	20	1.6
Fully Aware	40	3.2
Total	**1250**	**100.0**

Source: Primary Probe.

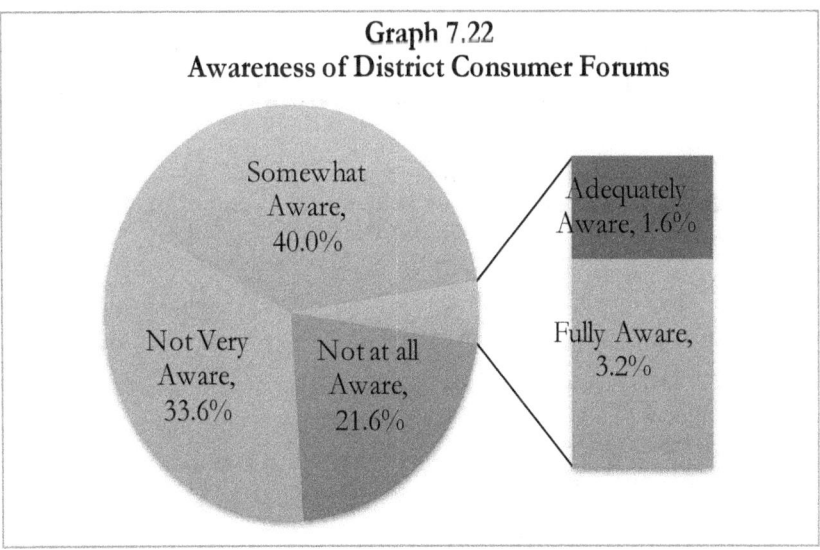

Graph 7.22
Awareness of District Consumer Forums

Table 7.26 shows that consumers by and large were not aware of district consumer forums. Table depicts that 33.6 per cent of respondents were not very aware, 21.6 per cent of respondents were not at all aware and 40.0 per cent of respondents were somewhat aware of district consumer forums. On the other hand, the percentage of those respondents who were fully aware and adequately aware was 3.2 per cent and 1.6 per cent respectively. Thus, it can be concluded that the majority of consumers are not aware of district consumer forums in Himachal Pradesh.

7.4.8. Awareness of District Consumer Forums in Himachal Pradesh

There are four whole time District Forums in the Himachal Pradesh. These are Shimla District Forum: For Shimla, Solan, Sirmour and Kinnaur Districts, Mandi District Forum: For Mandi, Kullu, and Lahaul Spiti Districts, Una District Forum: For Una, Hamirpur and Bilaspur Districts, and Kangra District Forum at Dharamshala: For Kangra and Chamba Districts. Data regarding the awareness about District Consumer Forums in Himachal Pradesh has presented in Table 7.27 and shown in Graph 7.23.

Table 7.27

Awareness of Location of District Consumer Forums in Himachal Pradesh

Awareness	Frequency	Percent
Not at all Aware	320	25.6
Not Very Aware	480	38.4
Somewhat Aware	375	30.0
Adequately Aware	25	2.0
Fully Aware	50	4.0
Total	**1250**	**100.0**

Source: *Primary Probe.*

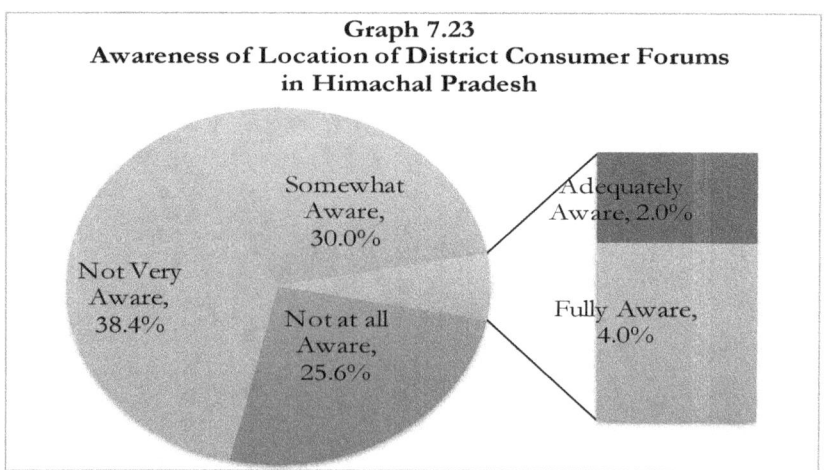

Graph 7.23
Awareness of Location of District Consumer Forums in Himachal Pradesh

Table 7.27 depicts rather shocking results that about 64 per cent of the respondents either not at all aware or not very aware of the location of district forum. have no idea or little idea of where the district forums of consumer protection are located in Himachal Pradesh and their jurisdictions.

Only 6 per cent of the respondents have indicated that they are adequately or fully aware of various district forums in Himachal Pradesh. Thus, government of Himachal Pradesh should make efforts to popularize district forums in its general public.

7.4.9. Awareness of State Commission

The State Consumer Disputes Redressal Commission deals with a pecuniary jurisdiction of only those complaints where the compensation sought is higher than twenty lakh but lesser than one crore. The State Consumer Forum usually hears cases of three types, viz. appeals from District Consumer Forums, cases against companies that operates an office or a branch in the state, and cases where the actual reason why one is filing the complaint (such as signing of an agreement or payment of a bill) partially or fully occurred within the state. The State Consumer Court also has the powers to transfer a case from one District Consumer Forum to another Forum provided there is such a request or it is in the interest of the law. The awareness about the state commission has been enumerated in Table 7.28 and shown in Graph 7.24.

Table 7.28 indicates a lower level of awareness among consumers regarding state commission and legal provisions related to state commissions. Out of total respondents, 38.0 of respondents were somewhat aware, 36.0 per cent were not very aware and 19.6 per cent of respondents were not at all aware of State consumer commission.

Table 7.28
Awareness of State Commission

Awareness	Frequency	Percent
Not at all Aware	245	19.6
Not Very Aware	450	36.0
Somewhat Aware	475	38.0
Adequately Aware	20	1.6
Fully Aware	60	4.8
Total	**1250**	**100.0**

Source: *Primary Probe.*

While on the other hand, about 6 per cent of respondents were either fully aware or adequately aware of state commission. Hence, it can be inferred that the consumer in Himachal Pradesh are not aware of state commission and provisions related to it.

271

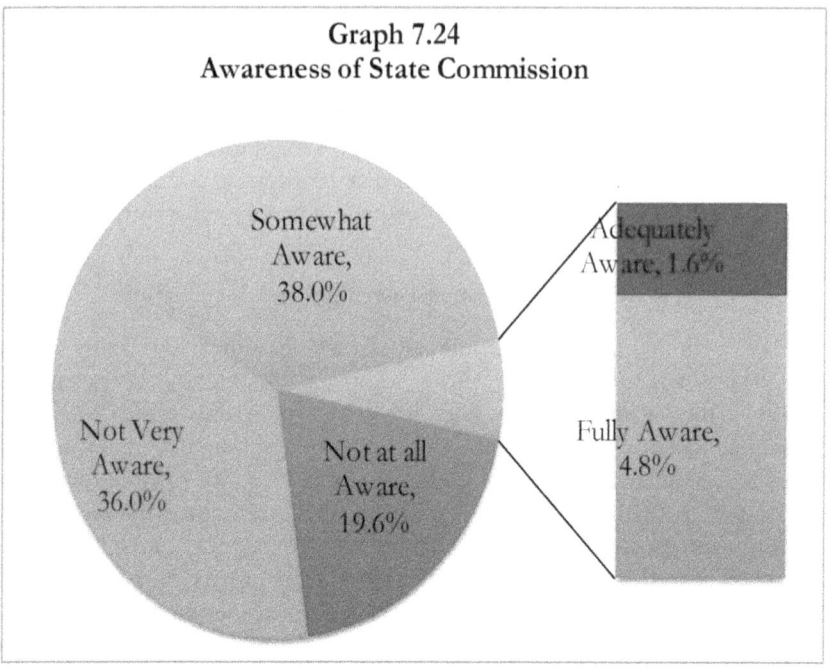

Graph 7.24
Awareness of State Commission

Somewhat Aware, 38.0%

Adequately Aware, 1.6%

Not Very Aware, 36.0%

Not at all Aware, 19.6%

Fully Aware, 4.8%

7.4.10. Awareness of National Commission

If the complaint seeks more than one crore rupees of compensation from a company, then the National Consumer Commission has the pecuniary jurisdiction over your complaint. The National Consumer Court must ordinarily be functioning in New Delhi and is presided over by a person who is currently or has been in the past a judge of the Supreme Court. The President of the National Consumer Disputes Redressal Commission (NCDRC) is appointed by the Central Government after consultation with the Chief Justice of India. The National Consumer Court handles five types of complaints viz. Complaints that has been sought or need to be transferred from one State Consumer Commission to another in the interest of justice, Appeals from State Consumer Disputes Redressal Commissions, Consumer complaints that occurred in India, except in the State of Jammu and Kashmir, Cases from State Consumer Commissions where there has been accusations or proof of material irregularity or illegal activities, and Cases where ex-parte (where verdicts have been passed in the absence of either parties) orders have to be set aside. The responses of respondents about the awareness of National Commission has been shown in Table 7.29 and in Graph 7.25.

Table 7.29
Awareness of National Commission

Awareness	Frequency	Percent
Not at all Aware	240	19.2
Not Very Aware	400	32.0
Somewhat Aware	475	38.0
Adequately Aware	60	4.8
Fully Aware	75	6.0
Total	1250	100.0

Source: Primary Probe.

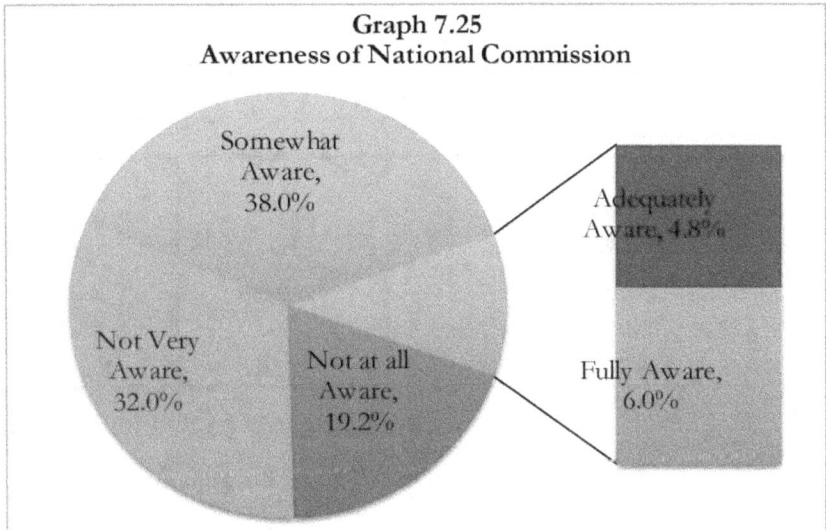

Graph 7.25
Awareness of National Commission

The analysis of respondent's opinion regarding their awareness of National Commission reveals that majority of respondents were not aware of this commission. Out of total respondents, 38.0 per cent of respondents were somewhat aware, 32.0 per cent of respondents were not very aware and 19.2 per cent of respondents were not at all aware of National Commission. 6.0 per cent of respondents were fully aware and 4.8 per cent of respondents were adequately aware of National Commission. Hence, the analysis depicts that more than two third of respondents were not aware of National Commission in Himachal Pradesh.

7.4.11. Awareness of Consumer Protection Laws - Process of filing complaints

A complaint in relation to any goods sold or delivered or agreed to be sold or delivered or any service provided or agreed to be provided, may be filed with a District Forum, by the consumer to whom such goods are sold or delivered, or by any recognized consumer association whether the consumer is a member of such association or not, or by one or more consumers, where there are numerous consumers having the same interest, or by the Central Government or the State Government, as the case may be, either in its individual capacity or as a representative of interests of the consumers in general. Every complaint filed is to be accompanied with such amount of fee and payable in such manner as may be prescribed. If a consumer knows the process of filing a complaint, the rest of the legal process is simplified. Hence, consumers must be aware of how to initiate legal proceedings by filing complaint. The responses of respondents about the awareness of the process of filing complaints have been presented in Table 7.30 and in Graph 7.26.

Table 7.30
Awareness of Consumer Protection Laws - Process of filing complaints

Awareness	Frequency	Percent
Not at all Aware	270	21.6
Not Very Aware	440	35.2
Somewhat Aware	440	35.2
Adequately Aware	40	3.2
Fully Aware	60	4.8
Total	**1250**	**100.0**

Source: *Primary Probe.*

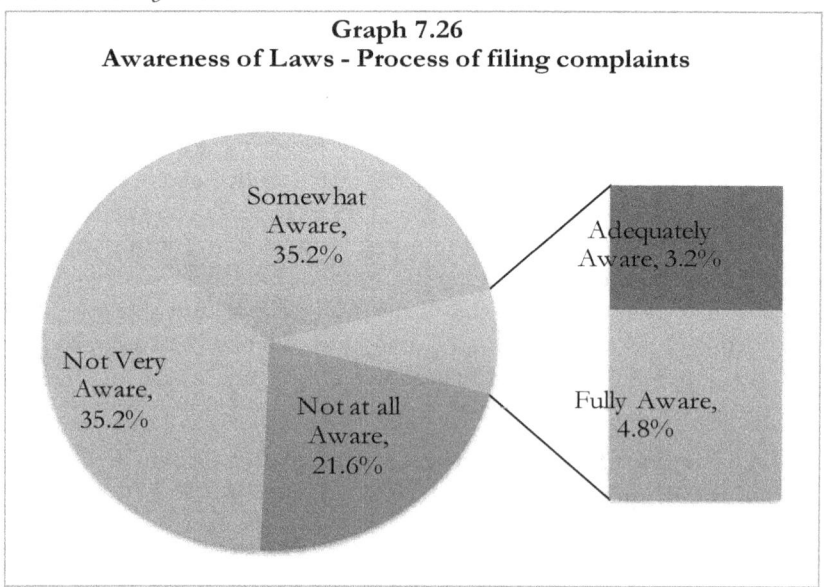

Graph 7.26
Awareness of Laws - Process of filing complaints

274

Table 7.30 shows that majority of respondents were not aware of the process of filing complaints, as 35.2 per cent of respondents were of the opinion that they are not very aware, 21.6 per cent of respondents opined that they are not at all aware and 35.2 per cent of respondents were of the opinion that they somewhat aware of the process of filing complaints.

Table 7.30 shows that majority of respondents were not aware of the process of filing complaints, as 35.2 per cent of respondents were of the opinion that they are not very aware, 21.6 per cent of respondents opined that they are not at all aware and 35.2 per cent of respondents were of the opinion that they somewhat aware of the process of filing complaints. The percentage of those respondents who were of the opinion that they are either adequately or fully aware was 3.2 per cent and 4.8 per cent respectively. Thus, the analysis indicates that consumers in Himachal Pradesh do not know the process of filing complaints.

7.4.12. Awareness of Documents Required for Filing Complaints

Various documents which may be necessary for filing any consumer complaint can be mainly the bill of payment for product or service. However, it can also be any receipt issued by the seller or service provider. Main purpose of such documents is to establish that there has been a transaction between the buyer and seller. Though, a complaint can be filed even without such documents, yet it is beneficial to attach such documents to speed up and strengthen the case. The data regarding the documents required for filing complaints have been illustrated in Table 7.31 and shown in Graph 7.27.

Table 7.31 indicates a lower level of awareness among consumers regarding documents required in filing complaints with consumer courts. 38.4 per cent of respondents were not very aware, 34.8 per cent were somewhat aware and 19.2 per cent of respondents were not at all aware of the documents required in filing complaints.

Table 7.31

Awareness of Consumer Protection Laws - Documents required for filing complaints

Awareness	Frequency	Percent
Not at all Aware	240	19.2
Not Very Aware	480	38.4
Somewhat Aware	435	34.8
Adequately Aware	50	4.0
Fully Aware	45	3.6
Total	**1250**	**100.0**

Source: *Primary Probe.*

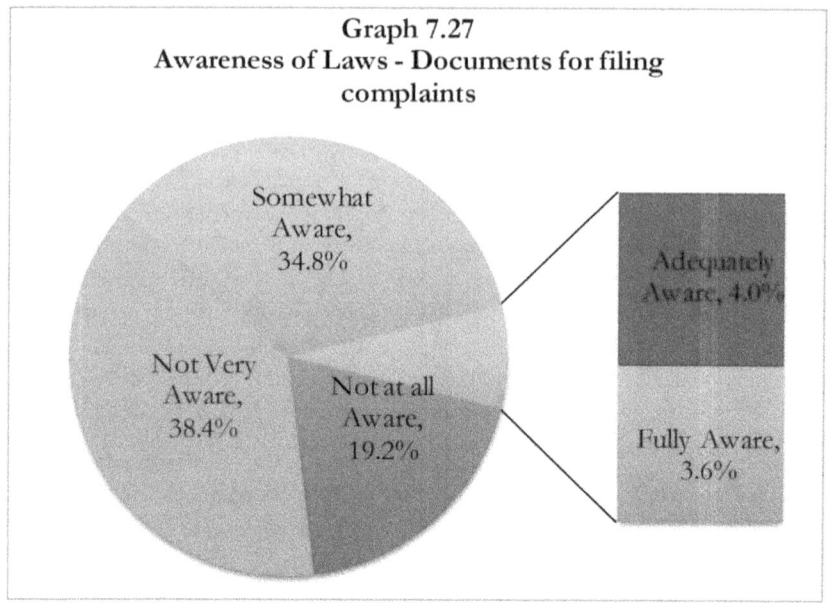

Graph 7.27
Awareness of Laws - Documents for filing complaints

Somewhat Aware, 34.8%

Adequately Aware, 4.0%

Not Very Aware, 38.4%

Not at all Aware, 19.2%

Fully Aware, 3.6%

Whereas, 4.0 per cent of respondents were adequately aware and 3.6 per cent of respondents were fully aware.

7.4.13. Awareness of Prescribed Fee for Filing Complaint

Under the original un-amended Act of 1986, no requirement of payment of Court-fee or any other formal procedure of Court was contemplated. However, after the amendment of 2002, there is a nominal fee you may have to pay for filing a complaint. For example in the District Forum located in Delhi the fee structure is as follows –

1. Up to 1 Lakh – Rs.100
2. 1 Lakh & above but less that 5 Lakhs – Rs.200
3. 5 Lakhs & above but less that 10 Lakhs – Rs.400
4. 10 Lakhs & above but less that 20 Lakhs – Rs. 500

The specified fee is to be paid in the form of a crossed demand draft drawn on a nationalized bank or through a crossed Indian Postal Order in favor of the Registrar of the State Commission & payable where it is situated. The concerned District Forum shall deposit the amount so received. Data regarding prescribed fee for filing complaint have been shown in Table 7.32 and in Graph 7.28.

Table 7.32 shows that more than half of the respondents were either not at all aware or little aware of the prescribed fee for filing complaints. Out of total respondents, 40.8 per cent of respondents were not at all aware, 33.6 per cent were somewhat aware and 18.0 per cent of respondents were not at all aware of the prescribed fee for filing complaints.

Table 7.32

Awareness of Consumer Protection Laws - Prescribed Fee for Filing Complaint

Awareness	Frequency	Percent
Not at all Aware	225	18.0
Not Very Aware	510	40.8
Somewhat Aware	420	33.6
Adequately Aware	55	4.4
Fully Aware	40	3.2
Total	1250	100.0

Source: *Primary Probe.*

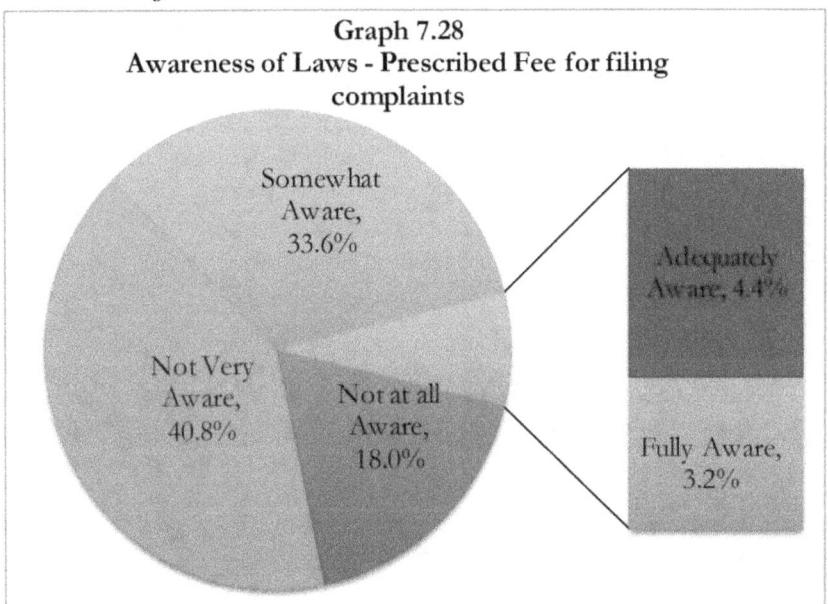

Graph 7.28
Awareness of Laws - Prescribed Fee for filing complaints

The percentage of those consumers who were either adequately aware or fully aware was 4.4 per cent and 3.2 per cent respectively. Thus, it can be inferred that people don't know the prescribed fee for filing complaints.

7.4.14. Awareness of Available Reliefs

Reliefs which are available to the consumers under the act include removal of defects from the goods; replacement of the goods; refund of the price paid; award of compensation for the loss or injury suffered; discontinue and not to repeat unfair trade practice or restrictive trade practice; not to offer hazardous goods for sale; to withdraw hazardous goods from sale; to cease manufacture of hazardous goods and desist from offering services which are hazardous in nature; if the loss or injury has been suffered by a large number of consumers who are not identifiable conveniently, to pay such sum (not less than 5 per cent of the value of such defective goods or services provided) which shall be determined by Forum; to issue corrective advertisement to neutralize the effect of misleading advertisement; and to provide adequate costs to parties. Data regarding the awareness about the available reliefs have been shown in Table 7.33 and in Graph 7.29.

Table 7.33
Awareness of Consumer Protection Laws - Available Reliefs

Awareness	Frequency	Percent
Not at all Aware	215	17.2
Not Very Aware	435	34.8
Somewhat Aware	505	40.4
Adequately Aware	40	3.2
Fully Aware	55	4.4
Total	1250	100.0

Source: *Primary Probe.*

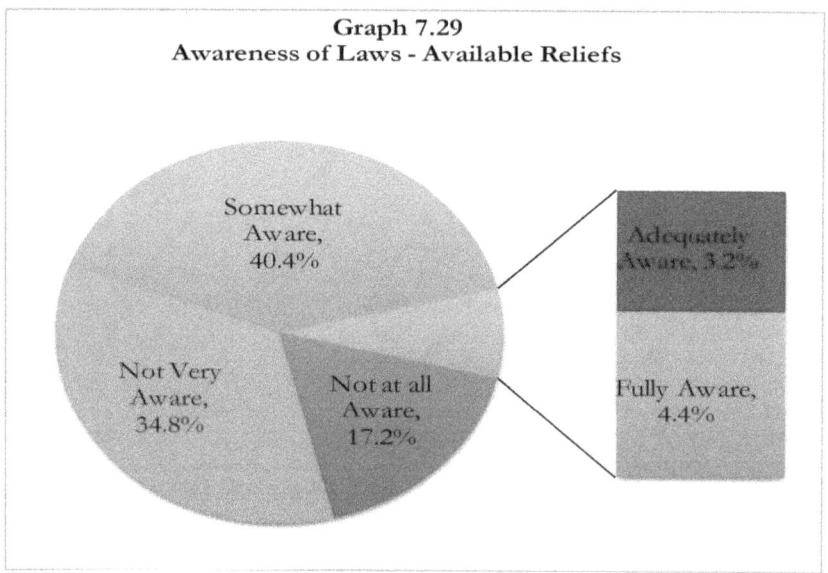

Graph 7.29
Awareness of Laws - Available Reliefs

Table 7.33 shows that consumers by and large were not aware various reliefs available to them under law. Analysis reveals that 34.8 per cent of respondents were not very aware, 40.4 per cent of respondents were somewhat aware and 17.2 per cent of respondents were not at all aware of available reliefs.

The percentage of awaked consumer was very low. It indicates that consumers in Himachal Pradesh are not aware of available reliefs under law.

7.4.15. Awareness of Unfair Trade Practices

A business practice may result in an unfair trade practice if it includes any false representation and misleading advertisement of goods and services, falsely representing second-hand goods as new, misleading representation regarding usefulness, need, quality, standard, style etc of goods and services, false claims or representation regarding price of goods and services, giving false facts regarding sponsorship, affiliation etc. of goods and services, and giving false guarantee or warranty on goods and services without adequate tests. Opinion of respondents about the awareness of unfair trade practices has been analyzed in Table 7.34 and shown in Graph 7.30.

Table 7.34
Awareness of Unfair Trade Practices

Awareness	Frequency	Percent
Not at all Aware	195	15.6
Not Very Aware	475	38.0
Somewhat Aware	495	39.6
Adequately Aware	65	5.2
Fully Aware	20	1.6
Total	**1250**	**100.0**

Source: *Primary Probe.*

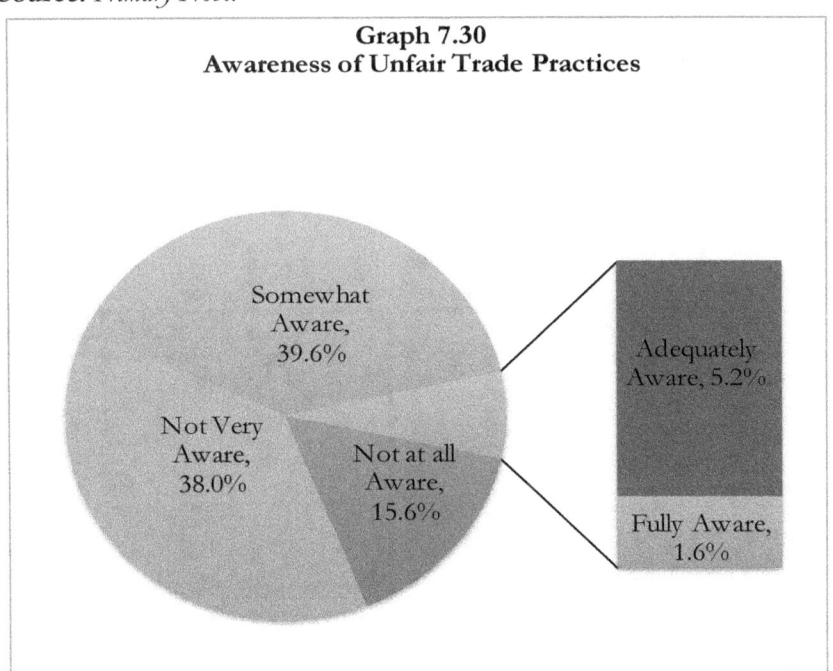

Graph 7.30
Awareness of Unfair Trade Practices

Table 7.34 depicts a lower level of awareness among consumers regarding concept of unfair trade practices or what practices fall under the purview of unfair trade practices. About 53 per cent of respondents were either not very aware or not at all aware. 39.6 per cent of respondents were somewhat aware of unfair trade practices.

Only 5.2 per cent of respondents were adequately and 1.6 per cent of respondents were fully aware in this context.

7.4.16. Awareness of Restrictive Trade Practice

Restrictive trade practice means a trade practice which has, or may have, the effect of preventing, distorting or restricting competition in any manner and in particular, which tends to obstruct the flow of capital or resources into the stream of production, or which tends to bring about manipulation of prices, or conditions of delivery or to affect the flow of supplies in the market relating to goods or services in such manner as to impose on the consumers unjustified costs or restrictions; These may include anti-competitive arrangements, Price fixing, Boycotts, Misuse of Market Power, Exclusive Dealing, and Resale Price Maintenance. If a consumer knows which activities of traders are restrictive under various acts, it can help the consumer to decide the course of action he wants to opt. Hence, consumers must be aware of activities which are restrictive in nature as per law. Data regarding the awareness of sample respondents about restrictive trade practices have been depicted in Table 7.35 and in Graph 7.31.

Table 7.35 shows that out of total respondents, 37.2 per cent of respondents were not very aware, 36.8 per cent of respondents were somewhat aware and 20.8 per cent of respondents were not at all aware of restrictive trade practices. Further, the full awareness and adequate awareness was found only in about 5 percent of respondents. Hence, it can be inferred that majority of consumers were not aware of restrictive trade practices in Himachal Pradesh.

Table 7.35
Awareness of Restrictive Trade Practice

Awareness	Frequency	Percent
Not at all Aware	260	20.8
Not Very Aware	465	37.2
Somewhat Aware	460	36.8
Adequately Aware	50	4.0
Fully Aware	15	1.2
Total	1250	100.0

Source: *Primary Probe.*

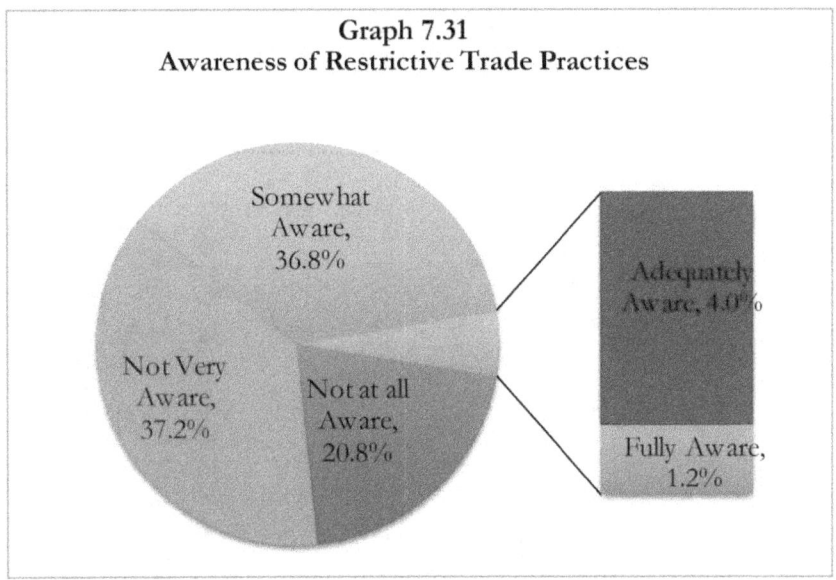

Graph 7.31
Awareness of Restrictive Trade Practices

7.4.17. Awareness of Spurious Goods and Services

The word 'Spurious' means lacking authenticity or validity in essence or origin; not genuine; false. Spurious goods and services mean such goods and services which are claimed to be genuine but they are actually not so. There is increasing supply of duplicate products. It is very difficult for an ordinary consumer to distinguish between a genuine product and its imitation. It is necessary to protect consumers from such exploitation by ensuring compliance with prescribed norms of quality and safety. The opinion of the sample respondents about the awareness of spurious goods and services have been analyzed in Table 7.36 and shown in Graph 7.32.

Table 7.36
Awareness of Spurious Goods and Service

Awareness	Frequency	Percent
Not at all Aware	240	19.2
Not Very Aware	415	33.2
Somewhat Aware	460	36.8
Adequately Aware	105	8.4
Fully Aware	30	2.4
Total	**1250**	**100.0**

Source: *Primary Probe.*

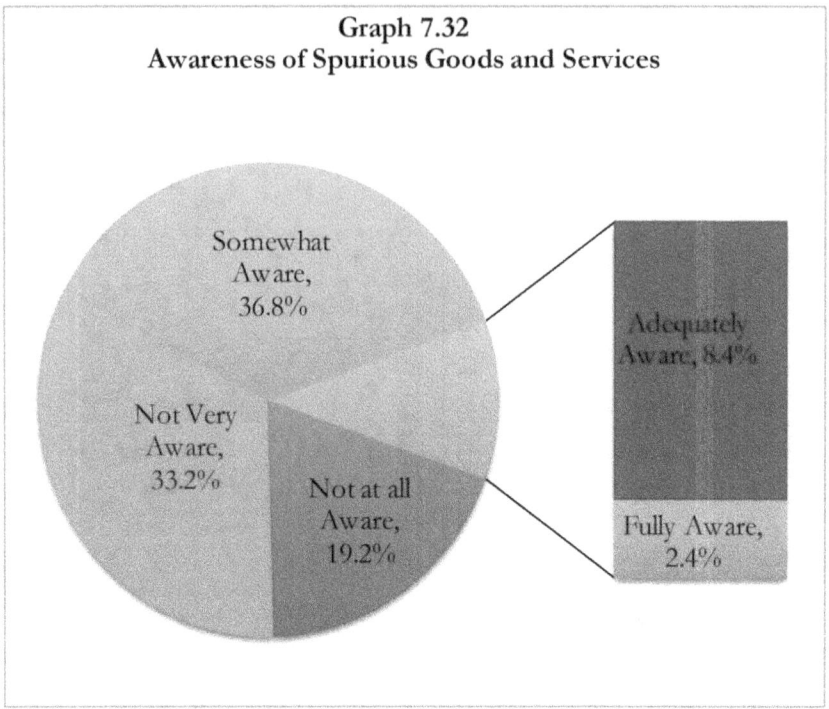

Graph 7.32
Awareness of Spurious Goods and Services

Table 7.36 shows that majority of respondents were not aware of spurious goods and services. The percentage of those respondents who opined that they are either not very aware or somewhat aware or not at all aware was 33.2 per cent, 36.8 per cent and 19.2 per cent respectively. 10.8 per cent of respondents were either adequately or fully aware of spurious goods and services. A reasonable degree of knowledge of such goods and services can help consumers to be alert at the time of buying goods and services, but the analysis reveals that consumer didn't have reasonable degree of knowledge of such goods and services.

7.4.18. Snapshot Comparison of Awareness of Consumer Protection Laws

This section deals with a brief comparison of awareness of all the concepts or provisions of consumer protection laws discussed above. The purpose here is to make a comparative analysis of level of awareness in case of all consumer protection laws. For this purpose, all these provisions or definitions have been put subject to mean value and standard deviation value. These have been divided in three codes. Code A deals with high awareness categories, code B deals with moderate awareness category, and finally code C deals with low awareness category.

Table 7.37

Descriptive Statistics Awareness of Consumer Protection Laws

Code		Mean	SD
A1	Awareness of Consumer Protection Laws - Definition of consumer	3.54	.792
A2	Awareness of District Consumer Protection Council	3.51	.777
B1	Awareness of National Commission	2.46	1.046
B2	Awareness of Consumer Protection Laws - Available Reliefs	2.43	.959
B3	Awareness of Spurious Goods and Service	2.42	.971
B4	Awareness of Unfair Trade Practices	2.39	.868
B5	Awareness of State Commission	2.36	.973
B6	Awareness of Consumer Protection Laws - Process of filing complaints	2.34	1.007
B 7	Awareness of Consumer Protection Laws - Documents required for filing complaints	2.34	.954
B8	Awareness of Consumer Protection Laws - Prescribed Fee for Filing Complaint	2.34	.932
B9	Awareness of District Consumer Forums	2.31	.935
B10	Awareness of Restrictive Trade Practice	2.28	.878
B11	Awareness of District Consumer Forums in Himachal Pradesh	2.20	.979
B12	Awareness of Consumer Protection Laws - Who can make complaint	2.19	.708
B13	Awareness of consumer protection act	2.13	1.097
C1	Aware of standards of weights & measures act	1.53	.622

Source: Primary Probe.

Graph 7.33

Average Awareness of Consumer Protection Laws

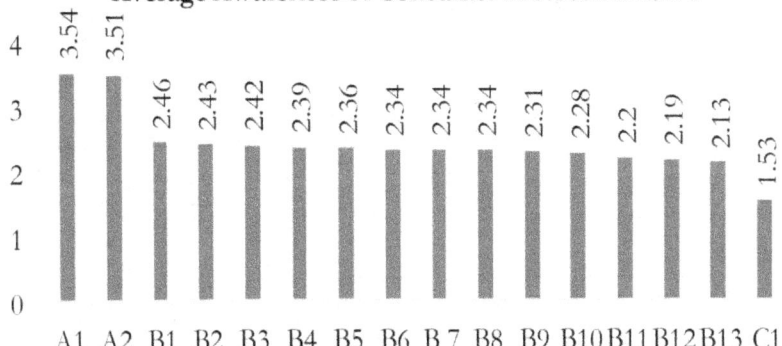

Table 7.37 shows that average level of awareness among consumers regarding consumer protection laws is quite good when it comes to knowledge of who is a consumer and what is a district consumer protection council. However, regarding consumer protection machinery like consumer courts, district forums, state and national commissions, they have a moderate degree of awareness. Same is the case with the procedures of consumer complaints like who can make a complaint, procedure of filing complaint, fee and documents required etc. Finally the level of awareness is really poor in case of The Standards of Weights & Measures Act.

7.5. Awareness of Consumer Protection Laws and Demographic Attributes

In this section, an effort has been made to see if any demographic attribute of the customer has any say in doing or not doing any particular activity. For this purpose, four demographic attributes viz., gender of the respondents, age of the respondents, occupation of the respondents, and qualification of the respondents have been covered and analyzed. Just like level of alertness, level of legal awareness has been calculated by totaling all the responses of respondents related to awareness of consumer protection law.

7.5.1. Gender Based ANOVA

This part deals with the exploration of difference, if any, in males and females with regards to knowledge of various concepts, machinery and procedures followed in consumer protection laws. Descriptive and ANOVA of gender vs. awareness of consumer protection laws have been depicted in Table 7.38 (a) and Table 7.38 (b).

Table 7.38 (a)
Descriptive – Gender vs. Awareness of Consumer Protection Laws

Gender vs. Awareness of Consumer Protection Laws	N	Mean	Std. Deviation
Male	875	61.3943	4.78971
Female	375	61.6267	6.35392
Total	**1250**	**61.4640**	**5.29536**

Table 7.38 (a) shows that the average awareness score which represents the sum of all awareness related activities is marginally high in case of females than males.

To find the significance of difference, ANOVA has been used. Null hypothesis for ANOVA states no difference between male and female respondents with regards to level of awareness of consumer protection laws.

However, ANOVA value 0.507 is quite low. Due to it, p-value of significance is 0.477. It indicates that no significant difference exists in male and female respondents in relation to level of awareness of consumer protection laws. Thus, the null hypothesis stating no difference in males and females in relation to their level of awareness of consumer protection laws stands accepted.

Table 7.38 (b)
ANOVA – Gender vs. Awareness of Consumer Protection Laws

Gender vs. Awareness of Consumer Protection Laws	Sum of Squares	df	Mean Square	F	Sig.
Between Groups	14.175	1	14.175	.507	.477
Within Groups	34896.705	1248	27.962		
Total	34910.880	1249			

7.5.2.   Occupation Based ANOVA

This ANOVA deals with the examination of differences, if any, in different occupational categories. Null hypothesis in this case states that respondents belonging to different occupational backgrounds have no difference in their level of awareness of consumer protection laws. Descriptive and ANOVA of occupation vs. level of awareness of consumer protection laws have been enumerated in Table 7.39 (a) and Table 7.39 (b).

Table 7.39 (a)
Descriptive – Occupation vs. Level of Awareness of Consumer Protection Laws

Occupation vs. Level of Awareness of Consumer Protection Laws	N	Mean	Std. Deviation
Business	325	61.5846	5.60104
Service	635	61.2677	5.24699
Student	160	61.9375	4.43547
Housewife	130	61.5385	5.94125
Total	1250	61.4640	5.29536

Descriptive in Table 7.39 (a) show that service sector people have the lowest mean Level of Awareness of Consumer Protection Laws whereas student respondents have a better degree of awareness of consumer protection laws.

ANOVA value in this case is 0.784 which is quite low. Also the p-value is 0.503 which indicates insignificant variation. Hence, it may be concluded that though difference exists in respondents with regard to awareness of consumer protection laws, but it is not very significant. Hence, null hypothesis assuming no difference of awareness of consumer protection laws among respondents belonging to different occupations stands accepted.

Table 7.39 (b)
ANOVA – Occupation vs. Awareness of Consumer Protection Laws

Occupation vs. Awareness of Consumer Protection Laws	Sum of Squares	df	Mean Square	F	Sig.
Between Groups	65.786	3	21.929	.784	.503
Within Groups	34845.094	1246	27.966		
Total	34910.880	1249			

7.5.3. Age Based ANOVA

Age based ANOVA has been calculated in this part to examine any possible difference of Level of Awareness of Consumer Protection Laws among respondents belonging to different age groups. Here null hypothesis statement is that respondents belonging to different age groups do not significantly differ on their Level of Awareness of Consumer Protection Laws while making purchases. Descriptive and ANOVA of age vs. level of awareness of consumer protection laws have been enumerated in Table 7.40 (a) and Table 7.40 (b).

Table 7.40 (a)
Descriptive – Age vs. Level of awareness of Consumer Protection Laws

Age vs. level of awareness of consumer protection laws	N	Mean	Std. Deviation
15 - 18	300	61.2667	5.09192
18 - 25	365	61.4932	6.11265
25 - 35	445	61.5618	5.14109
35 or above	140	61.5000	4.00463
Total	1250	61.4640	5.29536

Table 7.40 (a) shows that Level of Awareness of Consumer Protection Laws has been minimum in case of age group 15-18 years, followed by 18

years to 25 years and 35 years or above. The maximum awareness has been found in the respondents in age group 25 years to 35 years. Besides, standard deviation is not too high.

Table 7.40 (b)
ANOVA - Age vs. Level of Consumer Protection Laws

Age vs. Level of Consumer Protection Laws	Sum of Squares	df	Mean Square	F	Sig.
Between Groups	16.430	3	5.477	.196	.899
Within Groups	34894.450	1246	28.005		
Total	34910.880	1249			

F-value in this case is 0.196 which is low. That's why p-value is more than 0.05. It indicates insignificant difference. Thus, it can be stated almost all the age groups have the same Level of Awareness of Consumer Protection Laws. Hence, null hypothesis assuming no difference of awareness of consumer protection laws among consumers belonging to different age groups stands accepted.

7.5.4. Education Based ANOVA

In this case, ANOVA has been used to examine the possibility of significant difference of degree of awareness of consumer protection laws of various respondents having different levels of education. It has been assumed that education makes a person more aware and educated people cannot be cheated easily. Here the null hypothesis is that respondents having been from various levels of education do not differ significantly with respect to degree of such awareness. Descriptive and ANOVA of age vs. level of awareness of consumer protection laws have been enumerated in Table 7.41 (a) and Table 7.41 (b).

Table 7.41 (a)
Descriptive – Education vs. Level of Awareness of Consumer Protection Laws

Education vs. Level of Awareness of Consumer Protection Laws	N	Mean	Std. Deviation
Matriculate or below	280	61.4821	5.21184
Higher Secondary	375	61.6267	5.26532
Graduate	280	60.8571	5.60982
Post Graduate or above	315	61.7937	5.19975
Total	1250	61.4640	5.29536

Table 7.41 (a) shows that the degree of such awareness has been found

to be maximum in case of graduates followed by post graduates and higher secondary education. Matriculate or below people have been on the lower side.

As far as level of education is concerned, F-value has been quite low at 1.761 with p-value of significance at 0.153. This clearly indicates that Level of Awareness of Consumer Protection Laws has been almost similar in all categories of education.

Table 7.41 (b)
ANOVA– Education vs. Level of Awareness of Consumer Protection Laws

Education vs. Level of Awareness of Consumer Protection Laws	Sum of Squares	df	Mean Square	F	Sig.
Between Groups	147.363	3	49.121	1.761	.153
Within Groups	34763.517	1246	27.900		
Total	**34910.880**	**1249**			

Hence, the null hypothesis stating no difference of awareness of consumer protection laws among various education levels stands accepted.

7.6. Awareness of Consumer Rights

Consumer rights are the rights given to a "consumer" to protect him/her from being cheated by salesman/manufacturer/shopkeeper. Consumer protection laws are designed to ensure fair trade competition and the free flow of truthful information in the marketplace. The laws are designed to prevent businesses that engage in fraud or specified unfair practices from gaining an advantage over competitors and may provide additional protection for the weak and those unable to take care of themselves. Consumer Protection laws are a form of government regulation which aim to protect the rights of consumers.

7.6.1. Awareness of Right to Safety

Consumer right to safety is as vast in its purview as the market reach itself. It applies to all possible consumption patterns and to all goods and services. In the context of the new market economy and rapid technological advances affecting the market, the right to safety has become a pre-requisite quality in all products and services. For e.g. some Indian products carry the ISI mark, this is a symbol of satisfactory quality of a product. Similarly, the FPO and AGMARK symbolize standard quality of food products. The market has for long made consumers believe that by consuming packaged food or mineral water, consumers can safeguard their health. This notion has been proved wrong time and again due to rampant food adulteration in market products. Right to food safety is an important consumer right since it directly affects the health and quality of life of consumers. The data regarding the awareness of right to safety has been shown in Table 7.42 and in Graph 7.34.

Table 7.42
Awareness of Right to Safety

Awareness	Frequency	Percent
Not at all Aware	270	21.6
Not Very Aware	385	30.8
Somewhat Aware	440	35.2
Adequately Aware	90	7.2
Fully Aware	65	5.2
Total	1250	100.0

Source: *Primary Probe.*

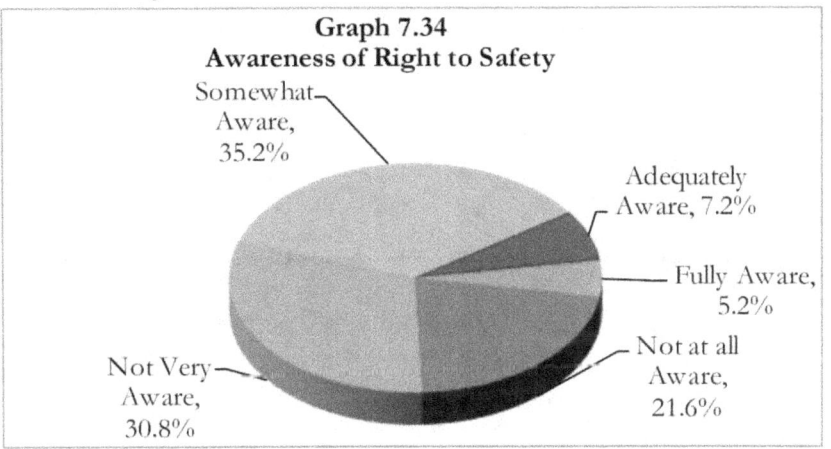

Graph 7.34
Awareness of Right to Safety

Table 7.42 shows that more than half of the respondents are either totally unaware or not very aware of this right to safety. This is surely a disappointing situation. Around 35 per cent of the respondents are somewhat aware of this right. Only 12.4 per cent of the respondents are adequately or fully aware of this right. Though this right is very generic, yet the lower rate of awareness can be a matter of concern.

7.6.2. Awareness of Right to Information

Right to information means the right to be given the facts needed to make an informed choice or decision about factors like quality, quantity, potency, purity standards and price of product or service. The right to information now goes beyond avoiding deception and protection against misleading advertising, improper labeling and other practices. For e.g. when you buy a product or utilize a service, you should be informed about a) how to consume a product b) the adverse health effects of its consumption c)

Whether the ingredients used are environment- friendly or not etc.

Due to the ever increasing influence of the market and the ever changing scene with price wars and hard-sell techniques, the consumer's right to information becomes even more important. The right to information means much more than simple disclosure of the product's weight or price. A consumer has the right to know how the product has been prepared, whether it has been tested or animals or not, if environmentally-sound techniques and resources have been used in its production processes, what kinds of chemicals are used into its manufacturing and what could be their impact on consumer health. Clearly, a consumer has to consider a lot of factors before s/he buys a product. The opinion of the respondents about the awareness of right to be informed have been presented in Table 7.43 and in Graph 7.35.

Table 7.43
Awareness of Right to be Informed

Awareness	Frequency	Percent
Not at all Aware	280	22.4
Not Very Aware	380	30.4
Somewhat Aware	395	31.6
Adequately Aware	85	6.8
Fully Aware	110	8.8
Total	1250	100.0

Source: Primary Probe.

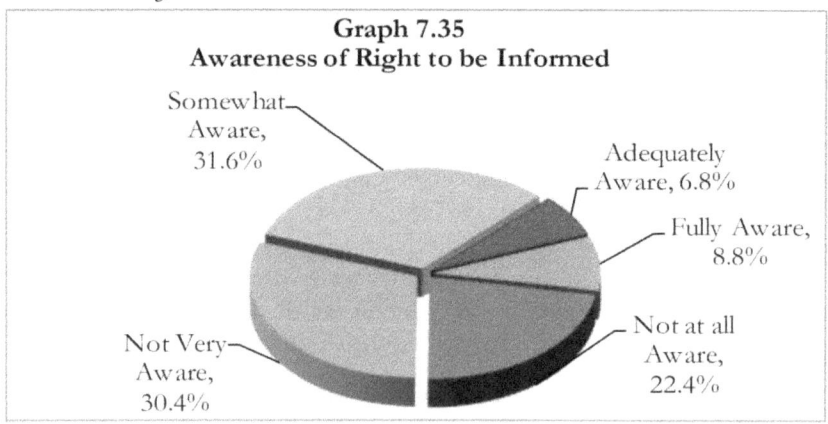

Graph 7.35
Awareness of Right to be Informed

Table 7.43 shows that right to information is not a well-known right available to consumers. Nearly 53 per cent of the respondents were either not at all aware of this right or they are not very aware of it. Around 32 per cent of the respondents are somewhat aware of this right. Finally about 16 per cent of the respondents believe that they are adequately or fully aware of right to information.

7.6.3. Awareness of Right to Choice

The right to choice has a very different definition in developing countries. For a population dependent on the environment for livelihood, the right to choice and other consumer rights need a shift in focus. The focus needs to be on choice of good practices like organic farming and conservation of natural heritage. In cities, people should be able to choose cleaner and safer ways of transportation over polluting ones. Similarly, healthy and fresh food should be chosen over junk food. The right to choose must essentially be a consumer's right to choose a safe and healthy product of good quality over an unsafe or defective product. This can give a consumer immense leverage not just to choose products that are safe but also to influence the practices adopted by the market. Opinion of the respondents about the awareness of right to choose have been shown in Table 7.44 and in Graph 7.36.

Table 7.44
Awareness of Right to Choose

Awareness	Frequency	Percent
Not at all Aware	265	21.2
Not Very Aware	395	31.6
Somewhat Aware	385	30.8
Adequately Aware	95	7.6
Fully Aware	110	8.8
Total	**1250**	**100.0**

Source: Primary Probe.

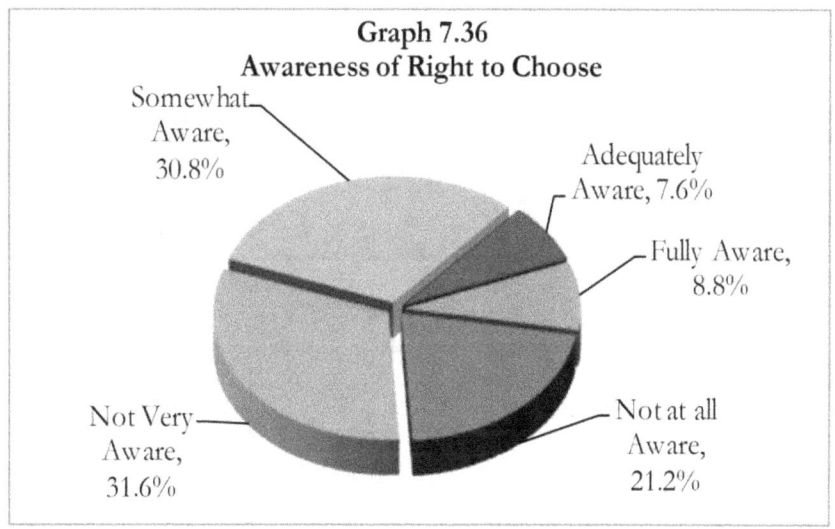

Graph 7.36
Awareness of Right to Choose

Somewhat Aware, 30.8%
Adequately Aware, 7.6%
Fully Aware, 8.8%
Not Very Aware, 31.6%
Not at all Aware, 21.2%

Table 7.44 again depicts that right to choice is not at all popular among consumers. Nearly 53 per cent of the respondents are either not at all aware of this right or they are not very aware of it. Around 31 per cent of the respondents are somewhat aware of this right. Finally about 16 per cent of the respondents believe that they are adequately or fully aware of right to information.

7.6.4. Awareness of Right to be Heard

The right to be heard means that consumers should be allowed to voice their opinions and grievances at appropriate forum. For e.g. if you have been cheated in the market place or deprived of the right quality of service, your complaint should be heard and given due attention by the authorities. Consumers should also have a right to voice their opinion when rules and regulations pertaining to them are being formulated, like the recent amendments in the Consumer Protection Act. The right to be heard holds special significance in the Indian context because Indian consumers are largely unaware of their rights and passively accept their violation. Even when they have legal recourse, they prefer not to use it for fear of getting embroiled in legal complexities. The data with regard to the awareness of right to be heard have been presented in Table 7.45 and shown in Graph 7.37.

Table 7.45
Awareness of Right to be heard

Awareness	Frequency	Percent
Not at all Aware	215	17.2
Not Very Aware	465	37.2
Somewhat Aware	350	28.0
Adequately Aware	120	9.6
Fully Aware	100	8.0
Total	1250	100.0

Source: *Primary Probe.*

Table 7.45 shows that the awareness level in case of right to be heard is quite low. Only about 18 per cent of the respondents believe that they are adequately or fully aware of this right. 28 per cent of the respondents have indicated a somewhat awareness degree for this right. However, a major chunk of respondents (around 54 per cent) are either does not know anything about this right or they have little knowledge on this issue.

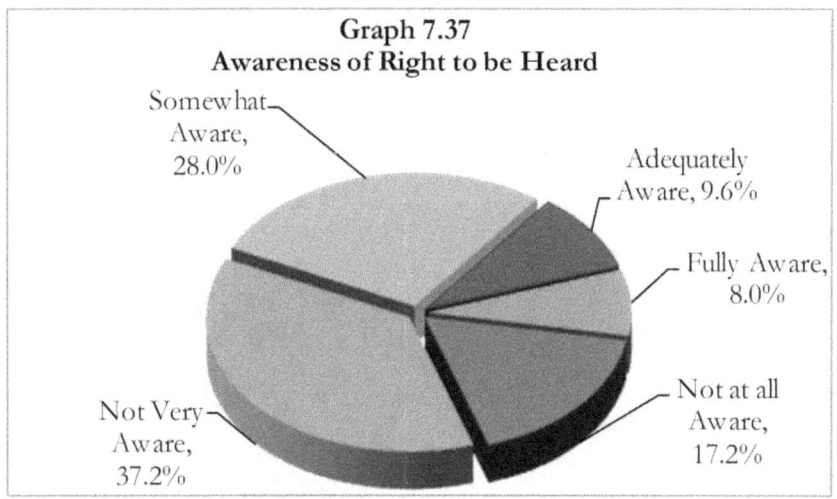

Graph 7.37
Awareness of Right to be Heard

Somewhat Aware, 28.0%

Adequately Aware, 9.6%

Fully Aware, 8.0%

Not Very Aware, 37.2%

Not at all Aware, 17.2%

7.6.5. Right to Seek Redressal

It is to protect consumer interests that consumers have been given the right to obtain redress. In India, we have a redress machinery called Consumer Courts constituted under the Consumer Protection Act (1986), functioning at national state and district levels. But it has not been made complete use of under due to lack of awareness of basic consumer rights among consumers themselves. While in the developed world, right to redress is perhaps the most commonly exercised consumer right, in developing countries, consumers are still wary of getting involved in legal redress system. There are consumer courts in India where any consumer can lodge a case if s/he thinks he or she has been cheated. The details of how to lodge a complaint have been explained elsewhere in the manual. The data regarding the awareness of right to seek redressal have been analyzed in Table 7.46 and in Graph 7.38.

Table 7.46
Awareness of Right to seek Redressal

Awareness	Frequency	Percent
Not at all Aware	185	14.8
Not Very Aware	450	36.0
Somewhat Aware	430	34.4
Adequately Aware	115	9.2
Fully Aware	70	5.6
Total	**1250**	**100.0**

Source: *Primary Probe.*

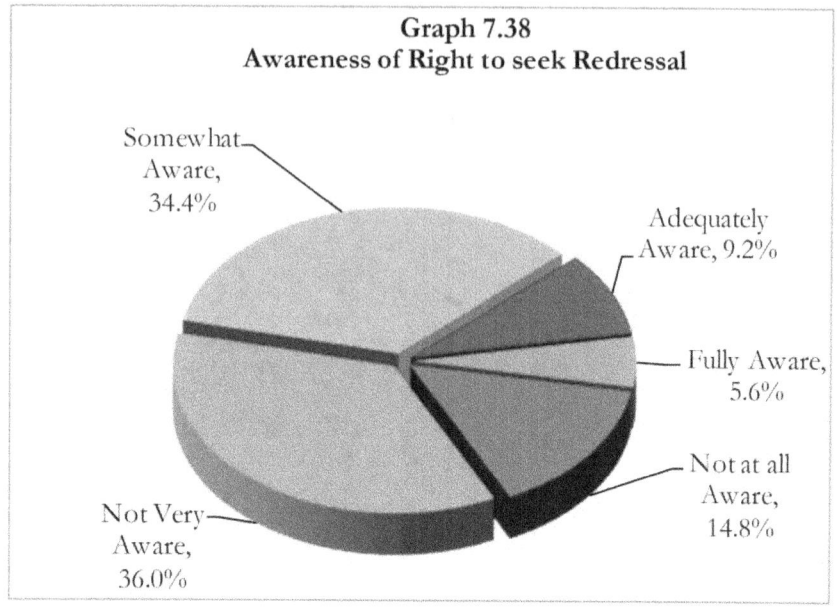

Graph 7.38
Awareness of Right to seek Redressal

Somewhat Aware, 34.4%

Adequately Aware, 9.2%

Fully Aware, 5.6%

Not at all Aware, 14.8%

Not Very Aware, 36.0%

Table 7.46 shows that out of total respondents, 36.0 per cent of respondents were not very aware of right to seek redressal, 34.4 per cent of respondents were somewhat aware and 14.8 per cent of respondents were not at all aware of this right. About 15 per cent of respondents were of the opinion that they either adequately or fully aware of this right. Thus, it can be concluded that majority of consumers Himachal Pradesh are not aware of the right to seek redressal.

7.6.6. Right to Consumer Education

Consumer education empowers consumers to exercise their consumer rights. It is perhaps the single most powerful tool that can take consumers from their present disadvantageous position to one of strength in the marketplace. Consumer education is dynamic, participatory and is mostly acquired by hands-on and practical experience. For instance, a woman who makes purchase decisions for the household and does the actual buying in the marketplace would be more educated about market conditions and 'best buys' than a person who educates himself about the market with the help of newspapers or television. Also, today, it is not just the market or products that a consumer needs to educate him about but s/he also needs to know about company profile, government policies and introduction of new technology. Respondent's opinion about the awareness of right to consumer education have been shown in Table 7.47 and in Graph 7.39.

Table 7.47
Awareness of Right to Consumer Education

Awareness	Frequency	Percent
Not at all Aware	240	19.2
Not Very Aware	390	31.2
Somewhat Aware	440	35.2
Adequately Aware	70	5.6
Fully Aware	110	8.8
Total	1250	100.0

Source: Primary Probe.

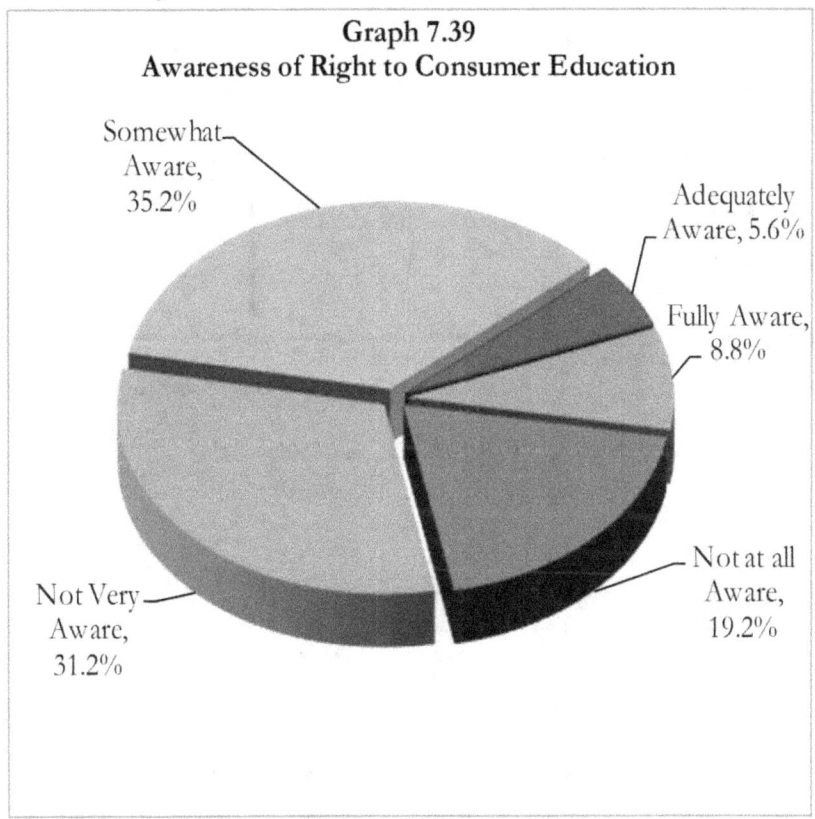

Graph 7.39
Awareness of Right to Consumer Education

Table 7.47 reveals that 35.2 per cent of respondents were of the opinion that they somewhat aware of the right to consumer education, 31.2 per cent of respondents opined that they are not very aware of this right and 19.2 per cent of respondents were not at all aware. Approximately 15 per cent of respondents were either adequately or fully aware of the right to consumer education.

Hence, it can be inferred that majority of consumers were either not aware or they have little knowledge of the right to consumer education.

7.6.7. Snapshot Comparison of Awareness of Consumer Protection Rights

This section deals with a brief comparison of awareness of all the rights discussed above. The purpose here is to make a comparative analysis of level of awareness in case of all consumer protection rights. For this purpose, all these rights have been put subject to mean value and standard deviation value.

Table 7.48
Descriptive Statistics of Awareness of Consumer Rights

Code		Mean	Std. Deviation
A1	Awareness of Right to seek Redressal	2.55	1.033
A2	Awareness of Right to be heard	2.54	1.127
A3	Awareness of Right to Consumer Education	2.54	1.130
A4	Awareness of Right to Choose	2.51	1.166
A5	Awareness of Right to be Informed	2.49	1.169
A6	Awareness of Right to Safety	2.44	1.067

Source: *Primary Probe.*

Graph 6.40
Average Awareness of Consumer Rights

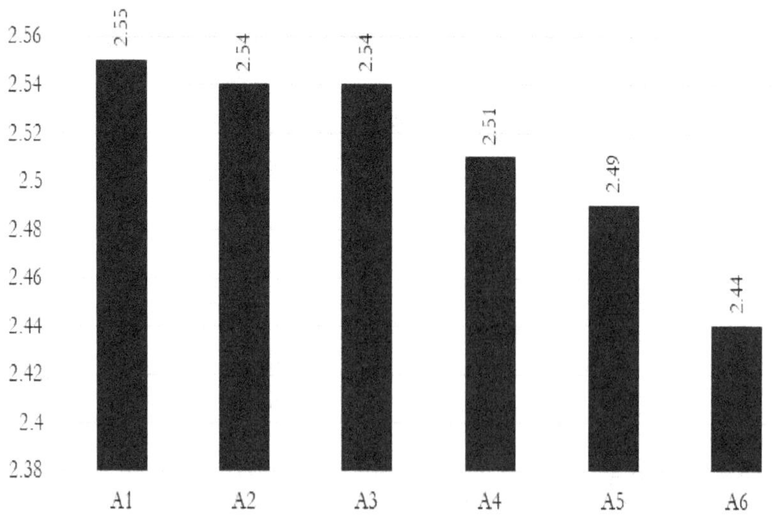

Values in Table 7.48 show that there has been a marginal difference in case of all the consumer protection rights. However, right to seek redressal has the maximum level of awareness among people of Himachal Pradesh followed by the Awareness of Right to be heard, Awareness of Right to Consumer Education, Awareness of Right to choose, and Awareness of Right to be informed. Right to safety has been the least known consumer protection right. Overall picture reveals that the awareness level about the consumer's rights among people in Himachal Pradesh is not good enough and there is a need to work in the direction of creating awareness about consumer protection rights.

7.7. Awareness of Consumer Rights And Demographic Attributes

In this section, an effort has been made to see if any demographic attribute of the customer has any say in his level of awareness of various rights of consumers. For this purpose, four demographic attributes viz., gender of the respondents, age of the respondents, occupation of the respondents, and qualification of the respondents have been covered and analyzed. Awareness score of each group has been calculated by totaling all the responses of respondents in relation to awareness of rights.

7.7.1. Gender Based ANOVA

This part deals with the exploration of difference, if any, in males and females with regards to knowledge of consumer Rights. Descriptive and ANOVA of gender vs. level of awareness of consumer rights have been given Table 7.49 (a) and Table 7.49 (b) respectively.

Table 7.49 (a)

Descriptive – Gender vs. Level of Awareness of Consumer Rights

Level of Awareness of Consumer Rights	N	Mean	Std. Deviation
Male	875	14.6629	3.11015
Female	375	16.0000	3.99324
Total	**1250**	**15.0640**	**3.44607**

Source: Primary Probe.

Table 7.49 (a) shows that the average awareness score which represents the sum of awareness of all rights of consumers is high in case of females than males.

To find the significance of difference, ANOVA has been used. Null hypothesis for ANOVA states no difference between male and female respondents with regards to level of awareness of consumer Rights.

However, ANOVA value 40.916 is relatively high. Due to it, p-value of significance is 0.000. It indicates that significant difference exists in male and female respondents in relation to level of awareness of consumer Rights.

Table 7.49 (b)
ANOVA– Gender vs. Level of Awareness of Consumer Rights

Gender vs. Level of Awareness of Consumer Rights	Sum of Squares	d.f.	Mean Square	F	Sig.
Between Groups	469.337	1	469.337	40.916	.000
Within Groups	14315.543	1248	11.471		
Total	**14784.880**	**1249**			

Source: Primary Probe.

Thus, the null hypothesis stating no difference in males and females in relation to their level of awareness of consumer Rights stands rejected. It may be interpreted that females have a higher degree of awareness of consumer rights.

7.7.2.   Occupation Based ANOVA

This ANOVA deals with the examination of differences, if any, in different occupational categories. Null hypothesis in this case states that respondents belonging to different occupational backgrounds have no difference in their level of awareness of consumer Rights. Descriptive and ANOVA in this regard has been shown in Table 7.50 (a) and 7.50 (b) respectively.

Table 7.50 (a)
Descriptive – Occupation vs. Level of Awareness of Consumer Rights

Occupation vs. Level of Awareness of Consumer Rights	N	Mean	Std. Deviation
Business	325	14.4615	3.21168
Service	635	15.5039	3.46839
Student	160	14.6875	3.34507
Housewife	130	14.8846	3.90207
Total	**1250**	**15.0640**	**3.44607**

Source: Primary Probe.

Descriptive in table 7.50 (a) show that business sector people have the lowest mean Level of Awareness of Consumer Rights whereas service sector respondents have a better degree of awareness of consumer Rights.

Table 7.50 (b)
ANOVA – Occupation vs. Level of Awareness of Consumer Rights

Occupation vs. Level of Awareness of Consumer Rights	Sum of Squares	d.f.	Mean Square	F	Sig.
Between Groups	267.726	3	89.242	7.660	.000
Within Groups	14517.154	1246	11.651		
Total	14784.880	1249			

Source: Primary Probe.

ANOVA value in this case is 7.660 which is high. Also the p-value is 0.000 which indicates significant variation. Hence, it may be concluded that people belonging to service class have relatively high level of awareness of consumer rights as compared to other occupational categories. Hence, null hypothesis assuming no difference of awareness of consumer Rights among respondents belonging to different occupations stands rejected.

7.7.3.   Age Based ANOVA

Age based ANOVA has been calculated in this part to examine any possible difference of Level of Awareness of Consumer Rights among respondents belonging to different age groups. Here null hypothesis statement is that respondents belonging to different age groups do not significantly differ on their Level of Awareness of Consumer Rights. In this respect descriptive and ANOVA has been depicted in Table 7.51 (a) and Table 7.51 (b) respectively.

Table 7.51 (a)
Descriptive - Age vs. Level of Awareness of Consumer Rights

Age vs. Level of Awareness of Consumer Rights	N	Mean	Std. Deviation
15 - 18	300	15.4333	3.77488
18 - 25	365	14.8082	3.43858
25 - 35	445	15.0449	3.41424
35 or above	140	15.0000	2.89316
Total	1250	15.0640	3.44607

Source: Primary Probe.

Table 7.51 (a) shows that Level of Awareness of Consumer Rights has been minimum in case of age group 18-25 years, followed by 35 years or above and 25 years to 35 years. The maximum awareness has been found in the respondents in age group 15 years to 18 years. Besides, standard deviation is not relatively too high.

The application of ANOVA in Table 7.51 (b) shows that the F-value in this case is 1.849 which is low. That's why p-value is more than 0.05. It indicates insignificant difference.

Table 7.51 (b)
ANOVA - Age vs. Level of Awareness of Consumer Rights

Age vs. Level of Awareness of Consumer Rights	Sum of Squares	d.f.	Mean Square	F	Sig.
Between Groups	65.537	3	21.846	1.849	.136
Within Groups	14719.343	1246	11.813		
Total	**14784.880**	**1249**			

Source: Primary Probe.

Thus, it can be stated almost all the age groups have the same Level of Awareness of Consumer Rights. Hence, null hypothesis assuming no difference of awareness of consumer Rights among consumers belonging to different age groups stands accepted.

7.7.4. Education Based ANOVA

In this case, ANOVA has been used to examine the possibility of significant difference of degree of awareness of consumer Rights of various respondents having different levels of education. It has been assumed that education makes a person more aware and educated people cannot be cheated easily. Here the null hypothesis is that respondents having been from various levels of education do not differ significantly with respect to degree of such awareness. The descriptive and ANOVA have been enumerated in Table 7.52 (a) and Table 7.52 (b) respectively.

Table 7.52 (a)
Descriptive - Education vs. Level of Awareness of Consumer Rights

Education vs. Level of Awareness of Consumer Rights	N	Mean	Std. Deviation
Matriculate or below	280	15.5179	3.73188
Higher Secondary	375	14.9067	2.78594
Graduate	280	14.9821	3.60551
Post Graduate or above	315	14.9206	3.78154
Total	**1250**	**15.0640**	**3.44607**

Source: Primary Probe.

Table 7.52 (a) shows that the degree of such awareness has been found to be maximum in case of matriculate or below people followed by graduates and post graduates. Higher secondary education category has been on the lower side.

Table 7.52 (a)
ANOVA - Education vs. Level of Awareness of Consumer Rights

Education vs. Level of Awareness of Consumer Rights	Sum of Squares	df	Mean Square	F	Sig.
Between Groups	75.309	3	25.103	2.126	.095
Within Groups	14709.571	1246	11.805		
Total	14784.880	1249			

Source: *Primary Probe.*

As far as level of education is concerned, F-value has been quite low at 2.126 with p-value of significance at 0.095. This clearly indicates that Level of Awareness of Consumer Rights has been almost similar in all categories of education. Hence, the null hypothesis stating no difference of awareness of consumer Rights among various education levels stands accepted.

7.8. General Consumer Protection Awareness

General consumer protection awareness relates itself to the knowledge of consumer protection environment, consumer awareness programs and other related aspects. In this section, a detailed analysis of general awareness regarding consumer protection among respondents has been carried out. The results have been as below.

7.8.1. Awareness of Jago Grahak Jago Move

The Consumer Awareness Scheme for the XI Plan was approved by the Cabinet Committee on Economic Affairs on 24.01.08. This scheme has been formulated to give an increased thrust to a multimedia publicity campaign to make consumers aware of their rights. The slogan Jago Grahak Jago is part of the publicity campaign undertaken in the last few years. Jago Grahak Jago has become the focal theme through which issues concerning the functioning of almost all Government Departments having a consumer interface can been addressed. To achieve this objective joint campaigns have been undertaken/are being undertaken with a number of Government Departments. In this move, consumer awareness is focused by showing a small clip related to various malpractices of shopkeepers and remedy available against such acts. Both radio and television broadcast it. Data about the awareness of Jago Grahak Jago Move have been shown in Table 7.53 and in Graph 7.41.

Table 7.53 shows that though there is awareness regarding this move among all the respondents, yet the level of awareness are not very encouraging. Around 68 per cent of the respondents have indicated somewhat awareness of this move. Only about 32 per cent of the respondents are adequately or fully aware of this move. Though this move is broadcast on television and radio very aggressively, yet the awareness is not to the extent it should have created.

Table 7.53
Awareness of Jago Grahak Jago Move

Awareness	Frequency	Percent
Not at all Aware	0	0.0
Not Very Aware	0	0.0
Somewhat Aware	845	67.6
Adequately Aware	210	16.8
Fully Aware	195	15.6
Total	**1250**	**100.0**

Source: *Primary Probe.*

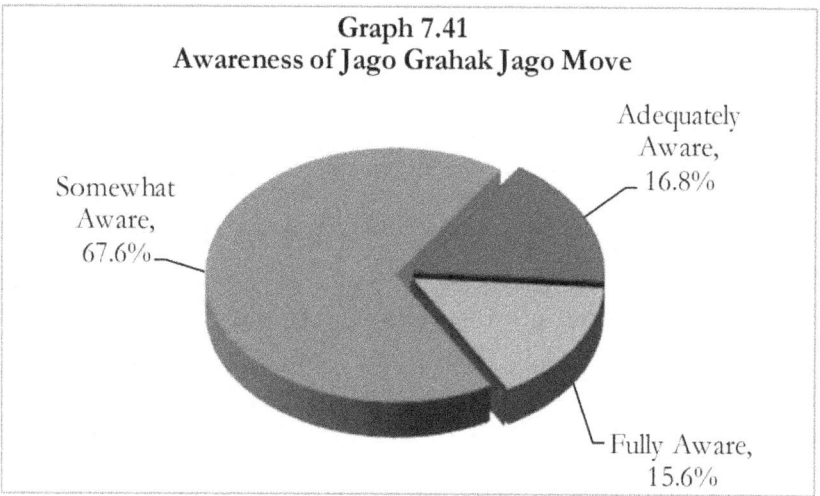

Graph 7.41
Awareness of Jago Grahak Jago Move

7.8.2. Awareness of Major Voluntary Consumer Organizations in India

Currently there are many active voluntary organizations working in the field of consumer protection. To quote a few, these can be Consumer Coordination Council (CCC), Consumer Guidance Society of India, Citizen Consumer and Civic Action Group, Association for Consumers Action on Safety and Health, Consumer Education and Research Centre, Consumer Protection Council, Consumer Unity and Trust Society, Consumers Association of India, Consumers' Forum, Mumbai Grahak Panchayat, VOICE Society, Grahak Shakti. These organizations can be a real helping hand in case consumers suffer from malpractices. Data regarding the awareness of major voluntary consumer organizations in India has been enumerated in Table 7.54 and in Graph 7.42.

Table 7.54

Awareness of Major Voluntary Consumer Organizations

Awareness	Frequency	Percent
Not at all Aware	235	18.8
Not Very Aware	475	38.0
Somewhat Aware	420	33.6
Adequately Aware	40	3.2
Fully Aware	80	6.4
Total	**1250**	**100.0**

Source: *Primary Probe.*

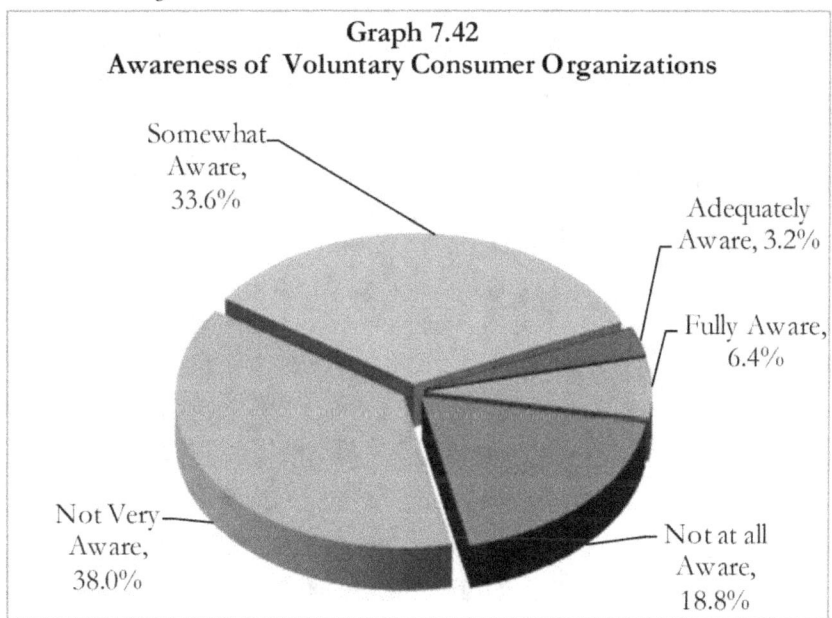

Graph 7.42

Awareness of Voluntary Consumer Organizations

Table 7.54 has produced disappointing result. 18.8 per cent of the respondents have no knowledge of such organizations. Further, 38.0 per cent of the respondents are not very aware of such organizations. Only about ten percent respondents are adequately or fully aware of such organizations. It is unfortunate that people do not even know about organizations which can help them in protection against malpractices.

7.8.3. Awareness of Agmark

Agmark is an acronym for agricultural marketing. Agmark is a quality certification mark provided by the Government of India. This certification confirms that the product or commodity in better term is scientifically laid down. It confirms the qualtiy control and the best hygenic condition of the food. This certification also marks the food standard keeping in mind the requirements of WTO. This certification benefits all including the producer and the consumer. The sellers can sell their products easily and obviously its a satisfaction mark for buyers. Analyses of opinion about awareness of agmark has been presented in Table 7.55 and in Graph 7.43.

Table 7.55
Awareness of AGMARK

Awareness	Frequency	Percent
Not at all Aware	0	0.0
Not Very Aware	0	0.0
Somewhat Aware	745	59.6
Adequately Aware	260	20.8
Fully Aware	245	19.6
Total	**1250**	**100.0**

Source: *Primary Probe.*

Table 7.55 shows that 59.6 per cent of respondents were somewhat aware of AGMARK, 20.8 per cent were adequately aware and 19.6 per cent of respondents were fully aware AGMARK.

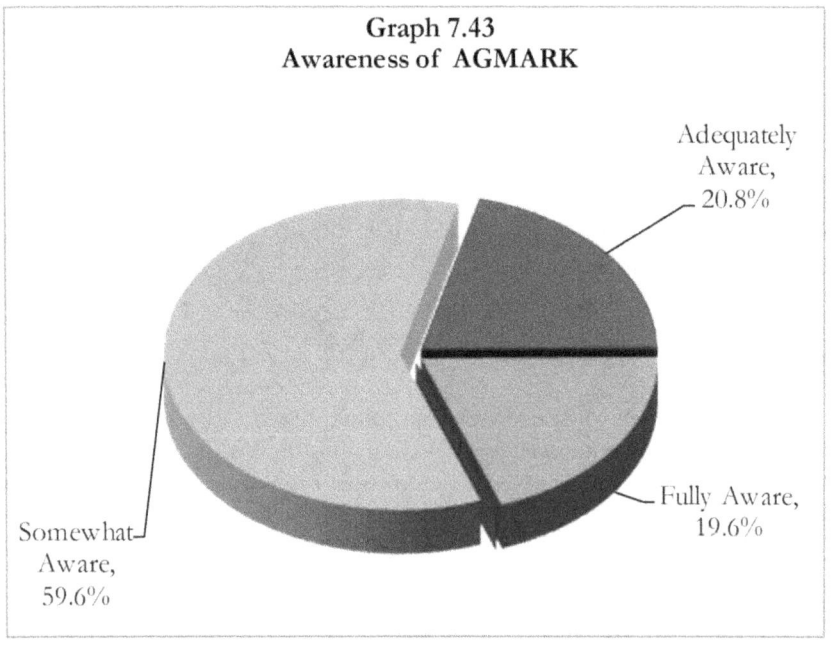

Graph 7.43
Awareness of AGMARK

Thus, the analysis of respondent's opinion about awareness of AGMARK reveals a positive indication. If consumers are aware of AGMARK and start using food products bearing AGMARK standards, then consumer protection related to health is highly assured.

7.8.4. Awareness of ISI Mark

The Indian Standards Institution (ISI) was, therefore, set up in 1947 as a registered society, under a Government of India resolution. To maintain the service and quality of a product is the main job of Bureau of Indian Standards (BIS). BIS allot the ISI mark to any product as third party guarantee after ensuring its quality, reliability and safety. Another job of BIS is to take action on the consumer complaints after making proper inquiry. Data with regard to the awareness of ISI mark have been enumerated in Table 7.56 and shown in Graph 7.44.

Table 7.56
Awareness of ISI Mark

Awareness	Frequency	Percent
Not at all Aware	0	0.0
Not Very Aware	0	0.0
Somewhat Aware	675	54.0
Adequately Aware	265	21.2
Fully Aware	310	24.8
Total	**1250**	**100.0**

Source: Primary Probe.

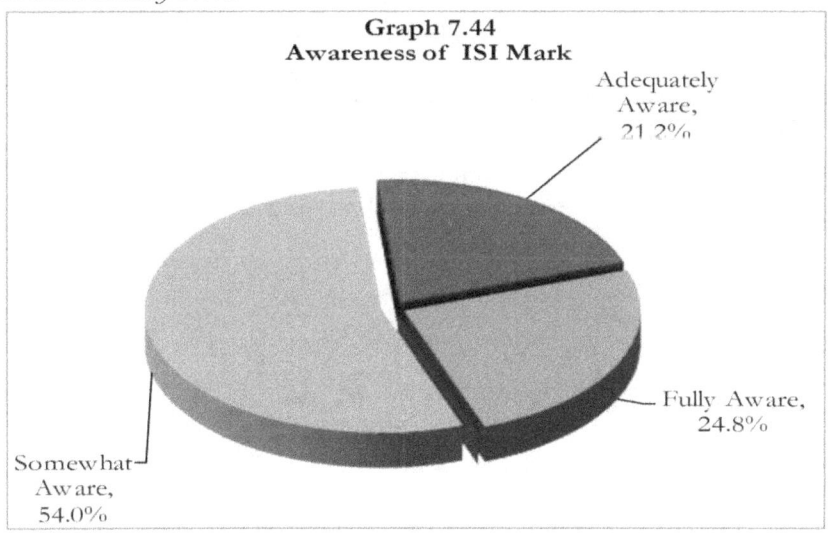

Graph 7.44
Awareness of ISI Mark

Table 7.56 shows that 54 per cent of the respondents are somewhat aware of ISI mark. Others are adequately or fully aware of ISI mark. This figure is somewhat surprising. ISI mark has an age old popularity and still known in electronic products. Using an ISI mark product itself states that quality testing has been carried out. However, still many people are not even aware of this mark. Hence, steps should be taken to make people aware of it.

7.8.5. Awareness of Gold Hallmarking

BIS hallmarking Scheme is voluntary in nature and is operating under BIS Act, Rules and Regulations. It operates on the basis of trust and thus it is desirable that aspect of quality control is in built in the system responsible for managing quality. The BIS Hallmarking Scheme has been aligned with International criteria on hallmarking (Vienna Convention 1972). As per this scheme, license is granted to the jewelers by BIS under Hallmarking Scheme. The BIS certified jewelers can get their jewelry hallmarked from any of the BIS recognized Assaying and Hallmarking Centre. The recognition to an Assaying and Hallmarking Centre is given against BIS criteria Doc: HMS/RAHC/GO1 which is in line with International criteria on Marking and Control of Precious metals. The analyses of data about the awareness of gold hallmarking has been presented in Table 7.57 and in Graph 7.45.

Table 7.57
Awareness of Gold Hallmarking

Awareness	Frequency	Percent
Not at all Aware	0	0.0
Not Very Aware	0	0.0
Somewhat Aware	690	55.2
Adequately Aware	280	22.4
Fully Aware	280	22.4
Total	**1250**	**100.0**

Source: Primary Probe.

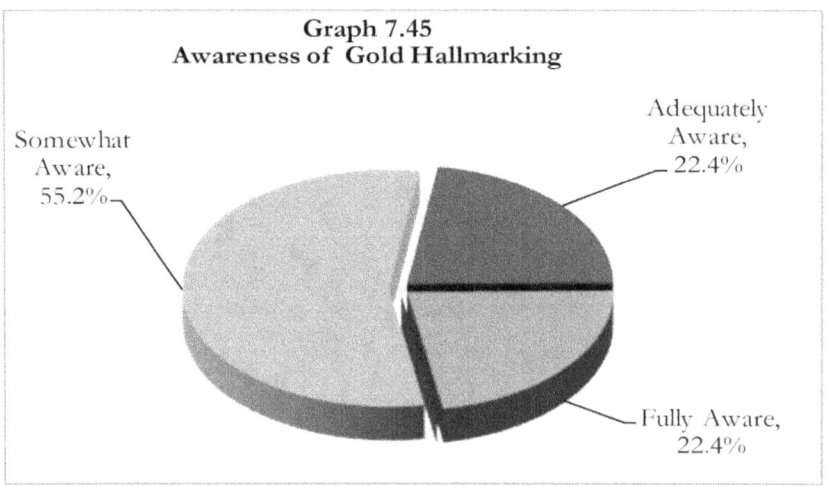

Graph 7.45
Awareness of Gold Hallmarking

Table 7.57 reveals that out of total respondents, 55.2 per cent of respondents were somewhat aware of gold hallmarking, 22.4 per cent of respondents were adequately aware and 22.4 of respondents were fully aware of gold hallmarking. Hence, the analysis reveals that the awareness level among consumers about the gold hallmarking is quit encouraging, as about 45 per cent of respondents either adequately or fully aware.

7.8.6. Awareness of BEE Star Rating

The Government of India set up Bureau of Energy Efficiency (BEE) on 1st March 2002 under the provisions of the Energy Conservation Act, 2001. The mission of the Bureau of Energy Efficiency is to assist in developing policies and strategies with a thrust on self-regulation and market principles, within the overall framework of the Energy Conservation Act, 2001 with the primary objective of reducing energy intensity of the Indian economy. This will be achieved with active participation of all stakeholders, resulting in accelerated and sustained adoption of energy efficiency in all sectors. Data in relation to the awareness of BEE Stars has been analyzed in Table 7.58 and in Graph 7.46.

Table 7.58
Awareness of BEE Stars

Awareness	Frequency	Percent
Not at all Aware	230	18.4
Not Very Aware	275	22.0
Somewhat Aware	235	18.8
Adequately Aware	230	18.4
Fully Aware	280	22.4
Total	**1250**	**100.0**

Source: Primary Probe.

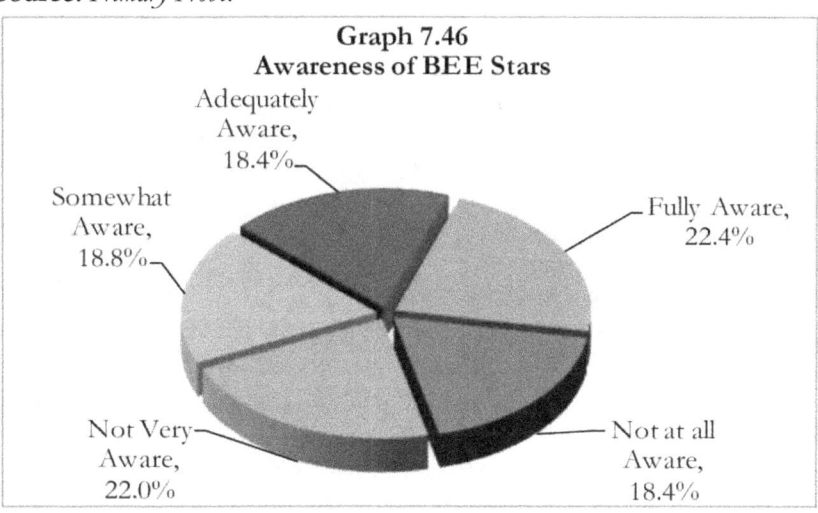

Graph 7.46
Awareness of BEE Stars

Data Table 7.58 depicts that 22.0 per cent of respondents were not very aware of BEE Stars, 18.8 per cent of respondents were somewhat aware and 18.4 per cent of respondents were not at all aware of BEE Stars. On the other hand, 22.4 per cent of respondents were fully aware and 18.4 per cent of respondents were adequately aware.

Thus, it can be inferred that the awareness level about BEE Star on product is not good enough.

7.8.7. Snapshot Comparison of General Consumer Protection Awareness

This section deals with a brief comparison of awareness of all the parameters mentioned above. For this purpose, all these parameters have been divided in two categories; one with higher than three average score of awareness, and the second category with lower than three mean value of awareness.

Table 7.59

Comparative Awareness of General Consumer Protection Scenario

Code		Mean	Std. Deviation
A1	Awareness of ISI Mark	3.71	.840
A2	Awareness of Gold Hallmarking	3.67	.819
A3	Awareness of AGMARK	3.60	.797
A4	Awareness of Jago Grahak Jago Move	3.48	.751
A5	Awareness of BEE Stars	3.04	1.429
B1	Awareness of Major Voluntary Consumer Organizations In India	2.40	1.034

Source: *Primary Probe.*

Table 7.59 shows that the minimum level of awareness has been recorded in case of awareness in relation to major voluntary consumer protection agencies in India. People do not know that in India, there exist many agencies and·non-government organizations, which continuously focus on activities related to consumer awareness and consumer protection.

High level of awareness has been found in case of ISI mark, AGMARK, and Gold Hallmarking. This is quite encouraging as people with this type of awareness can differentiate between good and bad quality products. However, the level of awareness of Jago Grahak Jago move is not very encouraging. The state government should take necessary steps to assure that people know about this move. Finally, BEE star rating is not very known among respondents. However, considering its inception of recent origin, it may happen that the awareness level of this rating goes high.

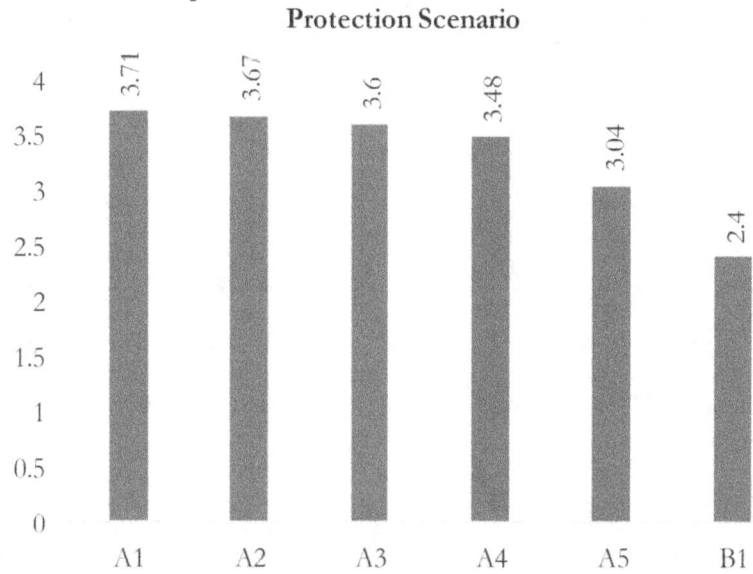

Graph 7.47
Comparative Awareness of General Consumer
Protection Scenario

7.9. General Consumer Protection Awareness and Demographic Attributes

In this section, an effort has been made to see if any demographic attribute of the customer has any say in his level of general awareness of consumer protection awareness. For this purpose, four demographic attributes viz., gender of the respondents, age of the respondents, occupation of the respondents, and qualification of the respondents have been covered and analyzed. The level of general consumer protection awareness has been calculated by totaling all the responses of questions related to general awareness of consumer protection.

7.9.1. Gender Based ANOVA

This part deals with the exploration of difference, if any, in males and females with regards to general consumer protection scenario. Descriptive and ANOVA in this regard has been presented in Table 7.60 (a) and 7.60 (b) respectively.

Table 7.60 (a) shows that the average awareness score which represents the sum of awareness of all general aspects of consumer protection is high in case of males than females.

Table 7.60 (a)
Descriptive – Gender vs. Awareness of General Consumer Protection Scenario

Gender vs. Awareness of General Consumer Protection Scenario	N	Mean	Std. Deviation
Male	875	20.0743	2.29697
Female	375	19.5200	2.22006
Total	**1250**	**19.9080**	**2.28394**

Source: *Primary Probe.*

To find the significance of difference, ANOVA has been used. Null hypothesis for ANOVA states no difference between male and female respondents with regards to level of General Consumer Protection Awareness.

Table 7.60 (b)
ANOVA– Gender vs. Awareness of General Consumer Protection Scenario

Gender vs. Awareness of General Consumer Protection Scenario	Sum of Squares	df	Mean Square	F	Sig.
Between Groups	80.649	1	80.649	15.693	.000
Within Groups	6413.771	1248	5.139		
Total	**6494.420**	**1249**			

Source: *Primary Probe.*

However, ANOVA value 15.693 is relatively large. Due to it, p-value of significance is 0.000. It indicates that significant difference exists in male and female respondents in relation to level of General Consumer Protection Awareness. Male respondents have relatively large level of general consumer protection awareness. Thus, the null hypothesis stating no difference in males and females in relation to their level of General Consumer Protection Awareness stands rejected.

7.9.2. Occupation Based ANOVA

This ANOVA deals with the examination of differences, if any, in different occupational categories. Null hypothesis in this case states that respondents belonging to different occupational backgrounds have no difference in their level of General Consumer Protection Awareness. In this regard descriptive and ANOVA have been shown in Table 7.61 (a) and Table 7.61 (b) respectively.

Table 7.61 (a)
Descriptive – Occupation vs. Awareness of General Consumer Protection Scenario

Occupation vs. Awareness of General Consumer Protection Scenario	N	Mean	Std. Deviation
Business	325	19.8769	2.24658
Service	635	19.8740	2.08925
Student	160	19.6250	2.47243
Housewife	130	20.5000	2.99666
Total	1250	19.9080	2.28394

Source: *Primary Probe.*

Descriptive in Table 7.61 (a) shows that the students have the lowest mean Level of General Consumer Protection Awareness whereas housewife respondents have a better degree of General Consumer Protection Awareness.

Table 7.61 (b)
ANOVA– Occupation vs. Awareness of General Consumer Protection Scenario

Occupation vs. Awareness of General Consumer Protection Scenario	Sum of Squares	df	Mean Square	F	Sig.
Between Groups	59.422	3	19.807	3.835	.059
Within Groups	6434.998	1246	5.165		
Total	6494.420	1249			

Source: *Primary Probe.*

ANOVA value in this case is 3.835 which is very low. Also the p-value is 0.059 which indicates insignificant variation. Hence, it may be concluded that though difference exists in respondents with regard to General Consumer Protection Awareness, but it is not very significant. Hence, null hypothesis assuming no difference of General Consumer Protection Awareness among respondents belonging to different occupations stands accepted.

7.9.3. Age Based ANOVA

Age based ANOVA has been calculated in this part to examine any possible difference of Level of General Consumer Protection Awareness among respondents belonging to different age groups. Here null hypothesis statement is that respondents belonging to different age groups do not significantly differ on their Level of General Consumer Protection Awareness. The descriptive and ANOVA about age vs. awareness of general consumer protection scenario have been depicted in Tab le 7.62 (a) and 7.62 (b) respectively.

Table 7.62 (a)
Descriptive – Age vs. Awareness of General Consumer Protection Scenario

Age vs. Awareness of General Consumer Protection Scenario	N	Mean	Std. Deviation
15 - 18	300	19.9167	2.28697
18 - 25	365	19.7397	2.37479
25 - 35	445	19.8652	2.20635
35 or above	140	20.4643	2.31712
Total	**1250**	**19.9080**	**2.28394**

Source: Primary Probe.

Table 7.62 (a) shows that Level of General Consumer Protection Awareness has been minimum in case of age group 18-25 years, followed by 25 years to 35 and 15 years to 18 years. The maximum awareness has been found in the respondents in age group 35 years or above. Besides, standard deviation is not relatively too high.

F-value in this case is 3.515 which is low. That's why p-value is more than 0.053. It indicates insignificant difference. Thus, it can be stated almost all the age groups have the same Level of General Consumer Protection Awareness. Hence, null hypothesis assuming no difference of General Consumer Protection Awareness among consumers belonging to different age groups stands accepted.

Table 7.62 (b)
ANOVA - Age vs. Awareness of General Consumer Protection Scenario

Age vs. Awareness of General Consumer Protection Scenario	Sum of Squares	df	Mean Square	F	Sig.
Between Groups	54.498	3	18.166	3.515	.053
Within Groups	6439.922	1246	5.168		
Total	**6494.420**	**1249**			

Source: Primary Probe.

7.9.4. Education Based ANOVA

In this case, ANOVA has been used to examine the possibility of significant difference of degree of General Consumer Protection Awareness of various respondents having different levels of education. It has been assumed that education makes a person more aware and educated people cannot be cheated easily. Here the null hypothesis is that respondents having been from various levels of education do not differ significantly with respect to degree of such awareness. In this regard descriptive and ANOVA have been presented in Table 7.63 (a) and Table 7.63 (b) respectively.

Table 7.63 (a)

Descriptive - Education vs. Awareness of General Consumer Protection Scenario

Education vs. Awareness of General Consumer Protection Scenario	N	Mean	Std. Deviation
Matriculate or below	280	20.0536	2.56848
Higher Secondary	375	20.2267	2.28138
Graduate	280	19.5714	2.26320
Post Graduate or above	315	19.6984	2.01314
Total	**1250**	**19.9080**	**2.28394**

Source: Primary Probe.

Table 7.63 (a) shows that the degree of such awareness has been found to be maximum in case of higher secondary education category followed by matriculate or below people. Graduates and post graduates surprisingly have been on the lower side.

As far as level of education is concerned, F-value has been quite low at 5.808 with p-value of significance at 0.031. This clearly indicates that Level of General Consumer Protection Awareness has been more in case of matriculate or below and higher secondary than graduate and post-graduate.

Table 7.63 (b)

ANOVA - Education vs. Awareness of General Consumer Protection Scenario

Education vs. Awareness of General Consumer Protection Scenario	Sum of Squares	df	Mean Square	F	Sig.
Between Groups	89.570	3	29.857	5.808	.031
Within Groups	6404.850	1246	5.140		
Total	**6494.420**	**1249**			

Source: Primary Probe.

Hence, the null hypothesis stating no difference of General Consumer Protection Awareness among various education levels stands rejected.

7.10. Services Prone to be Deficient

This section presents a brief discussion on various services, which consumers generally find on news regarding cases or disputes of consumer protection. These services have been categorized as prone to be deficient services. These services represent the industries where maximum number of malpractices have been heard or witnessed. Descriptive statistics of deficient services has been shown in Table 7.64 and in Graph 7.48.

Table 7.64
Descriptive Statistics of Deficient Services

Code		Mean	Std. Deviation
A1	Heard consumer cases in General Insurance	3.80	.751
A2	Heard consumer cases in Credit Cards	3.78	.772
A3	Heard consumer cases in Life Insurance	3.78	.748
A4	Heard consumer cases in Telecom	3.13	1.406
A5	Heard consumer cases in Tours & Travels	3.01	1.358
B1	Heard consumer cases in Motor Loans	2.98	1.356
B2	Heard consumer cases in Demat Accounts	2.90	1.440
C1	Heard consumer cases in Healthcare Services	1.87	.781
C2	Heard consumer cases in Real Estate	1.83	.768
C3	Heard consumer cases in Personal Loans	1.80	.764
C4	Heard consumer cases in Housing Loans	1.78	.695
C5	Heard consumer cases in Immigration Services	1.75	.713

Source: *Primary Probe.*

Graph 7.48
Descriptive Statistics of Deficient Services

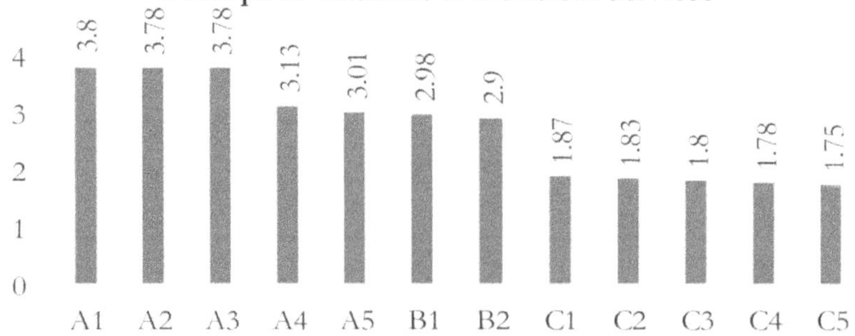

Table 7.64 shows that maximum number of cases of consumer disputes have been heard for general insurance industry covering medical and vehicle insurances. Also the number of heard cases in credit cards and life insurance

314

industry is very high. In this category, somewhat lower mean value is with telecom and tour & travel services.

Motor loans and demat account related cases have been relatively low. Finally services like healthcare services, real estate, personal loans, housing loans, and immigration services have the minimum number of cases as recalled by the respondents.

7.11.   Products Prone to be Deficient

This section deals with the physical or tangible goods or products in relation to which respondents recall any consumer dispute in news. That's why these products have been termed as prone to be deficient products. Under this analysis, the products have been divided in three groups viz. highly deficient, moderately deficient and low deficiency products. The results are as below. Descriptive statistics about deficient products have been analyzed in Table 7.65 and in Graph 7.49.

Table 7.65
Descriptive Statistics of Deficient Products

Code		Mean	Std. Deviation
A1	Heard consumer cases in Apparels	3.13	1.406
A2	Heard consumer cases in Automobiles	3.01	1.358
B1	Heard consumer cases in Domestic Appliances	2.98	1.356
B2	Heard consumer cases in Computers & Networking	2.94	1.416
B3	Heard consumer cases in FMCG (Except Food)	2.94	1.416
C1	Heard consumer cases in Consumer Electronics	1.83	.768
C2	Heard consumer cases in Food Items	1.75	.713

Source: Primary Probe.

Graph 7.49
Descriptive Statistics of Deficient Products

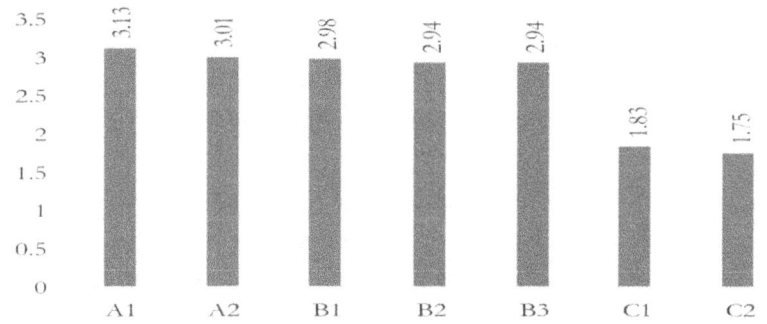

Table 7.65 shows that apparels and automobiles have been the two products where maximum number of respondents can recall or have heard any consumer related dispute in news. Thereafter, a moderate number of respondents feel that they have heard cases in domestic appliances, Computers & Networking, and FMCG (Except Food). Thus, this category can be termed as moderately deficient products. Finally, not many respondents have heard consumer disputes in relation to consumer electronics and food items. Thus, these are less deficient products.

7.12. Deficiencies in Products/Services Noticed by Consumers

This section deals with various experiences of consumers in relation to deficiencies in products or services purchased or used by them. In the earlier chapters, a detailed discussion on various malpractices of business concerns has been provided. Keeping that discussion as a base, the respondents have been asked to mention the deficiencies in products and services noticed by them. The effort here has been made to find which type of malpractice is more prevalent in Himachal Pradesh. Below is the discussion on results for a list of prominent deficiencies.

7.12.1. Price Charged More than MRP

MRP is the maximum retail price that can be charged from a customer. Charging price in excess of MRP is a malpractice to earn more profits. No shopkeeper or seller can charge price in excess of MRP. Rather many sellers offer discount on MRPs. Opinion of respondents about price charged more than M.R.P. has been analyzed in Table 7.66 and shown in Graph 7.50.

Table 7.66
Noticed - Price Charged more than M.R.P.

Response	Frequency	Percent
Occasionally	780	62.4
Frequently	235	18.8
Very Frequently	235	18.8
Total	**1250**	**100.0**

Source: *Primary Probe.*

As per table 7.66 reveals that about two third of respondents (62.4 per cent) were occasionally noticed that the price charged more than M.R.P., 18.8 per cent of respondents frequently and same percentage of respondents were noticed it frequently and very frequently respectively. The analysis indicated towards a serious malpractice.

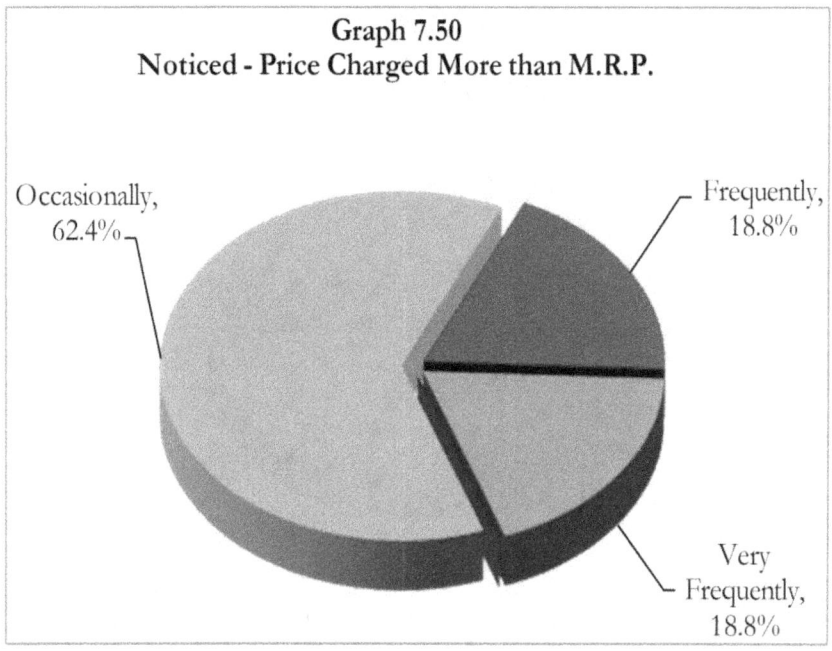

Graph 7.50
Noticed - Price Charged More than M.R.P.

Occasionally, 62.4%

Frequently, 18.8%

Very Frequently, 18.8%

7.12.2. Less Weight as Compared to Printed on Products

As per the standards of weights and measures act, many products are required to print on the label the price, gross weight and net weight when being packed. Consumers if in doubt, can cross check the weight of product with the one mentioned on the label. There should not be any significant difference in the weight mentioned on label and the actual weight. The opinion of the sample respondents about less weight as compared to printed on products has been presented in Table 7.67 and in Graph 7.51.

Table 7.67
Noticed - Less weight as compared to printed on commodities

Responses	Frequency	Percent
Very Rarely	550	44.0
Frequently	470	37.6
Very Frequently	230	18.4
Total	**1250**	**100.0**

Source: Primary Probe.

Figures in Table 6.67 show that in 44.0 per cent of respondents felt that in very rare cases the weight of product is less than the printed weight. In 37.6 per cent of cases respondents have frequently found this malpractice and 18.4 per cent of respondents noticed it very frequently while purchasing a commodity or product.

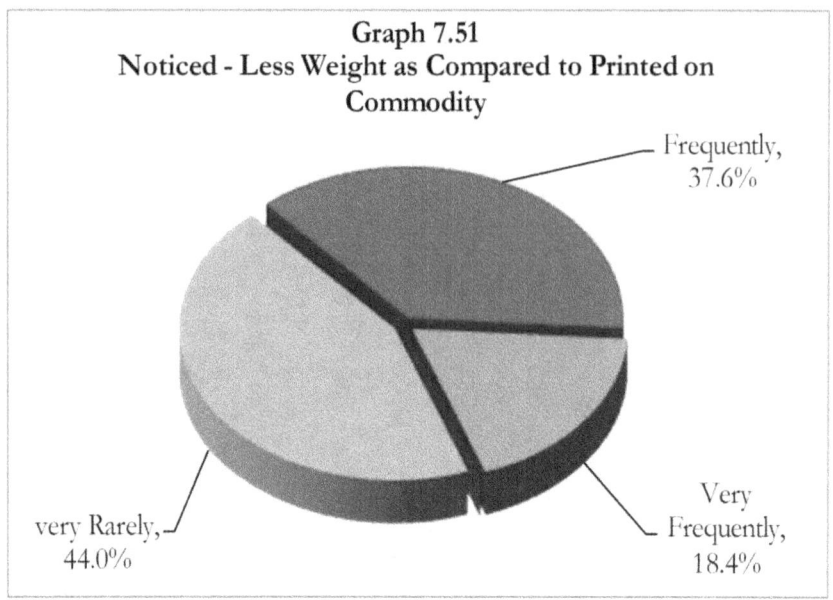

Graph 7.51
Noticed - Less Weight as Compared to Printed on Commodity

Frequently, 37.6%

very Rarely, 44.0%

Very Frequently, 18.4%

Thus, it can be interpreted that selling products with less weights is not a very common malpractice.

7.12.3. Discount/other Offers Stated on Products not Granted

Many companies, in order to increase their sales, use discounts or other promotional offers. But these can be of some benefit only if these discounts or offers reach the persons for whom these actually have been designed i.e., the end user or consumer. But retailers and shopkeepers sometimes refuse to grant such offers. This is also a malpractice in India. Opinion about discount/other offers stated on products not granted have been shown in Table 7.68 and in Graph 7.52.

Table 7.68
Noticed - Discount/other offers stated on products not granted

Response	Frequency	Percent
Very Rarely	495	39.6
Frequently	485	38.8
Very Frequently	270	21.6
Total	**1250**	**100.0**

Source: Primary Probe.

318

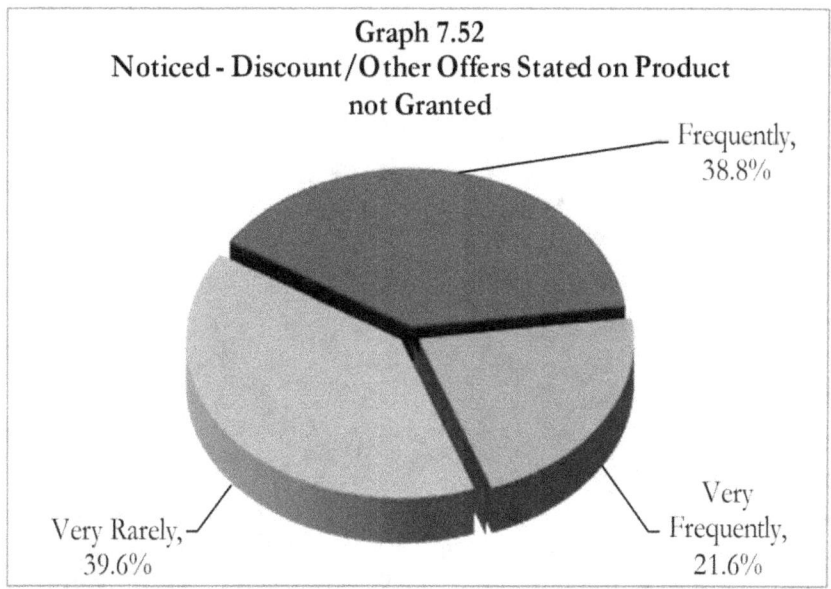

Graph 7.52
Noticed - Discount/Other Offers Stated on Product
not Granted

Frequently, 38.8%

Very Frequently, 21.6%

Very Rarely, 39.6%

Table 7.68 shows that 39.6 per cent of the respondents have very rarely faced this situation when they buy product with discount or promotional offer mentioned on it. However, 38.8 per cent of respondents have also frequently noticed it. Finally 21.6 per cent respondents have very frequently faced it. By and large, it may be said that this is not a very common phenomenon.

7.12.4. Breach of Warranties

This generally happens in electric and electronic products. Customers are provided with fixed period warranties on buying electric and electronic components. These warranties may include, free repairs, free component or full product replacement, or any compensation for damages. These warranties are another form of after sales services. Breach of these warranties can be a major setback for buyers. In this regard data have been presented in Table 7.69 and in Graph 7.53.

Table 7.69
Noticed - Breach of Warranties

Response	Frequency	Percent
Occasionally	750	60.0
Frequently	280	22.4
Very Frequently	220	17.6
Total	**1250**	**100.0**

Source: *Primary Probe.*

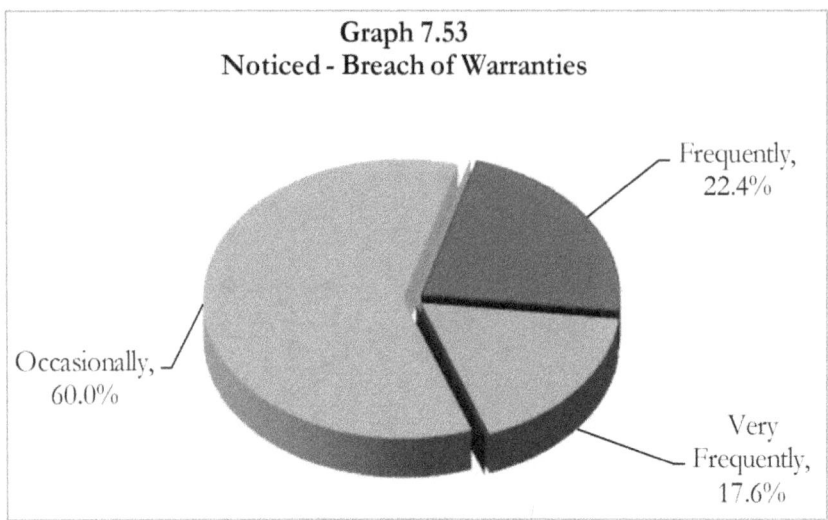

Graph 7.53
Noticed - Breach of Warranties

Frequently, 22.4%

Occasionally, 60.0%

Very Frequently, 17.6%

Table 7.69 witnesses a real disappointment on this front. 40 per cent of the respondents claimed that they evidenced a refusal warranties frequently or very frequently. Even remaining of the respondents has also noticed this problem occasionally. Hence, it can be said that breach of warranties is a common phenomenon in Himachal Pradesh.

7.12.5. Expired Medicines Sold

Medicines generally represent chemical mixtures mentioned in the list of ingredients on the labels. These mixtures mostly have a fixed useful life after which they are expected to be expired and not to be used or consumed. That's why medicines come with expiry dates. Consuming expired medicines can be a health hazard. Hence, expired medicines should be disposed off in proper manner and should not be sold to patients at any cost. The data collected about expired medicines sold have been enumerated in Table 7.70 and graphically shown in Graph 7.54.

Table 7.70
Noticed - Expired medicines sold

Response	Frequency	Percent
Very Rarely	435	34.8
Frequently	535	42.8
Very Frequently	280	22.4
Total	1250	100.0

Source: *Primary Probe.*

Table 7.70 shows a shocking result. More than 65 per cent of the respondents feel that they have noticed the sale of expired drugs to patients. Around 35 per cent of the respondents have rarely faced this malpractice.

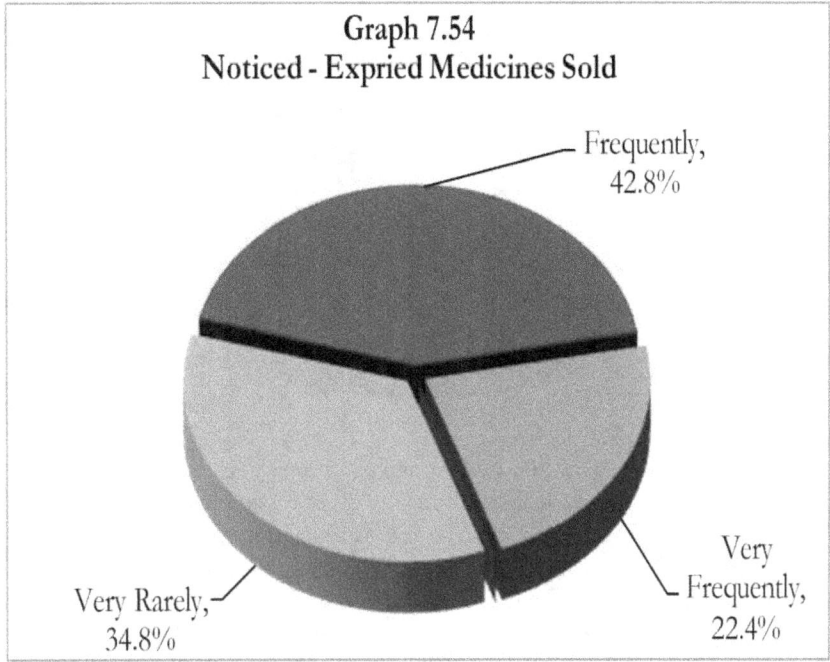

Graph 7.54
Noticed - Expried Medicines Sold

Frequently, 42.8%

Very Frequently, 22.4%

Very Rarely, 34.8%

The government should take necessary action to check this malpractice which allows sellers to play with the lives of innocent patients.

7.12.6. Bill not Issued

While buying anything, a bill of purchases can be asked for. A seller who issues bills automatically binds himself with that transaction and cannot deny the same. Also, a bill can be used to file a case in the consumer court. However, many a times, consumers either ignorantly or for tax avoidance and saving few rupees, ignore bills. This is not at all fair even on the part of consumers. The data with regard to bill not issued have been depicted in Table 7.71 and in Graph 7.55.

Table 7.71
Noticed - Bill not issued

Response	Frequency	Percent
Occasionally	750	60.0
Frequently	270	21.6
Very Frequently	230	18.4
Total	**1250**	**100.0**

Source: Primary Probe.

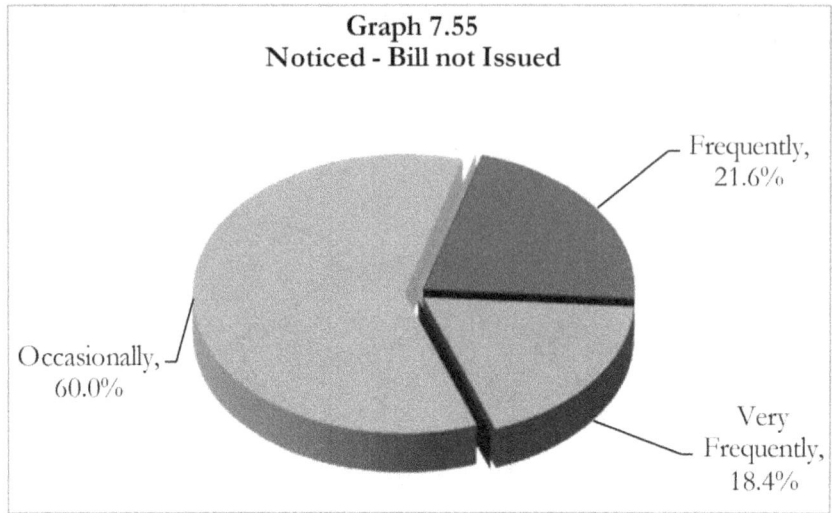

Graph 7.55
Noticed - Bill not Issued

Frequently, 21.6%

Occasionally, 60.0%

Very Frequently, 18.4%

Table 7.71 shows that 60 per cent of the respondents have occasionally noticed that the seller didn't issue bill for the purchase made by the buyers. Rest of the respondents had noticed this malpractice either very frequently or frequently. Thus, it can be interpreted that selling products without bills is a common practice in Himachal Pradesh, particularly in case of low price products. Buyers generally rely on the shopkeepers and even do not ask for bills.

7.12.7. Fake Product Sold

Fake product selling in this context is selling a duplicate product which resembles in color combination, size, shape and even in words to some very popular and costly brands in the market. But definitely there exists a problem related to quality with these products. The quality is no way near to those popular products. Respondent's opinion about fake products sold have been illustrated in Table 7.72 and in Graph 7.56.

Table 7.72
Noticed - Fake products sold

Response	Frequency	Percent
Occasionally	790	63.2
Frequently	230	18.4
Very Frequently	230	18.4
Total	**1250**	**100.0**

Source: *Primary Probe.*

322

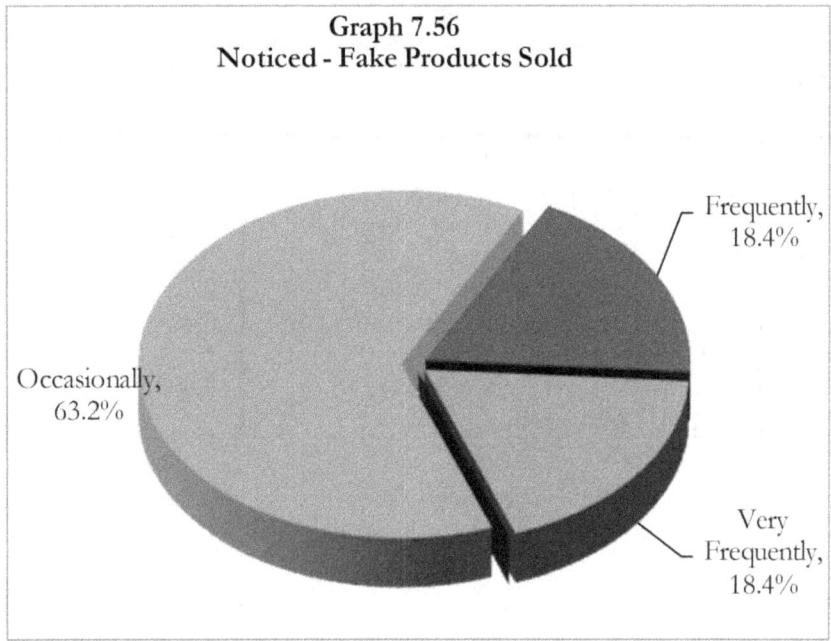

Table 7.72 shows that 63.2 per cent of the respondents have occasionally noticed sales of fake products. Remaining of the respondents has also noticed the same but frequently or even very frequently. However, it is only the consumer who can check this malpractice by refusing to buy such fake products. Consumers should be very alert and they should read the name of company and brand very carefully on the product they are buying. It would assure that no duplicate or low quality product is being sold to the customers.

7.12.8. Comparison of Various Malpractices

A high degree of mean value, i.e., more than three as against a maximum possible of five, indicates that almost all the problems have been noticed frequently or occasionally by the consumers. Statistics of noticed malpractices has been depicted in Table 7.73 and shown in Graph 7.57.

Table 7.73 reveals that making sales without issuing bills seems to be a more common malpractice. Customers remain silent on this issue because they may be asked to pay more on account of indirect taxes which becomes a burden on their pockets. But still, customers should ask for bills which can serve as proof of their transactions and can be used as sound evidence against cheating sellers. At the same mean value is also breach of warranty malpractice.

Table 7.73
Descriptive Statistics of Noticed Malpractices

Code		Mean	Std. Deviation
A1	Noticed - Bill not issued	3.58	.783
A2	Noticed - Breach of Warranties	3.58	.774
A3	Noticed - Price Charged more than M.R.P.	3.56	.790
A4	Noticed - Fake products sold	3.55	.786
A5	Noticed - Expired medicines sold	3.53	1.183
A6	Noticed - Discount/other offers stated on products not granted	3.42	1.214
A7	Noticed - Less weight as compared to printed on commodities	3.30	1.211

Source: *Primary Probe.*

Graph 7.57
Descriptive Statistics of Deficient Products

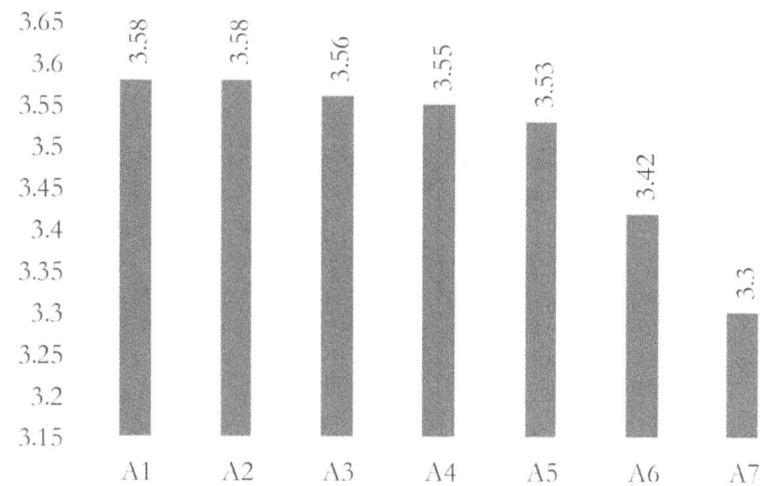

Malpractices which are at the bottom of this list are the refusal of discounts or other promotional offers mentioned on the product by sellers and less actual weight of products as compared to the one mentioned on the label. By and large, it should be the obligation on part of consumers also to be alert at the time of purchases and to keep one aware of various malpractices.

7.13. Major Sources of Information Related to Consumer Protection

This section deals with various sources of information for the consumers in relation to consumer protection in India. To examine the usage of various sources, major sources covered included newspapers, television, radio, websites, magazines, and friends/family etc. results related to each of these sources are as below.

7.13.1. Newspapers as a Source of Information

Newspapers are considered good source of instant information. These include daily news or weekly segments publication. Newspapers are generally good sources of collecting information related to various cases filed and results of such cases. Opinion of respondents about newspaper as a source of information has been given in Table 7.74 and in Graph 7.58.

Table 7.74
Source of Information - Newspapers

Response	Frequency	Percent
Occasionally	475	38.0
Frequently	520	41.6
Very Frequently	255	20.4
Total	**1250**	**100.0**

Source: *Primary Probe.*

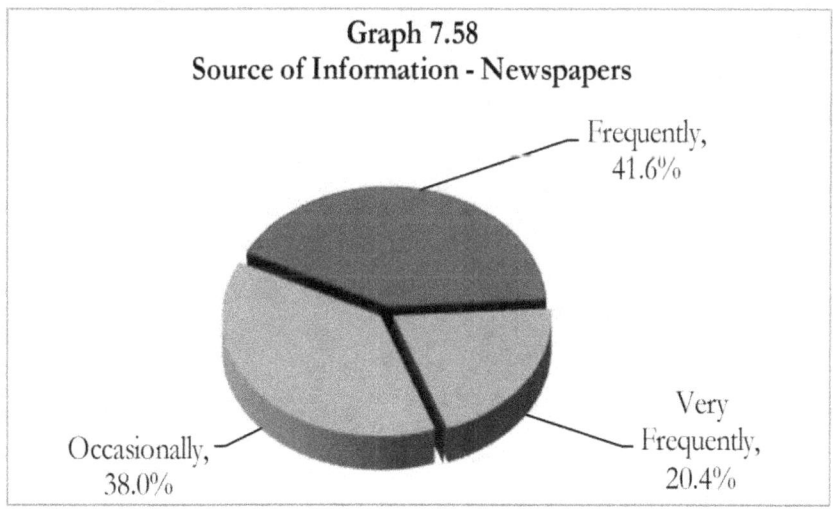

Graph 7.58
Source of Information - Newspapers

Results in table 7.74 show that the frequency of using newspapers as a source of information of consumer protection is quite high. 20.4 per cent of the respondents very frequently read or use newspapers, 41.6 per cent of the respondents use them frequently and 38.0 per cent of the respondents use newspapers occasionally. It seems to be a good indicator as cases related information can help respondents to find those sellers or business concerns which are involved in unfair or malpractices.

7.13.2.   Television as a Source of Information

Nowadays televisions are there in many households. Television channels broadcast information related to various products and services in form of advertising. Media industry is now largely dependent on television channels. Advertisements use channels to demonstrate various features of their products to lure customers. Opinion of respondents about television as a source of information has been given in Table 7.75 and in Graph 7.59.

Table 7.75
Source of Information – Television

Response	Frequency	Percent
Never	265	21.2
Very Rarely	295	23.6
Occasionally	235	18.8
Frequently	245	19.6
Very Frequently	210	16.8
Total	**1250**	**100.0**

Source: *Primary Probe.*

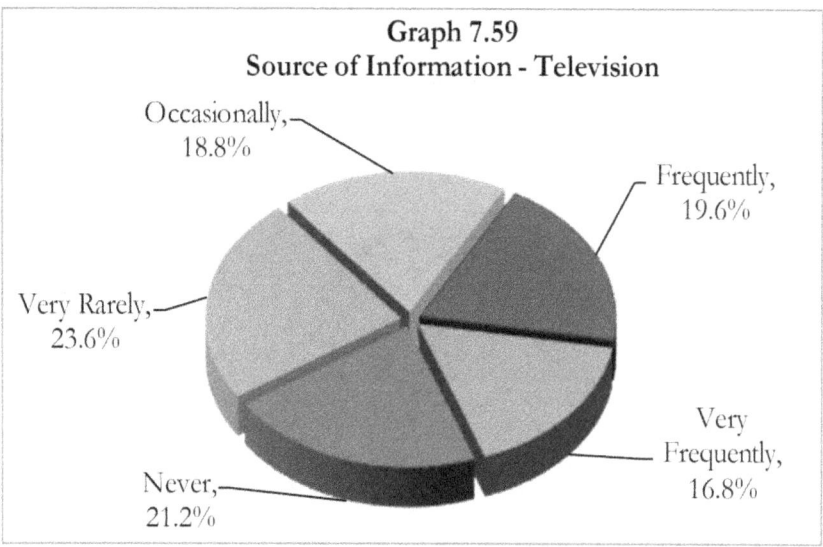

Graph 7.59
Source of Information - Television

Occasionally, 18.8%
Frequently, 19.6%
Very Rarely, 23.6%
Very Frequently, 16.8%
Never, 21.2%

Table 7.75 shows that in relation to use of television as a source of information, there are almost similar frequencies in all the classes. Maximum of the respondents (23.6 per cent) have very rarely used television as a source of information. However, the difference between the maximum and the minimum is not so big. Hence, it can be interpreted that for the purpose of consumer protection and its related information, television is not a widely used media.

7.13.3.   Radio as a Source of Information

As a source of information, even radio can work. Like television, radio channels are also used by companies to advertise their products. Television and radio channels can also be used by government to make people aware on various aspects of consumer protection. Moves like Jaago Re, and Jago Grahak Jago are very popular in these two media. The responses of respondents about radio as a source of information have been shown in Table 7.76 and in Graph 7.60.

Table 7.76
Source of Information – Radio

Response	Frequency	Percent
Never	245	19.6
Very Rarely	310	24.8
Occasionally	160	12.8
Frequently	250	20.0
Very Frequently	285	22.8
Total	**1250**	**100.0**

Source: *Primary Probe.*

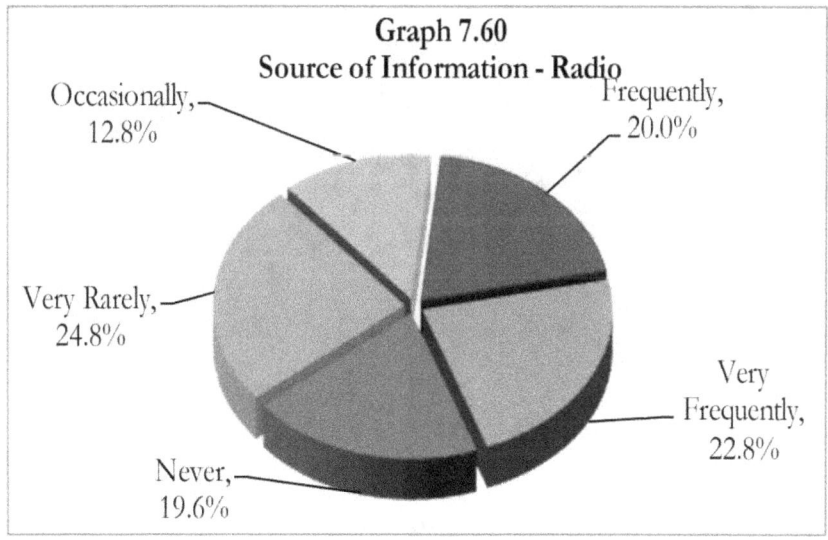

Graph 7.60
Source of Information - Radio
Occasionally, 12.8%
Frequently, 20.0%
Very Rarely, 24.8%
Very Frequently, 22.8%
Never, 19.6%

Table 7.76 shows that 19.6 per cent of the respondents have never used radio as a source of information. Nearly 25 per cent of the respondents have very rarely used it. Around 42 per cent of the respondents have either frequently or very frequently used radio as a source of information.

However, category of respondents using radio occasionally is very small. It indicates that either people use it frequently or they rarely use it.

7.13.4.   Websites as Source of Information

Due to technology enhancement and more dependence on using internet services, websites of various manufacturers, agencies, news, and government have recently emerged as a strong, useful and updated source of information. State governments have their own consumer protection forums on websites where necessary information is available all the times. Consumers can easily access this information. The responses of respondents about websites as a source of information have been analyzed in Table 7.77 and in Graph 7.61.

Table 7.77
Source of Information – Websites

Response	Frequency	Percent
Never	520	41.6
Very Rarely	250	20.0
Occasionally	480	38.4
Total	**1250**	**100.0**

Source: *Primary Probe.*

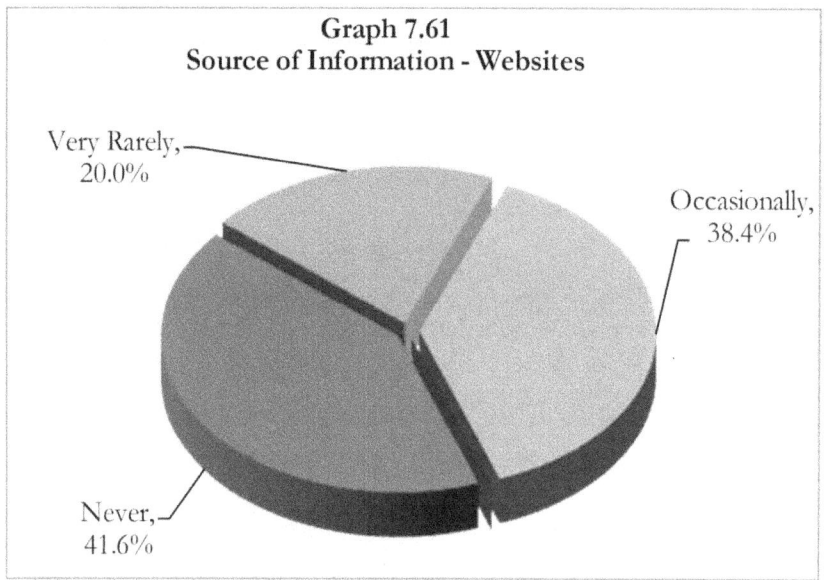

Graph 7.61
Source of Information - Websites

Table 7.77 shows that the spread of information technology in Himachal Pradesh is yet to achieve heights. Its penetration seems to be very low. More than 40 per cent of the respondents have never made any attempt to find or extract any information related to consumer protection using websites. Nearly 39 per cent of the respondents have used websites occasionally. Thus, internet websites are not very popular among consumers when it comes to access information related to consumer protection.

7.13.5.   Magazines as Source of Information

Many magazines are available in India which publish consumer related useful information weekly or monthly. Like newspapers, these can also be a highly useful source of information to the consumers. A habit of reading magazines can really help readers to keep themselves updated with all the happenings of consumer protection. The opinion of sample respondents about magazines as a source of information have been depicted in Table 7.78 and in Graph 7.62.

Table 7.78
Source of Information – Magazines

Response	Frequency	Percent
Never	485	38.8
Very Rarely	265	21.2
Occasionally	500	40.0
Total	**1250**	**100.0**

Source: Primary Probe.

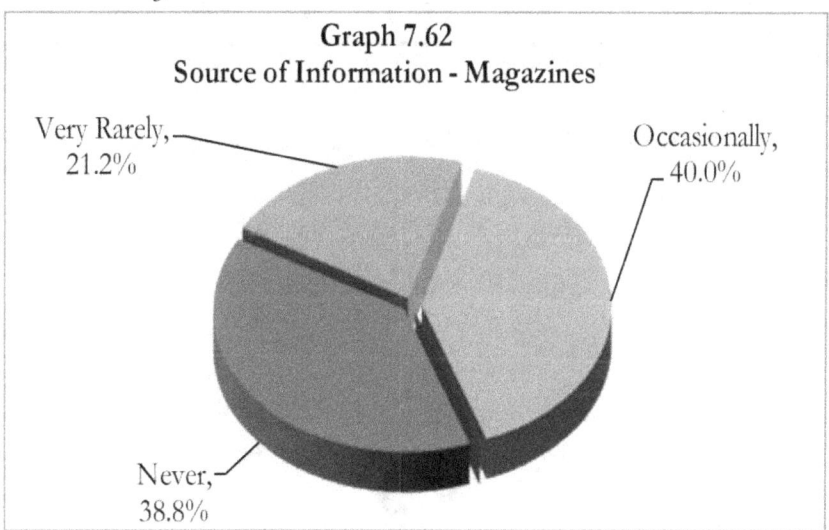

Graph 7.62
Source of Information - Magazines

Very Rarely, 21.2%

Occasionally, 40.0%

Never, 38.8%

Table 7.78 shows that even magazines are not very popular among respondents. Thus, they do not rely on magazines regarding consumer information. At the maximum, 40 per cent of the respondents use magazines occasionally. Remaining of the respondents have never used or rarely used magazines for extracting consumer related information.

Another reason for this lower rating can also be the access to such magazines. Unlike newspapers, magazines are not reachable in each of the nook and corner of the state.

7.13.6. Family & Friends as Sources of Information

Many a times, consumers can get the information shared by their family or friends in their network. This can be an effective source of information. Generally, information related to good or bad products, can be shared by family or friends. A similar sharing can be related to good or bad experiences of using any particular product or service. The opinion of sample respondents about family and friends as a source of information have been shown in Table 7.79 and in Graph 7.63.

Table 7.79
Source of Information - Family & Friends

Response	Frequency	Percent
Never	220	17.6
Very Rarely	255	20.4
Occasionally	225	18.0
Frequently	270	21.6
Very Frequently	280	22.4
Total	**1250**	**100.0**

Source: Primary Probe.

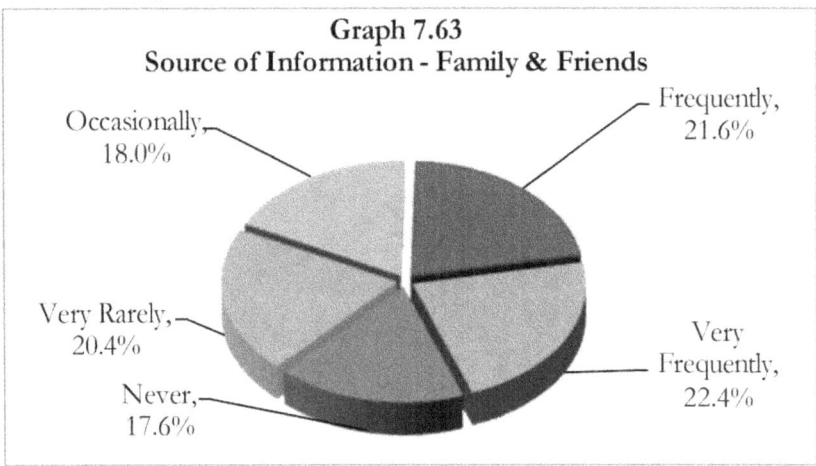

Graph 7.63
Source of Information - Family & Friends

Table 7.79 shows almost similar number of respondents for all types of responses. Around 44 per cent of the respondents frequently or very frequently used information shared with them by their family or friends. Around 38 per cent of the respondents perhaps do not rely on this source as their usage response of this source is never or very rarely. Thus, it may be said that a reasonably good number of people rely on information shared by family and friends.

7.13.7. Comparison of Different Sources of information

Mean response of each type of source of information has been calculated to find the relatively popular sources. Also standard deviation has been calculated to find the degree of deviation from mean values. Results of mean analysis have helped to divide sources in three categories. First category shows highly used sources of information. Against the maximum possible mean value of five, these sources have secured mean value in excess of three. These sources are newspapers, family and friends, and radio. The statistics regarding source of information have been illustrated in Table 7.80 and graphically in Graph 7.64.

Table 7.80
Descriptive of Sources of Information

Code		Mean	Std. Deviation
A1	Source of Information - Newspapers	3.82	.745
A2	Source of Information - Family & Friends	3.11	1.420
A3	Source of Information - Radio	3.02	1.467
B1	Source of Information - Television	2.87	1.394
B2	Source of Information - Magazines	2.01	.889
C1	Source of Information - Websites	1.97	.896

Source: Primary Probe.

Graph 7.64
Descriptive of Sources of Information

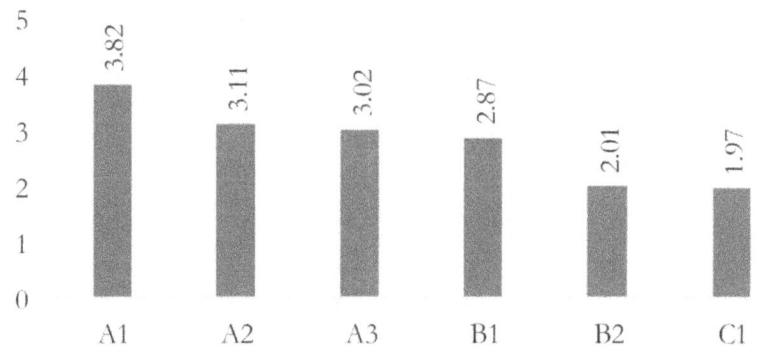

Among these, newspapers are the highly used source of information. Table 7.80 shows that sources with less than three but more than two mean values are television and magazines. These indicate average use of source for information. Finally websites having mean value less than two are the least used source of consumer related information.

Sum up

This chapter dealt with consumer awareness, consumer alertness, and various other aspects of consumer awareness related to consumer protection.

It is clear from the analysis that average level of awareness among consumers is very low. Consumers do not know various aspects related to consumer protection act and consumer redressal mechanism. The process of filing complaint and other matters is also very low. This really becomes a matter of concern for Himachal Pradesh State Government. Besides, in general, consumers also do not exercise necessary alertness while buying something. Billing, weight measurement, ingredients checking etc. are some of the ignored facts. Thus, consumer awareness campaigns should be initiated to increase consumer awareness. Here, the role of consumer NGOs can be critical.

CHAPTER – 8
SUMMARY, CONCLUSIONS AND SUGGESTIONS

The growing interdependence of the world economy and international character of many business practices have contributed to the development of universal emphasis on consumer rights protection and promotion. Consumers, clients and customers world over, are demanding value for money in the form of quality goods and better services. In present situation, consumer protection, though as old as consumer exploitation, has assumed greater importance and relevance. Consumerism is a recent and universal phenomenon. It is a social movement. Consumerism is all about protection of the interests of the consumers.

Consumer protection means and aims at protecting consumers from various unfair trade practices. In India, business organizations have certain advantages in form of well-organized firms, better informed and a better dominating position. Because of this, the companies are understandably in a position to easily exploit consumers. Many Indian consumers are still semi-literate and unaware of consumer protection and consumer rights. These consumers are highly vulnerable to business malpractices. Recent global scenario has contributed to increased awareness of consumer rights among consumers. Consumers are gradually becoming more and more conscious towards deficiencies in products and services.

It would be in fitness of the fact to recall the greatest of Arab historians, Ibn Khaldun saying: "That in civilization there is a limit that cannot be overstepped. When prosperity and luxury come to a people, they are followed by excessive consumption and extravagance, with which the human soul itself is undermined, both in its worldly well-being and in its spiritual life", particularly in context of globalization, liberalization and consumerism in India. This is what happening in India under the auspices of Multinationals and trade policies of developed countries which are supposedly formulated to devour the third world consumer kingdom. Consumers may be deceived in various ways by unscrupulous businessmen including traders, dealers, producers and manufacturers as well as service providers.

Though government is playing its role in protecting rights of the customers, but as long as the customer is not made aware, the problem cannot be addressed. Making laws would help but that is not the solution if the customer is not aware. Education and awareness is the most powerful means for the growth of the country and an educated individual is able to make rationale choice as a consumer. Consumer Protection Act was enacted in 1986 and has been recognized as one of the finest foundation of legislation enacted in any part of the world and India can boast of being only country having such specialized legislation for consumer protection. However, only aware consumers can make use of this legislation. Hence, the present study is an attempt to study consumer's alertness and awareness about consumer protection legislation in Himachal Pradesh.

The present study was conducted to achieve following objectives:

- To examine critically various laws and regulations for consumer protection in India.
- To understand the functioning of Consumer Organizations in Himachal Pradesh.
- To examine the level of alertness among consumers of Himachal Pradesh.
- To examine the level of awareness among consumers of Himachal Pradesh with regards to consumer protection laws, consumer rights and general consumer protection scenario.
- To examine the variation in alertness and awareness among the consumers in Himachal Pradesh with respect to demographic attributes like gender, age, occupation and educational qualification.
- To suggest measures that would help in enhancing consumer alertness and awareness and streamlining the implementation process of consumer protection laws and regulations.

To achieve the above said objectives various hypothesis has been developed and tested during the study.

8.1. Summary and Conclusions

Chapter-wise summary and conclusion of the present study has been discussed in the following paragraphs.

First Chapter is an introductory part. It discusses meaning of consumer, consumer protection and consumerisms. It also discusses the consumer's rights, needs and consumer's responsibilities. In simple words consumer protection is a form of social action which is created to attain the well-being of consumers. Since an individual consumer is considered more vulnerable in the modern world, to exploitation and harassment by the manufacturers and distributors or sellers, it is necessary that the various groups of society such as government, judiciary, voluntary associations of consumers play their role to protect the consumer interest (economic, social and environmental).

The necessity of adopting measures to protect the interest of consumers arises mainly due to their helpless position and the unfair business practices. No doubt consumers have the basic right to be protected from the loss or injury caused on account of defective goods and deficiency of services. However, consumers are unable to make use of their rights due to lack of awareness and ignorance. For example, as consumers we have the right to choose the goods of right quality from a variety of similar goods available in the market. But often we fail to make the right choice because of misleading advertisements by which we are carried away and buy sub-standard goods. Under certain circumstances, we are helpless in the sense of our inability to verify the quality of products.

It is true that the Constitution of India is enshrined with a number of Articles and Clauses to protect the various interests of the consumers. In addition to this, a plethora of Laws and Regulations have enacted in India by various Governments in Union and State to ensure the protection of consumers. But the important issue for ensuring protection of consumers is not the number of Laws and Regulations, but its qualitative aspects. The effective implementation of Laws Acts regarding consumers' right is multi-dimensional in nature and lack of proper implementation of this holistic as well as overreaching laws/Acts makes it difficult for the consumers to enjoy their rights as consumers

Second chapter is an attempt to review the literature concerning the problem in hand. The review of literature reveals that many scholars have studied the consumer awareness, consumer protection and consumer rights at the national and international level. The major finding emerging from the review of relevant studies on the subject is that there is hardly any research work, which has been undertaken to study the consumer awareness in Himachal Pradesh. As the consumer awareness about their rights is important to protect them from the unfair business practices, it is important to study consumer's alertness and awareness level. It is in this background that the present study was conducted. It also presents a picture of research design formulated for the present research work. It discusses the selection of the problem, importance, scope, objectives, hypotheses and research methodology of the present study. Present study was based on both primary and secondary data. Secondary data was collected from the office records of the Department of Food & Civil Supplies and Consumer Affairs. The secondary data have also been collected from the various books, research papers, journals and internet sites. Primary data was collected through administering questionnaire or schedule to the respondents selected through sampling. Multi-stage-cum- Convenience sampling was used to selected respondents. The present study was conducted in five districts, namely, Kangra, Kullu, Shimla, Solan and Una, of Himachal Pradesh. These districts were selected after taking into consideration the population and markets in these districts. At the second stage, sample of respondents was selected. 1250 respondents (250 from each district) were selected conveniently. All the respondents were the consumers of one or another goods. These respondents were selected after visiting the main markets of the selected district. As the present study was focused on the consumer alertness and consumer awareness regarding the consumer protection, the respondents were personally contacted alongwith schedule.

Third Chapter discusses consumerism and consumer protection movements at the international and national level. The consumer movement stands for the organized efforts of consumers seeking to redress, restitute and remedy for the dissatisfaction of the standard of living. It is a social movement seeking to challenge the rights and powers of the buyers in relation to those of sellers. Consumerism, like democracy, is a movement by the people and for the people where the role of common man is uncommon. Consumerism has weak links with the Western world, but is in fact an international phenomenon. People purchasing goods and consuming materials in excess of their basic needs is as old as the first civilizations (e.g. Ancient Egypt, Babylon and Ancient Rome). A great turn in consumerism arrived just before the Industrial Revolution. The industrial revolution and the development in the international trade and commerce has led to the vast expansion of the business and trade. Due to the international character of trade and industry having well organized and highly professionalized producers and traders on one side and illiterate and unorganized consumers with little time on the other, the exploitation of the consumers is common. Various international organizations like ILO, WHO, UNESCO, UNCTAD and UNICEF, have contributed a lot for the protection of the rights of the consumers in the international sphere. In addition, the world Industrial Property Organization, International Organization of Consumer Union and the Inter-Scandinavian Committee on Consumer Matters are also busy in protecting the interests of the consumers at the international level. Many factors and elements are responsible for the development of consumerism. These include technological development, uniformity and speed in manufacturing, development and expansion of transportation, emergence of new society, etc. in India, also, many organization and non-government organizations are working to improve awareness regarding consumer rights and advice on the legal recourse a user can take when his consumer rights are violated.

The fourth Chapter is an attempt to examine various legislations for consumer protection at the international level as well at the national level in India. The anonymity of urban living has been responsible for a number of malpractices on the part of the producers, sellers, suppliers, distributors, etc. These malpractices, in turn, resulted in a number of consumer protection legislations. Each of these legislations is designed to protect the interests of the consumers in one way or the other. Consumer Protection Act has been the major umbrella legislation or act which deals directly with consumer rights and problems. Apart from it, The Essential Commodities Act, empowers the Central Government to regulate production, supply, distribution, storage, transport, price, etc. of essential commodities. Likewise, the Prevention of Food Adulteration Act is designed to eradicate the evil of food adulteration and to ensure purity in the articles of food. Standards of Weights and Measures Act aims at introducing standards in relation to weights and measures used in trade, and commerce. The Trade and Merchandise Marks Act offers protection to the consumers by preventing the use of fraudulent marks.

'AGMARK' under Agricultural Produce (Grading and Marking) Act is an assurance of quality with respect to agricultural products. Then, the Indian Contract Act offers protection to consumers by declaring those contracts which are the result of fraud, misrepresentations, coercion, and undue influence as terminable at the option of the party aggrieved. Besides, damages can also be claimed. Against Sale of Goods Act, protects consumers by subjecting every contract of sale and purchase of goods to certain conditions and warranties. Sale by a person not having a clear title entitles the buyer at full refund of price. Buyer is also protected by latent defects in the goods rendering the un-merchantable.

The efficient and effective program of Consumer Protection is of special significance to all of us because we all are consumers. Even a manufacturer or provider of a service is a consumer of some other goods or services. If both the producers/providers and consumers realize the need for co-existence, adulterated products, spurious goods and other deficiencies in services would become a thing of the past. The active involvement and participation from all quarters i.e. the central and state governments, the educational Institutions, the NGO's, the print and electronic media and the adoption and observance of a voluntary code of conduct by the trade and industry and the citizen's charter by the service providers is necessary to see that the consumers get their due. The need of the hour is for total commitment to the consumer cause and social responsiveness to consumer needs. This should, however, proceed in a harmonious manner so that our society becomes a better place for all of us to live in.

The consumer protection Act, 1986 (68 of 1986) is a milestone in the history of socio-economic legislation in the country. It is one of the most progressive and comprehensive piece of legislations enacted for the protection of consumers. It was enacted after in-depth study of consumer protection laws in a number of countries and in consultation with representatives of consumers, trade and industry and extensive discussions within the Government.

The fifth chapter reviews the frameworks for consumer dispute resolution and redress in India. Consumer Court is the special purpose court, mainly in India that deals with cases regarding consumer disputes and grievances. These are judiciary set ups by the government to protect the consumer rights. Its main function is to maintain the fair practices by the sellers towards consumers. Consumers can file a case against a seller if they are harassed or exploited by sellers. The court will only give a verdict in favour of the consumers/customers if they have proof of exploitation, i.e., bills or other documents. If a consumer does not have the proper documents required for filing a case then it would be very difficult for the consumer to win or even file a case. A nation level court works for the whole country and deals with amount more than Rs 1 crore. A state level court works at the state level with cases valuing less than 20 lakhs and : A district level court works at the district level with cases valuing upto 20 lakhs. The District Consumer Forum is established in all the District of India, The State Consumer Commission is established in all the State Capitals of India, The "National Consumer Disputes Redressal Commission" situated in New Delhi and the governing law is "Consumer Protection Act, in India". It is important to note that the goods purchased or services availed for commercial purposes cannot be challenged under the Consumer Protection Act of India.

The sixth chapter examines the organizational setup for the consumer protection along with its evaluation in Himachal Pradesh. In brief, it may be said that the number of cases filed with both state commission and district forums have been increasing. However, more than ninety percent of the cases have already been resolved. Though, the crucial element of prescribed time limit has sometimes not been followed. After the year 2005, the speed of resolving consumer cases has increased. Finally, insurance and telecom services have been sued most of the times for deficiency in services. So these service providers should look for the major causes of such cases. And due to critical and technical assessment problems, it takes longer time to resolve cases in medical and banking services.

Seventh Chapter deals with the analyses of opinion and perception about consumer awareness and consumer alertness with regard to consumer protection. The major findings of this analysis have been discussed under various headings as follows:

8.1.1. Alertness among Consumers

It was found that in 40 per cent of cases consumers either never or few times check the expiry date of food products and medicines and about 10 per cent consumers sometimes check the expiry date. This indicates that consumers were not found alert while buying medicine and food product.

With regard to the bill it was found that 55 per cent of consumers either never ask for or few times ask for bill while making purchases. Majority of consumer either few times (36.8 per cent) or sometimes (19.2 per cent) check the name of the company on the product. Almost one fourth of the total sample has never checked the MRP of the products. Whereas 37.2 per cent of respondents opined that they few times check the MRP. It was found that 2.0 per cent of respondents always check it. This gives an impression that consumer are not alert of MRP.

More than 71 per cent of consumers were not found alert about looking ingredients detail of the product. In this respect, 34.0 per cent of respondents never checked the detail, 16.8 per cent checked it few times and 20.8 per cent of respondents sometimes check ingredients detail of product. Majority of consumer were not aware/alert about the standards or marks which assure good quality of product. About three fourth of consumers were either few times (32.4 per cent) or never (18.0 per cent) or sometimes (14.4 per cent) check the popular standard marks (such as, ISI, AGMARK) on the product. Such types of inattentiveness can leads to a safety hazard.

The study reveals relatively high degree of alertness among customers in relation to discounts or other promotional offers. Around 43 per cent of the respondents either always or very frequently check and make enquiry with the shopkeepers about discounts or free gifts available with the main products. However, around 41 per cent respondents are also such which never or few times make such enquiries. These customers can easily fall prey to shopkeepers' malpractices

In relation to cross checking of weight of product it was found that 36.8 per cent of customers never, 43.2 per cent few times and 20.0 per cent of customers sometimes cross checked the weight of product. 36.0 per cent of customers either never or few times checked the prices of goods from alternative sources. On the other hand, 40.0 per cent of customers either frequently or always checked the prices of goods from alternative sources.

About 40 per cent of the respondents frequently or always look for the trademarks mentioned on the product labels. However, around 43 per cent are also such respondents who never or few times look for the company trademarks on the products. Application of arithmetic mean and standard deviation reveals that average consumers frequently or sometimes verify the rate printed on the product cover/bottle/carton, look for the company's name on the product, examine the expiry date of the food items and medicines, check the prices from alternative sources, and enquire whether any discounts or any other offers available. Whereas activities such as to look for the trade mark on the product, ask for a bill while purchasing, check for the ISI/AGMARK or other Mark on the product, check the M.R.P.(Maximum Retail Prices) before buying the products, and look for ingredients details of the product were ignored by the consumers but sometimes do take interest in these activities. While in case of cross checking the weight of products by actually weighing the analyses reveals that this is the least performed activity. Not many customers like to cross check the weights of the products they buy.

8.1.2. Consumer Alertness and Demographic Attributes

The analyses with regard to see if any demographic attribute of the customer has any say in doing or not doing any particular activity reveals that the average alertness scores which represents the sum of all alertness related activities is marginally high in case of females than males. However, the application of ANOVA indicates that there is no significant difference exists in male and female respondents in relation to level of alertness. Occupation based ANOVA depicts that consumers belonging to different occupational background have significant difference in their level of alertness. Service and student class have higher levels of alertness as compared to other two categories (Business and Housewife).

When ANOVA is applied to age group versus level of alertness it denotes that F-value is 8.506 and p-value is 0.00, which indicates that there is significant difference among various age groups with regards to their level of alertness. Consumer in the age group of '15-18 yrs' tends to be alert. However, the alertness decreases with increase in age. As far as level of education is concerned, F-value is quite low at 1.464 with p-value of significance at 0.223. This clearly indicates that level of alertness has been almost similar in all categories of education, which gives an impression that there is no significant difference of alertness among consumers having different educational level.

8.1.3. Awareness of Consumer Protection Laws

Study shows that average level of awareness among consumers regarding consumer protection laws is quite good when it comes to knowledge of who is a consumer and what is a district consumer protection council

However, regarding consumer protection machinery like consumer courts, district forums, state and national commissions, they have a moderate degree of awareness. Same is the case with the procedures of consumer complaints like who can make a complaint, procedure of filing complaint, fee and documents required etc. Finally the level of awareness is really poor in case of The Standards of Weights & Measures Act.

8.1.4. Consumer Awareness of Consumer protection Laws and Demographic Attributes

The average awareness score which represents the sum of all awareness related activities is marginally high in case of females than males. The ANOVA value is 0.507 and p-value is 0.477 which indicates that there is no significant difference in male and female consumers in relations to level of awareness of consumer protection laws.

The study reveals that service sector people have the lowest mean Level of Awareness of Consumer Protection Laws whereas students have a better degree of awareness of consumer protection laws. ANOVA value in this case is 0.784 which is quite low. Also the p-value is 0.503 which indicates towards significant variation with regard to the awareness level about consumer protection laws.

Level of Awareness of Consumer Protection Laws was found minimum in case of age group '15-18 years', followed by '18 to 25 years' and '35 years or above'. The maximum awareness was found in among the consumers in age group of '25 to 35 years'. F-value in this case is 0.196 which is low. That's why p-value (.899) is more than 0.05, which indicates that almost all the age groups have the same Level of Awareness of Consumer Protection Laws.

It was found that degree of awareness was maximum in case of graduates followed by post graduates and higher secondary education. Matriculate or below people have been on the lower side.

8.1.5. Awareness of Consumer Rights

With regard to the awareness of consumer rights the study reveals that right to seek redressal has the maximum level of awareness among people of Himachal Pradesh followed by awareness of Right to be heard, awareness of Right to Consumer Education, awareness of Right to choose, and Awareness of Right to be informed. Right to safety has been the least known consumer protection right.

Business sector people have the lowest mean Level of Awareness of Consumer Rights whereas service sector respondents have a better degree of awareness of consumer Rights. Age group-wise analyses reveals that Level of Awareness about Consumer Rights was minimum among the consumers in age group of '18-25 years', followed by '35 or above' and '25 to 35 years'. The maximum awareness has been found in the consumers fall in age group of '15 to 18 years'.

It was found that the degree of awareness about consumer rights was found highest among post-graduate people followed by graduates and matriculate. Higher secondary education category has been on the lower side. ANOVA test in this regard reveals that there is no significant difference of awareness among people with different educational level.

8.1.6. General Consumer Protection Awareness

It was found that in 67.6 per cent of cases people were somewhat aware of Jago Grahak Jago Move. While 16.8 per cent of people were adequately aware and 15.6 per cent of people were fully aware of this move in Himachal Pradesh. This indicates that the awareness level in this regard is not very encouraging.

Awareness of people about the major voluntary consumer organizations in India was also found very low. About 9.6 per cent of people were either fully or somewhat aware. Remaining were either not very aware or somewhat aware or not at all aware. It is unfortunate that people do not even know about organizations which can help them in protection against malpractices.

Nearly 45 per cent of the respondents were adequately or fully aware of Gold Hallmarking. Even, remaining of the respondents is somewhat aware of it. Keeping in mind the recent introduction and popularity of gold hallmarking, the awareness rate is quite encouraging.

With regard to awareness of people about Bureau of Energy Efficiency the study reveals low of level of awareness. About 40 per cent of consumer were found either not very aware or not at all aware of BEE. Hence it can be concluded that there is a minimum level of awareness in relation to major voluntary consumer protection agencies in India. Also people didn't know the existence of various consumer organization engaged in consumer protection. While, High level of awareness was found in case of ISI mark, Agmark, and Gold Hallmarking. However, the level of awareness of Jago Grahak Jago move is not very encouraging. Finally, BEE star rating is not known to people.

Awareness of all general aspects of consumer protection is high in case of males than females. ANOVA value in this regard is 15.693 and p-value of significance is 0.000. It indicates that significant difference exists in male and female respondents in relation to level of General Consumer Protection Awareness. It was found that students has the lowest mean Level of General Consumer Protection Awareness whereas housewife respondents have a better degree of General Consumer Protection Awareness.

Level of General Consumer Protection Awareness was minimum in case of age group '18-25 years' followed by '25 to 35 years' and '15 to 18 years'. The maximum awareness was found in the people in age group 35 years or above'. Awareness level about general aspect of consumer protection was found maximum among people with educational level of higher secondary followed by matriculate or below. Graduates and post graduates surprisingly have been on the lower side.

8.1.7. Product and Services prone to be Deficient

In this regard it was found that maximum number of cases of consumer disputes have been heard for general insurance industry covering medical and vehicle insurances. The number of heard cases in credit cards and life insurance industry is very high. In this category, somewhat lower mean value is with telecom and tour & travel services. Motor loans and demat account related cases have been relatively low. Finally services like healthcare services, real estate, personal loans, housing loans, and immigration services have the minimum number of cases as recalled by the respondents.

The study reveals that apparels and automobiles have been the two products where maximum number of respondents heard recall any consumer related dispute in news. A moderate number of respondents feel that they have heard cases in domestic appliances, Computers & Networking, and FMCG (Except Food). Thus, this category can be termed as moderately deficient products. Finally, not many respondents have heard consumer disputes in relation to consumer electronics and food items. Thus, these are less deficient products.

8.1.8. Deficiency in Products/services noticed by Consumers

Customers remain silent on this issue because they may be asked to pay more on account of indirect taxes which becomes a burden on their pockets.

At the same mean value is also breach of warranty malpractice. Malpractices which are at the bottom of this list are the refusal of discounts or other promotional offers mentioned on the product by sellers and less actual weight of products as compared to the one mentioned on the label

It was found that 62 per cent of respondents occasionally noticed that the price charged is in excess of MRP. 38 per cent of consumers felt that price charge was either frequently or very frequently in excess to MRP. 56 per cent of consumers were experienced the problem of less weight as compared to printed on commodities. 44 per cent of consumer very rarely faced this problem.

About 60 per cent of consumers were of the opinion that they either frequently or very frequently didn't get discount or offers stated on products. It was found that in 78 per cent of cases consumers reported that they noticed sale of expired medicines to the patient.

40 per cent of consumers were of the opinion that they either frequently or very frequently were denied warranties on product.

60 per cent of the respondents have occasionally noticed that they were not issued bill for the purchases made by them. Rest of the respondents has more frequently noticed it. Thus, it may be interpreted that selling products without bills is a common practice in Himachal. 60 per cent of the respondents have occasionally noticed sales of fake products. Remaining of the respondents has also noticed the same but more frequently.

8.1.9. Sources of information related to consumer protection

Newspapers are the highly used source of information. sources with less than three but more than two mean values are television and magazines.

These indicate average use of source for information. Finally websites having mean value less than two are the least used source of consumer related information

8.1.10. Status of Hypotheses

Following Table shows the status of hypotheses stated earlier and tested during the study:

Table 8.1
Status of Hypothesis

Sr. No.	Hypothesis	Test Result
1	There is no significant difference of alertness in males and females.	Accepted
2	There is no significant difference of alertness in respondents belonging to different age groups.	Accepted
3	There is no significant difference of alertness in respondents belonging to different occupations.	Accepted
4	There is no significant difference of alertness in respondents belonging to different educational qualifications.	Accepted
5	There is no significant difference of awareness in males and females.	Partially Accepted*
6	There is no significant difference of awareness in respondents belonging to different age groups.	Accepted
7	There is no significant difference of awareness in respondents belonging to different occupations.	Accepted
8	There is no significant difference of awareness in respondents belonging to different educational qualifications.	Accepted

* It has been found that there is no significant difference in the level of awareness of consumer protection laws between male and female respondents. However, in relation to rights of consumers, female respondents have a significantly higher level of awareness. Hence, the stated hypothesis stands partially accepted.

It is now over two decades since the Consumer Protection Act, 1986 was passed after years of lobbying by the various consumer organizations. The redressal machinery, however, is not fully satisfactory. The number of cases pending in the district forums is piling high. Unless consumer groups take determined action to see that the institutions set up for their protection work effectively, the redressal agencies will go the way of civil courts, where litigants have to wait for years and spend fortunes for the settlements of their disputes. Making the Consumer Protection Act effective is therefore, the first challenge facing the consumer movement in India. There are now a number of voluntary organizations of consumers in existence, but all the cities and towns have not been covered. The rural areas where the greater part of our nine hundred million consumers lives are still virtually untouched by the consumer movement.

In Himachal Pradesh, though the aim is to have a Consumer Complaints Redressal Forum in every district, it is not easy for poor rural consumers to go to the forum with complaints, nor do many consumers have an awareness of ways to assert their consumer rights. The solution lies in training rural workers who are already active in the villages. Mass media should be used to penetrate rural houses. Creating consumer awareness in the vast reaches of rural India with its variety of customs, traditions and languages and little formal education is the second challenge for the consumer movement.

Another matter of concern for the consumer is the likely fall out of the liberalization policy adopted by the government. Undoubtedly, liberalization is going to bring us many benefits, notably, up to date technology, more competition and better products, more employment and investment opportunities. But some possible adverse effects must be taken into account. The export to India of drugs, pesticides and cosmetics which are sometimes banned in the countries from which they originate is likely to be much easier with liberalized import laws. Consumer groups will have to be on their guard against such products and services. For example, obesity treatments, hair restoration treatments and arthritis cures which were not approved in the countries of origin have been brought in here through collaboration and launched with tremendous publicity.

Consumer organizations need to take action against them for their misleading and highly exaggerated claim. Laws against cigarette and liquor advertising are being openly flouted through advertising on hoardings and through cable television. Consumer movement needs to be extremely alert regarding dubious or hazardous products entering the country in the wake of liberalization. Some other emerging areas of consumer protection are environment protection, investor protection and freedom of information. Relentless increase in environmental pollution of all kinds has totally impoverished the quality of our lives and is taking a heavy toll of our health. Consumer groups need to strongly support and work with environmentalists. Every consumer will have to join with others to reduce pollution in his/her own neighborhood.

8.2. Suggestions

The present study reveals that consumer awareness about their rights and protections is not upto the mark, which results in consumer's exploitation. Unawareness of consumers provides an opportunity to the clever seller to sell sub-standard, non-quality and fake products. Therefore, aware consumer is the need of the day. Following are some of the suggestions to enhance consumer awareness and streamline the consumer protection initiatives.

1. Consumer should not ask what the government, consumer organizations and media can do for them but first think what they can do for themselves. They should aware themselves through different sources and they should collect as much as information as they can.

2. Awareness camps should be organized to spread education and information about consumer rights and consumer protection legislations. In this government as well as non-government organization can play an important role. Such type of consumer awareness camps and programmes should be organized at the village level through Nukkar Nataks, workshops, and seminars so that rural people could be educated about different aspects of consumer rights and consumer protection legislations.

3. There should be proper publicity of consumer rights and consumer protection legislations on television, radio, newspapers, magazines and internet.

4. In spreading awareness, social media and new media can play an important role. Blogs, twitter, Facebook etc. should be used to educate people.

5. The number of internet user is increasing rapidly; therefore, a webpage to highlight different aspect related to consumer rights, consumer's responsibilities, consumer protection, consumer forums, etc., should be developed. This webpage could help the people to understand and get information instantly about different aspects of consumer rights and consumer protection.

6. Consumer, while purchasing products, should check the marks of standard, like, AGMARK, ISI, Gold Hallmarking etc. These marks ensure the quality of products and goods.

7. To avoid paying more price than the Minimum Retail Price, the consumer should check MRP on the packet.

8. There is a need to keep check on the weighing and measuring instruments used by traders. Government should conduct periodic checking of these instruments. Consumers should create a habit to check the weighing and measuring instruments while purchasing goods and products.

9. Consumer should collect bill at the time of every purchase. With this they should also collect the guarantee and warranty card from the traders/shopkeepers. This practice could be a check on tax evasion and also act as a proof if the good and product found to be sub-standard or fake.

10. Consumer should check the expiry date of the product, particularly that of eatable and medicines.

346

11. Consumers should always check the quantity as per the figure printed on the packet of the product.
12. People should avoid buying fruits and vegetables from unhygienic places.
13. The Manufacturers of the product should clearly mention the information manufacturing and expiry date, weight of products, ingredients, price, etc., on the packet of the products, so that the consumer can easily get the information about the product.
14. The consumer should collect the proper information of the brand, logo before the purchase of a particular brand and he should also compare the rate of the different brands of a particular product. So that consumer cannot be cheated with fake products.
15. The Government should encourage the voluntary consumer organizations to set up their branch offices at the district level or if possible at the block level. So that the consumers can get proper information related to consumer awareness, consumer rights and responsibilities and knowledge related to how to file the complaints.
16. Government should take stern action against those traders and shopkeepers who used to sell fake, sub-standard and non-quality products.
17. The consumer cases should be finalized within reasonable time period so that faith of the consumers on the consumer protection commission and forums could be enhanced.
18. Until and unless people bring any violation in their rights, malpractices and other bad activities to the notice of the concerned authorities, relief of any kind cannot be given to the affected consumers and also corrective measures cannot be initiated. Hence, it is the prime responsibility of a consumer to bring to the notice of the concerned authorities, any violation in their rights.

BIBLIOGRAPHY

Books

Adamson, C. (1982). *Consumer in Business*. London: National Consumer Council.

Agarwal, V. (1989). *Consumer Protection in India*. New Delhi: Deep & Deep Publication.

Ahluwalia, M.S. (1993). *History of Himachal Pradesh (2nd ed.)*. New Delhi: Intellectual Publishing House.

Anderson, J. (1998). *For the People: A Consumer Action Handbook*. California: Addition Wesky Publishing Company.

Antony, M. (1991). *Consumer Rights*. New Delhi: Clarion Books.

Balokhra. Jag Mohan. (2010). *The Wonderland Himachal Pradesh: An Encyclopedia on the State of Western Himalayas*. New Delhi: H.G. Publications.

Berger, M. (1975). *Consumer Protection Labs*. New York: The John Day Company.

Bijlani, D. (1990). *Role of Mass Media in Consumer Education*. Ahmedabad: Centre for Development Communication.

Blake, D. H. (1987). *The Politics of Global Economic Relations* (3rd ed.). Englewood Cliffs New Jersy: Prentice Hall Inclusive.

Borrie, G. (1984). *The Development of Consumer Law and Policy: Bold Spirits and Timorous Soul (Hamlyn Lecture Series)*. U.K.: Steven and Sons Ltd.

Bruun, Jensen B., Simovska, Venka & Schnack, K. (2001). *Critical Environmental and Health Education: Research Issues and Challenges*. Copenhagen: Research Centre for Environmental and Heal Education, The Danish University of Education.

Cattell, R. B. (1978). *The Scientific Use of Factor Analysis in the Behavioural and Life Sciences*. New York: Plenum Press.

Chamola, S. (2007). *Kautilya's Arthshastra and the Science of Management: Relevance for the Contemporary Society*. Gurgaon: Hope India Publications.

Chandra, J.P. (2004). *Rights of Consumers.* New Delhi.

Chaturvedi, B. (2006). *Kautilya's Arthshastra.* New Delhi: Diamond Pocket Books.

Chaturvedi, L. A. (1986). *Ensure LPG Consumer Safety: A Report.* Ahmedabad: Consumer Education and Research Centre.

Chaudhry, Minakshi. (2006). *Himachal: A complete Guide to the Land of Gods.* New Delhi: Rupa and Company.

Cooper, I. (1986). *Consumer Education.* Oxford: Oxford University Press.

Cooper, I. (1986). *Consumer Education.* Oxford: Oxford University Press.

Council., N. C. (1979). *Consumer and State: Getting Value for Public Money.* London: National Consumer Council.

Dave, N. (1987). *Speeding Towards Road Safety.* Ahmedabad: Consumer Education and Research Centre.

David, N. (1975). *Reference Guide to Consumer.* New York: R.R. Broker Company.

David, N. (1975). *Reference Guide to Consumers.* New York: R.R. Broker Co.

Dourglas, Mary & Isherwood, Baron. (1996). *The World of Goods: Towards an Anthropology of consumption.* London: Routledge.

Epstein, D. G. and Nickles, S.H. (1983). *Consumer Law.* USA: West Publishing Company.

Fauth, Julia. (2002). *Money Consumption and the Environment: Young Consumer at the Beginning of the 21st Century.* Frankfurt: Verlag Fritz Knapp.

Featherstone, Michael. (1992). *Consumer Culture and Postmoernism.* London: Sage Publications.

Fernando, A. (2009). *Business Ethics: An Indian Perspective.* New Delhi: Pearson Education India.

Fetterman, E. A. & Schiller, M.K. (1978). *Let the Buyer Be Aware Consumer Rights and Responsibilities.* New York: Fairchild Publications.

Fox, Richard Wightman & Lears, T.J. Jackson. (1983). *The Culture of Consumption: Critical Essays in American History 1880-1980.* New York: Pantheon Books.

Garg, O. (1990). *Consumer Protection Act.* New Delhi: Vinod Publishing House.

Ghatak, A. (1991). *Consumerism in India: A General Study.* New Delhi: Naurang Rai.

Giddens, Anthony. (1991). *Modernity and Self-identity: Self and Society in the Late Modern Age.* Cambridge: Polity Press.

Giordan, M. (1980). *Consumer Education: A Handbook for Teachers.* London: Methuen and Company Ltd.

Giri, H.N. (1987). *Consumer Crimes and Law.* New Delhi: Ashish Publishing House.

Gopal, M. (1935). *Mauryan Public Finance.* London: George Allen & Unwin Ltd.

Grada, H.T. (1985). *Promoting Consumer Education in Schools.* Emeryville, CA: Penang IOCU.

Groeneveld, J. (1984). *Simple Tests Manual.* Emeryville, CA: IOCU Penang.

Gulshan, S. (2007). *Consumer Protection and Satisfaction.* New Delhi: Deep & Deep Publishing House.

Gunter, Barrie & Furnham, Adrian. (1998). *Children as Consumers: A Psychological Analysis of the Young People's Market.* London: Routledge.

Gurg, M. (2003). *Consumer Rights.* New Delhi: Clarion Books.

Hall, R. H. (1972). *Organization: Structure and Process.* Englewood Cliffs, New Jersey: Prentice Hall Inc.

India., K. C. (1976). *Some Tips to Remember.* Bangalor: Karnataka Consumer Society.

Jacobson, Lisa. (2004). *Raising Consumers: Children and the American Mass Market in the Early Twentieth Century.* New York: Columbia University Press.

Jayadevan, R. (1993). *Banking Service and Consumer Protection (Dissertation).* Cochin: Cochin University.

Jayapalan, N. (2000). *Public Administration.* New Delhi: Atlantic Publishers and Distributors.

Jha, A. K. (2003). *Consumer Protection, Consumer Rights and Consumer Disputes Redressal Commission in India.*

Jreat, Manoj (2004). *Tourism in Himachal Pradesh.* New Delhi: Indus Publishing Company.

Judit, C. K. (2005). *Competition Law and Consumer Protection.* The Heagu, Netherland: Kluwer Law International.

Kamath, K. (1987). *Servants, Not Masters: A Guide for Consumer Activists in India.* Karnataka : Consumers' Forum Udupi.

Karnik, S. (1995). *Consumer and Law.* Ahmedabad: Consumer Education and Research Centre.

Katona, G. (1960). *Powerful Consumer: Psychological Studies of American Economy.* New York: MacGraw Hill Book Company.

Krishana, P. L. (1984). *Consumer Protection and Legal Control.* Lucknow: Eastern Book Company.

Krishna, P. L. (1984). *Consumer Protection and Legal Control.* Lucknow: Eastern Book Company.

Krishna, P. L. (2002). *Consumer Protection and Legal Control.* Lucknow: Eastern Book Company.

Lee, M. J. (2000). *The Consumer Society Reader.* Blackwell: Malden MA.

Lewis, D. A. (2000). *The Soul of the New Consumer: Authenticity- What We Buy and Why in the Economy.* London: Nicholas Brealey.

Lizzy, E. (1996). *Women and Consumer Protection (Ph. D. Thesis).* Cochin: Cochin University.

Lowe, R. A. (1980). *Consumer - Law and Practice.* London: Seet & Maxwell Ltd.

Lowe, R., & Woodroffe, G. (1980). *Consumer - Law and Practice.* London: Sweet & Maxwell Ltd.

Malhotra, G. (2006). *Public Administration.* New Delhi: Murari Lal and Sons.

Misra, V. (2007). *Ancient Indian Dynasties.* Mumbai: Bharatiya Vidya Bhavan.

Muller, F. (2004). *The Laws of Manu: The Sacred Books of the East.* Oxford: Oxford University Press.

Nadel, M. (1971). *The Politics of Consumer Protection.* Indianapolis: Bobbs-Merril Company Inc.

Nagarajan, V. (1992). *Evolution of Social Polity of Ancient India.* New Delhi: Dattsons.

Narayan, R. (1989). *Consumer Awareness and Business Ethics: An Annual Report.* Ahmedabad: Consumer Education and Research Centre.

Padma, G. (1990). *Media and Consumer Protection - A Manual.* Ahmedabad: Consumer Education and Research Centre.

Painter, A. (1978). *Guide to Consumer Protection Law.* London: Barry Rose Publishers Ltd.

Patrick, O. (2004). *Manu's Code of Law: A Critical Edition and Translation of the Manava Dharmsastra.* Oxford: Oxford University Press.

Promod, K. (1986). *Inadequate Information on Lebel of Product: An Annual Report.* Ahmedabad: Consumer Education and Research Centre.

Rangarjan, L. (1992). *Kautilaya: The Arthashastra.* New Delhi: Penguin Books.

Rarlph, B. J. (1963). *Administration and Economic Development in India.* Durham NC: Duke University Press.

Riswadkar, S. (1983). *Unfair Fair Price Shops.* Ahmedabad: Consumer Education and Research Centre.

Robbins, S. A., Judge, T. &. Sanghi, Seema (2008). *Organizational Behaviour.* New Delhi: Pearson Prentice Hall, Dorling Kindersley (India) Pvt. Ltd.

Saraf, D.N. (1990). *Law of Consumer Protection in India.* Bombay: N.M. Tripati.

Sarkar, A. (1989). *The Problem of Consumer in Modern India* (1st ed.). New Delhi: Discovery Publication House.

Sekaran, U. (2004). *Organizational Behaviour: Text and Cases* (2nd ed.). New Delhi: Tata McGraw Hill Publishing Company.

Selvasdas, M. (1998). *A Study on the Consumer Protection Movement in Kerala (Ph.D. Thesis).* Kerala: University of Kerala.

Shah, M. (1981). *Public Interest Groups and Development Journalism.* Ahmedabad: Consumer Education and Research Centre.

Shah, P. (1987). *Some Safety.* Ahmedabad: Consumer Education and Research Centre.

Sharma, L.R. (1987). *The Economy of Himachal Pradesh: Growth and Structure: A Study in Development Performance.* New Delhi: Mittal Publications.

Shobhana, R. (1983). *Unfair Price Shops.* Ahmedabad: Consumer Education and Research Centre.

Silber, N. (1983). *Test and Protest: The Influence of Consumers' Union.* London: Holmes & Meier Publishers.

Singh, Mian Goverdhan. (1999). *Wooden Temples of Himachal Prades.* New Delhi: Indus Publishing Company.

Singh, S., & Singh, M. (2006). *Rural Development in 21st Century: A Multi-Dimensional Study.* New Delhi: Deep & Deep Publications Pvt. Ltd.

Spengler, J. J. (1971). *Indian Economic Thought.* Durham NC: Duke University Press.

Sreevidya, K. (1993). *Consumer Justic and Public Utility Services (Unpublished).* Cochin: Cochin University.

Subhojyoti, A. (2005). *Consumer Protection and Law: A General Study from India's Perspective.* New Delhi: New India Publications.

Subhojyoti, A. (2007). *Consumer Protection and Law: A General Study from India's Perspective.* New Delhi: New India Publications.

Thakur, Laxam S. (1996). *The Architectural Heritage of Himachal Pradesh: Origin and Development of Temple Styles,* New Delhi: Munshiram Manoharlal Publishers.

Tiwari, A.K. (2007). *Spatial Dimension of Socio-Economic Development: A Case Study of Himachal Pradesh.* New Delhi: Kanishka Publishers and Distributors.

Trivedi, K. (1999). *Organization and Administrative Theories.* Jaipur: Research Publication.

Veblen, T. (1994). *The Theory of the Leisure Class: An Economic Study of Instutitions.* Mineola, N.Y.: Dover Publications.

Wells, T., & Sim, E. (1987). *Till They Have Faces: Women as Consumers.* Penang: International Organization of Consumers Union.

Journals and Research Article

Abbokar, S. (2009, Februray 15). Consumer Protection in India: Some Reflections. *Southern Economists.*

Arndt, Jonan, Cran, Edgar & Tallhaug, Knut (1977). Opinions of Consumerism Issues Among Present and Future Norwegian Business Executives. *European Journal of Marketing,* 11(1): 13-20.

Arndt, Jonan, Barksdale, Hiram C. & Perreault, William D. (1980). Comparative Study of Attitudes Toward Marketing, Consumerism and Government Regulation: The United States versus Norway and Venezuela. In Day, Ralph L. & Hunt, H. Keith. *New Findings on Consumer Satisfaction and Complaining.* St. Louis,MO: 66-72.

Bakshi, P. (1989, May 24). Consumer Law and Voluntary Agencies. *Financial Express.*

Barker, A. T. (1987). Consumerism in New Zealand. *International Marketing Review, 4.*

Benn, Jette. (2004). Consumer Education between Consumership and Citizenship: Experience from Studies of Young People. *International Journal of Consumer Studies*, 28; 108-116.

Bloom, P. N., & Greyser, S. A. (1981, November-December). The Maturing of Consumerism. *Harvard Business Review*, 59: 130-139.

Barksdale, Hiram C. et.al. (1982). A Cross National Survey of Consumer Attitude towards Marketing Practices, Consumerism and Government Regulations. *Columbia Journal of World Business*, 17: 71-86.

Brigitte, M. N. (1987). Consumerism and Marketing Mangement's Responsibility. *European Journal of Marketing, 21*(3).

Brown, Karen, McIlveen, Heather & Christopher, Strugnell. (2000). Young Consumer's Food Preferences within Selected Sectors of the Hospitality Spectrum. *International Journal of Consumer Studies & Home Economics*, 24(2): 104-112.

Bruun, Jensen B. & Schnack, K. (1985). Action and Action Competence as Key Concepts in Critical Pedagogy Studies. *Educational Theory and Curriculum*, 12.

Campbell, C. (1990). Character of Consumption: An Historical Action Theory Approach to the Understanding of Consumer Behaviour. *Culture & History*, 7: 37-48.

Choudhary, Y. (2010, January 10). Conumer Preference on Mobile Connections and Buyer Behaviour towards Reliance Mobile in Chennai City. *SSRN*. Retrieved from http://papers.ssrn.com/sol3/Delivery.cfm/SSRN_ID1623429_code1327817.pdf?abstractid=1623429&mirid=1

Clifford, Mark. (1988, September). Citizens Begin to Battle for Their Rights. *Far Eastern Economic Review*, 8: 96-97.

Dahat, P. R. (2010, April 14). *Medical Neglinece and Consumer Protection Law*. Retrieved from Social Science Research Network: http://ssrn.com/abstract=1589192

Daniel, O. (1988, August). How the FTC Serves the Consumer. *Consumer Research*.

Dickinson, Roger. (2000). Food and Eating on Television: Impacts and Influence. *Nutrition & Food Science*, 30(1): 24-29.

Dixit, V. (1989, May 25). Consumers Don't Take Things Down. *Social Welfare*.

Dowd, Ann Reilly. (1997, August). How to Protect Your Privacy. *Money*.

Drucker, P. (1987, September). Consumerism and A Shame of Modern Marketing. *Journal of Marketing, 25*.

Elliott, Richard. Existential Consumption and Irrational Desire. *European Journal of Marketing*, 31(3/4): 285-296.

Evers, M. (1983, August). Consumerism in the Eighties. *Public Relations Journal*.

Frech, W.A. Barksdale, Hiram C. & Perreault, William D. (1982). Consumer Attitude toward Marketing in England and the United States. *European Journal of Marketing*, 16(6): 20-30.

Gaedeke, Ralph M. and Udo, Udo Aka. (1974). Toward the Internationalization of Consumerism. *California Management Review*, 27: 86-92.

Gambhi, C. (2002). Consumer Protection: Law and Practice. *Indian Journal of Marketing*, 32, 17-20.

Goldsmith, E. & McGregor, S. (2000). E-Commerce: Consumer Issues and Implications for Research and Education. *Journal of Consumer Studies and Home Economics*, 24: 124-127.

Grant, N. (1989, May 22). Indian Consumer Must Shake off His Apathy. *Times of India*.

Gupta, A., & Agarwal, R. (2003). The Consumer Financing Busienss in India's Building Blocks for the Future. *Social Science Research Network*. Retrieved from http://ssrn.com/abstract=619721

Gupta, P. K. (2008). Internet Banking in India - Consumer Concerns and Bank Strategies. *Global Journal of Business Research*, 2(1), 43-51.

Gupta, S., & Anurag. (1988, May-June). Business Ethics and Consumer Interest. 8(5).

Hamilton, J., Macllveed, H., & Christopher, S. (2000). Educating Young Consumer - A Food Choice Model. *Journal of Consumer Studies & Home Economics*, 24(2): 113-123.

Hans, W. M. (2006). Consumers and Competition - Access and Compensation under the EC Law. *European Business Law Review*, 17(1), 69-75.

Harland, D. (1987, September). The United Nations Guidlines for Consumer Protection. *Journal of Consumer Policy*,: 245-266.

Harland, D. (1988, March). The United Nations Guidelines for Consumer Protection, Reply to the Comment by Weidenbaum. *Journal of Consumer Policy*, 10(4): 111-115.

Hasalkar, S., & Ashalatha, K. (1998). Awareness of Home-Makers About Indian Standard Marks on Consumer Goods. *Karnataka Journal of Agricultural Science*, 11(4), 1148-1151.

Hendon, Donald W. (1975, August). Toward a Theory of Consumerism. *Business Horizons*,: 16:24.

Herrmann, Robert O. (1970, October). Consumerism: Its Goals, Organizations and Future. *Journal of Marketing*, 34: 55-60.

Herrmann, Robert O. (1980, May). Consumer Protection: Yesterday, Today and Tomorrow. *Current History*, 78: 193-227.

Herrmann, Robert O. & Rex, H. Warland. (1976). Nader's Support: Its Sources and Concerns. *The Journal of Consumer Affairs*, 10: 1-18.

Hinds, Michael DeCourcy. (1988, September 12). Consumer Protection 101 for Chinese. *The New York Times,*: IV-1.

Hong, Liu. (1989, November). Association Champions Consumer Rights. *China Reconstructs*, 38: 41-43.

Imam, Z. (1989, October 18). Consumer not the King. *Hindustan Times*.

Joshi, N. (1990, December 21). Creating Consumerism. *Financial Express*.

Jones, Gill & Martin, Chris D. (1999). Young Consumer at Home: Dependence, Resistance and Autonomy. Hearn, Jeff & Rosenell, Sasha, *Consuming Cultures: Power and Resistance*, Macmmilan Press Ltd.

Kulkarni, M., & Murali, D. (1990). Study on Purchasing Practices of Consumers of Parbhani Town. *Indian Journal of Marketing, 26*, 3-7.

Kumar, A. (2011, April 4). *Celebrity Endorsements and Its Impact on Consumer Buying Behaviour.* Retrieved from SSRN: http://ssrn.com/abstract=1802531

Kumar, N., & Batra, N. (1990). Consumer Rights - Awareness and Action. *Indian Journal of Marketing, 21*(4), 21-23.

Malik, A. (2006). Rural Development Administration in India. In S. Singh, & S. Mohinder, *Rural Development in the 21st Century: A Multi-Dimensional Study.* New Delhi: Deep & Deep Publication Pvt. Ltd.

Mathew, S. (1975). Awareness of Housewives towards Food Adulteration and the Extent of Adulterated Foods Sold in the Local Market of Udaipur City. *Indian Journal of Home Science, 9*(3), 81-85.

McGregor, Sue. (1999). Towards a Rationale for integrating Consumer and Citizenship Education. *Journal of Consumer Sutdies & Home Economics,* 23(4): 207-211.

Mehta, P. (1990, January 22). Blow for the Consumer. *Indian Express*.

Narayan, R. (1989, October 25). Hope for Harried Consumers. *Indian Express*.

Natarajan, K. (1990). Consumer Awareness Towards ISI Mark. *Indian Journal of Marketing, 20*(6), 16-19.

OECD. (2008). Interference Between Competition Law and Consumer Welfare. Retrieved from http://www.oecd.org/competition 01/07/2009

Parigi, V. (1990, March 20). Safer Products for the Consumer. *The Hindu*.

Ramesh, M. (1989, December 4). Consumer Interest in Legal Profession: Problems and Perspectives. *Cochin University Law Review*(13), 405-425.

Rebellow, A. (1989, November 6). Long Wait for Redressal Panels. *Indian Express*.

Rebellow, A. (1990, April 11). Is Service Sector any the Better. *Indian Express*.

Reddy, N., & Ramesh, A. (1998). The Role of an Independent Agency to Protect the Consumer Interest: An Empirical Study. *Indian Journal of Marketing, 28*, 2-11.

Roy, S. (2011, January 29). *An Overview of Retail Industry in India: Its Growth, Challenges and Opportunities.* Retrieved from SSRN: http://ssrn.com/abstract=175079

Sahoo, S., & Chatterjee, A. (2009). Consumer Protection - Problems and Prospects. *SSRN.* Retrieved from http://sssrn.com/abstract=1452526

Sawarkar, J., & Giram, S. (1996). Consumer Awareness: A Survey Analysis. *Indian Journal of Marketing, 25,* 13-21.

Sayeedun, N. (2007). FDI in Indian Retail Industry. *SSRN.* Retrieved from http://ssrn.come/abstract=983711

Shah, S. (1989, March 22). Confused Customer Diffused Movement. *Times of India.*

Shourie, H. (1989, August 10). Consumer Protection - Pass Lows and Sleep. *Hindustan Times.*

Singh, J. (1989, January 25). Consumer Complaint Interion and Behaviour: Definition and Issue. *Journal of Marketing,* 93-107.

Sivaraman, S. (1989, March 19). Combating Consumer Exploitation. *Economic Times.*

Suresh, G. (2010). Consumers Attitude and Green Advertisement: An Evaluation. *SSRN.* Retrieved from http://ssrn.com/abstract=1640006

Thanulingam, N., & Kochadai, M. (1989). An Evaluation of Consumer Awareness. *Indian Journal of Marketing, 19*(8), 3-8.

Thomas, B. (1978). The Legal Framework of Consumer Protection. In J. Mitchell, *Marketing and the Consumer Movement.*

Thorelli, H. B. (1981). Consumer Policy for the Third World. *Journal of Consumer Policy, 3.*

Vedder, H. (2006). Competition Law and Consumer Protection: How Competition Law Can be used to Protect Consumers evern Better or Not. *European Business Law Review, 17*(1), 83-95.

Reports and government Documents

Department of Consumer Affairs (2004). *Annual Report 2003-04.* New Delhi: Ministry of Consumer Affairs, Food and Public Distribution (Government of India).

Department of Consumer Affairs (2007). *Annual Report 2006-07.* New Delhi: Ministry of Consumer Affairs, Food and Public Distribution (Government of India).

Department of Economics and Statistics (2011). Economic *Survey 2010-11,* Shimla: Government of Himachal Pradesh.

Department of Economics and Statistics. (2010). *Brief Facts: Himachal Pradesh 2009-10,* Shimla: Government of Himachal Pradesh.

Department of Economics and Statistics. (2012). *Economic Survey 2011-12.* Shimla: Government of Himachal Pradesh.

Department of Economics and Statistics. *Himachal in Figures 2010-11*, Shimla: Government of Himachal Pradesh.

Department of Economics and Statistics. *Himachal in Figures 2010-11*. Shimla: Government of Himachal Pradesh

Directorate of Census Operations, *Census of India 2011: Provisional Population Totals, Paper 1 of 2011 Himachal Pradesh Series-3*. Shimla: Government of Himachal Pradesh.

Government of Himachal Pradesh. (2004). *Brief Facts: Himachal Pradesh 2004* Shimla: Department of Economics and Statistics.

Ministry of Environment and Forest,. (2006). *Annual Report 2005-06*. New Delhi: Government of India.

Ministry of Environment and Forest,. (2007). *Annual Report 2006-07*. New Delhi: Government of India.

Minstry of Food & Civil Supply,. (1990). *Annual Report 1989-90*. New Delhi: Government of India.

Planning Department. (2010). *Draft Annual Plan 2010-11*. Shimla: Government of Himachal Pradesh.

Public Accounts Committee. (2000). *Annual Report*. New Delhi: Union Parliament.

World Bank. (2006). *The World Bank Annual Report*.

Websites and URL

http://www.india.gov.in/knowindia/state_uts.php?id=10, retrieved on 21st March 2012.

About the Organization. Retrieved September 24, 2013, from Akhil Bhartiya Upbhokta Uthan Sangathan: http://aicpo.org.in/about.htm

About us. Retrieved October 9, 2013, from Bharat Jyoti: Consumer Protection and Social Welfare Organization: http://bharatjyoti.org/aboutus.php

About us. Retrieved October 8, 2013, from Consumer Co-ordination Council: http://www.cccindia.co/aboutus.asp

About Us. Retrieved October 9, 2013, from Consumer Association of India: http://www.caiindia.org/about.aspx

About Us. Retrieved October 9, 2013, from EMPOWER.

About Us. Retrieved October 9, 2013, from Grahak Raja Jago Ho: http://www.grahakraja.org/

About Us. Retrieved October 1, 2013, from Mumbai Grahak Panchayat: http://www.mumbaigrahakpanchayat.org/CMS/2/About%20us

About us: Overview. Retrieved October 8, 2013, from Citizen Consumer and Civic Action Group: http://www.cag.org.in/overview

ACASH. *An Introduction*. Retrieved October 9, 2013, from Association for Consumers Action on Safety and Health: http://www.acash.org/index.htm

ACASH. *Objectives*. Retrieved October 9, 2013, from http://www.acash.org/objectives.htm

Adhikaar: The Right Path. Retrieved September 18, 2013, from http://adhikaar.in/

Areas of Work. Retrieved October 9, 2013, from Consumer Rights Education and Awareness Trust: http://www.creatindia.org/areas-of-work.html

Choudhary, Y. L. (2010, January 10). *Conumer Preference on Mobile Connections and Buyer Behaviour towards Reliance Mobile in Chennai City*. Retrieved from Social Science Research Network: http://papers.ssrn.com /sol3/Delivery.cfm/SSRN_ID1623429_code1327817.pdf?abstractid=1 623429&mirid=1

Consumer. Retrieved September 10, 2013, from Answer: http://www.answers.com/topic/consumer

Grahak Panchayat. Retrieved October 9, 2013, from virtualpune.com: http://citizencentre.virtualpune.com/html/grahak_panchayat.shtml

Mission. Retrieved October 9, 2013, from Grahak Raja Jago Ho: http://www.grahakraja.org/mission.html

Welcome to C reat India. Retrieved October 9, 2013, from Consumer Rights Education and Awareness Trust: http://www.creatindia.org/

What is CERC? Retrieved September 24, 2013, from Consumer Education and Research Centre: http://www.cercindia.org/index.php?option=com_content&view=arti cle&id=69&Itemid=80

CONSUMER PROTECTION ACT, 1986, Retrieved from http://www.vakilno1.com/bareacts/consumerprotectionact/consumer protectionact.html. 18 March 2013.

ANNEXURE
Questionnaire on Consumer Awareness
Part- A: General Awareness Related Questions

1. Do you examine the expiry date the food items and medicines when you buy them?

Always	Frequently	Sometimes	Few times	Never

2. Do you ask for a bill whenever you purchase something?

Always	Frequently	Sometimes	Few times	Never

3. Do you look for the company's name on the product?

Always	Frequently	Sometimes	Few times	Never

4. Do you look for the trade mark on the product you buy?

Always	Frequently	Sometimes	Few times	Never

5. Do you look for ingredients details of the product you buy?

Always	Frequently	Sometimes	Few times	Never

6. Do you verify the rate printed on the product cover/bottle/carton?

Always	Frequently	Sometimes	Few times	Never

7. Do you check for the ISI/AGMARK or other Mark on the product when you buy it?

Always	Frequently	Sometimes	Few times	Never

8. Do you inquire whether any discounts or any other offers available if you purchase the product?

Always	Frequently	Sometimes	Few times	Never

9. Have you ever cross checked the weights of the products mentioned on the item?

Always	Frequently	Sometimes	Few times	Never

10. Do you check the prices, of goods you buy, from alternative sources?

Always	Frequently	Sometimes	Few times	Never

11. Do you check the M.R.P. (Maximum Retail Prices) before buying the products?

Always	Frequently	Sometimes	Few times	Never

12. Have you ever noticed the following problems?

Problem	Very Frequently	Frequently	Occasionally	Very Rarely	Never
Price Charged more than M.R.P.					
Less weight as compared to printed on commodities					
Discount/other offers stated on products not granted					
Breach of Warranties					
Expired medicines sold					
Bill not issued					
Fake products sold					

Part – B: Awareness of Consumer Protection Machinery of India

13. Are you aware of consumer courts, for redressal of grievances of consumers?

Fully Aware	Adequately Aware	Somewhat Aware	Not Very Aware	Not at all Aware

- If yes, have you ever filed a case in the consumer court?

Always	Frequently	Sometimes	Few times	Never

14. Are you aware of Consumer Protection Act?

Fully Aware	Adequately Aware	Somewhat Aware	Not Very Aware	Not at all Aware

15. Are you aware of The Standards of Weights and Measures Act?

Fully Aware	Adequately Aware	Somewhat Aware	Not Very Aware	Not at all Aware

16. Are you aware of the following aspects of Consumer Protection Laws in India?

Aspect	Fully Aware	Adequately Aware	Somewhat Aware	Not Very Aware	Not at all Aware
Definition of consumer					
Who can make complaint					
District Consumer Protection Council					
District Consumer Forums					
District Consumer Forums in Himachal Pradesh					
State Commission					
National Commission					
Process of filing complaints					
Documents required for filing complaints					
Prescribed fee for making complaint					
Available Reliefs					
Unfair Trade Practices					
Restrictive Trade Practice					
Spurious Goods and Service					
Jago Grahak Jago Move					
Major Voluntary Consumer Organizations In India					
Agmark					
ISI Mark					
Gold Hallmarking					
BEE Stars					

17. Are you aware of the following rights of consumers?

Right	Fully Aware	Adequately Aware	Somewhat Aware	Not Very Aware	Not at all Aware
Right to Safety					
Right to be Informed					
Right to Choose					
Right to be heard					
Right to seek Redressal					
Right to Consumer Education					

18. Which of the following kinds of organizations have you got to hear maximum number of consumer cases?

-   **Services**

Services	Fully Aware	Adequately Aware	Somewhat Aware	Not Very Aware	Not at all Aware
Telecom					
Housing Loans					
Motor Loans					
Personal Loans					
Life Insurance					
General Insurance					
Credit Cards					
Healthcare Services					
Demat Accounts					
Real Estate					
Tours & Travels					
Immigration Services					

-   **Product**

Products	Fully Aware	Adequately Aware	Somewhat Aware	Not Very Aware	Not at all Aware
FMCG (Except Food)					
Consumer Electronics					
Automobiles					
Food Items					
Computers & Networking					
Apparels					
Domestic Appliances					

19. Please indicate the degree of your access to following sources of information related to consumer protection and consumer cases.

Source of Information	Very Frequently	Frequently	Occasionally	Very Rarely	Never
Newspapers					
Television					
Radio					
Websites					
Magazines					
Family & Friends					

Part – C: Demographic Information

20. Name: _____.

21. Gender:

        a) Male

        b) Female

22. Occupation:

        a) Businessman   b) Service

        c) Student   d) Housewife

23. Age (years):

        a) [15-18]   b) [18-25]

        c) [25-35]   d) [35+]

24. Qualification:

        a) Matriculate or below   b) Higher Secondary

        c) Graduate   d) Post Graduate or above

ABOUT THE AUTHORS

Dr. Parkash Chandel is presently working as Professor, Department of Commerce, Centre for Evening Studies, Himachal Pradesh University Shimla. He attained his Ph.D. and MPhil degree from Himachal Pradesh University Shimla (INDIA). During his 25 years of research and teaching, he published more than thirty research papers in National and International Journals. He has also participated and presented in more than twenty-five National and International conferences and Seminars in India and abroad. His area of interest is Project Management, Accounting, Organizational Behaviour, International Business, Marketing Research, Business Management and International Business. Dr. Chandel has supervised more than ten PhD scholars, more than twenty MPhil students and more than seventy students towards their project reports for the completion of various management/M.Com degree. Dr. Chandel is the member of selection Committees of various universities and is also in the panel of examiners/experts, member of Board of Studies and research committees of various universities. He is the life time member of Indian Commerce Association.

Dr. Shammi Minhas is presently working as Assistant Professor in MBBGRGC Girls College, Mansowal, Hoshiarpur Punjab (INDIA). She attained her Ph.D. and MPhil degree in Commerce from Himachal Pradesh University Shimla. She has seven years of teaching and research experience. During her teaching and research, she has published many research papers in National and International Journals. She has also participated and presented papers in more than eight National and International seminars and conferences.

www.ingramcontent.com/pod-product-compliance
Lightning Source LLC
Chambersburg PA
CBHW071248220526
45468CB00001B/39